CRAFTING THE 613 COMMANDMENTS

MAIMONIDES ON THE ENUMERATION, CLASSIFICATION AND FORMULATION OF THE SCRIPTURAL COMMANDMENTS

ACADEMIC
STUDIES
PRESS

CRAFTING THE 613 COMMANDMENTS:

MAIMONIDES ON THE ENUMERATION, CLASSIFICATION AND FORMULATION OF THE SCRIPTURAL COMMANDMENTS

ALBERT D. FRIEDBERG

Boston
2014

Library of Congress Cataloging-in-Publication Data :
The bibliographic data for this title is available from the Library of Congress.

ISBN 978-1-61811-167-8 (cloth),
ISBN 978-1-61811-189-0 (electronic),
ISBN 978-1-61811-387-0 (paperback)

Book design by Olga Grabovsky

On the cover:
Fragments of Maimonides' *Sefer ha-Mitsvot* manuscript from the Cairo Genizah,
Cambridge University Library T_S_AR_52_233__L2F0B0S2
Cambridge University Library T_S_MISC_27_4c__L1F0B0S1
London, British Library OR 5563C.23
Reproduced with permission of the Syndics of Cambridge University Library and the British Library board.

Published by Academic Studies Press in 2013, paperback edition 2014.

28 Montfern Avenue
Brighton, MA 02135, USA
press@academicstudiespress.com
www.academicstudiespress.com

CONTENTS

ABBREVIATIONS, CITATIONS, TRANSLATIONS, AND TRANSLITERATIONS

GP	*The Guide of the Perplexed*
HD	*Hilkhot De'ot*
MnT	Moshe ibn Tibbon's translation of *ShM* (the base text in Heller's and Frankel's editions)
MT	*Mishneh Torah*
PhM	*Perush ha-Mishnayot*
SE	"Short Enumeration of the Commandments" (*Minyan ha Qatsar*)
ShM	*Sefer ha-Mitsvot*
SP	*Shemonah Peraqim*
P, N	Positive, Negative commandment, according to Maimonides
Pq, Nq	Positive, Negative commandment, according to Qayyara
Ps, Ns	Positive, Negative commandment, according to Sa'adiah
M	Mishnah
T	Tosefta
JT	Jerusalem (Palestinian) Talmud
BT	Babylonian Talmud

EDITIONS USED

Quotations from *Sefer ha-Mitsvot,* Nahmanides' *Hasagot*, and the commentaries *Megillat Esther*, *Qinat Sofrim,* and *Lev Sameah̲* are cited to the Frankel edition of *Sefer ha-Mitsvot*, either by page or by the particular commandment under discussion. There are two Hebrew translations of the *Sefer ha-Mitsvot*, originally written by Maimonides in Judeo-Arabic, the classical medieval translation of Moses ibn Tibbon, and a recent translation by Joseph Kafih, based on an extant Arabic version. Fragments of a third Hebrew translation, those of Ibn Ayub, were recovered by Heller and noted in his critical edition of the *Sefer ha-Mitsvot*. It is obvious to the careful student of the *Sefer ha-Mitsvot* that differences in the translations are not simply due to translational techniques, but rather to differences in the *vorlage* that underlie their translations. That is, the Hebrew translations are based on different versions of the work and it is impossible at this stage to determine with any degree of certainty which of the versions can be said to represent the author's final say.

I have used Chavel's English translation of the *Sefer ha-Mitsvot*, itself based on Joseph Kafih's Hebrew translation and corrected where necessary by reference to that Hebrew translation. The Hebrew translations of Ibn Tibbon and of Ibn Ayub (when noted by Heller) were consulted and noted where differences against Kafih's translation proved relevant. I did not rely exclusively on Kafih's translation, despite the fact that it was based on an extant Arabic version which may appear to be more original because it is not obvious that the extant Arabic version is as final a draft as the version underlying the Ibn Tibbon or Ibn Ayub translations.

The *Mishneh Torah* and its traditional commentaries are cited from standard printed editions; references are to treatise, chapter, and *halakhah*. The *Eight Chapters of Maimonides on Ethics* (*Shemonah Peraqim*) is cited in *Ethical Writings of Maimonides*, edited by Weiss and Butterworth.

The *midreshe halakhah* are cited from the following editions:

Mekhilta de-Rabbi Ishmael, edited by H. S. Horowitz and Y. Rabin;

Mekhilta de-Rabbi Simeon b. Yohai, edited by Y. N. Epstein and A. S. Melamed;

Sifra, edited by I. H. Weiss;

Sifre al Sefer Bamidbar ve-Sifre Zuta ("*Sifre Numbers*"; "*Sifre Zuta*"), edited by H. S. Horowitz;

Sifre al-Sefer Devarim ("*Sifre Deuteronomy*"), edited by L. Finkelstein.

When possible, I provide page numbers in addition to chapter or paragraph numbers for ease of reference.

References to a particular commandment in Qayyara's enumeration follow Naftali Tsvi Hildesheimer, *Haqdamat Sefer Halakhot Gedolot*), while numerical references to Saadia's commandments follow Yeruham Fischel Perla, *Sefer ha-Mitsvot le-RaSaG*.

Full citations for all these works can be found in the bibliography.

ENGLISH TRANSLATIONS AND TRANSLITERATIONS

Quotations of lemmas from the "Short Enumeration" are from Moses Hyamson's translation of the *Mishneh Torah*. Quotations from the *Sefer ha-Mitsvot* are from C. D. Chavel's translation (*The Book of Commandments*). Quotations from *The Guide of the Perplexed* are from Shlomo Pines' translation, cited by book, chapter, and page (in italics). Quotations from the *Shemonah Peraqim* are from Weiss and Butterworth's English translation. I have followed all of these translations quite faithfully; in the rare places where I amend any of them, I note my change. In contrast, the English quotations from the *Mishneh Torah* are my own adaptations of the Yale University translation (multiple editors).

For scriptural quotations, I used J. H. Hertz's translation of the Pentateuch to match Chavel's use of biblical passages in his own translation of the *Sefer ha-Mitsvot*. There will be instances, however, when exegetical derivations will not quite conform to these scriptural translations. Any inconsistencies are likely a result of the nuanced and ambiguous language of Scripture. I did my best to adapt these translations so that the reader will follow the interpretation.

By *Sages* (with a capital "S"), I refer to the authorities of the talmudic period.

The proliferation of transliteration systems found in scholarly works is nothing short of bewildering. Preferences are often a function of the scholar's academic and geographical background. For example, a student from the Lithuanian yeshiva tradition would differentiate the tav (*t*) from the spirant variety (*th*). An Israeli student, accustomed to the modern Sephardic pronunciation, would not. The field of Biblical

Studies, because of its emphasis on grammatical and morphological features, has tended to use the scientific or academic system. This work, however, is less concerned with the morphology of biblical passages as it is with idioms of the interpreters, the Sages, and medieval rabbis. With the exception of commonly used spellings, I have therefore adopted what I considered the simplest transliteration system, the "general-purpose style" of the Society of Biblical Literature Handbook of Style, with some slight modifications (ignoring the spirants *gh*, *dh*, *fh,* and *th* in favor of *g*, *d*, *f*, and *t*). I retain original Hebrew words or sentence where the translation may leave doubts as to the precise intention of the original rabbinic text.

Throughout the work, I make a clear distinction between the terms *Mishneh Torah* and *Halakhot* (of the *Mishneh Torah*). The full work of the *Mishneh Torah* consists of treatises, divided into Introductions, Headings, and *Halakhot*. I use the term *Mishneh Torah* to refer to this full work. When referring only to the text of the *Halakhot* themselves, without their Headings, I use the term *Halakhot.* I capitalize the term "Headings" because I treat them as a separate work, likely composed at a different time from the *Halakhot*. While the Headings likely derive from the "Short Enumeration" and the *Sefer ha-Mitsvot,* they contain many important differences in formulation, which have legal and exegetical implications.

ACKNOWLEDGMENTS

The present work is a revised version of my University of Toronto dissertation, written under the supervision of Harry Fox. The revisions were more formal than substantive; the method, general analysis, and conclusions remained the same. I owe an immense debt of gratitude to Sara Meirowitz, who went over the manuscript endless times and never tired of making new suggestions, insisting on stylistic and structural changes and clarifications, despite all my frustrations and protestations to the effect that it was perfectly good as it was. Her patience and critical acumen turned my dissertation into something considerably better than it might otherwise have been. It is my hope that, as a result, this book will be intelligible enough to even a lay audience possessing only a minimal background in rabbinic literature in general and Maimonidean jurisprudence and hermeneutics in particular.

Many contributed to this multi-year project as it made its way from the research phase to the final product. In the dissertation, I acknowledged all those who helped me, without whom I may never have been able to bring the project to fruition. I have chosen not to repeat now those acknowledgements, in the understanding that they can be easily accessed at https://tspace.library.utoronto.ca/bitstream/1807/16809/1/Friedberg_Albert_D_200811_PhD_thesis.pdf. Needless to say, my debt of gratitude remains as sincere and as warm as ever.

This revision benefitted from the comments of a number of scholars, foremost among them Marc Shapiro and Ofer Livnat, who read the final stages of the entire manuscript with extraordinary care and a critical eye, catching various errors and imprecisions and saving me from some embarrassment. May their ongoing scholarly work be blessed with continuing success. Of course, the thesis and all remaining errors are entirely my own. David Henshke and Shmuel Rosenthal read parts of the revised work and offered valuable suggestions. To all of you, *yasher kochahem*!

The book is also a small monument to my father, Peretz ben Mordechai Yehudah z"l, who invested so much of his resources and interest in making sure that I receive an excellent education, and a belated gift to my mother, Frieda bat Yonah, may she recover, who gave me so much love and took so much pride in me but who unfortunately is no longer able to enjoy this small piece of *naches*.

The book is dedicated to my beloved *eshet neurim* Nancy, who endured for 10 long years my nearly single minded obsession with this work and the near absence from family life that it caused. With it all, she became my principal sounding board and task master during long walks in which I, insensitively, would monopolize the conversation with my latest findings. Her common sense and clear thinking continuously corrected my trajectory. She is truly a partner in this work.

CHAPTER I

INTRODUCTION

The *TaRYaG*[1] count—the traditional enumeration of the 613 commandments contained in the five Mosaic books (Torah)—holds a prominent place in Jewish thought. The tradition is based on an aggadah (rabbinic homily) found in the Babylonian Talmud and, with some variants, in *Midrash Tanhuma*. No one did more to see this count achieve its place of importance than Moses Maimonides, who used his construction of the list to structure his *Sefer ha-Mitsvot* (*ShM*) and frame the *Mishneh Torah* (*MT*), possibly the most important, and certainly the most comprehensive, code of law in Jewish history.

The talmudic passage reads:

> R. Simlai when preaching said: Six hundred and thirteen precepts were communicated to Moses at Sinai,[2] three hundred and sixty-five negative precepts, corresponding to the number of solar days [in the year], and two hundred and forty-eight positive precepts, corresponding to the number of the members of man's body. Rav Hamnuna said: What is the [biblical] text for this? It is: *Moses commanded us* torah, *an inheritance of the congregation of Jacob* [Deut. 33:4] [the word "torah" equaling six hundred and eleven in letter value. The two commandments] *I am* [Exod. 20:2] and *Thou shalt have no* [*other Gods*] [Exod. 20:3] [are not included in the count, because] we heard [them directly] from the mouth of the Mighty [Divine].[3]

1. *TaRYaG* is a mnemonic whose Hebrew letters, when read numerically, stand for 613 (T=400, R=200, Y=10, G=3).
2. "At Sinai" appears in all the principal manuscripts of the Talmud; it is omitted in the printed versions.
3. *BT Makkot* 23b-24a, Soncino translation. When quoting this aggadah, Maimonides does not give the attribution, as he generally does in his halakhic works, as if to underscore unanimity. See *Sefer ha-Mitsvot*, trans. Ibn Tibbon, n. 51. This, of course, is relevant to Nahmanides' question about the normative character of the aggadah.

This aggadah connects the idea of 613 commandments to the word *torah*, using the numerical value of the letters as a touchstone in its analysis. As with many aggadot, it is impossible to ascertain which came first, the tradition or the exegesis. Were the Sages in possession of an oral tradition that the Torah contained 613 commandments and now merely found a way to connect it homiletically to the word *torah*? Or were they looking for a way to exegetically validate a new idea, the all-encompassing nature of the Law? Regardless of the sources of their tradition, we see that this aggadah is not derived by means of the normal canons of legal interpretation; it is not a *derashah* based on inferential analysis of the text. Rather, it is based on the playful application of a widely-used homiletical technique called *gematria*, which assigns a numerical value to the letters of the Hebrew alphabet.

R. Simlai was a second-generation Palestinian amora, a talmudic sage who lived around the late third century C.E. Is there any evidence that the preceding generations of talmudic scholars engaged in this endeavor of counting commandments? There are some mentions of such a task, although other tannaim may not have provided a fixed total for the entire Pentateuch. In other rabbinic works, sages provide differing counts and classifications for commandments, systems that may complement or may contradict R. Simlai's. An interesting example can be found in the following midrash from *Pesiqta de-Rav Kahana*:

> R. Yo<u>h</u>anan said in the name of R. Shimon b. Yo<u>h</u>ai: Moses wrote for us three chapters [*parashiyyot*] in the Pentateuch, each containing sixty commandments [*mitsvot*]. These are: *parashat Pesa<u>h</u>im*, *parashat Neziqin* and *parashat Qedoshim*. R. Levi said in the name of R. Shila of the city of Tamarta: These chapters contain seventy commandments. R. Tan<u>h</u>uma said: They do not disagree, for he who proposes seventy commandments in *parashat Pesa<u>h</u>im*, includes in it the *parashah* of phylacteries [*tefillin*]; he who proposes seventy commandments in *parashat Neziqin* includes in it the *parashah* of the year of remission [*shemitah*]; and similarly he who proposes seventy commandments in *parashat Qedoshim* includes in it the *parashah* of the fruits of the tree in the first three years of planting [*orlah*].[4]

4. *Pesiqta de-Rav Kahana*, ed. Buber, *parashat ha-<u>H</u>odesh*, *pisqa* 5, *siman* 164, p. 51b. My translation. In the printed editions of *Leviticus Rabbah* 24, the dictum is attributed to R. Yudan in the name of R. Shimon b. Yo<u>h</u>ai. This midrash can also be found in

This midrash notes several legalistic sections of the Pentateuch where many commandments are enumerated, detailing the number of commandments that can be found in each of these *parashiyyot*. Here, then, is some evidence that the tannaim counted commandments, a partial count that perhaps formed part of a global enumeration. However, we have no clear criteria that we could use to reconstruct this global count. Later commentators advanced a number of ingenious theories to identify the proposed number of commandments, but none of the solutions came close to finding the sixty commandments that were ostensibly embedded in each of these three *parashiyyot*. Moise Bloch, who reviewed these solutions, was forced to conclude that the statement "Moses wrote to us three chapters...each containing sixty commandments" could not be taken in a rigorously precise manner.[5] In the end, it was not difficult for Bloch to arrive at this conclusion, since the *Pesiqta*'s midrash postulated a specific and measurable claim—sixty commandments within three clearly identified and limited pericopes—which Bloch could not corroborate by identification. The *Pesiqta* passage well illustrates the varieties of problems we are likely to encounter in identifying specific commandments in larger counts, like that of R. Simlai's, which are spread over a much greater amount of text.

---

the *Yalqut Shimoni, Mishpatim, remez* 307. Though all manuscripts have the example of *orlah*, Mandelbaum suggests that it ought to read forbidden relation (*ervah*), and points to the text of *Leviticus Rabbah*. See Mandelbaum, *Pesikta de Rav Kahana*, vol. 1, 99. The context in *Leviticus Rabbah* suggests that the reason these three *parashiyyot* were given directly and in the presence of the entire congregation of Israel is because of the great number of commandments that they contain. The midrash then proceeds to discuss the specific number of commandments in each.

5. Bloch, "Les 613 Lois," 201n2, cites a number of attempts. For example, Shlomo b. Eliezer ha-Levi in his *'Avodat ha-Levi* [incorrectly referenced by Bloch as *Sefer Huqe Eloqim*], counts, following the enumeration proposed by Maimonides, seventeen commandments in *parashat Pesahim*, forty-one in *Neziqin* and forty-six in *Qedoshim*. Slightly different results were obtained by Moses b. Jacob Hagiz in *Sefer Eleh ha-Mitsvot* and Gabriel J. Polak in *Huqe ha-Eloqim*. Buber, in his notes to *Pesiqta de-Rav Kahana*, suggested that the word *mitsvot* stood for verses, a suggestion already made by Wolf Heidenheim in his 1876 work on the ritual for Passover eve, according to Mandelbaum. To find the sixty verses, Buber divided the *parashiyyot* in a totally arbitrary fashion, replacing one problem with another. Others suggested that the midrash refers to details of the laws, a suggestion that runs counter to the definition of *commandment*, as we shall see.

To return to R. Simlai and his aggadah: did his teaching reflect a unanimous tradition? And were the preceding generations of rabbis, the mishnaic tannaim, aware of such an enumeration of commandments, even if they did not mention it explicitly? Nahmanides, Maimonides' most prominent critic and the author of the *Hasagot* ("Critiques") to the *ShM*, was one of the first medieval scholars to struggle with these questions. Pointing out that the tannaim never seemed to take into account the number of commandments in their talmudic disputations, Nahmanides wondered whether in fact the tannaim cared about preserving the count of 613 commandments. Perhaps, Nahmanides thought at first, R. Simlai's count was the product of his own reckoning, and not all tannaim agreed with his exegesis and his count. Still, Nahmanides was forced to observe that the count had become a part of normative rabbinic tradition, as seen from the number of talmudic passages and midrashim that cited the number 613 in their arguments. He therefore concluded that "because of the widespread nature of this count ... we will say that it was a tradition handed down from Moses at Sinai."[6] On the other hand, Yeruham Fischel Perla, while agreeing with Nahmanides' conclusion, found it "somewhat strange" that "nowhere do we find mention of the *TaRYaG* count, not in the Mishnah, nor in the Tosefta and nor in the Sifra...and neither this count nor any other count is mentioned in the entire Palestinian Talmud." He reviews some of the midrashim cited by Nahmanides as proof of the pervasiveness of the count but finds that variant readings of these same midrashim seem to make a deliberate point of avoiding the number 613. Nevertheless, he too concludes that the tannaim of the Mishnah, Tosefta, *Sifra*, *Sifre*, and Jerusalem Talmud probably did not disagree with the *TaRYaG* count, since no explicit alternative is propounded.[7]

Even more emphatically, E. E. Urbach declares that "in the tannaitic sources this number [613] is unknown, and in the passages where it appears in the printed editions it is only an interpolation that is wanting in the manuscript."[8] Similarly, after a careful review of the

6. Nahmanides, *Hasagot* to Rule 1, *Sefer ha-Mitsvot,* ed. Frankel, 13-15.
7. Perla, *Sefer ha-Mitsvot le-RaSaG,* vol. 1, 6.
8. Urbach, *The Sages, Their Concepts and Beliefs*, 343.

tannaitic manuscript evidence, David Henshke finds no usage of the *TaRYaG* count, even in places where the printed versions make mention of it. From this silence, Henshke concludes that the exercise of counting commandments was an amoraic affair ("following perhaps upon their systematizing approach"), though he grants that the *TaRYaG* tradition may have traveled orally from earlier times. He adds that one could safely conclude that the "*TaRYaG* idea was not part of the mainstream of tannaitic consciousness."[9]

The above discussion raises important questions with regard to the antiquity, character, and general acceptance of R. Simlai's aggadah of the 613 commandments. Yet this aggadah prompted the greatest halakhic and philosophical authority of the Jewish medieval world to write a reasoned treatise on the correct method of enumerating the commandments. Why?

EARLY MEDIEVAL EXEGETES AND THE 613 COMMANDMENTS

We saw that Nahmanides resolved his doubts about considering the *TaRYaG* tradition to be normative, and thus a worthy object of study, once he had established that the tradition was found, uncontested, in a relatively wide number of talmudic aggadot. Other medieval scholars were not so persuaded. In their estimation, the *TaRYaG* count was inconsistent with an appropriate definition of the term *mitsvah* and how such a list of *mitsvot* should be presented.

The great Spanish exegete Abraham ibn Ezra (1089-1164), in a book whose express purpose is listing and discussing the laws of the Torah, gave the following opinion:

---

9. Henshke, "Did the Tannaim Reckon with a Fixed Number of Commandments," 47-58. While arguments from silence are generally thought to be demonstratively weak, in this case they take on more significance. All these midrashim could have gainfully used the *TaRYaG* count in their arguments; its absence appears to be deliberate, a point that Perla alluded to when he called their silence "somewhat strange." Interestingly, in his conclusion Perla relies on the talmudic principle that "one does not [gratuitously] increase disputes."

> I need to raise a methodological point before I deal with the *mitsvot*, because I saw scholars count 613 *mitsvot* in many different ways. There are those who count the boiling of a kid [in its mother's milk] as one *mitsvah*, and there are those who count it as three *mitsvot* on account of the fact that it is written in the Torah three times and that our Sages expounded each of those instances. There are many such instances. There are those who count the particulars and the general, sometimes the particulars by themselves and sometimes the general by themselves. And there are those who count as one *mitsvah* that which is formulated in two ways but whose intent is the same.
>
> Truly, there is no limit to *mitsvot*, as the psalmist says, *I have seen that all things have their limit, but your commandment is broad beyond measure* [Ps. 119:96]. On the other hand, if we count only the general, the fundamental ones [*ve-ha-iqarim*] and the commandments that are binding for all time, the *mitsvot* do not add up to [*'asuyot*, lit. "are not made to be"] 613.[10]

Abraham ibn Ezra is one of the earliest exegetes, if not the first, to critically raise methodological concerns. For example, how does one define *mitsvah*? Implicit in his commentary lies a rejection of the tradition of *TaRYaG*; it is simply impossible to arrive at R. Simlai's total without first agreeing on a definition of the term *mitsvah*. In Ibn Ezra's opinion, the number of commandments is indefinite; the count could range from fewer than 613 to many multiples of 613. It appears that Ibn Ezra sees R. Simlai's

10. Abraham Ibn Ezra, *Yesod Mora ve-Sod Torah*, Second Gate, *pisqa* 3-4, 91-92. What did Ibn Ezra mean by *ha-iqarim*, which we translated as "fundamental ones"? One of his uses of the term in the Fifth Gate (p. 121) can shed some light on this question. These *iqarim* are fundamental commandments that underpin our reasons for performing other commandments, such as creation, which we remember by observing the Sabbath, and the exodus from Egypt, which we remember by observing Passover, matzot, and *tsitsit*. It is those very general commandments that are included in this count that does not reach 613. See also the suggestions made by the editors (*ad loc.*). Some texts read *'asirit*, "one-tenth," instead of *'asuyot*, "made," the sense being that these commandments do not equal one-tenth of 613, or approximately sixty-one (121, notes to line 24). Hanina Ben-Menahem has suggested (183n27) that the number sixty-one may not be as implausible as it sounds: perhaps this has some relationship to Maimonides' list of sixty obligatory positive commandments (which we will discuss in chapter 3). But surely this cannot be correct, since it is clear that Ibn Ezra was referring to the sum of positive *and* negative commandments, not just the sixty obligatory positive commandments!

statement as an aggadic flourish without real significance.

Judah ibn Balaam, another prominent eleventh-century Spanish exegete, was more explicit. Commenting on a dispute between two Babylonian geonim, Hefets b. Yatsliah and Samuel b. Hofni, on whether the verse "And you shall return to the Lord, your God" (Deuteronomy 30:2) commands one to repent or is merely a prediction, Ibn Balaam stated:

> However, Hefets, may his soul rest in Eden, was forced to bring this [*mitsvah*] in the count of *mitsvot* in order to fill the number mentioned by the early scholars in the dictum, "R. Simlai when preaching said: Six hundred and thirteen precepts the Israelites were commanded." To my mind, the dictum was said only as an approximation.[11]

Ibn Balaam's position was also based on a methodological rationale. He asserted that there are two basic categories of commandments. One category consists of historical or contingent commandments; these need not be counted after their time has passed. Examples include the commandments associated with the Passover lamb offered in Egypt and the commandments related to the building of the portable Tabernacle in the desert. A second category is made up of commandments that are binding for all time. Ibn Balaam argued that the latter total "does not reach 613. This is the reason why Hefets was forced to include in his count commandments that were not given at Sinai [and] commandments that were abrogated soon after the time of their performance." He is another exegete who believed that the number of binding commandments could not equal R. Simlai's count if they were subjected to rational criteria of selection. In his opinion, the number of commandments binding for all time did not reach 613 (although we do not know how close his count came).[12]

11. Harkavy, "Zikhron ha-Gaon Shmuel ben Hofni u-Sefarav," 41-42. Also cited by Perla in his introduction to *Sefer ha-Mitsvot le-RaSaG*.

12. Two post-Maimonidean medieval scholars, Levi ben Gershom (RaLBaG or Gersonides) (1288-1344) and Simeon b. Tsemah Duran (1361-1444), also doubted the precision of R. Simlai's dictum. The latter stated: "we do not rely on his [R. Simlai's] interpretation in deciding the halakhah...The reason why this number is mentioned everywhere is that we find no other Sage who counted them, and so we have accepted his enumeration, and even if it misses or exceeds the enumeration, it approximates it [*holekh sevivo*, lit., goes around it]" (Duran, *Zohar ha-Raqia*, 225). For the former's thoughts, see

The opinions of these two exegetes affect our appreciation of Maimonides' work. Maimonides had a high regard for Ibn Balaam's exegetical abilities, as we gather from a comment he makes in the *Essay on Resurrection*: "I was anticipated by the keen commentators on the meaning of the passage, men like ... Ibn Balaam."[13] Though we have no way of knowing whether Maimonides had seen Ibn Balaam's comment regarding the number of countable commandments in the Torah, it is possible that he was aware of it.[14] With regard to Ibn Ezra, Perla has suggested that Maimonides had seen and adopted some of Ibn Ezra's principles; if so, he also must have been aware of Ibn Ezra's dismissal of R. Simlai's count.[15] This tendency among the exegetical predecessors of Maimonides to dismiss R. Simlai's aggadah makes Maimonides' uncritical acceptance of the aggadah all the more puzzling.

Gersonides, *RaLBaG's Commentary to the Pentateuch,* Exodus, *Bo*, 194, where he points out that Maimonides went through "great stress" to arrive at the exact count of 613, but that this number contains only a "small approximation," and R. Simlai "did not care to be precise about his exposition" (*lo hashash bo,* lit., "was not anxious about it"). Also see Braner, "Yahaso shel ha-RaLBaG le-Darko shel ha-RaMBaM be-Minyan ha-Mitsvot," 228-242.

13. "Essay on Resurrection," in *Epistles of Maimonides,* 222.

14. See, for example, Henshke, "Le-ofiyah shel Parshanut ha-Rambam," 10.

15. Perla, *Sefer ha-Mitsvot le-RaSaG*, 15-16. For a contrasting view, see Twersky, "Did Ibn Ezra Influence Maimonides?" 21-48. Harry Fox argues that Maimonides may have been familiar with Ibn Ezra's commentaries, at least in the last years of his life. He bases this on the mention of Ibn Ezra's Torah commentary in a section of a will that he believes is authentically Maimonides'. Fox, "Maimonides on Aging and the Aged," 319-383, in particular 341 and nn. 123, 124, and 126. In this book, I show a number of examples of the common exegetical methods and outlook that Maimonides and Ibn Ezra shared, which may simply be a product of their common Spanish intellectual legacy. It appears that those exegetes who exhibited philological independence and were the least beholden to talmudic interpretation also espoused a more systematic approach to counting commandments. The incompatibility of R. Simlai's count with their systematic thinking and their independent exegetical approaches led them to deny normative status to R. Simlai's exposition. It also appears to me that, at least according to the account of Ibn Balaam, the gaon Samuel b. Hofni also did not see R. Simlai's count as normative, since he did not see the need to increase his own count to achieve the 613 total. As we shall see, Maimonides trimmed commandments from the popular geonic count by systematically applying a number of rules, leaving him with fewer than 613 commandments. Unlike Abraham Ibn Ezra or Judah Ibn Balaam, however, Maimonides worked to restore R. Simlai's full count by introducing innovative commandments.

R. Simlai's division of commandments into positive and negative was not popular among the early medieval halakhic taxonomists. As they saw it, Jewish law contained many legal categories other than the unconditional obligations of positive and negative commandments. For example, one can find indications of neutral (neither positive nor negative), optional, and supererogatory laws, as well as many laws that were strictly contingent on circumstances. In fact, H̲efets b. Yatsliah̲, who used these broader categories, was forced to reinterpret R. Simlai's dictum, saying that "both positive and negative [commandments] are the more common and the more explicit. We find many like these in Scripture."[16] In other words, in H̲efets' opinion, R. Simlai's count contained more than just positive and negative commandments—those understood to be obligatory—and the midrashic dictum was a convenient oversimplification.

Though the 613 total was preserved in all these cases, the two-part classification of commandments based on the 248 positive + 365 negative metaphor was ignored by the Sages in the Geonic period, in particular Simeon Qayyara, Isaac al-Bargeloni, Solomon ibn Gabirol and Sa'adiah Gaon. They adopted a four-part classification divided into punishments (*onshin*), negative commandments, positive commandments, and sections (*parashiyyot*, an unclear term). The four-part classification may have originated in a no-longer-extant amoraic or post-amoraic tradition. This can be inferred from a statement that Qayyara makes in the homiletic introduction to his list, which begins with a statement about *parashiyyot*. The statement opens with a formula typical of extra-tannaitic teachings (*baraitot*):[17] "Our Sages have taught [*shanu h̲akhamim*]: sixty-five sections [*parashiyyot*] are the essence of

16. Zucker, "Qetayim hadashim mi-Sefer ha-Mitsvot of H̲afets b. Yatsliah̲," *PAAJR* 29 (1960-1961): 19-20.

17. It is unlikely, though not impossible, that we are dealing with an actual *baraita*, since *baraitot* tend to be tannaitic, and there is little evidence that tannaim engaged in a detailed commandment count. Y. N. Epstein pointed out that the expression "*shanu h̲akhamim*" also appears in Qayyara's *Halakhot Gedolot* in connection with amoraic dicta. Epstein, *Mavo le-Nusah̲ ha-Mishnah*, 769 and n. 1. See Perla, *Sefer ha-Mitsvot le-RaSaG*, vol. 1, 7, for an allusion to this division in *Midrash Tehillim*, and see Guttmann, *Beh̲inat ha-Mitsvot u-Beh̲inat Qiyyum ha-Mitsvot*, 22, who points to sources for the use of *parashiyyot*.

Torah, and each section was explicated by the Sages of Israel." As we shall see (especially in chapter 3), the four-part classification better suited many of the types of commandments that came to be included.

In closing, I should note that R. Simlai's *derashah* about 613 commandments spawned a remarkably extensive body of *TaRYaG* lists throughout the Jewish world of the ninth through thirteenth centuries, many of which have been lost to us. The geonim Sa'adiah Gaon, Hefets b. Yatsliah, and Samuel b. Hofni made systematic attempts to classify the commandments, but I am not aware of any serious attempts to develop comprehensive criteria on which to construct these lists. Abraham ibn Ezra did not use his methodological insights in writing his *Yesod Mora*, which treats commandments loosely, without any sort of numerical constraint. It is also hard to discern any sort of halakhic significance attached to these types of lists. Most of the literary creativity associated with the composition of *TaRYaG* was channeled into liturgical poems (*piyyutim*) called *azharot*, which were read in synagogues on the Festival of Weeks (Shavuot). This fact alone may account for some of the extraordinary popularity of the *TaRYaG* count.

MAIMONIDES' AVOWED PURPOSE IN ENUMERATING THE COMMANDMENTS

What occasioned Maimonides' interest in the *TaRYaG* enumeration? In the introduction to the *ShM,* he writes:

> after having completed our previous well-known work, wherein we included a commentary to the whole Mishnah [*Perush ha-Mishnayot, PhM*]...I deemed it advisable to compile a compendium which would include all the laws of the Torah and its regulations, nothing missing in it.

Maimonides then proceeds to tell us that in the new work he would omit "differences of opinion and rejected teachings" as well as attributions, and that he would compose the compendium in the language of the Mishnah "so that it would easily be understood by most of the people." He writes further that "brevity with completeness" would be the goal of this work:

> so that the reader thereof might encompass all that is found in the Mishnah and Talmud, *Sifra*, *Sifre*, and Tosefta, and more than that, all decrees and ordinances of the later geonim, of blessed memory, as well as all that they have explained and commented upon concerning the prohibited and permissible, unclean and clean, invalid and valid, liable and free, pay and not pay, swear and free from swearing.

With supreme confidence, he declares, "Outside of this work there [is] to be no need for another book to learn anything whatsoever that is required in the whole Torah, whether it be a law of the Scriptures or of the rabbis."

After discussing the arrangement of the work that will follow, Maimonides finally explains why he needs a list of all scriptural commandments. He says:

> Now, on account of this plan I deemed it advisable to enumerate first in the introduction to that work the number of all commandments, positive and negative, so that the scope of the work embraces all of them, not one commandment being left without being fully discussed.

The implication here is that Maimonides wishes to discuss every one of the scriptural commandments and their derivations and can ensure this goal only by listing them all. Later in his introduction, he writes:

> All this [I would do] in order to guard against omitting *any topic* [emphasis added] from discussion, for only by including them in the enumeration of the commandments [heading the various treatises] would I insure against such omission.

While the earlier statement appears to say that Maimonides wished to make sure that he discussed every one of the commandments, this statement says that the commandments themselves are to serve as a guide for listing all halakhic topics. In other words, the list of commandments would serve as a comprehensive writer's outline. Indeed, he uses this list as a sort of outline when writing the *Mishneh Torah*, although he reorders the list commandments topically, placing a pertinent group of commandments at the head of each treatise.

It is difficult, however, to countenance the idea that Maimonides intended the list of scriptural commandments to act as a comprehensive outline for this later treatise. For one thing, the *MT* has a number of treatises that only cover rabbinically-ordained laws, such as *Hilkhot 'Eruvin* and *Hilkhot Megillah ve-Hanukkah*. No list of scriptural commandments could have prevented the omission of these *halakhot*. Much the same can be said about three other treatises that deal with purely rabbinically-conceived legislation, such as *Hilkhot Zekhiyah u-Matanah, Hilkhot Shekhenim,* and *Hilkhot Sheluhin ve-Shutafin*. Finally, from a practical point of view, the vast scope of the material, most of it rabbinically-derived or rabbinically-ordained, should have led Maimonides to create a far more comprehensive outline if he was truly concerned about the possibility of overlooking a topic.

Even were we to take Maimonides at his word that a list of scriptural commandments could serve as an outline for a comprehensive code of law, the idea of using the tool of *TaRYaG* to ensure that all commandments would be covered does not necessarily follow. Neither a list of commandments nor an outline for a code would need the constraint of the number 613, or indeed of any number. All that Maimonides needed to have done was to create a logically consistent classification of all the scriptural commandments, to which he would have added a number of independent, stand-alone, rabbinic commandments. This would have allowed him to proceed with his code of law in an organized and methodical manner. Again—and this bears repeating—the 613 numerical target presented an unnecessary and awkward constraint on his task, one which continually necessitated justifications and special explanations.[18]

Another surprising element is Maimonides' particular attachment to this aggadah, one that was largely dismissed by his intellectual forefathers and enjoyed a dubious halakhic status. Indeed, we note that Maimonides describes how the *TaRYaG* enumeration flourished among poets, in a creative rather than a legal environment:

> Similarly, whenever I heard the many *azharot* [lit. "admonitions," fig. "liturgical poems"] which have been composed among us in the land

18. See, for example, Positive Commandments 74-77 (P74-77), discussed in chapter 4. There are many other similar examples throughout the *ShM*.

> of Spain, *My pangs have come writhing upon me* [Dan 10:16], because I saw how popular and disseminated these were. True, these authors are not to be criticized; they are poets, and not rabbis, and as far as their art is concerned—namely, well-balanced expressions and beauty of rhyme—they have performed with perfection.

In an attempt to lend some credibility and halakhic weight to this poetic activity and thus justify his own incursion into that area, Maimonides makes the claim that these poets have all followed Qayyara, the tenth-century Babylonian gaon and author of the *Halakhot Gedolot*, "and some of the later rabbis," most probably referring to the Babylonian gaon Hefets b. Yatsliah.[19] One understands the implication that although these lists are written as poems, they must not be dismissed, since they stem from a scholarly tradition.

Having made the decision to use the fixed count of 613, Maimonides realizes that he cannot rely on the work of previous scholars to detail the precise 613 commandments. When he discusses the multiplicity of attempts to enumerate the commandments, Maimonides describes himself as having a "feeling of distress." He says, "Scholars engaged in enumerating the commandments, or in writing anything whatsoever on this topic, have all come forward with the strangest of theories that I could hardly describe their magnitude." The more he thinks "about their fantasies—counting as they did matters which even on first thought would appear that they should not have been included," the more he feels the "ill fortune" that has befallen his people. Maimonides further complains that

> knowing...how widely accepted is this [Qayyara's] enumeration among the people, I knew that if I were just to list the true and proper enumeration, without [advancing] proofs for it, the first person that will chance to read it will suppose that this is a mistake—his proof being that this is contrary to what some author had written.

19. In a future work, I plan to briefly survey some of the earlier enumerators and attempt to determine which ones were read by Maimonides. It is clear, however, from what he says here that he cared little about their differences and preferred to group them all together as followers of Qayyara. In effect, Qayyara became Maimonides' proverbial straw man.

As a result, he set out to write a special treatise, the *Sefer ha-Mitsvot*. Written in an argumentative form, this treatise would detail the methods that could produce a logically correct and consistent enumeration. In it, Maimonides purports also to identify and document each of the commandment claims he was making. Quite clearly, the construction of a consistent list of 613 commandments was no simple task.

THE CENTRAL PROBLEM

Thus far, I have noted that were he to have been honestly engaged in "guard[ing] against omitting any topic from discussion," Maimonides could have more easily produced a systematic and complete classifying outline without the constraint of a particular number of commandments. I have also shown that a number of prominent exegetes and halakhists did not see the aggadah as legally binding, scholars who belonged to the same intellectual tradition as Maimonides and whom he held in esteem. Moreover, the aggadah's particular explanation for the number 613 seems more appropriate for a homily rather than for a midrash with halakhic weight. R. Simlai compares the negative and positive commandments, respectively, to the days of the solar year (365) and the number of human limbs and organs (248), a metaphorical expression of ideas of constancy and dedication. It need not be said that a homily is hardly an appropriate basis for a serious jurisprudential work.[20]

---

20. It is worth noting R. Levi ben Gershom's comment, following his assertion that R. Simlai's count was only an approximation (note 12 above): "Just as the rabbis were wont to take a verse out of its context in order to extract from it an ethical lesson [*mussar tov*], so too did this scholar [R. Simlai] treat with certain lightness this sum [613] so as to be able to extract from it the extraordinary ethical lessons that derive from this sum, [the idea] that every limb of a human being, as it were, says 'perform with me a commandment' and every day of the solar year warns 'don't transgress [today].' This being the case, it is clear that if the commandments were only closely to resemble this numerical total, it would well serve to derive from it this ethical lesson: one need not insist on its exactness [lit., 'match it without deficiency or excess']."
In other words, the two metaphors and their numerical values were the sole basis for the claim that there were 613 commandments. In reality, the total number of commandments only approximated 613. Nevertheless, equating the number of commandments with the sum of the number of days of the year and limbs of the body served its intended homiletical purpose: to show that the commandments

Furthermore, I note that any such list of commandments would require the compiler to fix a set of individuating criteria, rules to divide the totality of the Torah's legal material into separate units. By necessity, such individuation is subjective. It cannot justify Maimonides' hyperbolic claim that his enumeration is "founded upon clear proof beyond a doubt" and that "the reader will see the mistake of all those who counted in a way contrary to ours."[21]

Contemporary and later scholars began attacking the methods and criteria of Maimonides' *ShM* as soon as the ink had dried. As I mentioned briefly, Nahmanides tackled some of the many problematic individuation issues. Though erudite and powerful, Nahmanides's critique is not sufficiently systematic. He leaves unchallenged a great many more questionable concepts, essentially preserving Maimonides' central scheme.[22] Maimonides' four major traditional apologists, Isaac de Leon (*Megillat Esther*), Abraham Alegre (*Lev Sameah̲*), Hananiah Kazis (*Qinat Sofrim*) and Aryeh-Leib Segal-Horowitz (*Marganita Taba*), did their best to uphold the scheme in its entirety against the attacks of Nahmanides, never once questioning the scheme's inherent subjectivity.

Of the early critics of Maimonides' enumeration, special mention should be made of the acerbic and short glosses of RaBaD (R. Abraham b. David of Posquières) that appear alongside the *MT* and of Daniel ha-Bavli's objections, appearing in a collection of queries sent to

---

require daily attention and dedication and must be performed with one's entire being. Gersonides, *RaLBaG's Commentary to the Pentateuch,* Exodus, 195.

21. From the introduction to the *ShM*, with almost the exact same words in Responsum #355, in *Responsa of Moses b. Maimon,* vol. 2, 631. See also Maimonides' letter to R. Efraim of Tyre, in *Iggerot ha-RaMBaM*, trans. and ed. Shailat, vol. 1, 223.

22. In his summary at the end of his critique, Nahmanides writes that he removed 26 entries from Maimonides' list of positive commandments, though not all as a result of disagreements on individuation. Rosanes, "Derekh Mitsvotekha," 416-417, argues that Nahmanides actually subtracted 27 entries and substituted them with 27 new positive commandments (Rosanes first states that Nahmanides made 32 subtractions, but later only lists 27), with an explanation for the slight inexactitude. At any rate, the number of deletions is minor compared with the potential differences that can arise from different individuation standards. As an aside, it is worth noting that Maimonides' enumeration became the definitive work of this genre. In one way or another, all subsequent enumerations either incorporated it *in toto*, as did the *Sefer ha-H̲inukh* (attributed to Aaron of Barcelona), or adopted it with only minor changes, as did *Sefer Mitsvot ha-Gadol* (by Moshe b. Yaakov mi-Coucy).

Maimonides' son Abraham. Their critical comments are not numerous enough to undo the structure but clearly merit consideration when assessing the overall claims. Of all scholars after Nahmanides, Perla best succeeds in raising serious objections against Maimonides' edifice, discussing source documentation, interpretation of these sources, and logical questions on individuations. Because Perla's main concern is justifying and supporting Sa'adiah's enumeration, his sympathies lie with Sa'adiah, against Maimonides and other enumerators. His frequent criticism of Maimonides' position is extraordinarily erudite, lucid, and thorough, though less than systematic. In dissecting the scheme Maimonides puts forth, we will have ample opportunity to discuss the comments of these and other critics.

Finally, returning to the question of individuation, I must not pass up an observation of Halbertal's, who noted that

> the creation of organizing categories is a very complex issue, constrained by what Scripture as well as what tradition say, and the categorizing criteria [itself] ....The demarcation between the particular and the organizing commandment is problematic and complex.[23]

In chapter 2, we will explore problems in individuation. The examples there all show how individuation choices can significantly impact the total number of commandments. The idea that one can craft an incontrovertibly definitive list of commandments is so absurd that we must seriously question whether Maimonides truly believed that he could compile such a list. Indeed, we must explain why Maimonides felt compelled to conflate his outline for a proposed code with the concept of 613 scriptural commandments.

THE THESIS

I argue that Maimonides' interest in *TaRYaG* was due to one particular reason: the need to demonstrate that two fundamental beliefs of the Jewish faith were actually enjoined by Scripture—that these beliefs

23. Halbertal, "Maimonides' Book of Commandments," 461-462, n. 8.

constituted scriptural commandments. The first of the two is the belief in the existence of a Lord of the universe that is defined as the First Cause of all existents. For Maimonides, such a belief necessitates a specific cognitive act; he disagrees with earlier views that the mere acceptance of commandments, because of its implications, fulfills the requirement to believe in God. The second fundamental belief is the belief in God's oneness. This belief also requires a separate cognitive act, aside from the action of proclaiming His oneness. In the next few chapters, and in chapter 5 in particular, I will attempt to demonstrate this thesis. Note that these two commandments are specifically mentioned in R. Simlai's aggadah of the 613 commandments (in R. Hamnuna's exegetical addendum).

In the *ShM*, I argue, Maimonides wanted to show that he could compete with the geonic (Qayyara's) scheme; he thus disingenuously engaged in an enumeration that he knew full well could not be incontrovertible. His goal was to displace the reigning geonic scheme and replace it with R. Simlai's structure of 613 commandments. Maimonides is now able to commence his legal *magnum opus* with the unchallenged claim that the beliefs in the First and Necessary Existent and the oneness of this Existent are positive commandments (*Hilkhot Yesode ha-Torah* 1:1-1:7).[24]

In chapter 2, I define a number of terms that will be used throughout the book. These terms and definitions are intended to help the reader grasp the tools of enumeration and thus better follow the subsequent analysis. In chapter 3, I discuss the types of commandments that are contained in Maimonides' enumeration and the assumptions that he had to make to include these types under the heading of *mitsvot 'aseh*. In addition to the obligatory commandments normally defined as *mitsvot 'aseh*, his list includes contingent commandments, procedural commandments, and descriptions, categories far from what one might

24. It is a sign of Maimonides' extraordinary success that all subsequent halakhic authorities found it natural to include these two fundamental beliefs in their enumerations. We note that after first strenuously defending Qayyara's omission of the first commandment (in the *Hasagot* to P1), Nahmanides concedes that the belief in the existence of God ought to be enumerated "as opined by the Master" (*Hasagot* to N1).

reasonably call *mitsvot 'aseh*. Toward the end of that chapter, I will show that Maimonides demonstrates the relativity of his enumeration with his list of sixty absolutely obligatory commandments that he appended to his section on positive commandments. The sixty obligatory commandments act as a foil to the larger list of 248 positive commandments, which is constructed on a much broader definition of the term *mitsvot 'aseh* than commonly used. It also provides the key to our understanding of the way Maimonides presented the commandments in the *Halakhot* of the *Mishneh Torah*.

In chapter 4, I use competing methods of individuation to evaluate some of Maimonides' individuations and conclude that Maimonides could not have believed that one could create an incontrovertible list of commandments. This exercise raises further doubts about the validity of Maimonides' project, namely, the idea that there either exists a fixed and objective count of commandments or that one can be faithfully constructed.

In chapter 5, I discuss a number of legal innovations that Maimonides introduces in his work vis-à-vis the previous enumerators. I divide these innovations into those for which Maimonides provides strong rabbinic evidence, such as a midrash that specifically states that a particular law is a commandment, and those for which he offers scant evidence for his claims. I focus on some of the latter and suggest that extra-rabbinic factors—ethical and philosophical considerations—may have played a role in their enumeration.

Later in that same chapter, I come to the high point of the thesis, namely Maimonides' innovation that beliefs are valid objects of command. At first, this might hardly appear to be an innovation: as we see from R. Hamnuna's exegetical addendum to Simlai's dictum, the belief in God and the belief in God's oneness are part of the *TaRYaG*. Despite this, neither Qayyara nor any of the composers of the *azharot* include these two articles of faith in their enumeration. To clarify: the geonim include in their counts a commandment to proclaim God's oneness through the recitation of the Shema, and they count a prohibition against having more than one God. What they do not do is require that the faithful explicitly cognize His existence and oneness through a philosophical and logical process of reasoning. One might assume that these geonim disregarded R. Simlai's aggadah as a homily irrelevant to lawmaking. I posit, however, that the geonim's neglect of this aggadah can be attributed to a fundamental doubt whether scriptural law can or does command one to believe. Alternately, while they may acknowledge that the law does command belief, they maintain that the law is content with an implicit belief in God, one that would result from undertaking to the fulfillment of commandments: no special act of cognition is required.

In this chapter, I show that prior to Maimonides' time, the prevailing opinion was that only actions could be commanded, not beliefs. Even during his time, the question of whether dogma could be the object of a commandment was a matter of great controversy among theologians and jurists. In his works, Maimonides defends the notion that the acquisition of metaphysical beliefs is a matter that can be commanded. He reaches far beyond the plain sense of R. Simlai's aggadah when he reinterprets this statement as a declaration of belief in a First Cause. I will examine the bold and unexpected transformation and the profound theological truth that Maimonides saw hidden in R. Hamnuna's explanation of R. Simlai's dictum.[25]

FROM THE *SEFER HA-MITSVOT* TO THE *MISHNEH TORAH*

The thesis that I develop in the first five chapters of this work, that Maimonides was not fundamentally attached to a specific commandment count,[26] comes from an analysis of the commandment enumerations in the *Sefer ha-Mitsvot*. This analysis, in turn, sensitizes us to the language that he uses in the *Halakhot* (legal rulings) of the *Mishneh Torah* (*MT*),

25. The Babylonian gaon H̱efets b. Yatsliaẖ was actually the first to propose that belief in God's existence and His unity represent formal commandments. H̱efets' description of the first commandment was preserved for us by Judah b. Barzilai in his twelfth-century commentary on *Sefer Yetsirah*. Judah ben Barzilai, *Perush Sefer Yetsirah*, 55-56. See chapter 5 for further discussion.

26. While our interest here lies with the *MT*, it is worth noting that Maimonides never once mentions the idea of the 613 commandments in his lengthy survey of the biblical laws in the *Guide*, a work that postdates even the *MT*. My thanks to Harry Fox for this observation.

illuminating his changing concept of what constitutes a commandment.

Maimonides heads the treatises of the *MT* with short captions, all taken from the list of 613 commandments in the Short Enumeration (*SE*) and the *ShM*. He shuffles the original list, allowing negative and positive commandments to mix (as opposed to the positive-negative division of the *SE* and *ShM*) and groups the commandments topically. The Headings to the treatises, in aggregate, constitute exactly 613 commandments. Yet, when we move to the actual *Halakhot* we find that, in a great many cases, Maimonides fails to designate a particular commandment as such. This discontinuity is the subject of chapter 6. We start that chapter by noting that a declaration of commandment appears at the beginning of many—but not all—of the commandments in the *MT*. These are formulaically expressed, as "It is a positive commandment to do X" or sometimes, "It is a positive commandment of [or from] the Torah to do X." This formula is absent in as many as 109 discussions of commandments that had been listed in the *ShM*—a surprisingly large number.

While some scholars, such as Masud b. Aaron Hai-Raqah and Joseph Kafih, noted some of these formulaic omissions, their investigation was incomplete and unsystematic. As a result (as I will demonstrate), their proffered solution fails to satisfy. My analysis purports to show that one of the keys to understanding these gaps is to see that Maimonides essentially changed his criteria for what represents a *mitsvat 'aseh*. Maimonides designates far fewer commandments as *mitsvot 'aseh* in the *Halakhot* of the *MT* than he did in the *SE/ShM* because he treats *mitsvot 'aseh* in the *Halakhot* as unconditional obligations, or as obligations that are contingent on the ordinary life of an ordinary person. I suggest that these criteria were already foreshadowed by the list of the sixty obligatory commandments discussed earlier. This change in criteria, along with some changes in a number of individuations, explains a substantial portion of the structural anomalies evident in the *Halakhot*.

In chapters 7 and 8, I attempt to solve the remaining failures to designate. In the process, I make some innovative suggestions with respect to Maimonides' legal theory and scriptural hermeneutics. In chapter 7, I propose that writing in the *Halakhot*, Maimonides used a new requirement for what constitutes a scriptural commandment: it can only be derived from a scriptural verse that is read in the light of its plain meaning (*peshateh di-qera*). This hermeneutic explains why a number of commandments designated in the *SE/ShM* are no longer designated as scriptural commandments; I suggest that Maimonides quietly reclassified these commandments, moving them from the category of *de-oraita* (scriptural) law into the category of *divre sofrim* law. I briefly discuss the legal status of *divre sofrim* laws: are they to be treated as scriptural laws or as rabbinic laws?[27] And in what practical ways are commandments classified as *divre sofrim* distinct from scriptural commandments: how would Maimonides' reclassification have affected these commandments? Towards the end of chapter 8, I offer a number of suggestions for decisive differences between *divre sofrim* and scriptural legislation unrelated to the binding force of such laws.

In chapter 8, I examine Maimonides' special use of the participle. The participle is a common mishnaic grammatical form, one better suited to convey "correct practices," in David Daube's words,[28] than scriptural obligations. These correct practices probably originate in some remote past, impossible precisely to locate along the continuum of the oral tradition, often supported by a scriptural passage of uncertain meaning. In the *Halakhot*, Maimonides tends to use participles when discussing commandments that he presented in the *SE/ShM* as scriptural commandments but that lack support from the *peshateh di-qera*. Some of the more dramatic examples of "correct practices" are the recitation of the Shema, the learning and teaching of Torah, the binding of phylacteries on the head and on the arm, and the affixing of a mezuzah.

In chapter 9, I discuss commandments previously designated as *mitsvot 'aseh* in the *SE/ShM* that are denoted simply as *mitsvot* (without the modifier *'aseh*) in the *Halakhot*. Whereas the construct phrase *mitsvat 'aseh* connotes an absolute obligation, the freestanding term *mitsvah* suggests something less demanding, such as a scriptural counsel or a non-absolute obligation. In many respects, the freestanding use of

27. For an excellent discussion of the differences between these two types of law, see Elon, *Jewish Law*, 212-223.
28. Daube, "Haustafeln," 295-296.

the term *mitsvah* carries its common meaning from rabbinic literature: a good deed. I note that behind each of these redefinitions stand one or more hermeneutic difficulties that would not permit its designation as a *mitsvat 'aseh*. Among the handful of precepts that Maimonides calls *mitsvah* rather than *mitsvat 'aseh*, are the commands to love God, to fear Him, and to imitate His ways. In all these cases, I suggest that Maimonides has refined the scriptural message, creating a sort of ethical or intellectual imperative that falls just short of an obligation.

WHY POSITIVE COMMANDMENTS?

As the title suggests, I have chosen to deal exclusively with the positive commandments. My interest in the positive commandments arose from the fact that it is far more difficult to identify positive than negative commandments. Negative commandments can be identified by two markers: scriptural language and punishment. Maimonides tells us that, for the most part, negative commandments can be identified linguistically by Scripture's use of four terms: *lo, al, pen,* and *hishamer*. (The exceptions are fully discussed in one of the *Sefer ha-Mitsvot*'s methodological rules.) *Crucially, there are no linguistic markers when it comes to positive commandments.* For this reason, Maimonides must lean heavily on rabbinic warrants that demonstrate that a particular scriptural sentence denotes an obligation. I discuss these ideas in more depth in chapters 2 and 5.

There is a second marker that enables one to identify and individuate negative commandments, and that is the presence of a punishment. Maimonides identifies an important number of negative commandments by bringing rabbinic evidence that state that these violations are liable to lashes. Conversely, he eliminates a significant number of prohibitions from being considered negative commandments because they are not punishable with lashes, thus considering these prohibitions as simply reinforcing exhortations. Besides lashes, Maimonides also asserts that the presence of the penalties of excision (*karet*) and the death penalty imposed by the court (*mitat bet din*) accompanying a prohibition are also markers of negative commandments. While some prohibitions are not punishable, such as those that involve no action, the overarching principle that all negative commandments are punishable greatly facilitates their identification. This explains why, in the *Halakhot*, Maimonides might refer to a negative commandment with language such as "one who transgresses X scriptural prohibition is to receive lashes" without first stating that the transgressor has violated a negative commandment. By contrast, no one is punished for failing to fulfill a positive commandment. The precise nature of positive commandments must thus be clearly defined.

In sum, the positive commandments allowed me to ask about them a number of interesting questions. How did Maimonides identify them? In the absence of punishments, are there various shades of positive commandments? And if there are, can we distinguish these shades from Maimonides' formulations?

One final point: on a number of occasions throughout the book, I note that Maimonides' hermeneutical enterprise would be best understood if we knew the precise order in which he wrote his various legal works, in particular the Rules of the *ShM*, the body of the *ShM*, the *SE*, and the Headings. This knowledge would allow us to observe his train of thought and perhaps many of the reasons for his shifting positions. In the absence of evidence from manuscripts and consistent cross-references, I am guided by conjectures and by assumptions about the way that Maimonides "ought" to have written these treatises. While I have drawn some highly tentative conclusions, they remain just that—tentative, conjectural, and intuitive. A methodical and systematic analysis of these issues of chronology remains an important desideratum for those wishing to understand Maimonides' halakhic *oeuvre* and the development of his ideas.

CHAPTER II

IMPORTANT DEFINITIONS AND CONCEPTS

As he writes in the introduction to the *Sefer ha-Mitsvot,* Maimonides felt overcome by a "feeling of distress" when evaluating earlier attempts to enumerate the commandments. He describes his predecessors' enumerations as being based on the "strangest of theories," products of their "fantasies," and accuses them of "counting matters that even on first thought would appear that they should not have been included." To replace these inconsistent tallies, Maimonides pledges to compose a reasoned count, one "founded upon clear proof beyond a doubt" that would ensure that its "reader [would] see the mistake of all those who counted" differently. He intended its composition to use argumentative and interpretative techniques based on a reasoned and consistent methodology. At the end of this process, Maimonides claims to have produced an authoritative list—*the* authoritative list—of all the commandments.

In his enumeration, Maimonides uses formal rhetorical processes of argumentation, interpretation, and methodology. To facilitate our discussion, this chapter will introduce a number of key terms. Some of these are expressions that Maimonides himself uses, while others are rhetorical terms that will be useful for our analysis. These terms are: *mitsvah* (cs. *mitsvat*, pl. *mitsvot*), *mitsvat 'aseh*, *claims*, *data*, *warrants*, *entries*, and *individuation*.

MITSVAH

In a recent article, Jacob Chinitz insightfully states:

> The Torah, for all its emphasis on law and legality, has a surprising lack of consistency in legal terminology. If it used just one term for obligation

> or command, such as *mitsvah*, and spoke only of such commands and the punishments for lack of compliance, it would have been seen as a systematic and consistent code of law. But such is not the case. The Pentateuch uses no fewer than 10 terms for "law," and there seems to be no particular, permanent meaning to these terms, except a degree of tendency in one direction or another.[1]

Chinitz here notes the multiplicity of biblical terms for *law*; we similarly note that the word *mitsvah* can have multiple roles and meanings. In the Pentateuch, *mitsvah* is used to mean a commandment given by God, such as the Passover ritual (Deut. 6:25), the seventh-year release (Deut. 15:5), or even all of the commandments together (Deut. 8:1). It is sometimes used as an injunction, as in the *mitsvot* that proscribe particular actions (Lev. 4:2), and sometimes it refers to a related group of positive and negative commandments (Deut. 7:11, referring to Deut. 7:2-5). *Mitsvot* (in the plural form) is used to represent a group of commandments, which may or may not be clearly specified (Num. 36:13). Outside of the Pentateuch, *mitsvah* is also used for a commandment issued by a human. In the construct form, we find "*mitsvat ha-levi'im*" (Neh. 13:5) to mean that which is lawfully due to the Levites (comparable to "*mishpat ha-bekhorah*," Deut. 21:17).

Though few specific scriptural commandments contain the word *mitsvah*, we generally can identify commandments by their grammatical form: either the imperative or the imperfect. Despite this generalization, their grammar can sometimes vary. In his exploration of the taxonomy of commandments, the eleventh-century Babylonian gaon Samuel b. H̲ofni struggled with this question. The table of contents for his *Treatise on the Commandments* describes the no-longer-extant chapters nine and ten accordingly: "Concerning the imperative, the words used for expressing an imperative, and that which makes an imperative to be an imperative," and "Concerning the form of the prohibition, the words used for expressing a prohibition, and that

1. Chinitz, "Ten Terms in the Torah for Teachings, Commandments and Laws," 113-119. The ten terms that he lists are *din, tsedaqah, davar, mishmeret, mitsvah, torah, mishpat, hoq, 'edut,* and *ot*.

which makes [a prohibition be a prohibition]."[2] In this particular case, the gaon's methodology shows the clear influence of contemporary Arab theologians and scholars of jurisprudence, rather than rabbinic frameworks.[3] Nevertheless, his concerns clearly highlight the difficulty of using grammatical modes to identify scriptural commandments.

The talmudic rabbis, too, differed in their interpretations, not only about what constituted a commandment but also (more importantly) about how obligatory Scripture intended each particular commandment to be. A few examples of such disagreements:

> [To turn to] the main text: *And he be jealous of his wife* [Num. 5:14]—this is voluntary [*reshut*, lit. "optional"] in the opinion of R. Ishmael, but R. Akiva says it is obligatory. *For her he may defile himself* [Lev. 21:3]—this is voluntary in the opinion of R. Ishmael, but R. Akiva says it is obligatory. *Of them shall ye take your bondmen for ever* [Lev. 25:46]—this is voluntary in the opinion of R. Ishmael, but R. Akiva says it is obligatory. (*BT Sotah* 3a)

In this talmudic passage, R. Ishmael and R. Akiva disagree about the Bible's usage of imperative commands: is a man *obligated* to suspect his possibly unfaithful wife, or merely *permitted* to suspect her? The exegetical distinctions between these readings are far-reaching, as this series of disagreements shows. Their disagreement demonstrates that Scriptural grammar required interpretation; it is not clear whether one *may* perform an action or *must* perform it.

In our next example, Scripture discusses a case where an involuntary manslayer leaves his city of refuge. The verse (Num. 35: 27) states: "And the blood avenger comes upon him outside the limits of the city of refuge, and the blood avenger kills [*ve-ratsaḫ go'el ha-dam*] the manslayer, there is no blood-guilt on his account." This translation

2. Sklare, *Samuel ben Hofni Gaon*, 197. In footnote 70, Sklare notes that the chapters discuss the linguistic forms that express imperatives and prohibitions; what may have been included can be inferred from the beginning of question nine of the gaon's *Ten Questions*, translated on pages 285-294. He further notes that "the question of how 'command' and 'prohibition' are expressed in Scripture, through the grammatical imperatives and other modes, is an important topic in *usul al fiqh* works."

3. Sklare, *Samuel Ben Hofni Gaon*, 52-53 and *passim*. With respect to the *Treatise*, see 177-189.

has already rendered an interpretation, reading "*ve-ratsah̲ go'el ha-dam*" as "and the blood avenger kills." But by taking the *vav* of "*ve-ratsah̲*" as conversive rather than conjunctive, we can alter the meaning significantly to read "the avenger *shall kill* the manslayer" (emphasis added). This difference in interpretation forms the basis for a tannaitic dispute (*BT Makkot* 12a):

> Our Rabbis taught: *And the avenger of blood shall slay the manslayer,* this means that it is an *obligation* [emphasis added] for the blood-avenger [to slay the vagrant murderer]; if there be no blood-avenger, it is permissible for anyone [to do so]: these are the words of R. Yose the Galilean.
>
> R. Akiva says: [it means] that it is *permissible* [emphasis added] for the blood-avenger [to slay the murderer], and everyone [else] is [not] responsible for him.

Our final example stems from the verse: "If your kinsman is in straits and has to sell part of his holdings, his nearest redeemer shall come and redeem [*vega'al*] what his kinsman has sold" (Lev. 25:25). Again we find the same grammatical form, *vav* prefixed to a perfect tense of the verb "to redeem." This gives rise to another tannaitic dispute (*BT Qiddushin* 21a):

> For it was taught: [*If your kinsman is in straits and has to sell part of his holdings, his nearest redeemer shall come*] *and redeem* [ve-ga'al] *what his kinsman has sold*: that is an option. You say, an option: yet perhaps it is not so, but an obligation? Hence it is taught: *And if a man have no kinsman* [Lev. 25:26]. But is there a man in Israel who has no kinsman? Hence it must refer to him who has [a kinsman,] who [however] refuses to repurchase it, [thus showing] that he has [merely] an option. These are the words of R. Joshua. R. Eliezer: *and he [shall] redeem what his kinsman has sold* [implies] an obligation. You say, an obligation; yet perhaps it is not so, but an option?—Hence it is taught: *and in all...you shall effect a redemption* [Lev. 25:24].

These quotations demonstrate the liminality of the grammatical imperative form: divine statements can be read as explicit commands or as granting permission.

As we move our focus to rabbinic law, we find there that the term *mitsvah* also has a number of possible meanings:

1) It can designate an absolute requirement, one that is indispensable for the performance of a ritual. This applies primarily to matters related to offerings and sacrifices. An example can be found in *BT Menahot* 9a:

> It was stated: If the meal offering was mixed outside the walls of the Temple court, R. Yohanan says: It is invalid; Resh Laqish says: It is valid. "Resh Laqish says, it is valid," for it is written, *And he shall pour oil upon it, and put frankincense thereon, and then, he shall bring it to Aaron's sons the priests; and he shall take out his handful* [Lev. 2:1-2]; hence from the taking of the handful begins the duty of the priesthood [*mitsvat kehunah*].

2) Even when contrasted with an indispensable or essential act (*le-aqev*) in sacrificial matters, *mitsvah* can still connote an obligation, as in *BT Zevahim* 37b. *M Zevahim* 4:1 discusses the number of blood sprinklings required for a sin offering to be effective. The House of Shammai (Bet Shammai) maintains that two sprinklings are required in the case of a sin offering, while the House of Hillel (Bet Hillel) maintains that one sprinkling is sufficient. The Talmud proceeds to examine their positions:

> Rav Huna said: What is Bet Shammai's reason? The plural form *qarnot* [horns] is written three times, denoting six [applications], [thus intimating that] four are prescribed [*le-mitsvah*] while two [at least] are essential [*le-aqev*]. But Bet Hillel [argues]: [The written forms are] *qarnat* [singular] twice, and *qarnot* [plural] once, which denotes four, implying that three [applications] are prescribed [*le-mitsvah*], while [only] one is essential [*le-aqev*].

Le-mitsvah does not mean that the sprinkling is merely preferable or commendable, as is often the case when the preposition *lamed* is prefixed to the term *mitsvah*. A later passage (80a) makes it clear that failing to apply the necessary number of sprinklings would "take away" (alluding to the scriptural prohibition) from the total number of God's positive commandments. In other words, these sprinklings have the force of a positive commandment. Therefore, the expression that three (or four) sprinklings are "*le-mitsvah*" simply means that this number of sprinklings is obligatory, although only one sprinkling is essential.[4]

4. *Entsiklopedyah Talmudit*, s.v. "*hovah*," n. 93. In this section I have used a number of other examples presented in this entry.

3) *Le-mitsvah* can represent a preference (*mitsvah le-khathilah*) that does not interfere with the execution of the commandment. One example concerns a betrothed woman who commits adultery. Scripture writes: "they shall bring out the damsel to the door of her father's house, and the men of her city shall stone her with stones so that she dies" (Deut. 22:21). In a discussion of such cases, *M Ketubbot* 4:3 states:

> One who had a father but no door to her father's house, or a door to her father's house but no father, is nevertheless subject to the penalty of stoning, [for the regulation stating] the door of her father's house was only intended as an [independent] precept [*le-mitsvah*].

The door mentioned in the injunction indicates a preferable location, one merely "*le-mitsvah*" rather than an indispensable element of the penalty.[5] A second example concerns one who is to be killed by stoning for having enticed another Jew to practice idolatry. Addressing the enticed person, Scripture says: "Let your hand be the first against him to put him to death, and the hand of the rest of the people thereafter" (Deut. 13:10). As the *Sifre* expounds: "It is a *mitsvah* that he be killed by the enticed person, thereafter by the rest of the people." While it is *preferable* that the enticed person be the one to execute the enticer, the people can execute the enticer if need be.[6]

---

5. Note that Tosafot *ad loc.*, s. v. "*en la petaḥ*," struggles with the text's liberal interpretation of the explicit stipulation and finds other cases where this is not done.
6. *Sifre Deuteronomy*, 89 (152). Classical rabbinic commentaries have also understood the command this way. See RaSHI, *ad loc.*, s. v. "*yadkha tihiyeh bo*," who paraphrases the *Sifre*. Compare *Hilkhot Sanhedrin* 14:8, where Maimonides rules that no one is authorized to execute the convict before the witnesses do so, to *Hilkhot 'Avodah Zarah* 5:4, where Maimonides states that it is a *mitsvah* for the enticed to execute the enticer. Some commentators conclude that Maimonides, too, reads the stipulation as a preference. See Pardo, *Sifrei d'Vei Rav*, 213. Ultimately, this is no proof that the *Sifre* intended to express a preference rather than an obligation (which would allow the enticed to refuse to carry out the execution). The idea that there could be a *mitsvah le-khathilah*, a preferred way of fulfilling certain commandments, is commonly accepted with respect to *qodashim* (lit. "hallowed things" or sacrificial matters). For the way that some of Maimonides' contemporaries understood this idea, see for example Tosafot, *BT Niddah* 66b, s. v. "*kol ha-raui le-bilah*." Whether or not the talmudic rabbis saw some scriptural commands as desiderata is a matter that requires a great deal of research and would take us too far off the scope of this book. I will argue in chapter 9 that Maimonides did think that they did and introduced this nuance in his legal classification.

4) *M Menahot* 10:5 states that after the bringing of the first sheaf of barley cut in the harvest (*omer*), sometime before noon, the new grain would be permitted immediately. In connection with this mishnah, the Talmud (*BT Menahot* 68a) makes the following comment:

> R. Yohanan and Resh Laqish both stated that even when the Temple stood, the [arrival of] daybreak [of the sixteenth day] rendered [the new grain] permitted. But is it not also written, *Until you have brought* [the offering of your God] [Lev. 23:14]?—This is only a recommendation [*le-mitsvah*].

Le-mitsvah here is not understood as a preference (*mitsvah le-khathilah*) but as a supererogatory act (*mitsvah min ha-muvhar*).[7]

5) *Mitsvah* can refer to a rabbinic obligation, as in *BT Shabbat* 21a: "Our rabbis taught: It is a mitsvah to place the Hanukkah lamp by the door of one's house on the outside." Lighting the Hanukkah lamp is a rabbinic obligation, as are all stipulations connected to its practice. Similarly, see *BT Gitin* 38b: "On one occasion R. Eliezer came into the synagogue and did not find [the quorum of] ten there, and he immediately emancipated his slave to make up the ten?—Where a mitsvah [has to be performed], the rule does not apply." Here, too, the term *mitsvah* is used even though the obligation to pray with a quorum of ten men is rabbinic.

6) *Mitsvah* may be interpreted as the performance of a good deed. Miriam's act of waiting to watch Moses after their mother had deposited him in the Nile there is referred to as *mitsvah ze'irah* (small *mitsvah*), and "for a small deed one will receive a great recompense."[8] Similarly, *BT Hullin* 106a, in connection with the rabbinic ordinance of washing one's hands before eating fruit:

> Raba, however, said to them: It is neither a duty [*hovah*] nor a meritorious act [*mitsvah*] but it is merely optional [*reshut*]. This opinion [of Raba] differs from that of R. Nahman, for R. Nahman said: Whoever washes his hands for fruit is of those that are haughty in spirit [*gassut ruah*].

---

7. See Tosafot, *BT Menahot* 5b, s. v. "*heir ha-mizrah matir.*"
8. *Targum Neofiti,* Num. 12:16.

In this hierarchy, *mitsvah* stands here as something desirable, clearly less than obligatory and clearly more than optional.

Aside from the last definition, no value judgment is attached to any of the forms of *mitsvah*. The vernacular connotation of *mitsvah* as a good deed has created great confusion at times, even among learned jurists. An interesting example can be found in the *Mishneh Torah, Hilkhot Bikkurim* 12:1, in connection with the commandment to break the neck of the firstling of an ass (Positive Commandment 82, hereafter P82). Maimonides rules that "there is a positive commandment [*mitsvat ʻaseh*] for every Israelite to redeem the firstling of an ass with a lamb. If one wishes not to redeem it, it is a positive commandment [*mitsvat ʻaseh*] to break its neck." This formulation prompts one of his sharpest critics, RaBaD, to exclaim:

> On my life, this comes neither from dialectics nor from calm reasoning—that this should be considered a *mitsvat ʻaseh*?!?...It is a transgression, and he is called a damager [*maziq*] and a destroyer of the property of a priest.[9]

In the *ShM*, Maimonides proves that breaking the neck (*ʻarifah*) is a commandment by quoting the Sages' expression "*mitsvat ʻarifah*." RaBaD thinks that the Rabbis only used this expression to parallel the term "*mitsvat pediyah*" ("the duty to redeem"), but that they never intended to call *ʻarifah* a *mitsvah*.[10] This is because RaBaD understood the term *mitsvah* to mean a good deed. Maimonides, on the other hand, used the term *mitsvat ʻaseh* to signify an obligation, and had no intention to make a value judgment in this respect.

MITSVAT ʻASEH AND *MITSVAT LO TAʻASEH*

In addition to the use of the plain term *mitsvah* in rabbinic sources, we also find the related terms *mitsvat ʻaseh* and *mitsvat lo taʻaseh* and their abbreviated forms *ʻaseh* and *lo taʻaseh,* with the negative particle

9. RaBaD, *Hasagot ha-RaBaD* (commentary to the *Mishneh Torah*), *ad loc.*
10. See Yosef Qurqus' interesting rebuttal of RaBaD, *ad loc.* Qurqus, "Commentary," *Mishneh Torah*, ed. Frankel.

lav or *lo* ("no") also functioning as a shortened form of *lo ta'aseh*. These terms are commonly translated in English as "positive commandments" and "negative commandments." While I will continue to use this translation for reasons of familiarity and elegance, the terms "positive" and "negative" do not accurately convey what is behind these rabbinic appellations. In effect, *mitsvat 'aseh* should literally be rendered as a "commandment of 'do,'" while *mitsvat lo ta'aseh* should literally be rendered as a "commandment of 'do not do.'" More idiomatically, one ought to translate them as "obligations" and "prohibitions."

There is a category of positive scriptural injunctions that do not instruct a specific action; rather, they are read as implying prohibitions. In what seems like a paradox, the Sages treated such a prohibition as a positive commandment, calling it a "prohibition derived from a positive statement [or command]," and labeling it as a *mitsvat 'aseh—"lav ha-ba mikhlal 'aseh, 'aseh."*[11] Although these prohibitions are treated as positive commandments, transgressors are not liable for lashes, as they would have been were the prohibition to have been stated explicitly. In the *ShM*, Maimonides makes occasional use of this hermeneutic for the purpose of enumerating positive commandments, maintaining that such inferred commands should be counted as a positive commandment. His main critics, RaBaD and Nahmanides, object strenuously, arguing that although these commandments are technically called *mitsvot 'aseh*, they do not represent countable obligations.[12] For example, the verse about the High Priest who is enjoined to marry says: "He shall take a

11. It is also called an *issur 'aseh* (a positive prohibition) in recognition of its being a prohibition derived from an *'aseh*.

12. See RaBaD's glosses on P7, P60, P146, P149-52, and P198 in the *MT*, "The Enumeration of the Commandments" in the introduction to *Sefer ha-Madda'*. While RaBaD had access to the "Short Enumeration of the Commandments" (*SE*), he did not have access to the *ShM* and thus could only infer the places where Maimonides makes use of the *lav ha-ba-mikhlal 'aseh* hermeneutic. In the *ShM*, we find Maimonides using this principle explicitly only in P38, P60, P84 (explained at N89), and P92, and implicitly at P149-P152. Nahmanides' strictures first appear in the *Hasagot* to Rule 1 (pp. 40 and 48) and are given full vent in the *Hasagot* to Rule 4 (p. 111) and to Rule 6 (pp. 131-132). I discuss this issue in a number of separate places in this book, for example, in the discussion of P142, P146 and P149-152 in chapter 5. I state above that Maimonides made occasional use of this hermeneutic for the purpose of advancing commandment claims. This is true only in the *ShM*; an important shift takes place in the *MT*, as I discuss in chapters 6-9.

wife in her virginity" (Lev. 21:13). The Sages, however, interpreted the verse as a prohibition on the High Priest's marrying a non-virgin. This did not deter Maimonides from arguing that the law requiring the High Priest to marry only a virgin is a positive commandment (P38):

> The Talmud says explicitly: "Rabbi Akiva held that even [the offspring of a union which was merely] contrary to a positive commandment was a bastard." As an example of a union which is merely contrary to a positive commandment they give the case of a High Priest who has a connection with a woman who is not a virgin. This is so because it is an accepted principle that a negative commandment which is derived from a positive commandment has the force of a positive commandment. It is thus clear that this is a positive commandment.

There is no positive obligation on the part of the High Priest to marry a virgin; rather, he is prohibited from marrying a non-virgin. Nevertheless, the positively worded command allows Maimonides to claim that it should be considered a positive commandment. In a sense, this is a *mitsvat 'aseh* in form but not in substance.

Can these commandments, positive in name but not in action, be counted as regular positive commandments? Nahmanides posits that a positive commandment needs to direct an action and not simply be a source for inferring a prohibition, basing his reasoning on the very same aggadah of the 613 commandments that Maimonides used to support his project. The full version of this midrash links the number of positive commandments to the number of limbs and organs in the human body: "It is as if each and every limb says to the person, 'Perform a commandment with me,'" and links the number of negative commandments to the number of days in a solar year: "It is as if each and every day says to the person, 'Do not do this day a transgression.'"[13] The implication, argues Nahmanides, is that positive commandments must comprise acts of commission. The aforementioned inferred prohibitions are simply acts of omission; as such, one ought to classify them as negative commandments. Furthermore, to avoid

13. *Midrash Tanhuma, Ki Tetse* and other places, with slight variants. See *Sefer ha-Mitsvot*, ed. Heller, 4n53.

double counting, Nahmanides suggests that this type of negative commandment should only be counted as a *mitsvat lo ta'aseh* if we find no other commandment that explicitly forbids what this positive statement forbids inferentially.[14]

Finally, it is useful to note this point that while the term *mitsvat 'aseh* is normally understood as an unconditional obligation, the category also applies to a conditional obligation. For example, one is under no obligation to acquire a house. If one were to acquire a house, however, one would be obligated to build a parapet on its roof. The building of a parapet can be called a *mitsvat 'aseh* even though it is only a conditional or contingent obligation.

Often, Scripture uses a case-based formulation to describe such contingencies; it uses the particles "when" (*ki*) or "if" (*im*) to introduce a law. Noting and listing several of these formulations, the Talmud declares that "when the *mitsvah* comes into your hands, you are bound to perform it [*atah zaquq la-'asotah*], and if it does not [come into your hand] you are not bound to perform it."[15] That is, obligations can also arise out of contingent situations. This relativity should be kept in mind, as it will become an important element in our evaluation of Maimonides' enumeration.

CLAIMS, DATA OR EVIDENCE, AND WARRANTS

Aside from the term *evidence*, for which Maimonides uses his term "proof," the terms that I am about to discuss are not used in the *ShM*. I bring them here in an effort to facilitate my analysis of Maimonides' hermeneutics. We will find these terms useful in parsing his language and systems of categorization.

Maimonides tells us in the introduction to the *ShM* that if he were to list just "the true and proper enumeration without [advancing]

---

14. Nahmanides, *Hasagot*, end of Rule 6, supporting Qayyara's omission of some of these entries.

15. *BT Derekh Erets Zuta, pereq ha-shalom*, para. 4, cited in the *Entsiklopedyah Talmudit*, s. v. "*hovah*," n. 236. Daniel Sperber's edition, *Masekhet Derekh Erets Zuta, pereq ha-shalom*, 193, does not have "and if it does not [come into your hand] you are not bound to perform it."

proofs for it, the first person that will chance to read it will suppose that this is a mistake—his proof being that it is contrary to what some author has written." In a later paragraph, he emphasizes the need to provide proof, stating that in order to support his enumeration of the commandments, he would "bring proofs from the verses of the Torah and from the words of the Sages, of blessed memory, concerning their interpretation."

With the exception of the nineteenth-century scholar Moritz Peritz, who examines the linguistic markers for Maimonides' proofs, most commentators have focused on the work's main agenda as defining commandments, ignoring its crucial argumentative and interpretative aspects.[16] Peritz was probably the first scholar to note the close connection between Maimonides' proofs and the manner by which midrashic and talmudic sources describe scriptural commands.[17] He details the many ways that Maimonides used specific and precise terms drawn from talmudic sources to support his claims. For example, Peritz notes Maimonides' use of the terms *mitsvat ʿaseh* (P173, 198), *ʿaseh* (P4, 22, 31, 60, 204), *mitsvah* (P29, 37, 90 and P188, "*milẖemet mitsvah*"), the *puʿal* participle *metsuveh* ("it is commanded," P38, P185) and *mitsvah ʿalenu* ("it is incumbent on us," P157), all referring to positive commandments that Maimonides adduced from *midreshe halakhah* and Talmud to support his claims. Maimonides uses similar terms to support negative commandments, such as *mitsvot lo taʿaseh* (N66, 154 and P198), *lo taʿaseh* (N229) and *lav* (N210) by themselves, and *over al* ("transgresses") in N201. Maimonides also makes argumentative use of the terms *ẖovah* ("obligation"), in P20, 44, 158 and 197; *de-oraita* ("from Scripture"), in P175 and 213; and *min ha-torah* ("from the Torah"), in P201 and 203. Peritz also notes Maimonides' use of composite terms such as *mitsvat qiddush yadayim ve-raglayim* (P24, the commandment of sanctifying of the hands and feet), *mitsvat hatavat ha-nerot* (P25, the

16. In the introduction to the *ShM*, Maimonides writes: "My intention, however, in this treatise is by no means to delve into the details of the laws of any of the commandments; only to enumerate them.... When a knowledge of the enumeration of the commandments will be attained in accordance with the proofs in this treatise, then I shall list them briefly at the head of that general work [the *MT*], as we have mentioned."

17. Peritz, "Das Buch der Gesetze, Nach Seiner Anlage un Seinem Inhalt Untersucht," 439-474.

commandment of trimming the lamps) and *mitsvat bigde kehunah* (P33, the commandment regarding the priest's clothes).[18]

Peritz points to Maimonides' use of even more remote and indirect terminology originally found in the *midreshe halakhah,* such as the expressions *al korho* ("against his will"; P23) and *ke-meqayem gezerat ha-melekh* ("fulfilling the decree of the king"; P33) to prove that we are in the presence of an obligation. He notes that

> from the words "Though the Torah has ordained an appointed time for the reading of the Shema, the Sages have appointed a time for prayer," Maimonides concludes that not only the recital of the Shema is a commandment but that the obligation to pray is of scriptural force (P10), though times for prayer are rabbinic.

Finally, Peritz points to two instances (N194 and P9), where, despite the lack of any special linguistic marker, Maimonides nonetheless draws complex inferences to deduce the existence of positive commandments. Examination of this use of language is a primary tool through which this book will analyze the implications of Maimonides' categorizations.

The *ShM* is primarily a rhetorical work; in line with his rhetorical tradition, Maimonides provides justification for his claims, expecting them to be challenged. The elements of its justificatory apparatus follow the outlines of Toulmin's basic theory of argumentation,[19] whose model I primarily use for terminological rather than analytical reasons. According to Toulmin, one can discern three elements in any basic argument: *claim*, *data*, and *warrant*. In the *ShM*, Maimonides begins each section by presenting a *claim* that a specific command is a Biblical commandment.[20]

After presenting his commandment claim, Maimonides begins his defense with a scriptural proof text, what Toulmin calls *data* or *evidence*

---

18. These last two terms cannot be found in the talmudic literature.

19. Toulmin, *Uses of Argument,* 87-134.

20. At this point in our discussion, I am not concerned with noting how these claims are stated differently in the *ShM* from how they are enunciated in Maimonides' other compositions (the *SE*, the headings to the treatises of the *MT*, and the *Halakhot* of the *MT*). In this section of the book, I focus my analysis on the argumentative apparatus surrounding the claims made in the *ShM*.

in his model. The scriptural proof text aims to answer the question: on what is this claim based? Sometimes, the proof text stands alone, appearing to offer sufficient proof. That is because the scriptural proof text is sufficiently clear, or because there may have been a contemporary scholarly consensus on the particular commandment, even if we are no longer aware of it now. See, for example, P15, P26, P27, and P39.

More often, however, the scriptural proof text does not provide an unambiguous proof, and Maimonides then needs to resort to interpretation. He needs to answer the question: how does the scriptural proof text lead to the proposed claim? Here we come to the heart of the *ShM*'s argumentative presentation, the *warrant*. Warrants act as a bridge between the data and the claim. In the *ShM*, warrants take the form of rabbinic statements, drawn from midrashim (principally *midreshe halakhah*), the Mishnah, the Tosefta, or the Jerusalem or Babylonian Talmud. It is crucial to note that Maimonides assumes that the rabbinic interpretations of Scripture accord with the biblical law's intentions, and that his audience accepts this premise.

Although in Toulmin's model, "data are appealed to explicitly, warrants implicitly,"[21] this is not always true in the *ShM*. Maimonides appeals to warrants both implicitly, as when he cites a general principle of rabbinic jurisprudence, such as "a positive commandment overrides a negative commandment" (P112), and explicitly, as when he resorts to a midrash to support his assertion that a particular verse expresses a *mitsvat ʿaseh*. In this latter instance, his warrant functionally resembles data/evidence. Rather than trying to distinguish functionally between data and warrant, and where relevant, I have simply adopted the term *warrant* to refer to *all* rabbinic evidence, while maintaining the term *proof text* for direct scriptural evidence.

ENTRIES

At this point, I want to make an important and basic distinction between Maimonides' work and that of Qayyara (as well as the composers of *azharot*). While Maimonides makes explicit claims,

21. Toulmin, *Uses of Argument*, 92.

defining each commandment and giving a brief evidentiary apparatus, Qayyara merely lists commandments as *entries* listed in the form of quotes or paraphrases of scriptural verses. Qayyara and the authors of the *azharot* never articulate the claims that lie behind these quotes. While the deciphering of these entries inspired a highly creative genre of work,[22] these attempts at deciphering are no more than highly speculative exercises, with little hope of ever definitively knowing the author's original intention. Moreover, these scholars share little or no consensus on a large number of entries. Ironically, while Maimonides himself engaged Qayyara with great zeal, we can never be absolutely sure that Maimonides understood Qayyara's true intentions.

INDIVIDUATION

Individuation is a concept that necessarily lies at the root of every attempt to enumerate commandments. As Joseph Raz notes:

> A theory of individuation [in the legal context] proffers a mode of dividing the totality of material constituting a legal system into separate units. Because of the vast amount of legal material which constitutes one legal system, we need to divide it into smaller units called laws in order to be able to refer to them. It is for legal philosophers to decide on principles of individuation. The division, undertaken by the legal philosopher to allow for exposition of the legal order, has *prima facie*, no practical consequences for the addressee of the law. It does not determine how the law is to be applied, and is, in essence, purely theoretical.[23]

Individuation is the logical process by which a body of law is divided into major coherent themes. There is no scientifically precise way of dividing such material; laws could logically be assigned to one unit or theme and

22. The best known of them are: Simeon b. Tsema<u>h</u> Duran's *Zohar ha-Raqia*, a commentary on the *azharot* of Ibn Gabirol; Abraham S. Traub's commentary in the introduction to Qayyara's *Halakhot Gedolot*; Shaul Cohen's *Netiv Mitsvotekha*, on the *azharot* of Isaac al-Bargeloni and Ibn Gabirol; and Yeruham Fischel Perla's monumental commentary to Sa'adiah's *Sefer ha-Mitsvot*, entitled *Sefer ha-Mitsvot le-RaSaG*, which also dicusses all the extant *azharot* and Maimonides' works.

23. Raz, "Legal Principles and the Limits of Law," 831. Cited by Ben-Menahem, "Maimonides' Fourteen Roots," 3-4.

just as logically assigned to another. An illustrative example: a traffic violation that causes the death of a pedestrian could be discussed in the section of the law code that covers traffic violations, but it could just as well be placed in a section of the code that covers manslaughter. Ben-Menahem refers to this type of individuation as "meta-legal individuation," and adds that meta-legal individuation "is constrained primarily by theoretical and aesthetic considerations." As he writes, "[a]ny metaphysical theory that seeks to classify the components of the system and determine their interrelations presupposes a division of the whole into distinct units amenable to categorization."[24]

While the subjects of our study are the distinct units called *mitsvot,* commandments, one should note that there exists at least one other enumeration whose distinct units were not the commandments but the Ten Articles (*dibberot*, colloquially called the Ten Commandments) given at Sinai. This is the enumeration system used by Sa'adiah Gaon in his *azharot*.[25] His highly stylized poem divides the 613 commandments unevenly, using thematic affinities to allocate each to one of the ten articles of the Decalogue.[26]

Maimonides was to his material what Aristotle had been to biology, a philosopher and logician in the service of taxonomy.[27] Yet unlike Aristotle, Maimonides' taxonomic effort was constrained by his efforts to arrive at a predetermined number of distinct units. This led Maimonides to make at least some individuation decisions that were, after a more detailed analysis, less than logically compelling and which appear to have been made for the sole purpose of gaming the outcome. Moreover, while his rules of individuation (which we will soon discuss)

---

24. Ben-Menahem, "Maimonides' Fourteen Roots," 5.

25. Beginning with the words "a fire consumes and lights more than all lights" (*esh okhla ve-noheret mi-kol noharot*), the *azharot* are found in the prayer book of Sa'adiah Gaon, interposed between the fourth and fifth blessings of the *'amidah*. Sa'adiah Gaon, *Siddur*, 184 and 191-216.

26. Sa'adiah may not have been the first scholar to have arranged the mitsvot in such a manner. See the discussion in Kasher, *Torah Shelemah,* vol. 16, 203-213. This pattern was common among Karaite jurists and exegetes—Sa'adiah may have been polemically motivated. His *azharot* attained semi-canonical status; RaSHi and Ibn Ezra cite them in their comments to Exodus (24:12 and 20:1, respectively).

27. I am grateful to David Novak, who pointed me in this direction.

were eminently logical, they were not always supported by the way the talmudic rabbis categorized the material. In pursuit of his objective, Maimonides would sometimes impose a logic and teleology on the material that was foreign to the rabbinic mind, as his critics note.[28] We shall discuss some of these instances in later chapters.

INDIVIDUATION RULES

In this section, I review the individuation rules, offering some light observations and tentatively raising some fundamental questions about the validity of these rules for defining *mitsvot*. A more sustained critique will follow in later chapters.

As defined by Maimonides in the introduction to the *ShM*, the individuation rules constitute nine out of the fourteen rules for defining *mitsvot*. According to Ben-Menahem's three-part division, the remaining five rules can be divided into rules of identification (Rules 1, 2 and 3) and rules of interpretation (Rules 5 and 8).[29] In a few cases, I follow the following descriptions of individuation rules with a few brief remarks. I will make frequent references to these Rules when examining individual commandment claims.

Rule 4: "We are not to include commands that cover the whole body of the commandments of the Torah." In other words, a commandment must enjoin one to do something specific. Maimonides notes that a statement like "Ye shall be holy" (Lev. 19:2) merely orders one to

28. In particular, see Perla's sharp criticism of Rules 7 and 11 in his introduction to *Sefer ha-Mitsvot le-RaSaG* (Perla, *Sefer ha-Mitsvot le-RaSaG*, vol. 1, 31-33 and 40-41). and his discussions on Ps76 and Ps101-102 (vol. 1, 581-586 and 680-688, respectively). ("Ps" stands for "positive commandment" according to Sa'adiah's enumeration.) For the contrary view that teleological thinking (usually assumed to be Aristotelian) can be found in the Babylonian Talmud among some of the later amoraim (especially Rava), see Novak, *Natural Law in Judaism*, 95-105.

29. I follow here Ben-Menahem's arrangement, with the exception of Rule 10, which I prefer to call a rule of individuation. The rules of identification, Ben-Menahem says, "identify the halakhic material that is to be itemized by specifying which material is to be excluded on external grounds, rather than because of the nature of the material itself, as in the case of the rules of interpretation, which exclude non-imperative material." Ben-Menahem, "Maimonides' Fourteen Roots," 10.

become holy by following all the Torah's laws—no specific action is enjoined. As a result, it is incorrect in his view to consider "Ye shall be holy" a commandment—as some of his predecessors did.

In the *ShM*, Maimonides tells us that to worship God (P5) violates this constraint, while I argue in chapter 9 that he must have felt the same way, though he did not spell it out, with respect to the commandments to fear God (P4). His son, Abraham Maimonides, was also asked whether the commandment to walk in God's ways (P8) might be a charge that covers the whole of the Torah.[30] Abraham ibn Ezra calls this sort of inclusive statement a "high principle" (*kelal gavoha*), but because he did not enumerate commandments, we cannot know whether he meant to eliminate such "high principles" from consideration.[31]

Maimonides' eliminating general commands from the count of commandments does not mean that he considers these charges to lack any halakhic value. For example, at the end of his discussion of Rule 4, Maimonides states that neither "And ye shall circumcise the foreskin of your heart" (Deut. 10:16) nor "and be no more stiffnecked" (ibid.) ought to be enumerated, as some of his predecessors thought. He explains that the former can be read as an exhortation to "humble yourself and listen to all the commandments which He has previously mentioned" and the latter as "do not rebel against accepting anything I have commanded you, and do not transgress it." We see these same verses in *GP* III:33:

> To the totality of purposes of the perfect Law there belong the abandonment, depreciation and restraint of desires in so far as possible, so that these should be satisfied only in so far as this is necessary.... Similarly, to the totality of intentions of the Law there belong gentleness

---

30. Maimonides, Abraham, "Teshuvot Rabbenu Abraham ben ha-RaMBaM le-Sheelot Rabbi Daniel ha-Bavli be-Inyane Sefer ha-Mitsvot," 218. See the discussion of this commandment in chapter 9.

31. Abraham ibn Ezra, *Yesod Mora*, 93. He also uses the expression "inclusive commandment" (*mitsvah kolelet*) on page 112. On page 134, Ibn Ezra calls the verse that enjoins one to fear God a "verse that includes all the commandments." Does this description carry enumerative implications? I am not sure and thus not confident in Perla's claim that "[Abraham ibn Ezra] anticipated him [Maimonides] in this type of work [methodology for counting commandments] in his book *Yesod Mora*," Perla, *Sefer ha-Mitsvot le-RaSaG*, 15.

> and docility; man should not be hard and rough, but responsive, obedient, acquiescent, and docile. You already know His commandment [*mitsvato*], may He be exalted: Circumcise therefore the foreskin of your heart, and be no more stiffnecked [Deut. 10:16].

By describing these verses as teaching specific *mitsvot*, this new reading contradicts Rule 4 from the *ShM*, which states that general charges should not be enumerated. This contradiction leads Perla to ask why Maimonides fails to count these injunctions as commandments if they enjoin a specific goal, a question Perla leaves unresolved.[32] From the narrow point of view of enumeration, this is a significant question. In any case, the *GP* quote indicates that Maimonides did attach a special value to these general commands, regardless of whether he thought they were commandments to be enumerated.

As he explicitly states at the start of the discussion, Maimonides uses the term *mitsvah* to refer to the Law's greater intentions rather than to its particular commandments. In the Maimonidean hermeneutics, non-specific commands generally denote intentions or goals towards which one must strive.[33] Occasionally, non-specific commands nudge or rouse a person to do a commendable action that may not be strictly obligatory. This point needs to be kept in mind for when we come to the discussion of the solo term *mitsvah*, in chapter 9.

Rule 6: "Where a commandment contains both a positive and a negative injunction, its two parts are to be counted separately, the one among the positive commandments, and the other among the negative."

Rule 7: "The detailed laws of a commandment are not to be counted [as separate commandments]." Maimonides called Rule 7 "'a central pillar' to lean on in the subject of our engagement." Commenting on a fuller hierarchy of Torah law, David Novak makes important use of this Rule:

32. Perla, *Sefer ha-Mitsvot le-RaSaG*, vol. 2, 98.

33. Nachum L. Rabinovitch points out that goals can have halakhic implications. See his comments to *Hilkhot Qeriyat Shema* 1:3, in *Mishneh Torah*, ed. Rabinovitch, 21, and also see Rabinovitch, "Tsivvuyyim, Hiyuvim u-Mattarot," 67-92.

> [It refers to] a specific prescription, having a number of particular details, which is commanded for the sake of a more general reason. Thus the more particular details (*diqduqim*) are subsumed under a specific commandment, and the specific commandment is subsumed under a more general reason (*ta'am*).[34]

Rule 9: "The enumeration is not to be based upon the number of times a particular negative or positive injunction is repeated in Scripture, but instead is to be based upon the nature of the action prohibited or enjoined."

Rule 10: "Acts prescribed as preliminary (to the performance of a commandment) are not to be counted."

Rule 11: "The different elements which go together to form one commandment are not to be counted separately." More precisely: when the commandment requires an assemblage of elements, the individual elements should not each be considered their own commandments. The commandment is defined by its desired purpose and *must encompass all the elements that fulfill that purpose*. For more clarity, note that Rule 7 deals with details or conditions of a general commandment that may not be present in all cases, while Rule 11 deals with the constitutive elements of a general commandment. What these rules have in common is that neither the details nor the constitutive elements can be counted as independent commandments.

An example of Rule 11: a leper accomplishes his ritual cleansing doing six specific prescribed actions. This rule dictates that these six actions are subsumed under the single commandment of the cleansing of the leper, regardless of the many actions that are required. A second example concerns the actions a leper must take to declare his leprosy: "His clothes shall be rent, and the hair of his head shall go loose, and he shall cover his upper lip, and shall cry: Unclean, unclean" (Lev. 13:45). These actions all have the same purpose—to make the leper recognizable—and thus are subsumed under one commandment.

34. See Novak, *Natural Law in Judaism*, 96. According to Rule 5, the "more general reason" should not be counted as a commandment.

In cases where the Rabbis say that performing one element incorrectly impairs (*me'aqev*) the validity of the entire assemblage, Maimonides says that "it is clear that [the actions] constitute one commandment." Similarly, "wherever it will be made clear to you that the desired goal [of a commandment] is not obtained by any one of its elements, it is also obvious that it is their totality that is to be counted." If the leper were to tear his clothes without performing the other three requirements, he would not have accomplished the goal of distinguishing himself. There is no rabbinic support for this fine teleologically-driven distinction, although I admit that I am not aware of any rabbinic opinion that expressly denies this point.

Maimonides acknowledges that there is a point of "great difficulty entailed in grasping this rule." Such a difficulty occurs in situations "when the Sages say concerning the elements of a certain commandment that 'they do not impair the validity of each other.'" The example he gives is the commandment of fringes (*tsitsit).* The Sages state: "The absence of the blue thread in the *tsitsit* does not impair the validity of the white nor does the [absence of the] white impair the validity of the blue." Since the commands to have two types of thread are not contingent upon each other, one might then think that the requirements to have blue and white threads constitute two separate commandments. According to Maimonides, however, because the commands to have blue and white threads have the same *telos,* we count *tsitsit* as one overarching commandment (P14). He bases his conclusion on the *Mekhilta*'s exegesis of the verse "And it shall be unto you for a fringe," which he reads as stating that the two types of thread share a single purpose.[35]

In sum, when a group of commanded elements shares a single purpose, that purpose is considered the commandment. No single element can be considered a commandment. Maimonides' teleological approach to the classification of commandments is quite evident here.

35. Nahmanides declares in amazement: "Did then the tanna [of the *Mekhilta*] come now to enumerate 248 positive commandments and to teach us that fringes (*tsitsit)* does not count for more than one entry? This is something about which it is not fitting that we make a mistake." *Hasagot* to Rule 11.

Rule 12: "The successive stages in the performance of a commandment are not to be counted separately." From a *categorizing* point of view, this rule is eminently logical. For example, the rituals prescribed for the burnt offering sacrifice—that the animal be slaughtered, flayed, cut into pieces, that its blood be sprinkled in a particular manner, and so forth—constitute a totality and can reasonably be counted as one commandment. To the best of my knowledge there is no support in the rabbinic sources, however, for the idea that the totality of the successive stages of this ritual is to be considered one single commandment. Here is an instance where the reader can note the lack of meaningful correspondence between taxonomic logic and commandment categorization.

Maimonides complains that "this principle was unknown" to the geonim (or if known, they "paid no attention to it"), since they counted all the details of the ritual of the meal offering as separate commandments, such as "pourings" (*yetziqot*), "mixings" (*belilot*), and "crumblings" (*petitot*). His classificatory logic saw these actions as merely details of the ritual. The geonim, however, were following rabbinic categorizations, where each of these actions was considered a separate duty (*'avodah*)[36] on a par with the rituals of the decapitation of the heifer, the purification of the leper, and the priestly blessings—all of which Maimonides also saw fit to count as separate positive commandments.

Rule 13: "Where a certain commandment has to be performed on more days than one, it is not to be counted once for each day." For example, this rule implies that all the *musaf* ("additional") sacrifices offered at the new moon ought to be counted as one commandment, even though they are offered in different months of the year. Similarly, all the *musaf* offerings for the Sabbath are counted as one commandment, and each festival's *musaf* offerings are counted as its own commandment—even though the same offering may be offered on different festivals. While there is some logic to this categorization, one could just as logically group all *musaf* offerings (Sabbath, new moon, and festivals) under one commandment, as Qayyara did,[37] emphasizing their common

36. *Sifra Tsav*, 16:9 (39d).
37. See the discussion of P41 in chapter 4.

characteristic of being *musaf* offerings and disregarding their specific differences. We see here that the individuating criteria are not firmly set and can vary almost whimsically, which we will discuss at greater length in chapter 4. For now, I ask again the question that I asked with respect to Rule 12: what exactly do these categories represent? How do we know that *mitsvot 'aseh* equate with categories and not with individual components—independent offerings, in this case? No rabbinic warrant was brought that would designate the elements in these categories as individual and separate *mitsvot 'aseh*.

Rule 14: "The modes of punishment are to be counted as positive commandments (and not each particular punishment)." In other words, we count the commandment to punish an offender with lashes as a single positive commandment, since it is a mode or category of punishment. We do not count as its own commandment each distinct instance where one is commanded to give a particular punishment. Maimonides argues that separately counting as positive commandments each instance where punishment is warranted for transgressing a negative commandment would result in one positive commandment for each negative commandment, resulting in more than four hundred positive commandments!

Nahmanides exposes the potential fallacy of this argument.[38] It is tradition, rather than the Torah, that stipulates flogging for nearly all infractions that involve transgressions of negative commandments. In fact, we find only one explicit reference to flogging in the Torah, in Deuteronomy 25:1-3, punishing the guilty party in litigation (see P224, N300). The Torah does stipulate punishments for specific other offenses, including stipulating excision and the death penalty. In an enumeration driven by textual references rather than logic, it would not be unreasonable to treat all these punishments as separate commandments, perhaps categorizing them in a slightly different way from other positive commandments. This is precisely what Qayyara and other geonim did by creating a section of punishments (*'onshin*) in their *TaRYaG* enumerations.

38. Nahmanides, *Hasagot* to Rule 14, 194.

Maimonides cites two reasons for breaking with the geonic scheme. His first concern is that the geonic scheme could produce confusion when it lists some transgressions twice, once as an admonition and once as a punishment, such as the prohibition against profaning the Sabbath and the punishment of death by stoning for one who profanes it. He says:

> [it is necessary to point out] that the reason for this error is that in counting the punishments as commandments they become entangled: sometimes counting them alone, and sometimes counting the punishment and also the action for which that punishment is incurred, establishing them all as negative commandments without contemplation.

Maimonides insinuates here that the reason is indeed a practical one: it would disrupt the outline on which he hopes to construct an ordered and systematic code of law.

The second objection to a logic that he describes as "still more perplexing" is that some of the stipulated punishments are meted out by God rather than by the human courts. As a result, we cannot count them as formal commandments. One of the proponents of including punishments in the enumeration was the gaon H̱efets b. Yatsliaẖ, author of his own *Sefer ha-Mitsvot*. Maimonides quotes from the first chapter of H̱efets' book, where he describes the section of punishments: "Among these are thirty-two subjects[39] wherein He informs us that He, blessed be He, is in charge of executing, not us." Maimonides thinks that it is absurd to believe that heavenly punishments (excision, death by the hand of Heaven) can be counted as commandments, since they clearly involve no judicial action.

In the chapters that follow, we shall question the theoretical viability of reaching a numerical target like 613. Maimonides foreshadows such difficulties in his explication of Rule 14. Discussing capital punishment, he writes: "As for counting them [in the enumeration of the commandments] we shall count the four death penalties inflicted by the courts as four positive commandments." To support this claim, Maimonides cites the following rabbinic warrant:

---

39. H̱efets later explains that the 32 cases comprised 23 cases of those liable to excision (*karet*) and nine liable to death by the hand of Heaven (*mitah bi-yede shamayim*).

> Such indeed is the language of the Mishnah: "This is the commandment of those that are to be stoned [*mitsvat ha-nisqalin*, lit. 'the command of the stoned ones']." Similarly [the Sages of the Mishnah] say: "In what manner is the commandment of burning performed [*mitsvat ha-nisrafin*, lit. 'the command of the burned ones']?"; "In what manner is the commandment of strangling [performed] [*mitsvat ha-nehenaqin*, lit. 'the command of the strangled ones']?"; "In what manner is the commandment of beheading [*mitsvat ha-neheragin*, lit. 'the command of the beheaded ones'] [performed]?"[40]

Disagreeing with Maimonides, Nahmanides argues that the court's obligation to deal out justice and extirpate evil, covered by the scriptural injunction "Thus you will sweep out evil from your midst" (Deut. 13:6), is the more encompassing category, the one that should be the sole enumerated commandment. Nahmanides dismisses Maimonides' warrant, claiming that the mishnah's usage of the construct chain containing the form *mitsvat* does not necessarily describe a commandment. Rather, it represents a handy rabbinic form that is used to refer to a scriptural command *in its ideal form of execution.* So for example *mitsvat ha-nisqalin* refers to the most correct form of carrying out the command to stone one liable for that form of punishment. Arguably, this command is itself a detail of a larger, overarching commandment to carry out justice.[41] Similar conclusions can be reached by examining a number of such construct chains (as we do below).

Maimonides' failure to adduce a more persuasive proof for the claim that these four punishments can be individuated[42] makes Nahmanides'

---

40. *M Sanhedrin* 7:1-4. Maimonides inverts the order of the last two. In the *SE/ShM*, these punishments are counted as P226-229.

41. Nahmanides, *Hasagot* to Rule 14, 198 and 200.

42. We should note that Maimonides makes here a second attempt to individuate each of the death penalties. He quotes *Mekhilta Vayaqhel* (347) on the verse "You shall kindle no fire throughout your habitations" (Exod. 35:3): "Lighting fire, which is included in the categories of work prohibited on the Sabbath, is singled out for special mention to teach us that just as the Sabbath laws cannot be disregarded in the specially-mentioned form of execution by burning [*aḫat mi-mitot bet din*], so they cannot be disregarded in the case of the other forms of judicial execution [*kol she'ar mitot bet din*]." While it is true that this passage individuates execution by burning, it does not make it an individual *mitsvat 'aseh*. Benveniste comes to the same conclusion, but only after he emends a passage in the Jerusalem Talmud that at first appears to provide

argument appear stronger. Nevertheless, one conclusion that *can* be drawn is that neither individuation nor enumeration can be absolutely convincing. On this basis, it would not be unreasonable to conclude that behind some of Maimonides' individuations, we can find the logic of an outline, a comprehensive and practical classification on which to base his code of law, rather than the logic of a commandment. Much as the mishnah had done earlier, Maimonides may simply have wanted to separate the various punishments to allow a detailed discussion of each of the forms of execution.

In sum, Maimonides appears to be pursuing two objectives at one time: a detailed outline for his future code of law, the stated objective of the *ShM*; and a precise numerical reconstruction of R. Simlai's 613 commandments. These objectives do not always correspond—indeed, why should they?—resulting in strained logical and hermeneutical demonstrations.

THE CONSTRUCT *MITSVAT* IN THE COMPOSITE TERM *MITSVAT*-X

We saw above that Maimonides used phrases such as *mitsvat ha-nisqalin* and *mitsvat ha-nisrafin* to individuate the four capital punishments (P226-229). As we saw, Nahmanides criticized the use of these phrases as evidence for individuation, arguing that they were never meant as such.

The capital punishment case is not the only instance in which Maimonides makes use of this composite phrase *mitsvat*-X for purposes of individuation. He also does so at P82, to justify the commandment of breaking the neck of the firstling of an ass (*'arifah*); at P217, to justify the commandment that obligates the ritual of removing the shoe (*ḫalitsah*); and at P233, to justify the commandment that one facilitate the redemption of a Hebrew maidservant (*pediyah*).[43] For all three cases, Maimonides brings a proof from *M Bekhorot* 1:7 that refers to *mitsvat*

some support to Maimonides' claim. This passage is not found in our editions of the Jerusalem Talmud. Benveniste, *Dina de-Hayy*, P99, 578.

43. Formally made at P234. Both *mitsvat yi'ud* and *mitsvat pediyah* are mentioned in *M Bekhorot* 1:7. Note that Scripture prefers *pediyah* over *'arifah*, *yibbum* over *ḫalitsah*, and *yi'ud* over *pediyah*, and that the activities named second are only second-best alternatives.

'arifah, mitsvat halitsah, and *mitsvat pediyah.* With this warrant, he trumps the logic of Rule 7, which would view these commands as details of the general commandments of redemption of the firstling (*pediyah*), levirate marriage (*yibbum*), and marriage to the maidservant (*yi'ud*). It is clear that the expression *mitsvat*-X held a special significance for Maimonides, functioning as a warrant for individuating a commandment.

It is therefore surprising to find that, across a wide range of rabbinic literature, the *mitsvat*-X expression is used in connection with commands that Maimonides does *not* designate as commandments. We see this in the very same mishnah (*M Bekhorot* 1:7) that Maimonides used to demonstrate the validity of his claims of *'arifah, halitsah,* and *pediyah.* The end of the mishnah states: "The duty of redeeming [*mitsvat geulah*] [an unclean beast that was dedicated to the Temple] falls upon its owner before all other men." Although the phrase *mitsvat geulah* is used to describe this duty, Maimonides does not include it in the list of commandments. Would this instance not represent a counterfactual example to the thesis that the expression *mitsvat*-X is an individuating marker?[44]

Following are some further counterexamples, instances where the phrase *mitsvat-X* is used, yet Maimonides does not individuate the given command as a positive commandment:

1) *M Sukkah* 4:5: "How was the rite of the willow-branch fulfilled?" (*mitsvat 'aravah ketsad*?)
Comment: In the *Halakhot,* Maimonides calls this rite a *halakhah le-Moshe mi-Sinai* rather than a *mitsvat 'aseh.* While Maimonides clearly had this mishnah in mind, given that he uses the mishnaic expression "*ketsad haytah mitsvatah,*" he does not categorize *mitsvat 'aravah* as a positive commandment (*Hilkhot Lulav* 7:20-21).

2) *M Menahot* 7:2: "If a man removes the sinews of the hip, he must remove all of it. R. Judah says: Only enough to fulfill the command to

44. In *Hilkhot 'Arakhin* (5:1, also 5:3), Maimonides formulates this *halakhah* as follows: "In the case of one who consecrates an ancestral (*ahuzzah*) field, it is incumbent (*mitsvah*) on him for him to redeem it, for the owner has priority." The principle is held valid for ancestral fields and unclean beasts according to *BT 'Arakhin* 27a.

remove it (*kede le-qayem bo mitsvat netilah*)."
Comment: Here, too, Maimonides does not count this as a positive commandment, despite R. Judah's use of the expression *mitsvat netilah*. The only commandment that Maimonides enumerates with respect to the sinews of an animal is the prohibition (N183) against eating them.

3) *M Nega'im* 14:6: "The command of the cedar wood [*mitsvat 'ets erez*]: It should be one cubit in length."
Comment: In P110, Maimonides subsumes the command of the cedar wood under the general commandment dealing with the purification of the leper: the stipulation to set aside cedar wood is treated as a detail of the general commandment. That is, although the mishnah refers to "*mitsvat 'ets erez*," Maimonides does not use the expression as a marker of a positive commandment. In the *MT*, Maimonides uses the term *mitsvato* when he refers to the cedar wood rite (*Hilkhot Tumat Tsara'at* 11:1), but it is used to refer to the correct measure of the wood: "and he takes [a piece] of a cedar tree, and the correct way [measure] (*mitsvato*) is ..."

Two similar expressions of the form *mitsvat-X* can be found in *M Parah* 11:9 (*mitsvat ezov*) and *Mekhilta de-Rabbi Simeon b. Yohai* (on Exod. 21:6) (*mitsvat retsi'ah*). Neither expression leads Maimonides to identify these rites as positive commandments. The next and final example suggests a different individuation scheme than the one Maimonides proposes in the *ShM*.

4) *Mekhilta de-Rabbi Ishmael* on Exodus 12:16: "From here they said: the command of phylacteries (*mitsvat tefillin*), the four sections [that go] on the arm are one bundle, the four sections [that go on, or belong on] the head are four divisions (*totafot*)."
Comment: Maimonides counts putting on each tefillin (head and arm) as two separate commandments (P12, P13) and provides proof for this decision.[45] Admittedly, this midrash deals with the making or description of the tefillin, not the wearing of them. Nevertheless, it refers to both

45. See Nahmanides, *Hasagot* to Rule 11, who argues that Maimonides should have treated tefillin as one commandment if he had followed the same logic as the one he used for the commandment of fringes.

tefillin together as *mitsvat tefillin*. Should Maimonides have changed his individuation and considered tefillin as one commandment?

In addition to the above, the expression *mitsvat*-X refers to a number of rabbinically-prescribed ordinances, suggesting that the term need not refer to scriptural commandments. Examples include *mitsvat megillah* (*T Megillah* 2:9), *mitsvat miun* (*T Yevamot* 13:1), *mitsvat ha-ner* (*Avot de-Rabbi Natan* B, 9) and *mitsvat ḫanukkah* (*BT Shabbat* 21b).

In this chapter, I defined a number of important terms and began analyzing Maimonides' rules of individuation. I raised some early questions about the relationship between classificatory logic and commandments, touching upon issues of indeterminacy in individuation decisions (to which I will return in chapter 4). Finally, I raised the issue of selectivity in using a particular linguistic marker as a warrant to support commandment claims. From the foregoing, it appeared that the enumeration project was not as hermeneutically compelling a project as Maimonides professed. These observations raise the possibility that some external criteria lay behind many of the enumerating decisions, rather than just the obvious linguistic markers (a topic I will cover in chapter 5). But I also want to go beyond the narrow issue of the selection of the commandment claims. In the following two chapters, I shall endeavor to show that the enumeration was neither fully consistent with rabbinic terminology nor as logically compelling as Maimonides might have wanted. The combination of all these problems should lead us once again to question the rationale for such a project.

CHAPTER III

TYPOLOGY OF *MITSVOT*

In the previous chapter, we saw Maimonides use the phrase *mitsvat 'aseh* to describe an unconditional obligation, a command to perform a specific action. What gives the term its literal meaning is the imperative form *'aseh* (lit. "do!") appended to the construct form *mitsvat*. Recall also that R. Simlai's midrash referred unequivocally to 248 *mitsvot 'aseh*. According to this definition, we would expect Maimonides' list to contain 248 unconditional obligations. Surprisingly, the list of commandments that Maimonides presents in the *ShM* looks more like a catalogue of laws than a list of unconditional obligations. Indeed, the so-called positive commandments contain a variety of types of laws: unconditional obligations, laws that specify a particular procedure but not an obligation, broad laws containing a number of provisions which are also not obligations, and descriptive laws which define the referents of other commandments.

Because they come from a different tradition of categorizing commandments, the geonic enumerations accommodate this varied typology somewhat better than does Maimonides. Positive commandments are called *mitsvot qum 'aseh*, literally "get up and do'" commandments.[1] Such commandments are generally unconditional obligations, although some of them are contingent on particular situations. Another of their categories is *parashiyyot*, literally

1. In talmudic literature, this term is quite common: see *M Makkot* 3:4, *T Hullin* 10:15, *BT Sanhedrin* 59a. In the Rome manuscript, Qayyara sums up the section thus: "These then are two hundred positive commandments (*mitsvot qum 'aseh*), that for each one individually reward is granted (*she-al kol ahat ve-ahat nottlin sekhar*)." For a discussion of the structure of commandments according to Qayyara and the importance of this mention of reward, see Guttmann, *Behinat ha-Mitsvot u-Behinat Qiyyum ha-Mitsvot*, 36-40.

"sections," 65 headings that agglomerate assorted provisions related to specific subjects, such as the "section on the Hebrew bondsman and bondswoman" or the "section on the Red Heifer." This scheme can accommodate conditional commandments, procedures, and even descriptive laws better than R. Simlai's single category of positive commandments could.[2]

In his remarks in the concluding section of positive commandments in the *Sefer ha-Mitsvot*, Maimonides takes notice of the broad variety of laws that he had included under the name "positive commandment." (For better comprehension, in the quotes that follow, I follow a slightly different commandment order than the one he uses.) Maimonides explains that there are commandments that

> are absolutely obligatory on every man, at all times, everywhere, and in all circumstances, as for instance, [those regarding] the fringes,[3]

2. Modern commentators differ on what commandments are defined by the term *parashiyyot*. Y. M. Guttmann (in *Be<u>h</u>inat ha-Mitsvot*, 23) maintains that *parashiyyot* only catalog obligations for the community, rather than those incumbent upon the individual. Perla (in *Sefer ha-Mitsvot le-RaSaG*, vol. 3, 193-208) thinks that the category also covers commandments whose practice is enforced by the community or the courts. However, these views fail to explain a number of entries. While Perla justified these questionable entries through a brilliant display of *pilpul*, such explanations seem unnecessarily convoluted. For examples of such forced arguments, see his discussion of the beautiful captive (vol. 1, 578), the Nazirite's obligation to shave after cleansing (vol. 1, 680) and *shemittah* (vol. 1, 554). In all these cases, *parashiyyot* can better be understood as laws that are only applicable under certain conditions, contrasting with the unconditional obligations called *mitsvot qum 'aseh*. M. Zucker (in *Mi-Sefer ha-Mitsvot shel <u>H</u>efets ben Yatslia<u>h</u>*, 11-12), suggests a more convincing definition, based on his reading of a passage in <u>H</u>efets's fragmentary *Sefer ha-Mitsvot*. These 65 *parashiyyot* do not represent commandments that devolve onto the community but rather commandments whose applicability depends on the opinion of the courts. It is worth noting that neither Maimonides nor Nahmanides thought that *parashiyyot* covered communal obligations. In his discussion of Rule 7, Maimonides makes some comments that approve of Qayyara's use of *parashiyyot*, since they resemble his own legal formulations. Subsequently, he criticizes Qayyara because "this matter was not completely clarified or apprehended by him; hence he counted among these sections matters he had already enumerated before, without being aware of [the repetition]." Nahmanides notes that Qayyara's "understanding of *parashiyyot* is not properly explained and I will not expand on it" (*Hasagot* to Rule 10).
3. Note that Maimonides considers here that the commandment of fringes consisted of making them (as per P14), not of wearing them, as he would later state in the

> the phylacteries, and the observance of the Sabbath. These we call unconditional commandments, because they are of necessity incumbent upon every adult Israelite at all times, everywhere, and in all circumstances. (*ShM*, 284)

I will discuss this category of unconditional commandments later in this chapter.

The next (and less obvious) type of positive commandment is the contingent commandment. As noted in our earlier discussion of the term *mitsvah,* these commandments consist of precise specifications of how to handle particular legal issues. The Hebrew particles *ki* or *im* specify and introduce the general topic under discussion. For example: "When (*ki*) you build a new house, you shall make a parapet for your roof" (Deut. 22:8). The circumstance that activates the commandment is the building of a new house. Such a contingency is introduced by the particle *ki*. In Maimonides' words, such commandments are

> obligatory on the individual who has performed a certain act, or to whom something has happened, as for instance the [commandments relating to] the sacrifices offered by one who has sinned unintentionally, or by a *zav*; and it is possible for a man to go through life without doing or experiencing any of these things. Again, there are among these commandments, as we have explained, certain laws, like the law of a Hebrew bondsman, of a Hebrew bondsmaid, of a Canaanite bondsman, of an unpaid bailee, of a borrower, and others mentioned above, which may never be applicable to a particular man, and which he may never be liable to carry out, throughout the whole of his life. Other commandments are binding only during the existence of the Temple.... Others are binding only on owners of property ... and it is possible for a man to be exempt from them because he has no property. (*ShM*, 284)

Contingent commandments are commandments conditional upon certain events or circumstances taking place. If the given events or circumstances never occur during the person's life, the person will be exempted from the commandment.

Similar to these contingent commandments are procedure-

Halakhot. See my discussion of the commandment to make fringes in chapter 6.

commandments, those that specify what procedure must be followed under certain circumstances. The classic example of such a commandment is the law of divorce (P222), which Maimonides formulates as follows: "We are commanded that divorce of a woman whom we wish to divorce must be accomplished by a bill of divorcement, and not otherwise." The first opportunity that he has to discuss procedure-commandments is at P95, where he claims: "we are commanded [Ar., *al-amar*] to apply the rules [laid down in Scripture] regarding the revocation of vows, that is, the rules [Ar. *al-tashria*] that we were taught to adjudicate these laws." Immediately after, he explains:

> This commandment, however, does not mean that we are bound in all cases to revoke vows. You must understand that precisely the same is true of every law that I enumerate: it is not necessarily a commandment to do a certain thing, but the commandment is that we must deal with the matter [in question] in accordance with this law.[4]

In his discussion of the commandment of immersing in a ritual bath (P109), Maimonides explains the logic of procedure-commandments once again. The commandment reads: "We are commanded to immerse ourselves in the waters of a ritual bath, and thus be cleansed of any of the kinds of uncleanness with which we may have been affected." He then explains:

> In treating immersion as a positive commandment we do not mean that every unclean person is bound to immerse himself, as anyone who wears a garment is bound to put fringes on it, or as anyone who has a house

4. Maimonides' notion that a particular law, teaching, or procedure is called a commandment "because we must deal with the matter in question in accordance with this law" can be seen in the special terminology that he used, *al-amar* in the first explanation of the commandment and *al-tashria* in the second. Aware that *al-amar* generally refers to a command and *al-tashria* does not, Maimonides' grandson Yehoshua ha-Nagid suggests that Maimonides used the two terms deliberately. Just as the annulment of vows is a teaching or instruction, not a direct order, but one that has specific parameters that must be followed, so too must one carry out any entries that contain the term *al-tashria* (e.g. P108, 114-5, 117, 145, 149, 190), even though they are only teachings. According to Yehoshua ha-Nagid, P95's equation of *al-amar* with *al-tashria* redefined all other uses of *al-tashria*. In talmudic jargon, we might say that P95 is a *binyan av* for all similar entries. See Yehoshua ha-Nagid, *Teshuvot*, 49.

> is bound to make a parapet [for its roof]; my meaning is only that by the law of immersion anybody who wishes to cleanse himself from his uncleanness cannot accomplish this purpose except through immersion in water, after which he becomes clean.

It is unclear why Maimonides felt the need to explain the significance of this type of commandment again.[5] Regardless, we see clearly that these types of commandments, be they contingent or procedural, are obligatory under certain circumstances: one who owns a Hebrew slave must free him after six years, one must give a bill of divorce to one's wife to effect a divorce, one must build a parapet for a house soon after acquiring it, and many more. While we may call these commandments "contingent," since they are tied to specific life circumstances, one who finds himself in those life circumstances is indeed obligated to fulfill these commandments. Seen in this light, contingent and procedural commandments can be described as obligations, albeit relative ones.

The fourth and last type of commandment that we find in the *ShM*'s enumeration is best called descriptive, rather than prescriptive. In effect, these commandments define the referents of other commandments. Unlike those previously discussed, this type of commandment never imposes an obligation, regardless of circumstance. A total of thirteen commandments fall into this category, all concerning types of uncleanness (P96-108). They are formulated as describing states of being, such as stipulating "that eight species of creeping things defile

5. The requirement to immerse in a ritual bath was a matter of contention between the Rabbanite and the Karaite communities. In fact, Maimonides was forced to issue a strong court order to uphold the Rabbanite practice. See *Iggerot ha-RaMBaM,* trans. and ed. Shailat, vol. 1, 175-185 for the *taqanah* and its background. We can detect traces of the polemic in the *ShM*, where Maimonides states: "The book of truth [Scripture] makes it clear that whoever has been unclean and undergoes immersion is rendered clean." Though Karaites rejected the Oral Law, they followed Scripture diligently. Maimonides' appeal to the "book of truth" is more rhetorical than actual, as the requirement to immerse is not specifically stipulated in Scripture. He may have wanted to emphasize the point that immersion was a procedure, not an obligation, to counter Karaite accusations that the Rabbanites were misconstruing Scripture by arguing that it was an obligation (as some Rabbanites did). Alternately, Maimonides may have wanted to emphasize his disagreement with his own coreligionists. For example, other enumerators, including Qayyara (Pq 171), counted "immersion in the proper time" (*tevilah bizmanah*) as a *mitsvat qum 'aseh*.

by contact (P97)" or "that a menstruating woman is unclean and defiles others (P99)." Maimonides introduces them as follows:

> The fact that we count each of the various kinds of uncleanness as involving a positive commandment does not mean either that it is an obligation, or that it is forbidden, to become unclean in one or other of these ways, as though this would entail a [violation of] a negative commandment. What we mean is that when the Torah says that one who touches this or that kind [of uncleanness] becomes unclean, or that this or that object makes one who touches it unclean in a certain way, this constitutes a positive commandment: that is to say, this law that we are bidden to observe is a [positive] commandment, that is, that which we said that one who touches a certain thing when it is in a certain condition becomes unclean, but if it is in a different condition, he does not become unclean. The actual becoming clean is optional: if a man wants to become unclean, he does, and if he does not, he does not.

The commandment requires us to declare that a person has become unclean under a certain set of conditions, or, conversely, clean under another set of conditions. We must not think, says Maimonides, that these laws *require* one to become clean or unclean.

In one of his fiercest attacks on Maimonides' claims, Nahmanides exclaims that, despite his prolixity, Maimonides does not present a convincing rationale for including the various kinds of uncleanness in his count. These kinds of uncleanness, writes Nahmanides, "are optional [*reshut*] from all angles, they have no connection to *mitsvah* [*ein ba-hem inyan mitsvah*] that they should deserve to be counted."[6] By "optional from all angles," Nahmanides notes (as I did earlier) that no possible circumstance exists that would *obligate* one to fulfill these directives. As Maimonides himself put it, "if a man wants to become unclean, he does, and if he does not, he does not." Moreover, Nahmanides continues, while the Torah does not prohibit one from becoming unclean, the Torah does forbid one from entering the sanctuary and/or eating sanctified foods while in a state of impurity. In connection with these prohibitions, the Torah describes what makes one unclean and what does not. This is comparable, he continues, to the prohibitions against

6. Nahmanides, *Hasagot* to P96, 248.

bringing blemished animals to the altar (P91-95), where knowing how to distinguish types of blemishes is a key element of fulfilling these commandments. Yet, Nahmanides argues, Maimonides does not enumerate separately all the relevant types of blemishes in those commandments. Why, then, does he count the types of uncleanness here? Nahmanides concludes that types of uncleanness and blemishes are referents of certain types of prohibitions: they cannot themselves constitute commandments.

Jacob Levinger suggests that these types of commandments are specifically intended to establish certain legal concepts. He calls these legal concepts the products of lawmaking, concepts which are part of the tradition from Sinai. These laws are conventions that neither have a basis in nature, as does medicine, nor in metaphysics, as does the belief in God's existence. "Certainly," Levinger opines, "it is this unique conceptualization of uncleanness that justifies their being called commandments." This is also the reason that a kabbalist like Nahmanides would not accept them as commandments; Nahmanides has a more ontological approach to uncleanness, even thinking that uncleanness has a basis in nature (a sort of spiritual pollution).[7]

As I understand Levinger, our difficulty in reconciling this category of commandments lies in our understanding of *mitsvah* as representing a command to do a particular action. Levinger argues that just as positive law differs from natural law—the former is the product of human action, the latter reflects innate beliefs or dispositions (like principles of morality)—so too do commandments differ from metaphysical truths and nature-based laws in that they are legal constructs. In this sense, the term *mitsvah* stands for divinely constructed positive law. It is this characterization that confers the status of commandments on the types of uncleanness, even though they command no specific action. Even if we agree with Levinger's argument, this reasoning does imply that Maimonides has changed the conventional meaning of the term *mitsvah*.

7. Levinger, *Darkhei ha-Maẖshavah ha-Hilkhatit shel ha-RaMBaM*, 73-74. On the difference between kabbalists and Maimonides, particularly on the question of whether impurity ontologically exists or whether it is merely a legal construct, see Kellner, *Maimonides' Confrontation With Mysticism*, 133-139.

Other scholars offer solutions to this conundrum—with little success. Hurewitz suggests that this group of commandments represents a specific goal: to caution the person contaminated by uncleanness to consciously avoid entering the sanctuary, eating sanctified food, and causing others to become unclean.[8] Though he admits that Maimonides did enumerate a number of explicit negative commandments prohibiting the faithful from entering into the sanctuary (N77)[9] and from eating sanctified food while in a state of uncleanness, he maintains that there is room for a positive commandment to reinforce a special guardedness. This reading seems quite strained. There is no precedent in the *ShM* for the idea that a positive commandment should denote the exact same thing as a negative commandment (notwithstanding the paired commandments discussed in Rule 6), and this reading would violate the spirit of Rule 9. More importantly, there is nothing in Maimonides' discussion to suggest that he intended this special guardedness; would he not have spelled out such an idea? In an attempt to rebut Nahmanides' objection, Hurewitz also argues that blemishes are of a "fixed nature and they do not possess such a wide diversity of provisions." The implication is that one is just commanded to recognize blemishes, not to analyze their types, while types of uncleanness require specific laws, due to their complexity and dependence on special circumstances. In response, one could counter that while such an argument may justify a detailed treatment of all types of uncleanness in a code of law, subsumed under one general heading of uncleanness, it does not justify entirely separate *commandments*.[10]

---

8. Hurewitz, *Sefer ha-Mitsvot im Perush Yad ha-Levi*, 117b.
9. He fails to note that there is an additional positive commandment to remove unclean people from the camp (P31).
10. Somewhat similar defenses are offered by de Leon, "Megillat Esther" and Alegre, "Lev Sameah," both in *Sefer ha-Mitsvot*, ed. S. Frankel, 248-250. Specifically, they argue that the various kinds of uncleanness impose a duty to behave in accord with their particular constraints, by secluding oneself, staying away from the sanctuary, neither touching nor eating holy objects, and so forth. It is interesting to note that Alegre concedes the value of Nahmanides' argument ("while his words here are good and correct"); he seems to lack conviction when he concedes: "it is possible to defend Maimonides." In my opinion, Nahmanides' objection retains its full force.

Were he to have shared Nahmanides' concerns, Maimonides could have included the laws of uncleanness in the section on laws of the sanctuary. As Nahmanides points out, while the Torah does not prohibit one from becoming unclean, it does prohibit one from entering the sanctuary and eating sanctified foods while unclean. The laws of cleanness are thus contingent upon the laws of the sanctuary. From an organizational point of view, however, the complex laws of cleanness would have represented an extremely lengthy addition to the section on laws of the sanctuary. Maimonides therefore streamlined the *MT*'s structure by dedicating a separate treatise to the laws of cleanness: *Sefer Taharah*. In this respect, Maimonides followed the arrangement of the Mishnah, where the "Order of Cleanness" (*Seder Teharot*) is distinguished from the "Order of Hallowed Things" (*Seder Kodashim*). I argue that the *ShM*'s separate enumeration of the types of uncleanness foreshadowed this organizational move. Maimonides' individuation of the types of uncleanness appears to be influenced more by compositional considerations regarding his future code than by questions of what constitutes a commandment.

UNCONDITIONAL OBLIGATIONS

Earlier in the chapter, I broached the subject of unconditional obligations and promised to return to them because of their special significance. At the very end of his concluding remarks on positive commandments, Maimonides offers a list of these 60 unconditional commandments. Levinger highlighted the significance of this list and some of its implications in the area of *halakhah* and jurisprudence.[11]

---

11. In the early manuscripts, we find that these commandments are simply referred to by their numbers in the enumeration, e.g. positive commandment #1, positive commandment #2, and so forth. One of the work's translators supplied brief captions, but, over time, mistakes began to enter the printed editions of the *ShM*. Jacob Levinger investigated the textual history of this list, diligently compared manuscripts and printed editions, and affirmed the accuracy of a certain group of manuscripts. See Levinger, *Ha-RaMBaM ke-Filosof u-ke-Poseq*, in particular chapter 6, "The Absolutely Obligatory Commandments (applicable) All the Time," 67-87. As our discussion unfolds, I will show the value of the list in understanding Maimonides' changing conception of the term *mitsvat 'aseh*.

This short list of sixty commandments demonstrates the relative nature of the term *obligatory*. Maimonides describes these commandments as the ones always obligatory upon a man (as opposed to a woman) who lives "in normal conditions: that is to say, that he lives in a house in a community, eats ordinary food, namely bread and meat, pursues a normal occupation, marries and has a family." He calls these commandments "compulsory commandments" (*MnT* and Kafih: *mitsvot hekhre<u>h</u>iyot*), a term likely synonymous with the rabbinic term *<u>h</u>ovah*. He does not call them *mitsvot 'aseh*, nor does he claim that these commandments count more authentically as *mitsvot 'aseh* than the others enumerated in his list. After the strenuous effort to assemble and justify a broad typology of commandments, it is surprising to see Maimonides attach special value to a different enumerating list.

I posit that this list reveals a degree of unease in Maimonides' mind about his system of enumeration, leading to a reaffirmation of the conventional understanding of the term *mitsvat 'aseh*, literally "a command to do," the requirement to perform a particular action. Maimonides here itemizes sixty commandments from his list of 248 that actually fit the conventional understanding of a *mitsvat 'aseh*, an unconditional commandment of action. These sixty commandments are incumbent upon the man who lives in "normal conditions." Maimonides is aware that much of the remainder of these 248 positive commandments can only be called absolute obligations through farfetched logic. Although he calls them *mitsvot 'aseh,* Maimonides does not intend that one *must* give his wife a writ of divorce, or that one *must* free a bondman, or that one *must* become unclean so as to become clean. The *mitsvot hekhre<u>h</u>iyot* are a subset of *mitsvot 'aseh*, but a subset that dovetails neatly with our conventional understanding of *mitsvot 'aseh*. They are not commandments describing a procedure, as is the commandment mandating the use of a writ of divorce. And they are certainly not descriptive commandments, as are those that detail the types of uncleanness. They are, as Maimonides says, commandments that are "absolutely obligatory on every man, at all times, everywhere, and in all circumstances, as for instance, [those regarding] the fringes, the phylacteries, and the observance of the Sabbath."

A few of the commandments on the list are indeed contingent commandments, contingent upon events that occur to ordinary men in "normal conditions." The list of sixty compulsory commandments thus contains the commandments of building a parapet to one's house, inspecting the tokens of an animal, and ritually slaughtering an animal for consumption. All these commandments are contingent upon a normal man's actions: owning a house and eating meat. The "normal conditions" transform a contingent commandment into a compulsory one.

The list of the sixty unconditional obligations will become relevant when I explore an important change in terminology between the *ShM* and the *MT*. I will return to this idea in the second part of the book, beginning in chapter 6.

CHAPTER IV

LOGICALLY INCONCLUSIVE INDIVIDUATIONS

In chapter 1, we briefly discussed the differing schemes that Qayyara and Maimonides used for their lists of commandments. Although Maimonides chose a two-part scheme for his list and rejected the four-part geonic scheme,[1] one might have imagined that he would have been able to incorporate many of Qayyara's commandments into his list. But even if we posit that Maimonides took Qayyara's list as a starting point, the strict methodological procedures enumerated in the *Sefer ha-Mitsvot*'s Rules disqualified many of Qayyara's claims from being accepted as *mitsvot*. Through analyzing Qayyara's list, I infer that an application of Maimonides' Rules would have reduced Qayyara's total of 200 positive commandments by approximately 64 entries.[2] Maimonides would have had to advance 112 new positive commandments, 64 to replace the ones eliminated and 48 new ones, to arrive at a total of 248 positive commandments. How he derived such commandments is the subject of the next two chapters of this work.

A note of clarification: I do not wish to imply that Maimonides drafted his list of commandments by literally revising Qayyara's list. For all we know, he composed his list without reference to Qayyara's, although I suspect that Qayyara's list did indeed hold Maimonides' "center of vision"[3] throughout his work. By analyzing his list as if Qayyara's was its basis, we can better understand the differences in their methods.

---

1. Recall that Qayyara counted 71 punishments (*onshin*), 277 negative commandments punishable by lashes, 200 positive commandments, and 65 sections (*parashiyyot*).
2. See Excursus 1.
3. This felicitous term, first coined by William James, was suggested to me by Bezalel Safran.

Maimonides took three approaches in revising Qayyara's list to fit his needs. First, he converted some of Qayyara's section (*parashah*) entries into individual positive commandments. For example: "the section of the cities of refuge" (*parashah* 3) became P182, the commandment to establish six cities of refuge; "the section of the Second Passover" (*parashah* 30) became P57, the commandment to slaughter the second Passover offering; "the section of the priestly blessings" (*parashah* 32) became P26, the commandment for the priests to bless Israel; "the section of the trumpets" (*parashah* 35) became P59, the commandment to sound trumpets in the Sanctuary; and many others. Second, he converted other sections into more than one positive commandment by applying different individuating criteria. An example examined below is Maimonides' treatment of the *musafin*, the additional offerings. While Qayyara listed these as "the section of the additional offering (*parashah* 41)," Maimonides moved *musafin* into the category of positive commandments and differentiated the single section into eight individual claims. These types of conversions will be the subject of this chapter, where I posit that many such individuation decisions were not logically convincing. Finally, Maimonides introduced entirely new commandment claims. Those innovations will be the subject of the next chapter.

The reader will note that the number of commandments discussed in this chapter and in the next does not total 112. Indeed, I do not intend the discussion of the conversion of individual sections into multiple commandments to be comprehensive. There are many conversions that do not merit special observation, if only because they have little to say about the topic of individuating criteria. Also, I do not explore the one-to-one conversions mentioned in the previous paragraph, since they are relatively straightforward.

In chapter 2, we saw that Maimonides used a linguistic marker to individuate the commandments obligating the court to carry out executions: the composite term *mitsvat-x*, as in *mitsvat ha-nisqalin* and *mitsvat ha-nisrafin*. In reviewing rabbinic passages containing this formula, I began to question the validity of Maimonides' individuation: I saw that the composite term was used on multiple other occasions without prompting Maimonides to individuate the command as a *mitsvat ʻaseh*. In this section, I will attempt to demonstrate that many of Maimonides' individuation decisions were not as logically conclusive as his language implies. This analysis casts doubt on the practical feasibility of reaching a firm and definitive commandment count, a doubt that Maimonides likely shared.

The reader might recognize that even one example should suffice to demonstrate this doubt. Still, any one example could be explained away. The classical apologetic commentaries on the *ShM* are proof of the extraordinary ability of scholars of Talmud to reconcile, harmonize, and rationalize even the thorniest problems. I have therefore used multiple examples to highlight the problems.

P41-43, P45, P47, P48, P50, P51. *MUSAFIN*

Maimonides enumerates eight commandments comprising the *musafin*, the special offerings for the Sabbath, New Moons, and festivals, in addition to the *temidin*, the daily offerings. Detailed in Numbers 28:9-29:39, the specific compositions of each of the *musafin* offerings differ only slightly from each other. The section regarding *musafin* closes with the words: "all these you shall offer to the Lord at stated times" (Num. 29:39). The geonim chose to count all these *musafin* as one commandment: Qayyara lists them as "the section of twenty additional offerings."[4] The twenty offerings are given on: Sabbath (1), New Moon (1), Sukkot (8), Passover (7), Shavuʻot (1), Rosh Hashanah (1), and Yom Kippur (1), paralleling their description in Scripture.

At the end of Rule 13, Maimonides faults the geonim for their analysis:

> They have committed a most serious and strange mistake in connection with this principle: they counted all the *musafin* [of the entire year]—the *musafin* of the Sabbath, of the New Moons, and of the festivals—as one commandment! By the same token they should have counted resting [from work] on all the festivals as one commandment! That they did not do. But the Lord knows and is witness that they are not to be held

4. Qayyara, *parashah* 41. See also Ibn Gabirol, "Azharot," positive commandment 187, sec. 65, s. v. "*musafin* twenty."

> accountable for that, since they have generally not followed one theory in their enumeration; instead, *They have mounted up to the heaven, they went down to the depths* [Ps107:26]. The clear truth is as I have mentioned it to you—that every *musaf* constitutes a commandment in itself, just as resting [from work, *shevitah*] on every [separate] festival constitutes a distinct commandment. This is the correct theory.

Maimonides himself counts eight *musaf* commandments: one for each of the seven occasions listed above, plus a *musaf* for the eighth day of Sukkot (Shemini 'Atseret), which he separates from the festival of Sukkot on the strength of a rabbinic warrant. He connects these individuations to the separately counted requirements to rest on each festival day. He uses Rule 13—"we count only the essential nature of what we have been commanded, regardless of the time element concerning its fulfillment"—to reject the notion of counting the separate *musaf* offerings for each individual Sabbath or New Moon as separate commandments. Similarly, he says, for each multi-day festival, we count only one commandment to bring *musafin* on that festival, even though these offerings are brought over many days.

While Maimonides' individuation seems logical, one could use his principles equally well to define the commandments differently. Invoking this principle of "the essential nature" of the offerings, one could argue that the *musafin* should all be counted as one inclusive commandment, as they all share the common nature of being a *musaf* offering. If one were to counter that the *musafin* for each of the festivals should be counted separately because the specific offerings differ (unlike the offerings for each of the New Moon days), one could respond by questioning why Maimonides subsumes all the *musafin* for Sukkot under one commandment, even though each day's offering is different.

There are arguments for either method of individuation, and it is readily apparent that neither individuation is more definitive than the other. Maimonides' decision to count them all separately is not justified by his critique of the geonic method: "By the same token they should have counted resting on all festivals as one commandment! That they did not do." While Qayyara could be faulted for inconsistency, his inconsistency does not justify Maimonides' individuation. Conversely,

Maimonides' association between discrete festivals and *musafin* is not airtight. One could easily argue that both the command to rest on all festivals and the command to bring *musafin* should be counted as their own overarching commandments, without any further individuation.[5]

P63-67. PRIESTLY OFFERINGS

In this group of commandments, Maimonides outlines the procedures that the priests follow for their various sacrifices: the burnt offering (P63), the sin offering (P64), the guilt offering (P65), the peace offering (P66), and the meal offering (P67). He provides no justification for his individuation decision. While each offering has its procedures explicated in its own separate section in Leviticus, Maimonides does not propose the existence of scriptural pericopes as one of the criteria for individuating commandments.

Without a rabbinic warrant to support his individuations, Maimonides' position is tenuous. As Nahmanides notes, earlier commandments stipulate that certain people must bring offerings under certain circumstances; it would be more logical to include the specifics of offerings as part of those commandments, rather than individuating each offering separately. For example, in P69, we are told that one who sins unintentionally must bring a sin offering. There should be no need to specify a separate commandment (P64) to tell the priest how to perform this duty.[6]

Despite its simplicity, Nahmanides' proposal does not further the goal of creating an outline for a comprehensive code. I postulate that one of the main motivations for Maimonides' organizing his list of commandments is to provide an outline for the comprehensive code of law he intended to write, the *Mishneh Torah*. In this case, he takes his

5. See below, P159.

6. Nahmanides admits that one could separate the requirement to bring the sacrifices from the priests' command to offer them, but he thinks that the scriptural pericopes do not support this bifurcation. In the end, Nahmanides appears to retract his criticism and offers a more general individuation, that all the provisions of the offerings be subsumed under: "And ye shall serve; I give you the priesthood as a service of gift" (Num. 18:7). *Hasagot* to Rule 12, 185-186.

inspiration from the Mishnah and partially follows its arrangement, placing prescriptive material in one section (when and for what reason does one bring an offering) and procedural material in another (how does one prepare each of the sacrificial offerings), much as *M Keritot* is separated from *M Zevahim* and *M Menahot*. Nahmanides' plan would have led to a code that would repeat the laws regarding particular offerings throughout the code, rather than grouping them together. I submit that Maimonides' need for an outline for the *Mishneh Torah* biased his commandment count and inspired his separating the sacrifices into five distinct groups. Here, his particular individuations were more concerned with organizing legal material than with distinguishing commandments. At the same time, the expansion of the list did help him meet his challenge of reaching 248 commandments.[7]

P68-9. SIN OFFERINGS

Here we find an example of Maimonides modifying a previously announced individuation criterion. In Rule 7, he writes, concerning the sin offering (*hatat*):

> Scripture has explained in Leviticus that he who unintentionally transgresses one of the commandments of the Lord—provided the error be in a matter for which the penalty is excision (*karet*) when committed willfully, and there is some act connected with it and the sin involves a negative commandment, as we have explained it in the commentary to tractates *Horayot* and *Keritot*—must bring a sin offering: this constituting a positive commandment. Following this, Scripture sets forth fully the laws pertaining to this offering, devoting many verses

7. Although Maimonides was less concerned about upholding a commandment count in the *Halakhot*, he also designated these procedures as positive commandments there. In that work, he may have used exegesis to interpret the scriptural pericopes of "this is the law of the sin offering" (*zot torat ha-hatat*), "this is the law of the guilt offering" (*zot torat ha-asham*), and so forth (Lev. 1:2-3, 6:7, 6:18, 7:1, and 7:11) as ordering the proper execution of these sacrifices. Admittedly, this argument could be used to justify Maimonides' stand in the *ShM*. Nevertheless, the point that I wish to emphasize is not that it is impossible to rationalize Maimonides' individuations; rather, his individuations can be inconclusive and valid alternatives exist, such as the ones proposed by Nahmanides.

> thereto, stating: if the person who commits the error is one of the common people, he is to bring a female sheep or goat; if he be the prince, he is to bring a male goat; and if he be the High Priest, he is to bring a bullock. And if the error committed be only with respect to idolatry, the transgressor—regardless of whether he be the prince, or one of the common people, or the High Priest—is to bring a female goat. Now [it is obvious that] changing of the kinds of animals from which the offering is brought does not alter the nature of the sacrifice itself—which is namely the offering for unintentional sin—into many, so that it may entail many commandments....[I]t is the charge to bring the offering which constitutes the positive commandment; that one person brings as his offering a female goat, and the other a male goat is merely a condition of that offering, and not every condition of a commandment is to be considered as a separate commandment.

One will note that Maimonides has grouped together the sin offerings of the common people, the prince, and the High Priest, because "it is the charge to bring the offering which constitutes the positive commandment." In the enumeration, Maimonides continues this idea: P69 is set as the general commandment prescribing a sin offering, regardless of who the sinner might be.

Surprisingly, however, he also enumerates another commandment regarding sin offerings: the commandment specifying that the court is to bring a sin offering if it gives a wrong decision (P68). This may be viewed as an inconsistency; how does the offering brought by the court differ from that brought by individuals? Maimonides has indicated that neither differences in the kind of animal nor in the type of sin would differentiate the commandment.[8] A subtler individuation criterion is at play: P68 covers a sin offering for the community; P69, a sin offering for

8. See P72, which contains many different infractions requiring "offering[s] of higher or lower value." This question vexed Kalinberg (*Seder ha-Mitsvot*, *Hilkhot Shegagot*, 48b, s. v. "*yiqshe lan*") who noted that: "It has been many years that I have been baffled by this [problem] and could not find a correct solution, one that would be acceptable." Kalinberg was baffled for three reasons: Rule 7 discards the differences in animals as a criterion for individuation; P72 discards the differences in transgressions as a criterion for individuation; and while the High Priest is fined with a sin offering for deciding incorrectly in matters of law, just as is the court (*Hilkhot Shegagot* 15:1-2), such a sin offering does not merit a separate entry.

the individual. Additionally, the court brings an offering for issuing an incorrect teaching that leads to sin even if the members of the court did not themselves transgress, while the individual brings an offering only for personally committing a transgression. The categorical differences between P68 and P69 may indeed justify their separation.[9]

Regardless, it seems evident that Maimonides made many individuation choices that were not clear-cut: within his rule system, he had the latitude to combine and to separate commandments. By using a nuanced and detailed individuation system, he created a more robust tool for constructing the later outline. And just as crucially, each added individuated *mitsvah* helps his count creep closer to the goal of 248.

P74-77. RITUALS OF ATONEMENT

This group of four commandments covers those needing a ritual of atonement (*meh̲usre kapparah*) before they are permitted to eat sanctified food, even though they have already been cleansed from impurity. They are: a man suffering a flux (*zav*), a woman suffering a flux outside of her menstrual period (*zavah*), a woman who has given birth (*yoledet*), and a leper (*metsora*).

Commenting on the last of these four commandments, P77, Maimonides voices the obvious question: why not enumerate them under an overarching commandment of "those in need of an atonement ritual"? His reply is that indeed this would be the case

> if the offerings incumbent upon those whose atonement is not complete were the same in all cases, and never altered....But because of the diversity of their offerings we are compelled...to count each offering separately.

Their offerings do all differ: the *zav* and *zavah* must bring two turtledoves or two pigeons, one for a sin offering and one for a burnt offering; a birthing woman must bring a one-year old lamb for a burnt offering and a pigeon or turtledove for a sin offering; and a leper must bring two male lambs, one for a guilt offering and one for a burnt offering, as well as

9. Hurewitz, *Sefer ha-Mitsvot im Perush Yad ha-Levi, ad loc.*, offers the differentiae but fails to note the changing criterion for individuation.

an ewe lamb for a sin offering. Indeed, from purely a teleological point of view, all four atonement rituals could be subsumed under one genus, yielding one commandment claim. In view of the diversity of their offerings, however, Maimonides chooses to make four separate claims.

This individuation strategy inspires a number of objections. In our earlier discussion of P68/69, we saw that Maimonides subsumes a number of different offerings[10] under the commandment to bring a sin offering (P69) because they all fulfill the same function. We also saw him explain in Rule 7 that "changing of the kinds of animals from which the offering is brought does not alter the nature of the sacrifice itself—which is, namely, the offering for unintentional sin—into many, so that it entails many commandments." In light of Rule 7, the different offerings required of the four *mehusre kapparah* should not distinguish them as separate commandments; we would expect all atonement rituals to be subsumed under one commandment.[11]

Maimonides' comments on P75 justify another objection to this individuation strategy. While *zav* and *zavah* are obligated to bring identical offerings, Maimonides differentiates these *mehusre kapparah* on physiological grounds. He connects their particular states of impurity to their differing discharges: semen from the male, blood from the female. Semen from the female (if such a thing were possible) or blood from the male would not constitute cause for impurity under these criteria. In contrast with this logic, he argues that he would only count all the *mehusre kapparah* as one commandment

> if the offerings incumbent upon those whose atonement is not complete were the same in all cases, and never altered....But because of the *diversity of their offerings* we are compelled...to count each offering separately. [emphasis added]

10. The common people bring a female goat or lamb; the ruler (*nasi*) brings a male goat; and the anointed priest, a young bullock.

11. This question is raised by Perla in *Sefer ha-Mitsvot le-RaSaG*, vol. 1, 684. Hurewitz, *Sefer ha-Mitsvot im Perush Yad ha-Levi,* ad loc., also notes this problem but blandly relies on the argument that while Maimonides might not differentiate modes of punishment, he does differentiate cleansing methods (P108, P109, P110). (As a side note, I find it interesting that Hurewitz frequently alludes to Perla but never mentions him by name and always tries to dismiss his questions.)

The implication is that if their offerings were identical, he would combine them under one commandment. We could thus imagine another logical arrangement. Taking into account the identical nature of the offerings of the *zav* and *zavah,* it seems more logical to propose three individuations/commandments—*zav/zavah*, the woman giving birth, and the healing leper—rather than the four individuations/commandments that he ended up proposing.

In short, there is nothing inherently logical about separating these atonement rituals into four commandments. Maimonides could have easily combined them into one overarching commandment; he also could have divided them into three, combining *zav* and *zavah* because of their identical offerings. This unconvincing individuation does stretch the count of commandments, bringing it closer to the desired total. It is also clear that four individuations instead of one or three make for a more detailed outline on which to base the intended code of law.

P91. BURNING THE REMNANTS

The following example shrinks the potential count of positive commandments by one; it also shows an inexplicable expansion of the list of negative commandments.

P91 is the commandment to burn the remnants of the consecrated offerings (*notar*). There are two scriptural proof texts enjoining such action: Exodus 12:10, discussing the Passover offering, which states that the remnants must be burned by the next morning; and Leviticus 7:17, covering peace offerings (*shelamim*), which states that the remnants must be burned on the third day. Despite the two proof texts that detail separate offerings with different stipulations, Maimonides only proposes a single positive commandment covering the burning of remnants from the various types of offerings.

The *ShM*'s exegetical warrant comes from the *Mekhilta* on Exodus 12:10, yet the evidence provided in the *SE* and the *Halakhot* is the Leviticus proof text. This single commandment claim contrasts with the individuation of the prohibitions against leaving the remnants of offerings, which he counts as four separate commandments: the remnants of the Passover offering (N117), the remnants of the festival offering (*hagigah*) of the fourteenth of Nisan (N118), the remnants of the second Passover offering (N119) and the remnants of the thanksgiving offering (*todah*) (N120). Duran noted this anomalous treatment, wondering why Maimonides did not specify two positive commandments, one for the *notar* of the Passover offering and one for the *notar* of the peace offerings. Without a good explanation, Duran was forced to note that the early enumerators individuated positive and negative commandments differently. He admits failing to understand their method and piously adds that "their apprehension is greater than ours."[12] Duran's puzzlement highlights the variable and perhaps inconsistent nature of some individuations.

P114-117. VALUATIONS

This group of laws covers valuations, vows to contribute to the Temple that are expressed by the metric of the value of one's life, someone else's life, cattle, a house, or a field. They follow the form "I vow my own valuation." P114 discusses one who pledges the value of a human life; P115, the value of an unclean beast; P116, the value of a house; and P117, the value of certain fields. The valuation scales are set by Scripture. These vows, called *'arakhin* in rabbinic parlance (from the word for valuation, *'arakhah*), are sequentially discussed in Leviticus 27:2-25, introduced by the words: "When a person vows to set aside [*ish ki yafli neder*] a votary offering to the Lord."

Qayyara lists only one entry: "The section of valuations [*parashat 'arakhin*]" (*parashah* 25). Maimonides appears to engage Qayyara when he says:

12. Duran, *Zohar ha-Raqia*, vol. 1, *siman* 40, p. 42; see also the summary at the end of his commentary, 229. See also Perla, *Sefer ha-Mitsvot le-RaSaG*, Ps115, pp. 721-722, who provides a reasonable rationale for the single positive commandment but does not explain the four negative commandments. In *Hilkhot Pesule ha-Muqdashin*, Maimonides appears to be subsuming all the prohibitions into one. But see Babad, *Minhat Hinnukh*, *mitsvah* 8, p. 54, s. v. "*'over 'al lav*." Many of our concerns about the enumeration of positive commandments are also present in the enumeration of negative commandments, which is unfortunately a topic beyond the scope of this work.

> Let no one think that these four kinds of valuations have so much in common that they should be counted as a single commandment. They are four separate commandments, each one with its own distinctive regulations, though the name "valuations" [*'arakhin*] is common to them all.[13] Hence it is not appropriate to count all the kinds of valuations as a single commandment just as it is not proper to count the kinds of offerings as a single commandment.[14] This becomes clear on careful consideration.

Maimonides compares these votary pledges to sacrificial offerings, each of which he lists separately (P63-67). But as we saw earlier, the separate individuation of offerings does not necessarily imply that their derivation is logical. Moreover, one might accept the separate individuation of offerings because their laws are discussed in discrete pericopes headed by the expression "this is the law of" (*zot torat ha-X*). With *'arakhin*, however, the four pericopes are not only listed sequentially but are also linked grammatically by the conjunctive *vav* and the conditional particle *im*, "and if" ("and if [*ve-im*] it be of an unclean beast ... and if a man shall sanctify unto the Lord part of the field of his possession ..."), or by the conjunctive *vav* by itself. This construction suggests that all the laws dealing with valuations are related to each other.

Indeed, the larger idea that each of these valuations should be counted as distinct terms is questionable. In P75, Maimonides explained that he might have combined *zav* and *zavah* under one commandment claim if the nature of their emissions were similar. While the words *zav* and *zavah* share a root, the emissions that give rise to their designations, semen and blood, come from pathologically distinct diseases. Then again, the "constituent element of the essence of each"[15] of the valuation laws is the monetary value of the

---

13. The phrase I translated as "common to them all" is a technical Arabic philosophical term (*astrakh*, translated by Tibbon as *shituf ha-shem*). Often translated in English as "homonym," Maimonides defines it as a "likeness in respect to some notion, which notion is an accident attached to both of them and not a constituent element of the essence of each one of them" (*GP* I:56, 131). See Efros, *Philosophical Terms in the Moreh Nebukim*, s. v. "*shituf*," 119. See also Wolfson, "The Amphibolous Terms in Aristotle, Arabic Philosophy and Maimonides," 155-173, and Wolfson, "Maimonides on Divine Attributes as Equivocal Terms," 37-51 (in particular 45).
14. In his translation, Chavel inexplicably omits the second half of this sentence, from "just" to "commandment."
15. To use the *GP*'s definition. See above, n. 13.

pledge of the votary. There are indeed sufficient grounds to argue that the four commandments of valuation could be subsumed under one heading.

We see the same difficulties here that we saw above with the individuation of offerings (P63-67). Maimonides stretches his logical vocabulary to find ways to individuate commandments, but the results remain unconvincing. While the four valuations do form a useful outline for their discussion in the *MT*, they have little to contribute to a forcefully compelling list of commandments.[16]

P159-160, 162-163, 166-167. FESTIVALS

These commandments discuss the six festivals, called here "the Sabbaths of the Lord" (Lev. 23:38; *shabbetot ha-Shem*) whose common denominator is that "no manner of work is to be done on [these festival days] except what is concerned with the preparation of food." These festivals are the first and last days of Passover, Shavu'ot, Rosh Hashanah, and the first and last days of Sukkot.

Maimonides uses complex exegesis to prove that these festival days are positive commandments. He interprets the term "holy convocations" (*miqrae qodesh*), which is found in the description of all six festival days, to refer to the action of "sanctify[ing] it [the day]" (*qadshehu*). Sanctification entails abstaining from work, except for what is needed for food preparation.[17] The idea that sanctifying the day entails abstaining from work stems from the term *shabbaton*, which derives from a root indicating the cessation of work. Moreover, the rabbis have stated that "*shabbaton* is a positive commandment." Finally, Maimonides encapsulates all six days by noting that "all the days of the 'appointed seasons' are called 'Sabbaths of the Lord' [*shabbetot ha-Shem*]." The positive commandment thus represents the obligation to abstain from work.

16. In the *Halakhot*, Maimonides apparently sees no problem in making the laws of *'arakhin* one commandment: "It is a positive commandment to adjudicate the laws of *'arakhin* as stipulated in the Torah." (*Hilkhot 'Arakhin ve-Haramin*, 1:2).

17. The fourth-listed festival day, the first day of Tishre (P163), is also described by Scripture as a day of "solemn rest" (*shabbaton*) instead of merely with the term *miqrae qodesh*, creating a convenient second exegetical bridge between the categories of *miqrae qodesh* and *shabbaton*.

As an introduction to the laws of festivals (that begin with P159), this exegesis is somewhat confusing and hard to follow.[18] More importantly, the exegesis does not specifically support individuating each of the days described as *miqrae qodesh*. At the end of P167, in an attempt to separate these six festivals from the Sabbath and Yom Kippur, Maimonides states:

> You must know that the same law applies to each of the six [festival] days on which we are enjoined to rest, and none of them is subject to a restriction which does not apply to the others. We are also permitted to prepare food on each one of them. Hence the same regulations regarding "rest" apply to all the festivals.

The principle that "the same law applies to each of the six festival days" is a perfectly good rationale for subsuming all the six festival days into one single commandment: the commandment to abstain from work on the festivals.

In sum, the individuation of each festival does not follow convincing logic. One could argue equally validly that "rest from all work other than the preparation of food" should be counted as one positive commandment, albeit one that takes place several times during the year. Indeed, all the festivals are included under the same directive: "These are My fixed times, the fixed times of the Lord, which you shall proclaim as holy convocations (*miqrae qodesh*)" (Lev. 23:2). One might assume that these "holy convocations" would be grouped together, much as the requirement to dwell in a sukkah for each of the seven days of Sukkot counts as a single commandment. Maimonides himself notes the absurdity of counting the daily offering (*tamid*) and the daily burning of the incense as separate commandments for each day (Rule 13).[19]

---

18. The confusion stems from a series of conflations and assumptions that Maimonides makes. First, the term *shabbaton* appears only in a few, but not in all, of the festival descriptions. To be able to substantiate that other festivals are also considered positive commandments, Maimonides equates the term *miqrae qodesh* with *shabbaton*, an equation that lacks scriptural basis. Nor is he more successful using the statement *shabbetot ha-Shem* to include all festivals where only some types of work are forbidden, because *shabbetot ha-Shem* includes also the Sabbath and the Day of Atonement, where all kind of work is forbidden.

19. To make all these festival days part of one commandment does not mean that one must transgress *all of them* to have transgressed the positive commandment; doing work

On previous occasions, I have noted that Maimonides often seems to derive his enumerations out of a desire to prepare a comprehensive outline for the anticipated code of law. I do not think that is the case here. In the *Mishneh Torah* (*Hilkhot Yom Tov*), Maimonides does not distinguish between the different festival days: "the same law applies to each of the six festival days." Perhaps this section is more evidence of the artificial manipulation needed to hit the exact numerical target of 248 positive commandments. I tentatively conjecture that, at some point in the exercise, Maimonides may have needed a few extra commandments to reach his target. It is at that point that Maimonides could have conveniently decided to follow here the practice of the other enumerators,[20] inflating his count to achieve the required total.

P191. ANOINTING A PRIEST FOR BATTLE

In this section, Maimonides writes:

> we are commanded to appoint a priest to speak to the people when they go forth to battle, and to send back any man who is unfit for battle, whether because he is faint-hearted, or because his thoughts are preoccupied with some matter that may prevent him from giving his mind to fighting.... This priest is called the Priest Anointed for Battle.

---

on *any one* of these days transgresses the positive commandment to rest from work. Conversely, resting on any one day fulfills the positive commandment, irrespective of what one does on other festival days. This is the intent of *Hilkhot Yom Tov* 1:2. One does not need to count six different commandments to achieve this result.

20. Solomon ibn Gabirol, in his "Azharot," clearly counted the festival days separately: two in *siman* 33, three in *siman* 41, and one in *siman* 42. It is not clear to me whether Qayyara individuated them separately or (as I think more likely) as one. See Pq 91-99, where we find: "rest [*shvut*], eight days" followed by a breakdown of the festival days. This breakdown may simply be a clarification and not a list of eight commandments, as Traub (in Qayyara, *Halakhot Gedolot,* ed. Traub) assumed. In Rule 13, Maimonides accused "some [scholars]" of counting the *musafin* as one commandment, something that they did not do with regard to resting on all festivals. The clear implication is that these scholars, whoever they were, counted the festivals individually. The fact that he speaks of "some scholars" and not the more personal "a certain other [scholar]" (as in Rule 2) suggests that he was *not* referring to Qayyara, contra Traub. Perhaps Maimonides was referring to Ibn Gabirol and his compatriots.

He further notes that

> all this procedure—the speech of the priest-anointed-for-war and its proclamation throughout the lines of battle—is binding only in the case of a non-obligatory, or permissible, war [*milhemet reshut*], to which alone this law applies. In the case of an obligatory war [*milhemet mitsvah*] there is no such procedure, neither speech nor proclamation.[21]

The appointment of this priest appears to be entirely dependent on the advent of war; it was not a permanent office. Since P190 permits the ruling powers to conduct non-obligatory wars in accord with scriptural provisions, one wonders why Maimonides did not subsume the appointment of this priest under that commandment. Indeed, to individuate this law seems to contravene Rule 7, which states that the particulars of a specific commandment should not be counted as separate commandments.

Maimonides advances this commandment claim uncritically.[22] Yet this claim not only represents an unnecessary individuation but it also appears to contravene Rule 7.[23] The utility of this enumeration is evident, both for serving as a useful reminder in the preparation of the future code and for assisting with the commandment count. I also wonder whether Maimonides may have had some pedagogic considerations in individuating this commandment. Speaking through the mouthpiece of the priest, Maimonides proclaims that all Israelites must be told "to lay down their lives for the triumph of the faith of the Lord, and for the punishment of the ignorants of the faith[24] who ruin the order of the city."[25] The expressions "ignorants of the faith" and "the order of the city" come from the Islamic political philosophy lexicon,

21. The distinction disappears in the *Halakhot* (*Hilkhot Melakhim* 7:1), however, where the procedures for conducting war apply to both types of wars. Maimonides there states: "a priest is appointed to speak to the people at a time of war in both an obligatory war and a permissible war [*ehad milhemet mitsvah ve-ehad milhemet reshut*]."
22. Enumerated by Qayyara in "the section of the Anointed Priest," *parashah* 50 and by Ibn Gabirol, "Azharot," in *siman* 85 as a *qum 'aseh*.
23. I note that the *Halakhot* does not designate this requirement as a positive commandment. See chapter 6.
24. Chavel: "ungodly ones." In *MnT*: "*ha-sikhlin bah*."
25. Chavel: "social order." In *MnT*: "*yosher ha-medinot*."

particularly from the works of Al-Farabi, a ninth-century philosopher whom Maimonides esteemed.[26] Maimonides here asserts that one must give one's life to punish those who ruin the order of the good polis. Individuating this commandment gives him an opportunity to emphasize this important political point.

P233/234. THE HEBREW MAIDSERVANT

These two commandments itemize the ways in which one can give a Hebrew maidservant her freedom: one can either marry her off before the end of her period of servitude (P233) or help her buy back her own freedom (P234). Arguably, these stipulations offer two alternative methods of fulfilling *one* obligation: to give the maidservant her freedom, "espouse ... or in the alternative, facilitate." To meet this possible objection, Maimonides resorts to a mishnah (*M Bekhorot* 1:7) which states: "The duty of espousal has precedence over the duty of redemption" (*mitsvat yi'ud qodemet le-mitsvat pediyah*). As we showed at the end of chapter 2, there is little or no reason to believe that construct chains using the term *mitsvat* denote the idea of positive commandment in its overarching sense.[27]

P237, 238, 240, 241. DAMAGES AND INJURIES

Maimonides here discusses four claims relating to the damages paid when one's property harms another: the harm caused by an ox to people

26. See Al-Farabi, *Al-Farabi on the Perfect State*. For a useful summary, see Fakhry, *Al-Farabi: Founder of Islamic Neoplatonism*, 101-122. On Maimonides' debt to Al-Farabi, see Berman, "Maimonides, the Disciple of Alfarabi," 154-178.

27. Maimonides may have thought that he had offered a single commandment in the place of these two claims. In his comments on P233, he writes: "You must know that the laws concerning a Hebrew bondsman and the *law* [emphasis added] concerning a Hebrew bondsmaid are in force only when the law of the Jubilee is in force." He again mentions "the law of a Hebrew bondsmaid" in his concluding remarks on the positive commandments. One can conjecture that at one time, P233 and P234 were united under the claim "the law of the bondsmaid," and only later did Maimonides separate them, based on his terminological proof. Qayyara, in "the section of the Hebrew maidservant," *parashah* 2, offers the other logical alternative: "*parashat ama 'ivriyah* [the section of the maidservant]; *parashat 'eved 'ivry* [the section of the slave]."

and to property (P237, based on Exod. 21:28, 35); the harm to animals caused by a pit (P238, based on Exod. 21:33); the harm to property caused by a beast (P240, based on Exod. 22:4); and the harm to property caused by fire (P241, based on Exod. 22:5). Why does Maimonides individuate these four laws, rather than including them in one overarching law: "the law of injuries and damage caused by one's property"?

While one might be able to find differences that justify individuating these four circumstances, one could just as easily have drawn different distinctions. For example, in P237, one could have differentiated between damage done to humans and damage done to property. Lacking a rabbinic warrant explicitly stating that we are in the presence of four *commandments*, we must conclude that this enumeration is not logically compelling.[28]

In the *Halakhot*, Maimonides subsumes these commandments under the heading of the laws of damage to property (*Hilkhot Nizqe Mamon*), which he then subdivides into these four commandments. This is similar to how he treats the laws regulating those who require atonement rituals (*Hilkhot Me<u>h</u>usre Kapparah*): a heading subdivided into four commandments (*zav, zavah*, birthing woman, and leper). The code's outline structure, moving from general law to specific enumeration, is foreshadowed here with these four individuated laws.

P242-244. BAILEES

Maimonides advances only three claims relating to the laws of bailees. According to rabbinic interpretation, Scripture describes four kinds of bailees: an unpaid bailee (Exod. 22:6-8), a paid bailee (Exod. 22:9), a borrower (Exod. 22:13), and a hirer (Exod. 22:14). *M Shevu'ot* 8:1 lists the four bailees, but *BT Shevu'ot* 49b explains that these four types of bailees are governed by only three principles, with the same principle applying to the paid bailee and to the hirer.

Indeed, Maimonides cites *BT Shevu'ot* 49b as a warrant for his

28. Hurewitz, *Sefer ha-Mitsvot im Perush Yad ha-Levi*, on P241, defends the arrangement based on *M Bava Qamma* 1:1, which discusses "the four principal causes [*avot*, lit. "fathers"] of damages." However, Maimonides never uses the term *avot* (unlike *mitsvah*) as a linguistic marker for individuation. Moreover, *avot* is used here in contradistinction to *toledot*, subordinate or derivative causes. Finally, and more importantly, since Maimonides does not quote this source, one must assume that he did not find it convincing.

abridging the count to three bailees: the law of an unpaid bailee (P242), the law of a paid bailee (P243) and the law of a borrower (P244). Despite this warrant, these talmudic categories do not necessarily provide the most logical individuation rationale on which to base commandments.[29] To complicate matters, we see that Maimonides revised his classification system in the *Halakhot*. There, he placed the paid bailee and the hirer in *Hilkhot Sekhirut*, and the unpaid bailee and the borrower in *Hilkhot Sheelah u-Fiqqadon*.[30] This classification might suggest that the scriptural bailees should be seen as representing two rather than three commandments.

To summarize: while Scripture discusses four types of bailees, in the *ShM*, Maimonides uses a talmudic passage to turn the four bailees into three commandments. Later, in the *Halakhot*, he divides the categories of bailees into only two parts. These changing divisions seem almost arbitrary.

Interestingly, in *parashah* 4, Qayyara places the laws of bailment into a broader category of civil laws (*dine mamonot*, "the laws of monies"). Would this constitute a more logical individuation?

P245. BUYING AND SELLING

With regard to this commandment, Maimonides writes: "we are

---

29. Consider, for example, the following *baraita* (*BT Bava Qamma* 4b): "Rav Oshaia taught: There are thirteen principal categories of damage: The Unpaid Bailee and the Borrower, the Paid Bailee and the Hirer, Depreciation, Pain [suffered], Healing, Loss of Time, Humiliation, and the four enumerated in the mishnah, thus making [a total of] thirteen." In this tannaitic teaching, we see some of the categories that Maimonides individuated as independent commandments, such as the paid and unpaid bailees and the borrower. Yet alongside these individuated commandments, we see other categories that seem to be details of the overarching rubrics of damages, such as depreciation, pain, healing, loss of time, and humiliation. Such tannaitic lists fulfill objectives other than counting commandments and cannot be read as shorthand for individuation.

30. There is some evidence that Maimonides originally wanted to separate *Hilkhot Piqqadon* from *Sheelah*. See *Hilkhot H̱ovel u-Maziq*, end of chapter 7, where Maimonides refers to the treatise *Sheelah u-Fiqqadon* by the name "*'inyan ha-piqqadon*," echoing the *Sefer ha-Piqqadon* monographs written by Sa'adiah Gaon, Samuel b. H̱ofni and Hai Gaon. Indeed, based on an autograph fragment of the *MT*, Assaf shows that before the final editing, Maimonides had planned to write *Sheelah* and *Piqqadon* separately. Assaf, "Qeta'im mi-Sefer Yad ha-H̱azaqah," 150. Regarding the laws of bailees, the original arrangement of the *Halakhot* thus followed the meta-halakhic individuation of the *ShM*, where Maimonides individuated three types of bailees.

commanded concerning the law of buying and selling; that is to say, the procedure by which a sale is to be effected between the vendor and the vendee." Maimonides' argumentation, given in the remainder of the explication, proceeds in a roundabout and vague fashion, perhaps unsurprising when one notes the lack of explicit scriptural evidence for this commandment. He begins by commenting that the talmudic rabbis find allusions in Scripture to mnemonically support their enactments (*taqanot*). For example, a rabbinically-enacted provision that one purchases a movable object by drawing it to himself is supported by this scriptural description of a transaction: "And if thou sell aught unto thy neighbor, or buy of thy neighbor's hand" (Lev. 25:14). The word "hand," the rabbis assert, alludes to a commodity that is "purchased from hand to hand" and acquired when the purchaser draws it to himself. Maimonides notes that while "it has been shown that by scriptural law, the payment of money secures the purchase,"[31] rabbinic provisions regulate the purchase and sale of movables. He adds that "other modes of procedures by which lands and other things are acquired, namely writ, and seizing, they base on scriptural verses." Problematically, these verses are drawn from extra-Pentateuchal sources.[32]

Maimonides' exegetical grasping is disconcerting. The scriptural verse he quotes bears no relation to laws of buying and selling, nor does it allude to such laws; it merely offers an extremely veiled hint—since the word "hand" is contextually best understood as "control" or "ownership"—that in certain commercial dealings, objects would pass from hand to hand. Moreover, as we noted, Maimonides only adduces proof for ways to regulate the acquisition of non-movable property from extra-Pentateuchal sources, hardly a valid move.[33] Given

31. As per R. Yo<u>h</u>anan in *BT Bava Metsi'a* 47b (and contra R. Simeon b. Lakish, who maintains that Scripture prescribes acquiring an item by drawing it near, rather than by using money). While R. Yo<u>h</u>anan offers no scriptural support for his thesis, RaSHI (*BT Bava Metsi'a* 46b, s. v. "*savar la ke-rabi yo<u>h</u>anan*") quotes a scriptural verse in support (although he cites it inexactly). Also see Tosafot, *BT Bekhorot* 13b, s. v. "*devar torah*," for an alternative source. At best, the evidence stems from Scripture's silence on the methods by which movables can be acquired, which implies that commerce follows the terms of common usage, i.e. money.

32. See *BT Qiddushin* 26a.

33. When offering exegetical support for this commandment, Maimonides does not use

this hermeneutical weakness, we conclude that there is no basis for believing that the laws of acquisition have a scriptural basis.[34]

It is hard to imagine why Maimonides would have made such a farfetched commandment claim[35] other than to fill an important gap in his outline of the *MT*. In effect, I suggest that Maimonides created an entry on this most tenuous of warrants to provide the proper reference to an important treatise in the *MT*, the Laws of Acquisition (*Hilkhot Mekhirah*). The absence of such a commandment from his enumeration would have disproved his claim that "all this [enumeration] [I would do] in order to guard against omitting *any topic* from discussion, for only by including them in the enumeration of the commandments would I insure against such omission."[36]

---

the typical formula: "this (injunction) is contained in X verse." Instead, he uses the phrase "this procedure has been learned," implying that the commandment is *not* actually contained in the verse.

34. See chapter 7 for a discussion of Maimonides' scriptural hermeneutics, one clearly grounded on contextual reading. Perla ("Introduction," *Sefer ha-Mitsvot le-RaSaG*, vol. 1, sec. 8, 47) also concludes that there is no scriptural passage that may cover the laws of acquisition as defined by Maimonides.

35. In discussing this commandment, Hurewitz, in *Sefer ha-Mitsvot im Perush Yad ha-Levi*, P245, exclaims that "the words of our master are astounding." After noting that Maimonides proved that all the modes of acquisition are only rabbinic ordinances, he asks: "What commandment claim did he advance here that can be considered as having been given to Moses at Sinai?" His apologetic answer is also astounding. The Torah, he says, did not legislate modes of acquisition, although it was mindful of such modes' benefits to society. The verse "And if thou sell aught unto thy neighbor, or buy of thy neighbor's hand" make it obvious that commercial transactions occurred in early days, although the text does not specify the types of transactions. Instead, Hurewitz asserts, the Torah suggests (Hurewitz does not explain how) that such standards should be adopted, either through rabbinic decrees or through commercial practice. The fallacy of this argument is readily exposed. While laws of acquisition can benefit some or most societies, a distance remains between seeing the value of such laws and asserting that the Torah wished to see such laws prescribed. Perhaps the Torah remained silent with regard to civil laws, allowing the market to develop its own mechanisms guided by an overall proviso of fairness and justice? See also Perla, "Introduction," *Sefer ha-Mitsvot le-RaSaG*, vol. 1, sec. 8, 47.

36. Having said this, I also note that Maimonides does not propose a single commandment to reference the laws of gifts (*Hilkhot Zekhiyah u-Matanah*), neighbors (*Hilkhot Shekhenim*), and agencies and partnerships (*Hilkhot Sheluhin u-Shutafin*). It appears that in contrast to the laws of buying and selling, these laws do not have even the most minimal connection to scriptural law.

CHAPTER V

INNOVATIVE COMMANDMENTS

In the previous chapter, we saw how certain individuation strategies helped Maimonides partially achieve his goal of enumerating 248 positive commandments. While he provided substantiations for a large number of claims, many of his arguments were not incontrovertible. One might say that some of these individuations resembled equations with more than one valid solution, with Maimonides arbitrarily choosing among them. Moreover, even when he used these individuation strategies to maximize the number of commandments, his total remained short. Maimonides had to find more commandment claims if he wanted to buttress R. Simlai's dictum. The way to accomplish this was with innovative claims, positing commandments that Qayyara had neither listed on his list of *qum 'aseh* nor on his list of *parashiyyot*.

Before we begin our analysis, I offer a word of caution. Qayyara's list is inconveniently terse, often vague, lacking in punctuation, and formatted differently than Maimonides' list. No definitive comparison between the two is possible. What we read as a Maimonidean innovation might indeed have been referenced by Qayyara, either as its own commandment or subsumed under a different rubric.[1] While this difficulty should not be ignored, scholars have come to a consensus on how to interpret Qayyara's list, developed through years of identifying

1. A good example is Qayyara's entry "faith" (Pq39), discussed in the second part of this chapter: does he use the term to mean belief in God or to mean acting in good faith in business? Or Qayyara's entry "to cheer a bride" (Pq149): does it refer to the rabbinic commandment to gladden a bride on her wedding day (perhaps supported by a *derashah*, as Traub suggests; see Hildesheimer, *Haqdamat Sefer Halakhot Gedolot*, 86n387), or to the scriptural commandment to give happiness to a new wife for a full year? See my discussion of these ideas in chapter 9. Many similar examples exist.

entries and reconciling lists of *azharot*. Building on the work of generations of scholars, Hildesheimer tabulates 37 innovations in Maimonides' list of positive commandments, commandments that do not appear as part of Qayyara's list or on other canonical enumerations.[2]

In this chapter, I first examine some of these 37 innovations, assess the arguments in their favor, and explore other factors that may have led Maimonides to posit these claims. The discussion of innovations leads directly into a discussion of Maimonides' greatest innovation, the introduction of dogma into *halakhah*. I show the critical role that R. Simlai's aggadah and R. Hamnuna's exegesis play in this new theology. This analysis will help the reader gain a more nuanced appreciation of the *TaRYaG* project. In the second part of the chapter, I examine two additional innovative claims, assessing Maimonides' arguments in their favor and exploring their extraordinary theological significance.

I preface this endeavor by quoting an insightful observation made by one of the most erudite and astute commentators on enumerations, Yeruham Perla. In the introduction to his monumental work on Sa'adiah's *Book of Commandments*, Perla raises an obvious question: given that a pious Jew is obligated to keep all commandments, both scriptural and rabbinic, why did the early rabbis (the *rishonim*) spend so much time analyzing the list of 613 commandments? Why does tradition restrict the number of commandments to 613, subordinating individual details under larger commandments and relegating other obligations to rabbinic status? What juridical motivations can exist for restricting the count to this precise number? He answers:

> These questions come from a basic lack of understanding, for it is clear that this enumeration has an important bearing on many of the scriptural commandments, according to the various views. In fact, it is clear that

2. Hildesheimer, *Haqdamat Sefer Halakhot Gedolot*, "Introduction," in particular 37-41. The number of innovations identified by Hildesheimer should be viewed as a minimal estimate. All major commentators agree that there are 37 innovative commandments; thus, I have used it as the focus of my analysis. However, given the commentators' strong propensity to harmonize the lists and their highly imaginative skills, a simple reading of Qayyara's entries would likely produce a much higher estimate. My own imprecise estimate yields a number of innovations slightly in excess of 70 commandments, about twice as many as found by Hildesheimer.

> there is no explicit evidence in Scripture—or even in the *Mekhilta*, *Sifra*, *Sifre*, Talmud and other such sources—for many of the positive and negative commandments enumerated by the various scholars. These commandments depend on the methodological underpinnings on which these enumerations were constructed. For it is clear that if, for example, following his Rules, Maimonides eliminated from Qayyara's count many positive and negative commandments that ought not to be included ... by necessity he must search for other commandments that respond to his criteria so as to be able to complete the count of 613 commandments. And it is quite possible that he [Maimonides] would not be able to draw support from among rabbinic sources for this large number of commandments, positive and negative, that would be consistent with his own Rules. Therefore, relying on the fundament that the scriptural commandments cannot total less than 613, he [Maimonides] *added such commandments from his own opinion, based on some tenuous allusions contained in the scriptural text, coupled with his own interpretation, even though the evidence is not sufficiently compelling.* Were it not for the fact that the number [*TaRYaG*] is fixed and known, he [Maimonides] would not have innovated these commandments. (emphasis added)[3]

Perla suggests that because the rabbinic tradition so prized the importance of 613 commandments, jurists—Maimonides among them—had a special impetus to find commandments in the scriptural text that were not obvious to the casual reader. It is this creativity that is at the heart of the *TaRYaG* project for Maimonides and his fellow enumerators. As Perla maintains, Maimonides' innovations are most original and interesting when he presents claims "based on some tenuous allusions in the scriptural text and coupled with his own reasoning." I add one qualification to Perla's thesis: Maimonides' philosophical views, both theoretical and politico-ethical, inform his individuations. He premises his analyses on the assumption that the Torah is a teaching guide whose purpose is to instill in Jews correct and necessary beliefs.

Maimonides' politico-philosophical views are encapsulated in *GP* III:27. There he suggests that the true law, the "Law of Moses," has two aims: the welfare of the body as a first aim; and the "indubitably greater in nobility" welfare of the soul, achievable only after reaching

3. Perla, *Sefer ha-Mitsvot le-RaSaG*, "Introduction," sec. 10, 56.

the first aim. The welfare of the body consists of "being healthy and in the very best bodily state," achieved by satisfying one's needs for food, shelter, and other similar needs. But because people are social animals, they tend to satisfy their needs through political association. Therefore, the Law aims to enable "the governance of the city and the well-being of the states of all its people according to their capacity," and it accomplishes this "through the abolition of reciprocal wrongdoing and through the acquisition of a noble and excellent character." The Law's ultimate aim is to perfect man's soul through the empirical research and metaphysical speculation that enable sound beliefs and correct opinions. Such beliefs and opinions, Maimonides tells us, lead to eternal life.

According to this scheme, all the commandments of the Torah can be classified according to one of three categories: practical, moral, or intellectual commandments. The former two categories operate on the welfare of the body, while the latter operates on the welfare of the soul. This scheme leads Twersky to say:

> Given these guidelines, established at the beginning of this section in chapter 27 of the *Moreh* [the *GP*], the remaining task is completely deductive. One has to relate each of the 613 commandments to one of the three goals: (a) establishment of civilized society—principles of social utility and justice; (b) development of the ethical personality—principles of goodness and love of fellow man; or (c) intellectual perfection—true knowledge and experience of God. Had the remaining chapters of the *Moreh* been lost, we could have undertaken to reconstruct the correlation between each commandment and these three goals.[4]

As we review some of Maimonides' innovative claims, particularly those not supported by conclusive rabbinic warrants, we note that his deductive process does not always work in the direction that Twersky posits. As Warren Zev Harvey writes:

> What is not explicit in Twersky's analysis is the extent to which Maimonides' legal teleology is *prescriptive* [Harvey's italics]. Are Maimonides' teleological explanations of the commandments merely

4. Twersky, *Introduction to the Code of Maimonides*, 388.

> descriptive of how he understood the received law, or is it possible to detect in the *Mishneh Torah* an ongoing effort by Maimonides to decide the law in such a manner as to bring (or keep) it in line with the *teloi* of peace and knowledge? [5]

My analysis leads me to believe that the latter pattern is frequently true. Maimonides formulates some of his commandments based on his underlying goals—and only then finds an appropriate supporting text. While he does not state it explicitly, Perla implies that this is often Maimonides' approach.

EXAMINING THE EVIDENCE

To identify the most original of Maimonides' contributions, I exclude from my analysis all those claims for which Maimonides provides strong evidentiary support. I contend that the remaining commandments, supported by inconclusive evidence, are at least partly driven by his philosophical goals.

Before I begin my analysis, I mention again the work of Moritz Peritz, discussed in some depth in chapter 2. Peritz was unusually sensitive to Maimonides' use of rabbinic language and evidentiary claims, particularly to the types of rabbinic expressions on which Maimonides relies. He highlights terms such as *mitsvat 'aseh, metsuveh, mitsvah, 'over 'al, ḫovah, de-oraita,* and *'al korḫo* as examples of tannaitic language that Maimonides appropriates for his arguments. Indeed, many of the inferences that I will draw in this chapter were first noted by Peritz.[6]

STRONG EVIDENCE

This category includes those innovative claims supported by strong rabbinic proofs for their positive commandments. For the most part, these warrants, taken mainly from the *midreshe halakhah*, describe

5. Harvey, Review of *Introduction to the Code of Maimonides*, 200-203.
6. Peritz's work can be found in Bacher, "Zum Sprachlichen Charakter des Mischne Thora," 439-474. See in particular 455-59. See chapter 2 of this book for a more detailed explication of his linguistic theories.

a particular scriptural passage as a *mitsvat 'aseh*. A word of caution: Maimonides understands these midrashim to be designating the commandments as scriptural, even though the midrash may not be applying Maimonidean criteria for designating positive commandments. That is, the *midrash halakhah* might sometimes use the phrase *mitsvat 'aseh* to define a command as obligatory without intending to count it as an enumerated commandment. For example, the obligation referred to as an *'aseh* may only be a detail or condition (*mishpat*, in the language of Rule 7) of a larger, overarching, commandment. In such a case, it would not qualify as an independent and individuated claim according to the guidelines of Rules 7 and 10-13. For the purposes of our analysis, I assume that Maimonides has used his Rules to test the evidence and has only enumerated those commandments that passed the required criteria. Although the linguistic markers are given prominence, it is Maimonides' considered judgment, through the prism of his Rules, which enables these commandments to be enumerated.

I list briefly some of the innovations supported by key linguistic markers, providing in parentheses the specific term used:

> P22. To watch over this edifice [*bayit*, holy house] continually (*be-'aseh*);
> P84. To offer all sacrifices in the Sanctuary (*be-'aseh*);[7]
> P87. That an exchanged beast [*ha-temurah*] is [or becomes] sacred (*'aseh*);
> P90. To burn meat of the holy [sacrifice] that has become unclean (*'aseh*);
> P142. To exact the debt of an alien (*zo mitsvat 'aseh*);
> P146. To slay, according to the ritual, cattle, deer, and fowl, and then their flesh may be eaten (*nitstaveh*);
> P198. To lend to an alien with interest (*zo mitsvat 'aseh*).

As we can see, this list contains commandment claims supported by derivatives of the term *mitsvat 'aseh*.

With respect to P142 and P198, the *midrash halakhah's* understanding that these are obligations is unique and highly controversial. The

7. For a lengthier discussion of this commandment, see Maimonides' remarks at N89, where the counterpart negative commandment is discussed.

simple meaning of the biblical verses is that while one is permitted to exact the debt of an alien and charge an alien interest, these actions are not specifically commanded: rather, the verses specify that one is *prohibited* from doing thus to an Israelite. Commentators have also pointed out that the Talmud supports the simple interpretation, and that the interpretation of the *midrash halakhah* should be subordinated to that of the Talmud.[8] Maimonides' use of midrash is highly selective and appears to respond to his strong concerns regarding contact with idolatrous people and practices. Restricting business dealings with pagans can prevent their potential integration into Jewish society.[9]

Maimonides also used other terms in his evidentiary work. The next two innovations use the terms *be'al korho*, "against his will," implying that one must do an action even when one does not want to, and *hayav*, "obligated to":

> P23. That the Levite shall serve in the Sanctuary (*be'al korho*);
> P32. To show honor to a descendant of Aaron, and to give him precedence in all things that are holy *(be'al korho)*;
> P85. To take trouble to bring sacrifices to the Sanctuary from places outside the land of Israel (*hayav)*.

On a number of occasions, Maimonides made novel commandment claims based on explicit scriptural verses without invoking a supporting rabbinic warrant. This is the case with:

> P175. To render the decision according to the majority, when there is a difference of opinion among the members of the *Sanhedrin* as to matters of law. This commandment is based on the verse "to incline after many" (Exod. 23:2) (despite its being a syntactically awkward clause);
> P179: To examine witnesses thoroughly. This commandment is based on the verse, "Then shalt thou enquire and make search and ask intelligently" (Deut. 13:15), found in a jurisprudential context.

---

8. Regarding P142, see di Tolosa, "Maggid Mishneh" (in standard editions of the *MT*), *Hilkhot Malveh ve-Loveh* 1:2, reflecting the opinion of post-Maimonidean commentators. With regard to P198, see Nahmanides, *Hasagot* to Rule 6; and RaBaD in his gloss to the *SE*.
9. Also see P187, where he says that the aim of destroying the Seven Nations is "to safeguard us from imitating their apostasy."

It is highly unlikely that any jurist preceding Maimonides disagreed with his contention that these two commandments are biblically commanded.[10] More likely, those who did not enumerate them did not see them as thematically independent laws, laws that needed to be individuated.[11] Earlier enumerators (such as Qayyara) may have subsumed these commandments under more general rubrics, such as *parashah* 1, which includes court law and criminal and monetary laws. Indeed, Maimonides' special individuation of these two laws calls for an explanation. I submit that Maimonides may have wanted to exhibit worthy examples of procedural concerns found in the Torah.[12] A complementary explanation is that these two laws could function as intermediate sub-headings in the long exposition on the laws of courts and witnesses, included to aid his avowed goal of drafting a useful working outline.

Another novel commandment claim based on a scriptural verse and lacking a rabbinic warrant is P30, which states that the priests are to lift off (*le-harim*)[13] some of the ashes from the altar.[14] The removal of ashes from the altar is neither an integral part of the sacrificial ritual nor a provision of it. It represents an independent cultic service, or as the rabbis would call it, the "removal [from the altar] service" (*'avodat siluq*). The "removal service" sits a notch below the "offering [unto the altar] service" (*'avodat matanah*) in importance, a distinction that carries legal consequences.[15] While the commandment is clearly biblically obligated, its individuation is somewhat more problematic.

---

10. For example, they appear as Ps96 and Ps97 in Sa'adiah's list of commandments. Perla, *Sefer ha-Mitsvot*, vol. 1, 648-662.

11. Maimonides could also have subsumed the command to follow majority opinion under "In righteousness shalt thou judge thy neighbor" (P177). This is suggested by Duran, *Zohar ha-Raqia, siman* 52, 60.

12. In my article, "Cross Cultural Influences and the Possible Role of Competition in the Selection of Some Commandments," 410-414, I discuss the individuation of P175, P178, and P179, suggesting that Maimonides may have wanted to show his Muslim colleagues that, just like Muslim jurisprudence, the Torah prioritized matters related to procedural law.

13. Hyamson's translation gives a correct interpretation of the literal text.

14. In the *ShM*, the commandment is stated (less precisely) as "to remove the ashes daily from the altar." See Perla, *Sefer ha-Mitsvot le-RaSaG*, vol. 1, 757.

15. For more on this distinction see *BT Yoma* 23b; *Hilkhot Biat ha-Miqdash* 9:8.

Maimonides could well have subsumed this activity under the general heading of *ma'arakhah* (lit. layout, array),[16] a category which could have included feeding a fire on the altar and maintaining a perpetual fire (P29), based on Leviticus 6:1-6. His outline requirement, however, may have necessitated a somewhat more specific claim. Alternatively, perhaps he considered the removal of ashes from the altar to be a truly independent commandment, expressing a specific *telos*: decorum and cleanliness in the service of the Lord.[17]

P201 is a novel commandment, one deserving of mention for two reasons. The claim states that the hired laborer shall be permitted to eat (while he is on hire).[18] Maimonides begins by referencing *M Bava Metsi'a* 7:2 to demonstrate the scriptural right of a harvesting worker to eat from the produce. The mishnah states: "These may eat [of the fruits among which they labor] by virtue of what is enjoined in the Law [*min ha-torah*]: he that labors on what is still growing after the work is finished."

Note that the commandment merely confers on the laborer the permission to eat while he is working. There is no obligation on the part of the owner to feed the laborer, although we presume he has an obligation to acquiesce to the demands of the laborer. In chapter 2, I analyzed the various ways in which Maimonides uses the term *mitsvat 'aseh*. In this instance, we see Maimonides broaden the term *mitsvat 'aseh* to include rights. Maimonides might not have individuated such law as a commandment if not for his outline in progress; this right represents a necessary rubric in his comprehensive outline. Laborers' rights while performing farming services are quite complex and detailed, covering all of chapter 12 of *Hilkhot Sekhirut*, 14 *halakhot* in all. The advancement of this claim appears therefore to stem from

---

16. Qayyara, *parashah* 9 (found only in the Oxford manuscript).

17. Note that in the *Halakhot*, which does not normally give explanations of a non-halakhic nature, Maimonides uses this type of reasoning to justify the priest's changing his special clothes in order to remove the ashes, noting that "it is not proper [*derekh erets*] that he [the priest] should pour wine for his master in the same clothes in which he cooked his food." *Hilkhot Temidin u-Musafin* 2:10, quoting a *baraita* attributed to R. Ishmael, *BT Yoma* 23b.

18. I have followed a more literal translation of the Hebrew text. Hyamson has "of the produce which he is reaping."

Maimonides' goal of producing a useful outline rather than from any inner logic justifying it.

I would also like to note that the laborers' right to eat is reformulated in the *Halakhot* while given a different *telos*. I will return to this discussion in chapter 9.

The aforementioned innovations all share the common feature of formal evidentiary support. Maimonides proves his claims adducing rabbinic warrants and/or relatively straightforward scriptural proof texts. The next group of enumerated commandments, all formulated as obligations, are either presented without formal evidence or presented with unconvincing evidence.

I organize the rest of this section by commandment, each followed by a very brief comment summing up Maimonides' proof(s). Here and throughout the rest of this work, I quote the positive commandments as they are formulated in the Short Enumeration (*SE*).

> P34. That, when the ark is carried, it should be carried on the shoulder, as it is said, "They shall bear it upon their shoulder" (Num. 7:9).

While the nonspecific language of the *SE* does not identify who is to carry the ark, the *ShM* clearly identifies the command's subject: "*the priests* are to bear the ark upon their shoulders" (emphasis added). The *SE's* ambiguity resurfaces in the tenor and formulation of the *Halakhot* (*Hilkhot Kele ha-Miqdash* 2:12), which omits the subject of the command.[19]

Proof: The proof text for this claim is the verse: "But unto the sons of Kehat he gave none [of the wagons and animals], because the service of holy things belonged unto them: they bore them upon their shoulders" (Num. 7:9). Note the lack of evidence of a direct or mediated command to the sons of Kehat[20] to carry the ark on their shoulders. The biblical text recounts that they did so without detailing a reason.

To prove that carrying the ark was a divine command, Maimonides quotes two passages from the Hagiographa (*Ketuvim*). The first refers to

19. This may be an indication that the *ShM* preceded the *SE* chronologically, and that Maimonides changed his interpretation of this commandment between these two works. See note 53 in this chapter and note 40 in chapter 9.

20. The priests were descendants of Kehat.

David's commanding the priests and the Levites to bring up the ark for the second time. Chronicles records: "And the children of the Levites [here referring to the priests] bore the ark of God on their shoulders with the bars thereon as Moses *commanded* according to the word of the Lord" (1 Chr. 15:15). The second passage discusses the division of the priests into twenty-four groups: "These were the orderings of them in their service, to come into the house of the Lord according to the ordinance given unto them by the hand of Aaron, their father, as the Lord, the God of Israel, had *commanded* him" (1 Chr. 24:19). On this passage, Maimonides comments:

> The Sages explain this verse as implying that it is the task of the priests to perform the service of bearing the ark upon their shoulders, and that this is what the Lord, the God of Israel commanded.
>
> The Sifre says: According to the ordinance unto them ... as the Lord, the God of Israel, had commanded him: where did He so command him? [In the verse,] *But unto the sons of Kohat he gave none, because the service of holy things belonged unto them: they bore them upon their shoulders* [Numbers 7:9]. (*Sifre Numbers* 46 (51-52))

The last line of the previous section of *Sifre Numbers* 45 (52), which Maimonides did not quote, explains: "Thus the Levites did not innovate at all: everything was commanded by Moses, and Moses was commanded by the Almighty [God]." This bit of inter-textual citation is Maimonides' putative evidence that the priests were commanded to carry the ark on their shoulders when it had to be moved.

> P86. To redeem cattle, set apart for sacrifices, that contracted disqualifying blemishes, after which they may be eaten by anyone, as it is said, "Nevertheless thou mayest kill (and eat flesh in all thy gates) whatever thy soul lusteth after" (Deut. 12:15). By tradition it is learned that this verse refers only to sanctified animals, and teaches us that they ought to be redeemed if and when they become unfit.[21]

Proof: The tradition to which Maimonides refers can be found in *Sifre Deuteronomy* 71 (134). He is the only enumerator to name an obligation

---

21. Chavel: "items that must be redeemed" for *she-yipadu* is interpretative.

to redeem a blemished animal reserved for sacrifice, selectively using sources to support his point. Other commentators maintain that redemption is voluntary and find other talmudic sources to support this view.[22] Note that even the midrash quoted by Maimonides does not necessarily obligate one to redeem the unfit animal; it merely states that it should be redeemed, presumably so that one can eat it.

> P157. To discourse concerning the departure from Egypt on the first night of the Feast of Passover, as it is said, "And thou shalt tell thy son on that day, saying . . ." (Exod. 13:8).

Proof: Maimonides brings two proofs, first citing a well-known rabbinic saying (found in the Passover Haggadah): "Even if we were all of us wise, all of us men of understanding, all of us learned in the Law, it is a *mitsvah* to speak of the departure from Egypt." On closer look, this is not a particularly persuasive proof for the obligation to recount those events, since *mitsvah* in rabbinic terminology can represent a good deed or a rabbinic obligation, as we saw in chapter 2.

The second proof is drawn from an exposition found in the *Mekhilta de-RaSHBY* on Exodus 13:3:

> Since it is said, *And it shall be when thy son asketh thee*, etc., one might think [*yakhol*] that you are to tell your son if he asks you, but not otherwise. Scripture therefore says [*talmud lomar*], *thou shalt tell thy son*—even though he does not ask you. Again, one might think that [the duty rests only on one] who has a son [with him]; whence do we infer that it applies also to one who is alone, or among strangers? From the words of Scripture: *Moses said unto the people: Remember* [zakhor] *this day* [Exod. 13:3].

22. See di Boton, *Lehem Mishneh* (in standard editions of the *MT*), *Hilkhot Isure Mizbeah* 1:10. A review of talmudic sources leads Perla (*Sefer ha-Mitsvot le-RaSaG*, vol. 1, 758-760) to conclude that the redemption of blemished animals is strictly voluntary (*reshut*). In contrast, Hurewitz, *Sefer ha-Mitsvot im Perush Yad ha-Levi*, ad loc., finds sufficient evidence to declare this verse an unconditional obligation. For Maimonides' apparent prioritization of *midreshe halakhah* over Talmud, see *Sefer ha-Mitsvot*, ed. Heller, N72, n. 19. I concede that it is possible to read the *ShM* as saying that one must redeem the animal *if and when* one wants to eat it, in effect a contingent obligation.

The midrash likely means that apart from the specific obligation to teach one's child about the exodus (Exod. 13:3), Moses also instructs all Israelites to remember the exodus, irrespective of the presence of children. Maimonides then adds his own[23] crucial explanation: "That is, Moses told the people that God commanded us to remember the exodus just as he ordained *Remember the Sabbath day, to keep it holy*." Since the remembrance of Sabbath is a positive commandment (P155), by analogy, this exhortation is one as well.[24] The analogy stretches the midrash well beyond its simple meaning.

It may be more plausible to consider that Maimonides turned the re-telling of the exodus into an obligation rather than simply into a recommendation because he thought that a belief in miracles was a necessary opinion.[25] The account of the miracles that God performed for the Israelites proves to the faithful that God is a volitional, interacting deity, a foundational concept in Judaism. The memory of these miracles must be perpetuated through constant repetition because, over the course of time, miracles can easily be rationalized away.[26]

> P172. To heed the call of every prophet in each generation, provided that he neither adds to nor takes away from the Torah, as it is said, "unto him ye shall hearken" (Deut. 18:15).

Proof: Maimonides resorts to a midrash that uniquely inteprets the verse "unto him ye shall hearken" (Deut. 18:15): "Even if he tells you to violate temporarily one of the commandments enjoined in the Torah, you must hearken unto him."[27] This commandment includes two prohibitions: that a prophet may not disobey his own prophecy

23. It does not appear in our text of the *Mekhilta*; this addition is Maimonides' own. So Shem Tov ibn Gaon (*Migdal Oz*) understands it. See also Kasher, *Ha-RaMBaM ve-ha-Mekhilta de-RaSHBY*, 61.

24. That Maimonides is satisfied with this exegesis is apparent from his repeating it in the *Halakhot, Hilkhot Hamets u-Matsah*, 7:1.

25. Cf. *GP* III:43, 572. On the connections between miracles, a willing deity, and religion, see "Iggeret Tehiyat ha-Metim" in *Iggerot ha-Rambam*, ed. Shailat, 356-357 and 367.

26. See *GP* III:50, 615-16: "all miracles are certain in the opinion of one who has seen them; however, at a future time their story becomes a mere traditional narrative, and there is a possibility for the hearer to consider it untrue." Also see the end of that long passage.

27. *Sifre Deuteronomy*, *Shoftim* 175 (221).

and that a prophet may not suppress a prophetic message. The Talmud (*BT Sanhedrin* 89a) derives these various prohibitions from the verse: "Whosoever will not hearken unto My words which he shall speak in My name, I will require it of him" (Deut. 18:19). Maimonides notes that, according to the Talmud, the scriptural verse indicates that transgressors will receive divine punishment.

No special linguistic marker, similar to the ones we had seen earlier, backs up the claim that we are in the presence of a *mitsvat 'aseh*. Furthermore, it is unclear why this claim should be designated a positive commandment rather than a prohibition (i.e. negative commandment) against ignoring the prophet's words. In fact, as Maimonides notes at the end of his explication, "transgressors will be punished"—which implies that this is a negative rather than a positive commandment.[28]

Maimonides could have based a similar claim on an explicit prohibition, "be no more stiffnecked" (Deut. 10:16) as Sa'adiah did,[29] making this a negative rather than a positive commandment. I suspect, however, that Maimonides needed the *Sifre*'s explication of Deuteronomy 18:15 to support his highly original exposition of the fundaments of prophecy presented in his "Introduction to the Mishnah" and in *Hilkhot Yesode ha-Torah* (chapters 7-10). He makes a brief reference to these principles of prophecy in the explication of the commandment in the *ShM*, when he states that the commandment is

> to hearken to any genuine prophet [lit., prophet from among the prophets] and to do whatever he bids, even if it be contrary to one or more of the [scriptural] commandments, provided that it is only temporary, and does not involve a permanent addition to or subtraction from [the Law], as we have explained in the Introduction to the Mishnah.

28. In *Hilkhot Sanhedrin* 19:3, when discussing the punishment applicable to transgressors of this injunction, Maimonides suggests that "unto him ye shall hearken" is a positive statement that yields an inferred prohibition (*lav ha-ba-mikhlal 'aseh*). As we saw, this principle allows the court to treat the inferred prohibition more leniently (i.e. no lashes as punishment) than if it were couched as an outright prohibition. In chapter 2, I call these positive statements *mitsvot 'aseh* in form rather than in substance because they legislate a prohibition rather than a positive act. Though Maimonides does not mention this hermeneutic in his gloss in the *ShM*, it is not impossible that he had it in mind here. See the further discussion of this commandment in chapter 9.

29. Perla, *Sefer ha-Mitsvot le-RaSaG*, vol. 2, Ns 49, 97.

Maimonides grounds his discussion of prophecy in the "Introduction to the Mishnah" on Deuteronomy 18:15-19 and on the *Sifre*'s interpretations of that passage. I conjecture that because of their fundamental importance, Maimonides deigned to craft a commandment out of this verse, despite the hermeneutic difficulty.[30]

> P178. That one who possesses evidence shall testify in Court, as it is said, "and if one is a witness, and hath seen or known [if he do not tell, then he shall bear his iniquity]" (Lev. 5:1).

Proof: Scripture proclaims that anyone who withholds evidence will suffer serious consequences: "And if any one sin, in that he heareth the voice of adjuration, he being a witness, whether he hath seen or known, if he do not utter it, then he shall bear his iniquity" (Lev. 5:1). The verse does not literally enjoin witnesses to present evidence, but rather admonishes and threatens witnesses for withholding evidence. Effectively, this appears to be an admonition rather than a precept—a negative rather than a positive commandment. Maimonides confirms this understanding in a little-noticed statement contained in his explications to N297, the prohibition against neglecting to save an Israelite in danger of losing his life and/or his money. After stating that "[t]he Sages say[31] that this prohibition covers also the case of one who withholds evidence," he adds, "Scripture again refers to this matter: *if he do not utter it, then he shall bear his iniquity* [Lev. 5:1]." In other words, at N297, Maimonides construes Leviticus 5:1 as conveying an admonition, a negative commandment, rather than a positive commandment.

---

30. Maimonides' enumeration here follows several other enumerator-jurists, although Qayyara is not among them. Although Sa'adiah lists this precept in his Decalogue-based *azharot* (under the third utterance), describing it as "my inheritance listens to the words of the prophet of God," he omits it in the *Sefer ha-Mitsvot*. Perla does a reasonable job explaining the omission (Perla, *Sefer ha-Mitsvot le-RaSaG*, vol. 2, Ns49, 97-99). H̲efets b. Yatsliah̲ also lists this precept: "It is our duty to listen to the words of the prophet" (ninth utterance). See Zucker, "Mi-Sefer ha-Mitsvot shel H̲efets b. Yatsliah̲," 34. In note 21, Zucker points out that both Sa'adiah, in his Arabic *Sefer ha-Mitsvot*, and Samuel b. H̲ofni counted this obligation.

31. Maimonides is referring to *Sifra Qedoshim* 4:8 (89a), on Leviticus 19:16, which he quotes later.

Commentators have struggled to read some type of affirmative injunction into the text. David b. Zimra (RaDBaZ) suggests that we ought to read the verse by adding the active verb "must tell" after "whether he hath seen or known." [32] RaDBaZ's solution is self-serving: he supplies a non-existent verb to support the claim that this is a positive statement. While this type of solution is sometimes offered in cases where a clear rabbinic tradition supports such a reading, we have no such tradition here.[33] Equally unsatisfactory is Duran's solution, which conjures a syntactically impossible imperative, interpreting "he being witness" to mean that he is obligated to be a witness.[34] Nor does Maimonides cite a rabbinic warrant in support of this claim.

In the *ShM*, Maimonides states, "Sages adduce as proof of this obligation to give testimony" the Leviticus proof text; however, he fails to cite the rabbinic source.[35] In sum, there is no evidence of a positive commandment urging one to offer testimony, neither in Scripture nor in rabbinic literature. As Maimonides comments at N297, the verse "if

---

32. RaDBaZ's commentary to *Hilkhot 'Edut*, 1:1, s.v. *"ha-ed metsuveh."*

33. The best examples are the ones in which Maimonides cites tradition in his reading of the verse. These are introduced by the formula "tradition taught" (*lamdu mi-pi ha-shemu'ah*), as in P85, P86, P109, P128, and others. Indeed, these interpretations involve *con*textual rather than textual manipulation—giving a novel meaning to the verse by providing a new context. Where some textual manipulation is required, where words and/or sentences do not appear to bear a clear meaning, Maimonides can cite a number of traditions to support the difficult reading, as he does in N194, for example.

34. Duran, *Zohar ha-Raqia*, *siman* 53, 61. See also Perla, *Sefer ha-Mitsvot le-RaSaG,* vol. 1, Ps 31-32, 368a.

35. The *Kesef Mishneh* commentary on *Hilkhot 'Edut* 1:1 points to *BT Bava Qamma* 56a, but that talmudic passage does not support the existence of an obligation to provide testimony. Instead, the passage warrants that the verse, which promises an unspecified retribution, concerns the case of two witnesses who withhold evidence, while R. Joshua maintains that even one witness who withholds evidence incurs heavenly disfavor. While there is a scripturally commanded punishment for withholding evidence, where is the command to bring the evidence? Bothered by this lack of direct evidence, Yosef b. Habiba, in the beginning of his *Nimuqe Yosef* commentary to the sixth chapter of *BT Bava Qamma*, asserts that the obligation to testify is only a supererogatory act (*gemilat hesed*). Other commentators find their source in *M Sanhedrin* 4:5. The mishnah has the witnesses complain about having to testify under strain and admonishments: "And if perchance ye would say: Why should we be at these pains? Was it not once written 'and he being a witness, whether he hath seen or known, if he do not utter it, etc.'?" Implicit is the obligation to provide testimony, although one could read the retort as articulating the gravity of the sin of withholding testimony, rather than implying a positive commandment.

he do not utter it, then he shall bear his iniquity" is only a special case of the overall prohibition against standing by while an Israelite is in danger of losing his life or his money.

This commandment, nonetheless, can be seen as serving as a pillar of an effective judicial system. This could explain Maimonides' desire to craft a positive commandment out of the verse "if he do not utter it, then he shall bear his iniquity"—despite scant scriptural or rabbinic evidence.[36]

> P187. To exterminate the seven Canaanite nations from the land of Israel, as it is said, "But thou shalt utterly destroy them" (Deut. 20:17).

Proof: Maimonides provides no direct rabbinic warrant in support of his claim, which he refers to as "an obligatory war" (*milhemet mitsvah*).[37] At the start of his discussion, he identifies the obvious problem: these nations no longer exist. While one might think that this commandment is no longer binding (and thus not a positive commandment, as per Rule 3), Maimonides writes that such an idea "will be entertained only by one who has not grasped the distinction between commandments that are binding for all time and those that are not." After acknowledging that "no trace of [the nations] remains," he notes that "it does not follow that the commandment to exterminate them is not binding for all time, just as we cannot say that the war against 'Amaleq is not binding for all time, even after they have been consumed and destroyed."[38] The core of his

36. For a possible motivation, see Friedberg, "Cross-Cultural Influences and the Possible Role of Competition in the Selection of Some Commandments."
37. According to *BT Sotah* 44b, the Sages and R. Judah agree that the category of obligatory wars includes the conquest wars against the seven nations, the war against the 'Amaleqites, and all defensive wars, though the Sages term an obligatory war *milhemet mitsvah* while R. Judah calls such a war *milhemet hovah*. (Maimonides follows the opinion of the Sages and calls such a war *milhemet mitsvah*.) From the fact that *tannaim* disagree about these categories, one can suppose that these categories specify active laws and commandments rather than historical events that only hold an antiquarian interest—thus Maimonides' warrant for the existence of a commandment to destroy the seven Canaanite nation. Nevertheless, it should be noted that Maimonides could have retained the concept of *milhemet mitsvah* and applied it only to "a war to deliver Israel from the enemy attacking it," as he does in *Hilkhot Melakhim* 5:1, without having to mention 'Amaleq and the seven nations.
38. The proof from the analogy to 'Amaleq (P188) is circular, for one may well question the validity of that claim since it seems that 'Amaleq, too, has perished and disappeared.

argument is that "no special condition of time and place is attached to this commandment, as is the case with those commandments specially designed for the desert or for Egypt." This fine distinction is difficult to accept, since the biblical command to exterminate the seven Canaanite nations also seems to apply to a historically circumscribed period, the conquest and settlement of the Land of Israel.[39] Even if no "condition of time and place" were attached to this commandment, Maimonides would still have to address Daniel ha-Bavli's objection that a precept is not incumbent on later generations once the objective of the precept has been realized.[40]

Regardless of whether this commandment should be counted, its practical value seems to be negligible, as the seven nations have long since lost their national identities. I believe that Maimonides posits this claim and defends it vigorously for didactic reasons. The opening line of his explication betrays a key concern: these nations had to be exterminated "because they constituted the root and very foundation of idolatry ... the object was to safeguard us from imitating their apostasy." [41] Maimonides sees Scripture as enjoining Israel to battle idolatry and heresy, not a specific people or ethnic group, a theme to which he returns throughout his works.[42] The abiding value of this commandment lies in its theological message: all traces of idolatry

---

39. This plain-sense reading of the text is defended by Tosafot. See *BT 'Avodah Zarah* 20a, s. v. "*de-amar qera*."

40. Daniel ha-Bavli, *she'elah* 2, in Abraham Maimonides, "Teshuvot Rabbenu Abraham ben ha-RaMBaM," 543. He gives the examples of "thou shalt set thee up great stones ... and thou shalt write upon them all the words of this law" (Deut. 27:2-3) and "thou shalt set the blessing upon Mount Gerizim and the curse upon Mount Eval" (Deut. 11:29).

41. I note that in his practical code of law, the *MT,* Maimonides sees no need to justify the commandment. It suffices there to posit the ever-present possibility that one might be able to fulfill this commandment. The underlying rationale for the commandment is revealed only in the teleologically-driven *ShM*, where he posits that the commandment is to destroy "the root and very foundation of idolatry." To Maimonides, this commandment indeed functioned as an eternal obligation.

42. Compare N48, for example, which forbids one from making a covenant with the seven nations. In the *ShM*, Maimonides ignores the ethnic divisions and writes: "We are forbidden to make a covenant with the heretics and leave them undisturbed in their heresy." See also N51, N52, and N58, where the emphasis is on heresy rather than ethnicity. In other words, making a peace treaty with the seven nations is a religious problem, not a racial one.

must be destroyed, lest they cause Israelites to apostatize.[43]

> P189. To always keep in remembrance what 'Amaleq did, as it is said, "Remember what 'Amaleq did unto thee" (Deut. 25:17).

More specifically, he writes in the *ShM*:

> We are commanded to remember what 'Amaleq did to us in attacking us unprovoked. We are to speak of this at all times, and to arouse the people to make war upon him and bid the people to hate them, to the end that this matter[44] be not forgotten, and that hatred of him be not weakened or lessened with the passage of time.

Proof: The scriptural evidence for this obligation and the parallel obligation not to forget 'Amaleq's deeds is found in Deuteronomy 25:17-19: "Remember what 'Amaleq did unto thee" (v. 17) and "thou

43. Stern (in "Maimonides on 'Amaleq") reaches a similar conclusion with respect to 'Amaleq and the seven nations. In my opinion, however, he misreads an important passage in the *GP* which leads to an unjustified claim regarding Maimonides' interpretation of the Torah. On the basis of *GP* III:50, 614, Stern claims that Maimonides reads Gen. 36:12 as introducing a corrective to the obligation to exterminate 'Amaleq (Deut. 25:17): because the descendants of Esau were "fully assimilated" with the children of Seir, it was "impossible 'today' to identify the real, authentic, pure 'Amaleqites as opposed to those who are 'Amaleqites in name only" (364-365). He conjectures that Maimonides was attempting to restrain individuals living in his time from persecuting Christians whom they identified as descendants of 'Amaleq (369). This conclusion is speculative and unwarranted if we read Maimonides' words in their proper context. He writes: "Consequently, Scripture explained their tribes [i.e., the tribes of Esau] and said that those whom you see today in Seir and the kingdom of 'Amaleq are not all of them children of 'Amaleq, but some of them are descendants of this or that individual and are only called after 'Amaleq because the latter's mother belonged to them." To prove that the corrective did not exempt the Israelites from the obligation to exterminate 'Amaleq, Maimonides adds: "All this was an act of justice on the part of God *lest a tribe be killed indiscriminately* in the course of the extermination of another tribe" (emphasis added). Maimonides states that Scripture's concern was to prevent errors in identification, not to state that 'Amaleq had been assimilated. Nowhere does Maimonides say that it had become "impossible" to identify 'Amaleqites or that they had been "fully assimilated" in biblical times. Indeed, the Israelites battled the descendants of 'Amaleq a number of times, both in the wilderness and in the time of Saul.
44. By "this matter" he means 'Amaleq's unprovoked attack. The *MnT* reads *mitsvah* instead of *davar*, which can be interpreted as the commandment to destroy 'Amaleq or as the commandment to remember his misdeeds.

shalt not forget" (v. 19). To prove that these statements are normative and not mere rhetorical flourishes, Maimonides quotes two similar *midreshe halakhah*. The first is found in *Sifre Deuteronomy*: "*Remember what 'Amaleq did unto thee* means [remembrance] in the spoken word; *thou shalt not forget* means [remembrance] in the heart,"[45] to which Maimonides adds, "That is, you are to speak such things as will ensure that the hatred of 'Amaleq is not removed from men's hearts." The second is found in the *Sifra*:[46]

> *Remember what 'Amaleq did unto thee*: one might think that this means in thy heart. But *thou shalt not forget* refers to forgetfulness of the heart: how then can one obey the injunction *Remember* [if that also refers to the heart? We must conclude that *Remember* means:] in the spoken word.

While the cited midrashim do not label these verses as positive and negative commandments (as the *Sifre* does, for example, when commenting on a similarly-structured phrase in Deuteronomy 22:8[47]), their analysis does buttress the idea that these verses represent formal and distinct acts.[48] Maimonides draws further support from an incident related in 1 Samuel 15:1-33. Just before sending King Saul on a mission to slay 'Amaleq, the prophet Samuel formally recounts 'Amaleq's wicked deeds, likely in order to fulfill the commandment to remember their nefarious acts.[49]

A further difficulty remains. Scripture's call to recount 'Amaleq's

45. *Sifre Deuteronomy, Ki Tetse* 296 (314).
46. *Sifra be-Huqotai* 1:3 (110c). Some printed versions incorrectly referenced it as the *Sifre*. See *Sefer ha-Mitsvot*, ed. Heller, ad loc., n. 5.
47. *Sifre Deuteronomy, Ki Tetse* 229 (261), states: "*Thou shalt make a parapet for thy roof* [is] a positive commandment, *that thou bring not blood upon thy house* [is] a negative commandment."
48. Nahmanides turns Maimonides' evidence against him by arguing that, on the basis of this or similar midrashim, Maimonides should have enumerated one or two additional commands (Nahmanides, *Hasagot*, "Additions to the Positive Commandments," no. 7, 288). See also de Leon, "Megillat Esther," 289. This is one of the rare instances in which the Maimonidean apologist de Leon agrees with Nahmanides.
49. So-called proofs adduced from non-Pentateuchal books were commonplace among Karaite jurists and exegetes, but rare among Rabbanites, who tended to rely on the oral tradition for interpretation. See, for example, Levi b. Yafet, *Sefer ha-Mitsvot, passim.*

past misdeeds might only represent a motivation or justification for the commandment to exterminate the nation, not an independent commandment. Or, going one step further, one might even understand the exhortation to recollect ʻAmaleq's evil deeds and intentions as merely a required step in the act of killing an ʻAmaleqite. The passage from 1 Samuel could be read as teaching that one must verbally announce the justification for destroying ʻAmaleq just as one is about to execute a member of their nation. Indeed, Samuel's actual words—"Thus said the Lord of Hosts: I am exacting [*paqadeti*] the penalty for what ʻAmaleq did to Israel" (1 Sam. 15:2, JPS translation)—read more like a justification for the coming destruction than a daily recounting of ʻAmaleq's evil. As we have seen, under Rules 10, 11, and 12, any command that forms part of another commandment or that is a preparation for another commandment cannot be enumerated as an independent commandment. If recalling ʻAmaleq's evil deeds is a declaration that one makes before destroying him, then remembering his deeds cannot be considered an independent positive commandment.

Maimonides avoids this problem in his definition of the obligation: "to speak of this at all times, and to arouse the people to make war upon him and bid the people to hate them, to the end *that this matter be not forgotten, and that hatred of him be not weakened or lessened with the passage of time*" (emphasis added). Accordingly, "Remember" is not a declaration that one makes when one exterminates ʻAmaleq. Rather, it is a daily reminder of ʻAmaleq's viciousness, so that "this matter be not forgotten, and that hatred of him be not weakened or lessened with the passage of time." Based on this definition, Maimonides can posit an independent commandment. But whence such an understanding? How does Maimonides know that the *Sifre* intended this commandment, rather than a justificatory declaration?

Interestingly, neither Qayyara nor any of the other extant enumerators who preceded Maimonides include this commandment on their *TaRYaG* lists.[50] Perhaps these enumerators saw these verses

50. In discussing this passage, Abraham ibn Ezra ridicules the *baale azharot*, charging that the enumerators are like those who count the number of blades of grass in their books of medicine without recognizing the medicinal utility of these blades. Shifting

as simple reminders of the obligation to destroy ʻAmaleq. Maimonides gleans from this verse and midrashim a totally novel concept: the duty to remember and to remind others of those who have tried, unprovoked, to destroy the Israelite nation, so as to keep hatred of them fresh in the communal memory. This is a commandment independent of the duty to exterminate ʻAmaleq. This new commandment can be fulfilled unconditionally—precisely at a time when the commandment to *exterminate* ʻAmaleq is practically impossible to fulfill. As Maimonides has already noted (in P187), by post-biblical times, ʻAmaleq could no longer be identified.[51]

PROBLEMATIC IDENTIFICATIONS

Maimonides is at his most inventive when fashioning the next group of obligations. In particular, the claims he advances do not seem to flow from the scriptural texts that he brings in support. In many cases, I believe that external criteria were involved in the selection of these commandments, and I offer some possible suggestions for what those may be.

I will focus more on this difficulty in later chapters (chapter 7 in particular), when I discuss Maimonides' scriptural hermeneutics. For now, I ask the reader to accept as correct my assumption that Maimonides defined commandments by using the plain sense of the text, rather than rabbinic exegetical understandings.

> P17. That every person shall write a scroll of the Torah for himself, as it

---

to the singular, he then charges that "he thinks that they ["thou shalt not forget" and "remember"] are two [commandments]." The shift to the singular suggests that he was referring to one *paytan* in particular. After noting that there are many such mirrored phrases in the Torah, Ibn Ezra concludes that these poets do not pay attention to the plain sense of the text, preferring to focus on the formal structure of the verse. Abraham ibn Ezra, *Yesod Mora*, 108. The *paytan* to which he refers remains unknown; I have not found an extant geonic work that counts these two commandments separately.

51. I do not understand why Maimonides omits P189 from the list of sixty unconditionally obligatory commandments (discussed in chapter 3), especially as he reconfirms its obligatory status in *Hilkhot Melakhim* 5:5. While one could argue that P187 and P188 (to destroy the seven nations and the seed of ʻAmaleq), should not be enumerated because their subjects have disappeared or can no longer be identified, the same cannot be said with respect to P189.

is said, "Write ye for yourselves this song" (Deut. 31:19).[52]

Proof: Maimonides offers two textual analyses as proofs for this commandment. The first is based on the verse "Write ye for yourselves this song" (Deut. 31:19). The simple meaning of the verse is that it refers to the writing of the song of *Ha'azinu* (Deut. 32:1-43). Yet in *BT Sanhedrin* 21b (quoted below), Rabbah uses this verse as a proof text for the individual's obligation to write a scroll of the Torah, possibly taking the word "song" as a metaphor for Torah. Not satisfied with this homily, Maimonides offers a rational but convoluted and hair-splitting interpretation of Rabbah's dictum: since one is not permitted to write individual sections of the Torah,[53] the instruction to Moses to write "this song" must have entailed the writing of an entire scroll of Torah. The proof strains the imagination, and the reader might conclude that Rabbah's proof text is but a scriptural hook on which Maimonides has hung a well-known tradition.

The second demonstration comes from the same talmudic passage:

> Rabbah said: Even if one's parents had left him a Scroll of the Law, he is nevertheless commanded to write one of his own, as it is said, *Now therefore write ye this song for you*. Abaye objected: The king is commanded to write a Scroll of the Law for himself, for he should not seek credit for

52. In all of the versions of the *ShM*, this commandment appears as P18. The *SE* uses a more logical arrangement, first listing the commandment for the individual to write a scroll, and then the commandment for the king to write a second scroll, "besides the one which every individual should write." Being essentially an argumentative work, the *ShM* may have listed the king's obligation first because it helped Maimonides to derive the individual's obligation. This may be further evidence that Maimonides wrote the *ShM* before writing the *SE*, a matter that I hope to explore in the future. See above, note 19. In his edition of the *MT*, Rabinovitch offers a similar explanation for the reversed presentation in the *ShM*, arguing that Maimonides proved the individual's obligation from the passage in *BT Sanhedrin* 21b, which itself is based on the law regarding the king's obligation (*Mishneh Torah*, ed. Rabinovitch, 112). To preserve the logical order of his analysis, Maimonides needed to address the obligation of the king before he could address the obligation of the individual. While my argument is similar, I argue that the *only* basis for the general commandment is the one found in the king's pericope.

53. Even granting the (questionable) scriptural force of this law, one could believe that Moses was given a special instruction to write just the song of *Ha'azinu*, much as one writes individual sections of the Torah in making tefillin. For this and other difficulties in Maimonides' argument, see Perla, *Sefer ha-Mitsvot*, vol. 3, sec. 60, 425-426.

> one written by others, and [this surely implies that] it is only a king [who is enjoined to write a Scroll even if his parents have left him one] and not a commoner? To this the reply was: The rule is necessary only to oblige the king to write two scrolls, as we have been taught: *He* [*the king*] *shall write him a copy of this law* [*mishneh ha-torah ha-zot*] means that he is to write for himself two copies. (*BT Sanhedrin* 21b)

From this passage, Maimonides infers that "the difference between the king and a commoner is that every man must write one Scroll of the Torah, but the king must write two." The simple meaning of the phrase "*mishneh ha-torah ha-zot*" is "a copy of this Torah": the king is commanded to write himself a copy of the Torah that Moses had handed down.[54] There is no good philological justification for reading "*mishneh ha-torah*" as meaning *two* copies of the Torah; most likely, this interpretation uses this scriptural intimation to support a rabbinic law.[55]

While Maimonides' proofs are unconvincing, his motivation for advancing this commandment is not. The act of writing the Torah inculcates a special reverence for its content and disseminates its teachings. As Maimonides writes in the *GP*, this commandment brings about "useful opinions"—in this case, the wisdom learned from the words of the law book itself.[56]

---

54. See, for example, Tg. Onqelos, ad loc.

55. In chapter 7, I will expand on Maimonides' crucial distinction between the plain sense of the text and the category of *asmakhta*, a term that generally covers scriptural intimations, hints, and mnemonics that can underpin a rabbinic ordinance, and explore the ways that he uses these categories to define his commandments.

56. *GP* III:44. In listing there the commandments included in the ninth class of commandments (the equivalent of those listed in *Sefer Ahavah* of the *MT*), Maimonides mentions "acquiring a book of the Torah and reading in it at certain times." Two observations are worth making in this respect. First, the commandment listed here is to acquire a book of the Torah, rather than to write such a book, as he had ruled in the *MT*. Second, while one could argue that the mention of reading in the book of the Torah could be counted as a separate commandment, wholly independent of the acquisition of the book, this is unlikely, as we do not find in the *MT* such a commandment. (Note that learning and teaching are included in *Sefer ha-Madda'*.) More likely, one should understand the sentence to mean that the acquisition of the scroll of Torah is *for the purpose* of reading in it at certain times. Thus it would appear that the acquisition is only a preparatory step. No such rationale is given in the *MT*, where writing a scroll of Torah appears to be the primary consideration regardless of what one does with it. (But note Deut. 17:19: "And it shall be with him, and he shall

> P36. That the priests shall serve in the Sanctuary, in watches [*mishmarot*], but on festivals, they all serve together, as it is said, "And if a Levite come . . .[then he shall minister in the name of the Lord]" (Deut. 18:6-8).

Proof: In the *ShM*, Maimonides quotes parts of a long passage containing three verses:

> And if a Levite come [from any of thy gates out of all Israel, where he sojourneth,] and come with all the desire of his soul [unto the place where the Lord shall choose]; then he shall minister in the name of the Lord his God, as all his brethren the Levites do, who stand there before the Lord. They shall have like portions to eat, beside that which cometh of the sale of his patrimony. (Deut. 18:6-8)

The *Sifre* expounds upon these verses:

> *And come with all the desire of his soul*: one might interpret this verse to mean that he might come at any time to participate in the service of the sanctuary; Scripture therefore says *from any of thy gates;* that is, when all Israel is assembled in one gate [i.e. in one city—Jerusalem] during the three festivals.[57]

Maimonides concludes from this interpretation that the visiting Levites had a right to participate equally with their Jerusalemite brethren at the time of the festivals.

The second part of this midrash is critical to his argument that the watches (*mishmarot*) were instituted by Scripture:

> One might think that all the divisions [of priests] shared equally in the festival offerings, even in these which were not occasioned by the festivals themselves [namely, the daily burnt offerings brought in the morning and at dusk every day of the year]; Scripture therefore says *beside that which cometh of the sale of his patrimony.* What is meant by *sale of patrimony*? [One priestly elder says to another,] "Do thou [minister] in thy week, and I [will minister] in my week."

---

read therein all the days of his life."). At any rate, it is clear that, at least in its final formulation, the utility of this commandment "is manifest."

57. *Sifre Deuteronomy, Shoftim* 168 (216-217).

The midrash understands the words "sale of patrimony" to mean "do thou [minister] in thy week, and I [will minister] in my week," implying that a rotation was in effect. As Maimonides describes it: "they agreed on the rotation of the watches; [the priests gave] their consent to the whole arrangement of the service into watches, a new watch ministering in turn every week."

Nahmanides vigorously contests Maimonides' last claim. He argues that, in their desire to certify the watches' scriptural authority after they were instituted, the Rabbis searched for an exegetical way to authorize the praxis. Thus, claims Nahmanides, the midrash rests on an *asmakhta*, a scriptural hook that the Rabbis used to support their own laws, and not a legitimate exegesis.[58] The essence of his objections is that the watches were instituted by the prophets and were not scripturally ordained.[59]

Along similar lines, while Maimonides does provide some scriptural indication that a cooperative rotation system operated in the Temple, one fails to find any evidence in his scriptural and rabbinic citations for there being a *commandment* to institute priestly watches. An external agenda, however, is suggested by the broader formulation of the commandment, given in the *ShM*:

> We are commanded that the priests are to minister in divisions [*mishmarot*], every division ministering one week, and that all divisions are not to minister at the same time,[60] except during the festivals when

58. To determine when a midrash is a genuine interpretation of Scripture and when it is merely an *asmakhta* is critical for the construction of commandment claims. Disagreements between Maimonides and Nahmanides on this topic are the basis of some of their many disagreements on what constitutes a scriptural commandment. There are no shared and definitive criteria for categorizing such midrashic explications; see chapter 7, note 10 for some proposed criteria.

59. *Hasagot*, ad loc. Nahmanides notes that Maimonides presented a revised formulation in the *Halakhot* and that "this formulation is more precise than what he presented here [in the *ShM*]." Indeed, the emphasis in the Heading to *Hilkhot Kele ha-Miqdash* ("That all the watches be equal on the festivals") and in *Hilkhot Kele ha-Miqdash* 4:4-5 is on the equal sharing of the festival service, or, more specifically, that all priests be allowed to share equally in the offerings of the festivals. There is no indication in these *Halakhot* that Scripture was mandating this institution of watches; the verse simply appears to reflect an old and established practice.

60. Literally, "and that everyone's hand should not busy itself at the same time (*ve-lo tihiye*

> all divisions are to share equally in the service and any [priest] who is present may sacrifice.

We have already seen that Maimonides wishes to emphasize the decorum and orderliness of the Temple service in order to strengthen the "greatness of the sanctuary and the awe felt for it." Perhaps this motivation underlies his insistence that the watches should have their own individuated *mitsvat 'aseh*.

> P37. That the priests defile themselves for their deceased relatives, and mourn for them like other Israelites, who are commanded to mourn for their relatives, as it is said, "for her, he shall defile himself" (Lev. 21:3).

This commandment consists of two parts: the priests must defile themselves for deceased relatives, and they must mourn for their dead, as must all Israelites. The second part of the claim is intended to be inferred from the first, but the inference is difficult to sustain. Maimonides supports this strained exegesis with a talmudic source that assumes that one day of mourning is a scripturally mandated commandment, despite no explicit scriptural command to that effect.

Proof: Maimonides takes evidence that mourning is a scriptural obligation from the talmudic position that one must not mourn during a festival. The talmudic passage (*BT Moed Qatan* 14b) reads as follows: "If the mourning begins before the festival, the positive precept affecting all Israel [to rejoice in the festival] overrides that affecting only the individual commandment enjoining one [to mourn over his deceased relative]." Maimonides concludes: "It is clear that the obligation of mourning is scriptural, but is scripturally obligatory only on the first day, while the remaining six days [of mourning are obligatory only by] rabbinic ordinance." The conclusion that the Sages consider mourning a scriptural obligation follows the opinion of many geonim, in particular, Maimonides' principal halakhic authority, Isaac Alfasi.[61]

---

yad ha-kol mitasseqet ya<u>h</u>ad)," an idiomatic expression that conveys a sense of chaos and disorder.

61. Alfasi's ruling can be found in his *Hilkhot ha-RIF, BT Berakhot* 10a and *BT Moed Qatan* 11b in the Alfasi pages (Vilna ed.).

In his search for scriptural evidence for the commandment to mourn, Maimonides quotes the following midrash in the *ShM*: "*For her he shall defile himself* is a positive commandment. If he [a priest] does not wish to defile himself, he is made to do so against his will."[62] Priests must defile themselves for their dead relatives—helping to bury the dead person, even if they come into contact with the corpse—despite the general prohibition that forbids them to defile themselves for the dead. Maimonides goes on to argue that "this itself is the commandment of mourning; that is to say that every Israelite person[63] is obligated to mourn his relatives, that is, the five[64] dead [relatives] for whom there is a duty [*mete mitsvah*]." Using an *a fortiori* inference, Maimonides explains that

> it is to confirm this obligation that He has expressly declared in the case of the priest, who is [ordinarily] forbidden to suffer defilement, that [in respect of the five relatives] he must defile himself at any rate like all other Israelites, so that the law of mourning may not be lightly esteemed.

Towards the end of his comments, Maimonides repeats this analysis, noting that "even a priest is bound to observe mourning on the first day, and to defile himself for his [deceased] relatives. Understand this." Aware that the demonstration is forced, he wants the reader to accept his reasoning. Karo objects to Maimonides' suggestion:

> This proof is puzzling, for defilement is one matter and mourning another. One cannot draw an implication that a priest must mourn his relatives from the fact that He commanded that [the priest] defile himself for his relatives.[65]

Maimonides struggles to fill an evidentiary gap in the oral tradition that maintains that there is in fact a positive commandment to mourn

---

62. *Sifra Emor* 1:12 (94a).
63. In the Arabic, the word *shkhts*, "person," is used, but the phrase *kol ish*, "every man," is used in the *MnT* translation.
64. Some versions have six; see "Tsiyunim," *Sefer ha-Mitsvot*, ad loc., and see *Sefer ha-Mitsvot*, ed. Kafih, ad loc., n. 26.
65. Karo, *Kesef Mishneh, Hilkhot Avel* 1:1, s. v. "*mitsvat 'aseh le-hitavel.*"

at least on the first day. Surely if there is such a scriptural obligation, some proof text ought to be found. As Karo complains, Maimonides' attempt does not satisfy. This obvious difficulty forces Maimonides to make a second, but still unsuccessful, attempt in the *MT*[66] before abandoning the connection altogether in the *GP* (III:47).[67]

In my opinion, there is no special politico-philosophical or theological motivation behind this claim. Instead, I believe that Maimonides' forced attempts to find a scriptural basis for this practice stemmed exclusively from his extraordinary respect for the oral tradition, which maintained that there was a scriptural obligation to mourn at least one day, despite the lack of scriptural evidence. This respectful attitude was foreshadowed in Rule 2, where he makes a rare concession and states that "if the Sages themselves clearly affirm that 'it is of the essence of Torah' or that 'it is of scriptural authority,' it is proper to count that particular law [among the commandments] even though the law is not scripturally explicit."[68]

---

66. See *Hilkhot Avel* 1:1. I say "unsuccessful attempt" because the new proof text, "Had I eaten sin offering today, would the Lord have approved" (Lev. 10:19), can hardly be taken as an admonition. (For an interpretation of the reasons for this proof, see RaDBaZ, ad loc.)

67. David Hartman notes (I believe correctly) that "the lack of any explicit biblical text dealing with the commandment of mourning may very well explain why Maimonides in the context of the *Guide of the Perplexed* does not mention the laws of mourning." Lawrence Kaplan believes, however, that he found "the 'missing' cross-reference to the Laws of Mourning of the *Mishneh Torah*" in a section of the *Guide* dealing with "the commandments concerned with the clean and unclean," *GP* III:47. Maimonides there notes: "Every priest in particular was forbidden to expose himself to being made unclean by a corpse unless it were a case of strong necessity in which it would be difficult for nature to avoid this; I refer to avoiding contact with one's parents, children and brothers." Kaplan comments: "The rites of mourning, on the biblical level, are not self-directed and commanded for the therapeutic benefit of the mourner, but rather are other-directed." They are, he says, "forms of personal *kevod ha-met*, of honoring one's deceased relatives." Thus, according to Kaplan, Maimonides redefined the scriptural concept of mourning in *GP* and ceased seeking a scriptural reference for the traditional concept of mourning. As attractive as this argument is, the passage in III:47 does not indicate a qualitatively different, other-directed obligation to mourn; the words "unless it were a case of strong necessity in which it would be difficult for nature to avoid this" seem to imply, instead, some sort of unavoidable need to waive the laws of defilement. Hartman's view is cited by Kaplan. See Kaplan, "The Unity of Maimonides' Thought," 393-412.

68. Much the same can be said with regard to the scriptural prooftext adduced in the

> P112. That the leper shall be universally recognized as such by the prescribed marks: "His garments shall be rent and the hair of his head disheveled and he shall cover his upper lip and shall cry 'unclean, unclean'" (Lev. 13:45). So too, all other unclean persons should declare themselves as such.

Proof: The *Sifra* infers that Scripture requires anyone "in whom the plague is" to rend his clothes and grow his hair from the redundant prepositional phrase in "the leper *in whom the plague is*" (Lev.13:45, emphasis added). This requirement, the midrash asserts, includes the High Priest, despite the prohibition against his normally doing so.[69] Maimonides discusses this waived prohibition:

> It is an accepted principle among us that wherever you find a positive commandment and a negative commandment [applying at the same time] if you can fulfill both, well and good; but if not, the positive commandment overrides the negative commandment (*yavo 'aseh ve-yidhe et lo ta'aseh*) ... since we find it laid down [by the Sages] that if a High Priest is leprous he must let his hair go loose and rend his clothes [the negative commandment notwithstanding], it follows that this is a positive commandment [for every leper to be unkempt].

Building on the midrash, Maimonides uses a rabbinic principle to infer this commandment. Since the midrash teaches that a leprous High Priest is required to become unkempt, despite the general prohibition, and a positive commandment overrides a negative commandment, the command for a leper to become unkempt must be a *mitsvat 'aseh.* Maimonides' inference is not entirely convincing, since the midrash

---

MT (see above, note 67). While the commandment could be inferred from the text, such an inference would need to follow the exception clause of Rule 2. The *ShM* and *MT* proof texts assume that mourning was one of those exceptions. However, in a celebrated responsum (*Responsa*, ed. Blau, vol. 2, no. 355, 631-632), Maimonides states that there were no more than "three or four" such exceptions, and better candidates could be found for these few exceptions. See Feintuch, *Sefer ha-Mitsvot im Perush Pequde Yesharim,* vol. 1, 43-45. In his analysis, Feintuch concludes that Maimonides did not mean that there were only three or four exceptions; rather, he meant that the number of exceptions is very small, and thus perhaps this commandment could represent a further exception.

69. *Sifra Tazri'a* 12:5 (67d).

derives the law's applicability to the High Priest from the redundant prepositional phrase "in whom the plague is," rather than by using the talmudic principle of "*yavo 'aseh ve-yidhe et lo ta'aseh.*" According to the midrash, the talmudic principle is not necessary: Scripture provides the exception by means of a redundancy.[70]

As we noted, the *Sifra* concludes that even the High Priest must rend his clothes and grow his hair if he becomes a leper. Maimonides does not simply subsume this requirement as a particular of the laws of the leper[71] under P101 ("that a leper is unclean and defiles"). Instead, he crafts a new commandment that reflects an original understanding of the purpose and essence of the requirement that the leper must allow himself to be recognized universally as a leper.[72] His insistence on individuating such a requirement may well have something to do with what he sees as a justification for the disease.

Maimonides avers that a slanderer is miraculously stricken

70. See Perla, *Sefer ha-Mitsvot le-RaSaG*, vol. 1, P189, 808-810. While Hurewitz (in *Sefer ha-Mitsvot im Perush Yad ha-Levi,* 121n5) acknowledges the problem, he dismisses it by reading the midrashic exegesis as based on the hermeneutic principle. This reading, however, does not fit the literal text of the midrash, which draws a typical inference from the verse.

71. In *Hilkhot Tumat Tsara'at* 10:7, Maimonides categorizes the requirement that a leper be secluded, derived from "he shall dwell apart; his dwelling shall be outside the camp" (Lev. 13:46), as a specific provision of the commandment (*din ha-metsora'*) rather than an independent commandment. I assume (although it is not clear) that Maimonides means this to be a provision of P101 (as does de Leon, "Megillat Esther," 291). Nahmanides (in *Hasagot*, "Addenda to the Positive Commandments," no. 14, 290) says that Maimonides counted "he shall dwell apart; his dwelling shall be outside the camp" as an independent commandment. De Leon comments in response that while perhaps Nahmanides counted it as an independent commandment, Maimonides certainly did not. Duran (in *Zohar ha-Raqia, siman* 80, 92), proposes to make P112 part of the independent commandment of "he shall dwell apart; his dwelling shall be outside the camp." For a short bibliography on authors who take up this point, see 92n469; see also ibid., *siman* 45, 46 and notes. It is possible that both Nahmanides and Duran understood the leper's obligation to remain secluded as a more general form of the obligation to keep others away from himself. For both of these jurists, the overarching commandment was "he shall dwell apart; his dwelling shall be outside the camp," and the requirements to rend clothes, keep his head covered, and such constituted details of the commandment. In contrast, Maimonides held that the leper's obligation to display his impurity constituted the more general principle while the precept to live secluded was a detail.

72. For a discussion of Maimonides' wider teleologically-driven conclusions, see my comments in chapter 2.

with leprosy because the revolting nature of the disease[73] raises two natural barriers: one barrier between the slanderer and his wicked circle of friends to keep him from continuing to engage "in evil talk, which consists of mockery and malicious gossip," and a second barrier between the slanderer and the person wishing to be virtuous. As he writes in *Hilkhot Tumat Tsara'at* 16:10: "it is fitting for someone who wishes to set aright his ways to distance himself from their presence and from speaking with them so that he does not become entrapped in the net of wicked people and their follies." Maimonides sees leprosy as a way to keep society away from the sinner rather than as a punishment for the sinner. In this sense, the public voicing of his own uncleanness is unrelated to the particulars of his uncleanness and defilement. Therefore, this requirement is not subsumed under P101.[74]

> P149. To examine the marks in cattle, as it is said, "these are the beasts which ye may eat" (Lev. 11:2).
> P150. To examine the marks in fowl, so as to distinguish between the unclean and the clean, as it is said, "Of all clean birds ye may eat" (Deut. 14:11).
> P151. To examine the marks in locusts, so as to distinguish the clean from the unclean, as it is said, "(yet these may ye eat of every flying, creeping thing that goeth upon all four) which have legs (above their feet)" (Lev. 11:21).[75]
> P152. To examine the marks in fishes, as it is said, "These shall ye eat of all that are in the waters" (Lev. 11:9).

As in other instances where Maimonides struggles with formulating a commandment or with its supporting hermeneutic, traces of the struggle can be found in the linguistic variants of the extant versions of the *ShM* (and the *MT*). While one cannot assert with certainty which of the extant versions represents the final one, all of the versions carry a similar message: the conscious act of separating the pure from the

73. Cf. *GP* III:47, 597.
74. In the gloss to P112, Maimonides extends this law to stipulate that all who become unclean must make themselves recognizable (not merely the leper).
75. Note that this verse contains a description of the locusts, not the typical proof text for the commandment. See our discussion below.

impure, separating that which may be consumed from that which may not. Maimonides pursues this agenda by means of a forced, somewhat confusing, but nonetheless creative exegetical exercise. For purposes of the ensuing discussion, I follow the formulaic expression "to examine" found in all the versions of the *SE* and assume that it represents Maimonides' final viewpoint.[76]

Proof: After explicitly prohibiting the consumption of living things that do not possess the requisite tokens (as detailed in N172–N174), Scripture further enjoins: "These are the living things which ye may eat among all the beasts that are on the earth. Whatsoever parteth...among the beasts, that may ye eat" (Lev. 11:2-3). As a proof text for P149, Maimonides cites the opening line of the verse: "these are the living things which ye may eat," together with the *Sifra*'s exposition on the closing statement of verse 3: "*That may ye eat*: only *that* may be eaten, but not the unclean beast."[77]

Maimonides explains that the midrash uses an hermeneutic rule that infers a prohibition from the positive statement. This type of inferred prohibition, called "a negative commandment that is inferred from a 'do' statement" ("*lav ha-ba-mikhlal 'aseh,*" also "*issur 'aseh*"), is not punishable as a negative commandment because Scripture does not articulate the prohibition in the form of an explicit interdiction. The positive statement coupled with the fact that the law calls the injunction an *'aseh* ("*lav ha-ba-mikhlal 'aseh*, *'aseh*") provides the hermeneutic basis for Maimonides' claim that examining for clean animals is a positive commandment. Maimonides shows himself satisfied with this proof ("thus it has been made clear that His words *that ye may eat* are a

---

76. The *ShM* versions appear to reflect at least two different literary or compositional stages. The *MnT* translation is similar to the language of the *SE*. It claims that the commandment mandates one to "examine" [*livdoq*] the tokens of the various animals and "[only] then would their consumption be permitted." The Arabic versions (including Kafih's) and the Shlomo ibn Ayub translation cited by Heller in the notes to his *ShM* edition read instead "that we were commanded about [Hebrew *al*; Arabic *b*; or "concerning"] the tokens" of the various animals. The former version would obligate one to examine particular animals for tokens of fitness; the latter, simply to know the characteristics of animals that are fit for consumption. The difference in formulation is also present in Maimonides' later compositions, as we shall see.

77. *Sifra Shemini* 3:1 (48b).

positive commandment").[78]

But does this exegesis support Maimonides' actual claim? The midrash sees Leviticus 11:3 as adding a new prohibition against eating living things that do not possess the requisite tokens onto the existing negative prohibitions, using inference from a positive statement ("that ye may eat"). This is at least how Maimonides' critics understood the midrash.[79] This reading seems to have little to do with examining or ascertaining the nature of the tokens.

By assuming, however, that Maimonides made a slight mistake in failing to match the appropriate proof text with the pertinent midrash, we can make some sense out of this exegesis. A close read shows that the proof text adduced for his claim "to examine the tokens" is "*These* are the living things which ye may eat" (v. 2, emphasis added). This proof text, however, is not the one that the midrash uses to infer a prohibition on eating. Rather, the midrash uses verse 3, which contains the words "that may ye eat." It is verse 2 that supports Maimonides' commandment—not verse 3, as his critics suppose—although Maimonides bears responsibility for this confusion by juxtaposing the proof text and the midrashic exposition. To Maimonides, the deictic "these" (*zot*) conveys an act of choosing or ascertaining, implying the need to examine tokens of fitness. Indeed, this is how the *Sifra* itself understands this term. On verse 2, "These are the living things which ye may eat," the midrash expounds: "It teaches us that Moses held the living thing, and on showing it to the Israelites, would say, 'this you

78. See above, chapter 2, in particular note 12, for further discussion of this hermeneutic.

79. So for example, Daniel ha-Bavli, who infers an additional, non-explicit prohibition against eating non-kosher animals (Abraham Maimonides, "Teshuvot Rabbenu Abraham ben ha-RaMBaM," *siman* 10, 277, s.v. *u-le-shitato*) from this verse (and fowl and fish from similar verses). Nahmanides, too, fails to see here anything other than a prohibition against eating non-kosher living things. Furthermore, since an explicit prohibition against eating non-kosher living things already exists, Nahmanides sees no reason to enumerate this additional injunction and finds Qayyara's omission justified. See Nahmanides, *Hasagot*, Rule 6, 131, s.v. "*ve-ani roeh*." However, what Maimonides derives from the cited verse is an injunction to examine the tokens of animals before eating them and not a prohibition to eat non-kosher animals! While Nahmanides could have questioned the relationship between the midrash and the presumed claim, he surely would not have misread the claim. I am thus at a loss to understand his critique.

may eat, this you may not eat.'"[80]

For whatever reason, Maimonides is not fully satisfied with the exegetical basis of this group of claims, and we see him changing his exegesis towards the end of his explications. There he offers a further clarification on these four commandments in the form of a restatement—but one that surely represents an entirely new explanation:

> And that which we said—that it is a positive commandment—is what I already mentioned to you:[81] we are commanded to decide on the basis of these tokens that one fish is permitted food, and another is not permitted, as Scripture clearly says: *Ye shall separate between the clean beast and the unclean (and between the unclean fowl and the clean)* [Lev. 20:25].

With this comment, Maimonides shifts the weight of the exegetical proof away from the earlier proof texts and their accompanying hermeneutic principle to an entirely new verse. The new proof text explicitly commands one to differentiate a clean animal from an unclean one. Despite its greater clarity, however, the new proof text is not as comprehensive as Maimonides indicates; it refers to beasts and birds but omits fish and grasshoppers.[82] Soon thereafter, Maimonides returns to the earlier-cited midrash to differentiate four separate commandments:

> The separation can be made only by means of the [prescribed] tokens, and therefore [the injunction to search for] the tokens in each of the four types [of living creatures]—animals tame and wild, birds, grasshoppers, and fish—is a separate and distinct commandment. We have already shown that [the Sages] regarded each of them as one of the positive commandments.

---

80. *Sifra Shemini, parshah* 2:2 (47d).
81. In the Hebrew, "*ve-ha-inyan be-amrenu she-hi mitsvat 'aseh, mah she-hizkarti lekhah,*" is an idiomatic expression of re-statement. On Maimonides' intellectual dynamism and his ability to add a new rationale to revitalize a rejected position, see Henshke, "Maimonides as His Own Commentator", 117-163.
82. Cf. Daniel ha-Bavli, in Abraham Maimonides, "Teshuvot Rabbenu Abraham ben ha-RaMBaM," *siman* 10, 277, s. v. "*ve-od hinneh bier.*"

Maimonides does not explain how the particular breakdown of the various prohibitions, presumably against eating non-kosher animals, can supplement or illuminate the new commandment to examine the tokens of these creatures. This is a problematic gap,[83] unless one was willing to accept the explanation regarding the confused use of the midrash. In sum, the various scriptural verses and their rabbinic warrants fail to sustain and differentiate these commandments clearly.

Whether the problem is four individuations, loosely based on a midrashic interpretation, or one individuation based on an incomplete proof text, the basic motivational question remains: what drove Maimonides to individuate these commandments when the essential prohibition against eating the flesh of unclean animals had already been individuated? I submit that Maimonides' political views were at least partly responsible for this move. Maimonides views the law as a political instrument for bringing order to society, a notion well documented in his philosophic works.[84] As with those of contemporary Islamic philosophers, Maimonides' political ideas are informed by Plato's views of the City and its organization,[85] its emphasis on social stratification and its use of different metals as symbols for the hermeticism of social classes. Consistent with these views, Maimonides saw the law as drawing clear and categorical boundaries between domains: between clean and unclean animals, between states of cleanness and uncleanness, between priests and Levites, between Levites and Israelites, and between Israelites and pagan nations.[86]

---

83. What stands out is Maimonides' desire to preserve four claims for his enumeration, a fitting objective if he intended the count to be a detailed outline. See the discussion of individuation in chapter 2.

84. See *GP* II:39-40 and III:27.

85. On the Platonic influence on Maimonides, see Strauss, "Quelques remarques sur la science politique de Maïmonide et de Farabi," 14: "And because the political science that is known and deemed worthy of some attention by Maimonides is a Platonizing form of politics, it will be, in the end, the doctrines of the Republic and the Laws that will determine the manner according to which Maimonides will understand Torah." (Quotation translated by Jean-Marc Liling and Oshrat Diane Cohen.)

86. Maimonides calls the fifth book of the *MT* the "Book of Holiness" (*Sefer Qedushah*) because, as he states in the introduction to the *MT*, "with these two matters [forbidden relations and forbidden foods] God had sanctified us and separated us from the nations," and continues to quote two scriptural verses in support.

As I conclude this review of Maimonides' innovations, I return for a moment to Twersky's categorical assumption. Recall that Twersky understood that Maimonides assumed that the 613 commandments were fixed. The enumeration was based purely on internal considerations, rabbinic exegesis, and individuation methods. Only after the enumeration was established did the philosopher set out to do his task: to ascertain how the commandments relate to the welfare of the body and the soul. In other words, Maimonides' explanations of the goals of the commandments are after-the-fact justifications. As we saw, Harvey doubted that matters were so simple and wondered, "can we detect...an ongoing effort by Maimonides to decide the law in such a manner as to bring (or keep) it in line with the *teloi* of peace and knowledge?"

I believe that the answer to Harvey's question must be yes. Based on our analysis, at least some of the innovations appear to owe their existence to external considerations, to the ethical and political themes that Maimonides wished to emphasize. When we peruse these innovations, we find a number of recurrent themes. Maimonides appears preoccupied with the needs of a well-ordered state, the concern of the political philosophers of his day. This includes the concepts that worship and sacrifices should be conducted at only one location (P85). It also includes appeals to orderliness (P36) and cleanliness (P30). The law must instill reverence towards the "guardians of society," the priests, (P32 and P34), because they are the keepers of the sanctuary and its objects; reverence towards the sanctuary is also important so that "man should be affected by a sentiment of submission and servitude" upon seeing its glory and greatness (P22).[87] Maimonides' concerns with maintaining clear demarcations are also quite noteworthy, as between ritually clean and unclean things (P149-52), and between those who have been secluded because of their wicked ways and those who "direct their ways aright"[88] (P112). We also find that the Law is concerned

87. *GP* III:45, 577.

88. As per *Hilkhot Metsora'* 16:10. Maimonides' concern with demarcations can also be seen in his dedicating an entire treatise to concepts of holiness (*qedushah*), which he read as signifying separation. See note 86 above.

with a well-functioning judicial system and with the adoption of just procedures (P175, P178 and P179), possibly influenced by the Muslim courts and their interest in procedural matters. Useful beliefs and necessary opinions are crucial for the proper conduct of the Platonic society, which fully justifies the acquiring or writing of a scroll of the Torah (P17) and the retelling of miracles (P157). Similarly, obeying the words of the true prophet (P172) brings about a belief in the validity, immutability, and eternal nature of Mosaic prophecy (P172), itself a useful belief since "belief in prophecy precedes belief in the Law."[89] Lastly, the masses must be instilled with an unceasing hatred for deceit and evil (P189) and for idolatry and paganism (P187), even when their perpetrators and practitioners can no longer be located or identified.

In the next section, we find Maimonides introducing a momentous idea in Jewish *halakhah*: dogma. The case for external factors driving the composition becomes even more compelling.

THE UNCERTAIN PLACE OF DOGMA IN *HALAKHAH*

Many of the commandments that Maimonides innovated were concerned with particular aspects of creating a well-ordered and moral society. The laws he delineated were specific actions to be carried out in body and form. But what did he believe about commandments for the mind—more precisely, could dogma be legislated? Maimonides includes on his list of positive commandments the obligations to believe in the existence of God and to believe that God is one, despite their not having a component of physical action. The remainder of this chapter will analyze Maimonides' philosophical writings on the rational faculties and assess the uncertain place of belief in a world of commanded action.

DOGMA AND COMMANDEDNESS

In his introduction to *M Avot*, referred to as *Shemonah Peraqim* (*SP*), Maimonides posits that the soul is made up of five faculties: the nutritive, the sentient, the imaginative, the appetitive, and the

89. *GP* III:45, 576.

rational. These ideas are adaptations of Aristotle's taxonomy of the soul, as expanded and mediated by the Islamic philosopher Al-Farabi.[90] In chapter two of *SP*, Maimonides discusses the faculties in which transgressions, observances, virtues, and vices reside. He writes:

> Know that disobedience and obedience of the Law are found only in two parts of the soul, namely, the sentient part and the appetitive part. All the transgressions and the commandments involve these two parts. There is no obedience or disobedience in the nutritive or imaginative parts, since thought and choice do not act upon them at all. By his thought, man is not able to suspend their action or to limit them to a certain action.[91]

He posits here that conscious or voluntary acts are connected to the sentient and the appetitive parts of the soul; thus these parts of the soul can be called the media of transgression and obedience.

Maimonides defines the rational part of the soul as "the power found in man by which he perceives intelligibles, deliberates, acquires the sciences, and distinguishes between base and noble actions. Some of these activities are practical and some are theoretical."[92] He then asks whether the rational part can transgress or obey, to which he responds:

> Although there is perplexity concerning the rational part, I say that this power too may bring about obedience and disobedience, namely, belief in a false or a true opinion. But there is no act in it to which the terms commandment or transgression would apply.[93]

---

90. *The Aphorisms of the Statesman* (*Fusul al-Madani*) served as Maimonides' blueprint for *SP*. See Davidson, "Maimonides' *Shemonah Perakim* and Al-Farabi's *Fusul al-Madani*," 33-50.
91. *Ethical Writings of Maimonides*, ed. Weiss and Butterworth, 64.
92. Ibid., 63.
93. Ibid., 64-65. Shailat (in *Haqdamot ha-RaMBaM la-Mishnah,* ed. Shailat, 273) suggests that Maimonides could have resolved this question by referring to the commandment of learning Torah, an activity centered in the mind that also involves the appetitive and sensitive faculties. Shailat refutes this demonstration by arguing that Maimonides was seeking an activity that solely and exclusively resided in the mind. I believe, however, that one can posit a more fundamental distinction between Torah study and doctrinal belief. One studies Torah neither to assert nor to demonstrate the truth of its commandments, but rather to acquire sufficient knowledge to perform them. However, the truth of beliefs is subject to investigation and demonstration. It is this latter activity to which Maimonides refers when he discusses commanding the rational

Maimonides does not tell us what thinkers are behind this "perplexity" or why it should even be a matter of doubt. Yet there is some evidence that a significant number of early medieval rabbinic authorities did not consider beliefs to be valid objects of commandments.[94] We learn this from remarks in the work *The Duties of the Heart* (*al-Hidaya ila Faraid al-Qulub*, or *H̲ovot ha-Levavot* in the Hebrew translation). Little is known about its author, Bah̲ya b. Joseph ibn Paquda, other than that he was an eleventh-century rabbinic scholar in Muslim Spain. As its title suggests, Bah̲ya wrote this work because he believed that even those most punctilious about performing commandments neglected the duties of the heart.

By all accounts, the work was extremely popular from the moment of its appearance and had a profound influence on Jewish pietistic practice and literature.[95] In his apologia for undertaking this work, Bah̲ya offers an interesting classification of the commandments. He divides the obligations of the religious person into two parts: the duties of the body and its limbs, with which one expresses outward obedience, and the duties of the heart, with which one expresses inward obedience. Duties of the body include

> Prayer, fasting, almsgiving, learning his book and spreading the knowledge of it, fulfilling the commandments concerning the Tabernacle, the palm branch, the fringes, the doorpost, the railings on the roof, and

---

faculty. I thank my grandson, Tsvi Horowitz, for making this fine distinction. I have also noticed that the distinction between the Law and wisdom is made very clearly in *GP* III:54, 633.

94. There are indications, however, that at least some talmudic rabbis held that there was room for correct beliefs in *halakhah*, as in the passage: "[*And that ye not go*] *after your own heart* [Num. 15:39]: this refers to heresy; and so it says: *The fool hath said in his heart, There is no God* [Eccl. 14:1]" (*BT Berakhot* 12b). See also *Sifre Numbers, Shelakh-Lekha* 115 (126), on Num. 15:39, which Maimonides uses as his proof text for N47. Since this violation does not involve an act, transgressors are exempt from lashes; nevertheless, it constitutes a transgression. Scripture thus forbids the denying of the existence of God. Qayyara lists "After your own heart" among the negative commandments (Nq117), although, as we cautioned earlier, we have no way to know to which prohibition Qayyara was referring, since he simply listed scriptural verses or close paraphrases.

95. The consensus of modern scholars is that Maimonides was not only well acquainted with Bah̲ya's work but may have been influenced by it (private communication with Haggai ben-Shammai).

the like, all of which can be wholly performed by man's physical body.[96]

Inward obedience, on the other hand, is expressed through the duties of the heart. Some of the most important active duties of the heart include: "to believe in the Creator of the world, who brought the world into existence from nothingness; to believe in pure monotheism, free from a belief in any other gods; to assent to obeying God in our hearts;" and others. Negative duties of the heart consist of emotions such as rancor, envy, and vengeance, and by a denial of the theological doctrines listed above.[97] For Bahya, inward obedience must both precede and accompany outward obedience: "Thus I have come to know for certain that the duties of the members are of no avail to us unless our hearts choose to do them and our soul desires their performance."[98]

Bahya relates a statement relevant to our project in his discussion of enumerating the duties of the heart. When he counted the duties of the heart, he writes, "I found that their details were very numerous...for the duties of the members are limited in number, about 613 commandments in all, while the duties of the heart are many and their details innumerable." Since the duties of the heart include the belief in the Creator and the belief in pure monotheism, it follows that Bahya did not count these two beliefs in his *TaRYaG* count: in his philosophy, commandments include only acts "that can be wholly performed by man's physical body."[99]

Although Bahya separates the duties of the heart from a listing of biblical commandments—while giving them priority of knowledge and importance—Maimonides incorporates two of these beliefs, the belief in the existence of a particular God and the belief in pure monotheism,

96. Bahya ibn Paquda. *The Book of Direction to the Duties of the Heart,* 89.

97. Ibid., 87.

98. Ibid., 89. Or see: "What determines the punishment is the participation of both heart and body in the act—the heart in the intention and the body in carrying out the heart's intention .... Since now, the foundation and the pillar of action is the intention of the heart and conscience, the knowledge of the duties of the heart should come before and stand above the knowledge of the duties of the members" (ibid., 91).

99. Ibid., 89. Maimonides clearly alludes to the idea that commandments can only include bodily acts when he writes that the rational part "may bring about obedience and disobedience, namely belief in a false or a true opinion." The rational part is thus able to be commanded, despite the fact that "there is no act in it to which the terms commandment or transgression would apply."

into his *TaRYaG* count. How he accomplishes this feat is the subject of the next section.

We appreciate the significance of Maimonides' innovation when we notice that these two affirmations are not found in Qayyara's list of commandments. While Hildesheimer places these two commandments under the header of Qayyara's entry Pq39, "and belief" (*ve-emunah*), also listed as "and truth" (*ve-emet*),[100] this is almost certainly mistaken. Pq39 follows immediately after a group of commandments devoted to the relationship between man and his fellow man: "to clothe the naked" (Pq33), "to bury the dead" (Pq34), "to console the mourner" (Pq35), "to visit the sick" (Pq36), "to love peace" (Pq37), and "and justice" (Pq38). It seems likely that Qayyara intended this commandment to stand for the obligation to conduct business in an honest manner, as in the rabbinic expression, "did you carry out transactions with honesty" (*nasata v-natata be-emunah*). If Qayyara had indeed intended to list the commandments to believe in the existence of God and His oneness, one should have expected to find these entries next to "love of God" (Pq23) and "fear of God" (Pq24), or at the very head of the list, given their obvious importance.[101]

This observation is confirmed by none other than Nahmanides, Qayyara's principal apologist, who declares: "I saw that the author of the *Halakhot* [Qayyara] did not count this commandment [the existence of God] among the 613."[102] According to Nahmanides, Qayyara omits the commandment to believe in God's existence from his count because commandments by necessity presuppose His existence. God is the "fundament and root" from which all commandments issue. Therefore, belief in God cannot be counted *among* the commandments.

100. Hildesheimer, *Haqdamat Sefer Halakhot Gedolot*, 74n335.

101. The *declaration* of His oneness, through the recitation of the *Shema*, is the first entry in Qayyara's list of positive commandments.

102. Nahmanides, *Hasagot*, P1, 206. Shelomo ibn Gabirol, who tends to follow Qayyara's enumeration, also omits belief in God from his enumeration. Moses ibn Tibbon, the first expositor of Gabirol's *Azharot*, thought that Gabirol had counted this commandment in line 11: "I took you out, I admonished you, I guided you, in righteous ways." This line, however, appears to be a preamble to the list of commandments that follows. Duran, *Zohar ha-Raqia*, ad loc., 3-4, disputes Ibn Tibbon's reading on interpretive grounds.

On Nahmanides' explanation, one would have to conclude that a vast theological divide exists between jurists like Qayyara, who presuppose the existence of a divine lawgiver (and do not need to enumerate the commandment to affirm it), and jurists like Maimonides, who require an explicit, reasoned affirmation of God's existence. It is reasonable to presume that Qayyara would be satisfied with almost any understanding of a superior being, even an anthropomorphic one, if that persona could form the basis for obedience of the laws. For Maimonides, however, who incorporates into the commandments a refined philosophical definition of God, such a conception of a supreme lawgiver would have constituted heresy. An explicit affirmation of God is how Maimonides ensures that the correct vision of divinity undergirds the foundation of commandments.

Maimonides was not the first scholar to propose that belief in the existence of God is a commandment. That distinction belongs to the Babylonian gaon, H̲efets b. Yatsliah̲, who writes:

> The first precept enjoins us to unite our mind and thoughts on the truths of the matter; to make our Creator exist in our heart, and to consider Him Lord of all things without a shadow of doubt, and without any other thought; to know that He is truth; as it is written: *Know therefore this day, and lay it to thy heart, that YHWH is Eloqim, there is no-one else besides Him* [Deut. 4:39].[103]

---

103. H̲efets' description of the first commandment was preserved for us by Judah b. Barzilai in his twelfth-century commentary on the Book of Creation (*Sefer Yetsirah*) (above quotation from Judah b. Barzilai, *Perush Sefer Yetsirah*, 55-56). H̲efets explains the two divine terms and references the end of the verse as proof that "He is one and that there is no other." H̲efets later adds that he is obliged to explain his proof that God exists, "that He is one and that there is no other," so that one "may be strengthened in the belief that He is one, and is the creator of all things." H̲efets, *A Volume of the Book of Precepts*, trans. Halper. Missing from H̲efets' apparatus is a rabbinic warrant to support the commandment claim. Davidson notes that Maimonides had "precedents... for viewing belief in, or the knowledge of, the existence of God as a formal commandment of the Law," among them Bah̲ya, H̲efets, Samuel b. H̲ofni, and Ibn Ezra. Davidson shows that there is a "modicum of corroboration" for the idea that H̲efets' formulation of the first two positive commandments of the Law "was a springboard for Maimonides." Davidson, "The First Two Commandments," 127-133. Hyman also notes: "By the time of Maimonides it was accepted at least by philosophers, that belief in the existence of God and similar beliefs formed part of the system of *mitsvot* and that their affirmation was a matter of religious observation." Hyman, "Rabbi Simlai's Sayings and Beliefs Concerning God," 52. I must insist, however, that none of these

In contrast to Hefets, who adduced only scriptural support, Maimonides provided a rabbinic warrant to prove this innovative claim (as we shall soon see). This lent great halakhic authority to his claim and undoubtedly became the main reason for the unquestioning reception of his idea in later generations.

I now return to Maimonides and his remarks in the second chapter of *SP*. While other thinkers did not necessarily connect transgression and obedience to the rational part of the soul, Maimonides did not doubt this connection. He does not explain how he knows that the rational part can be commanded, but this thesis correlates with his ethical-philosophical worldview, with its emphasis on correct notions and moral dispositions.[104] Maimonides sees the law as commanding the acquisition of these correct notions. If the law truly aims to enhance the welfare of the soul, then the law would necessarily encourage and inculcate correct opinions. In his words:

> Among the things to which your attention ought to be directed is that you should know that in regard to the correct opinions through which the ultimate perfections may be obtained, the Law has communicated only their end and made a call to believe in them in a summary way—that is, to believe in the existence of the deity, may He be exalted, His unity, His knowledge, His power, His will, and His eternity. All these points are ultimate ends, which can be made clear in detail and through definitions only after one knows many opinions (*GP* III:28, 512).

In short, to obtain the "ultimate perfections" (which would lead to ultimate happiness), man must acquire a correct notion of God and His oneness. His innovation is that the "Law had made a call to believe in them": it commanded the acquisition of these notions.[105]

---

exegetes cited rabbinic warrants for the formal claim, thus failing to integrate these beliefs into the halakhic world of commandments.

104. In this and related respects, Maimonides follows very closely on the footsteps of one of his principal philosophical mentors, Al-Farabi. Compare this discussion with Al-Farabi's *Aphorisms of the Statesman, Fusul*, in particular the early paragraphs and para. 49. See Davidson, "Maimonides' *Shemonah Perakim* and Al-Farabi's Fusul al-Madani," 33-50.

105. At this point, I am short-circuiting the subtle distinction that Maimonides makes between welfare and perfection, as some scholars have suggested. See Galston, "The Purpose of Law According to Maimonides," 27-51, and Harvey, "Political Philosophy

In the *ShM*, Maimonides gives a proof that these beliefs constitute a commandment. In support of his first commandment claim, to know God, Maimonides references the end of *BT Makkot*, paraphrasing the familiar aggadic passage found there:

> Six hundred and thirteen [*TaRYaG*] commandments were declared unto Moses at Sinai, as the verse says, *Moses commanded us a Law* [*Torah*] [Deut. 33:4]; that is, he commanded us to observe as many commandments as are signified by the sum of the letter-numbers *ToRaH*. To this it was objected that the letter-numbers of the word *ToRaH* add up to only six hundred and eleven; to which the reply was: "The two commandments *I am the Lord thy God* and *Thou shalt have no other gods before Me* [Exod. 20:2-3] we heard from the Almighty Himself." That is, the Lord commanded 611 commandments to the Israelites through Moses, thus *Moses commanded a Law*, and two commandments directly.

As we saw earlier, this exegesis is attributed to R. Hamnuna. Maimonides ends his short comment by stating: "*Thus it has been made clear to you* that the verse *I am the Lord thy God* is one of the 613 commandments, and is that whereby we are commanded to believe in God, as we have explained" (emphasis added).

To understand the compelling legal nature of this aggadah, we need first to understand the profound truth that Maimonides believed lay hidden in it. *GP* II:33 is dedicated to explaining the unique event of the revelation at Sinai. After offering an interpretation of the text based on the "external meaning,"[106] he then proceeds to tell us that the Sages "also have a dictum formulated in several passages of the midrashim

---

and Halakhah in Maimonides," 198-212. This difference may lie at the heart of Maimonides' pedagogy. The uninitiated individual accepts the existence of God with some minimum rational support, while the enlightened individual seeks perfection through a thorough demonstration of His Existence and Oneness.

106. The "external" (*zahir*) and "internal" (*batin*) meaning of parables, explained in the Introduction to part I of the *GP*, is a critical tool in understanding the *GP*'s project. Maimonides writes that while the external meaning of parables "contains wisdom that is useful in many respects, among which is the welfare of human societies," the internal meaning "contains wisdom that is useful for beliefs concerned with the truth as it is" (12). For a detailed discussion of this hermeneutic, see Stern, *Problems and Parables of Law*. For a critique of Stern's work, see Kaplan, "Review of Josef Stern's Problems and Parables of the Law," 361-364.

and also figuring in the Talmud."

The dictum to which Maimonides refers and which describes revelation in allegorical terms is contained in none other than R. Simlai's aggadah of the 613 commandments. It reveals the "internal meaning" of the fateful events that occurred at Sinai by drawing a sharp categorical distinction between the first two commandments and the rest of the Torah. According to the "external meaning" of the verses, Moses had relayed all the commandments to the Israelites after receiving them directly from God; according to the "internal meaning," Moses relays to the Israelites all the commandments *except* for the first two. These first two commandments are apprehended intellectually by each member of the entire nation, each in his own way and according to his own capacity. This, suggests Maimonides, is the true meaning of the midrashic dictum "The two commandments *I am the Lord thy God* and *Thou shalt have no other gods before Me* [Exod. 20:3] we heard from the Almighty Himself." In effect, two different types of commandments were "heard" on Sinai: those which Moses and Israel apprehended intellectually—the existence of God and His unity[107]—and those which Moses relayed to the Israelites—all the remaining commandments. The first two commandments, Maimonides asserts,

> are knowable by human speculation alone.[108] Now, with regard to everything that can be known by demonstration, the status of the prophet and that of everyone else who knows it are equal; there is no superiority of one over the other. Thus, these two principles are not known through prophecy alone. The text of the Torah says *Unto thee it was shown [that*

---

107. The plain meaning of "Thou shalt not have other gods before Me" is that it represents an admonition against believing in other gods—polytheism. Arguably, believing in God's composite unity can be viewed as believing in more than one god. Compare *Hilkhot Yesode ha-Torah* 1:7.

108. This statement confirms Efodi's understanding that Maimonides reads the words "we heard from the Almighty Himself" in the midrash as referring to human speculation; by means of his intellect, man can prove the existence and unity of God. The identification of intellectual apprehension with "hearing from the Almighty" is admittedly a bit stretched, but Maimonides leaves little doubt that that is what he thinks the allegory represents. Efodi, in *Moreh Nevukhim (with the Commentaries of Efodi, Shem Tov, Crescas and Abarbanel)*, trans. Ibn Tibbon, II:33:70*b*, s. v. "*rotsim be-zeh ha-maamar.*"

> *thou mightest know that the Lord, He is God; there is none else beside Him*] [Deut. 4:35]. As for the other commandments they belong to the class of generally-accepted opinions and those adopted in virtue of tradition, not the class of the *intellecta*.[109]

As Maimonides saw it, there was a profound qualitative difference between the first two commandments and the other eight. The first two commandments represent demonstrable propositions, the type of statements that philosophers and logicians are wont to make. These truths do not require the mediation of a prophet. The rest of the commandments, on the other hand, represent conventions, the type of laws that a wise and rational lawgiver—a prophet being the epitome of such a wise lawgiver in Maimonides' political philosophy—would promulgate for the benefit of a well-ordered society.

We should note that this qualitative distinction between the two sets of commandments does not hold up in the rabbinic accounts of the Sinaitic revelation. As recounted in Deuteronomy 5:22-24, Moses mediated God's message at the behest of the Israelites, frightened as they were by the voice of God. In *Song of Songs Rabbah*, the Sages disagree as to when this mediation occurred: R. Joshua says it was after the second commandment, and the rabbis say after the tenth.[110] Regardless of which interpretation one accepts, neither tradition hints at an intrinsic difference between the first two pronouncements and

---

109. The distinction between "the class of the *intellecta*," on which demonstrative syllogisms are based, and "generally accepted opinions," on which dialectic syllogisms are built, has been ascribed to Aristotle. The term "generally accepted opinions" corresponds to the Greek term *endoxa*, defined as "those which commend themselves to all or to the majority or to the wise—that is, to all of the wise or to the majority or to the most famous and distinguished of them." Aristotle, *Topica*, 1.1, 100b, 21-23, in Aristotle, *Posterior Analytics, Topica*, 275-277. The Arabic term used here, *almushhurath* (*mefursamot* in the Hebrew rendering), has a slightly different connotation, referring to things that are generally known. See *Les Guide des Egarés*, trans. S. Munk, 39n1. In *GP* I:2, "generally accepted opinions" refers to the categories of good and bad (as opposed to true and false) and can also refer to the particular notions of certain societies. See the short bibliography on this concept in *Moreh Nevukhim*, ed. Schwarz, vol. II, 378n5. See also "Maimonides' Treatise on Logic [English Translation]," ed. and trans. Efros, 47-49.

110. Song of Songs Rabbah 1:2. See also the commentary on the Pentateuch by H̲izkiyahu ben Manoah̲ (H̲izkuni), *Torat Chaim Chumash*, Exod. 20:1.

the remaining ones. Maimonides' reading of the aggadah, inferring the existence of two types of revelations at Sinai, is undoubtedly motivated and informed by his philosophical worldview.[111]

We have shown that, as Maimonides sees it, the aggadah of the 613 commandments was interpreted by the rabbis in ways that match Maimonides' radical understanding of the difference between the first two commandments and the remaining ones. This appears to be sufficient cause for Maimonides to take this aggadah, or at least a part of it, as more than just a pious homily. Furthermore, the aggadah gives Maimonides the opportunity to prove not only that dogma could be commanded, but also that the belief in God's existence and His oneness are commandments that belong in the *TaRYaG* count: they form part of the halakhic corpus. In light of Qayyara's enumeration and Ba<u>h</u>ya's description of what was commonly thought to be contained in the 613 commandments, this last assertion indeed represented a major halakhic innovation.

THE TWO COMMANDMENTS OF BELIEF

In the *ShM*, Maimonides turns the dogmas of God's existence and His unity into commandments. In this section, I shall examine the way Maimonides formulates these two commandments.

> P1. To know that there is a God, as it is said, "I am the Lord, thy God" (Exod. 20:2; Deut. 5:6).

The *ShM* states the claim thus: "We are commanded in the belief[112] of

111. This philosophical reading did not go unnoticed in rabbinic circles. Yitz<u>h</u>aq b. Sheshet (RiBaSH; 1326-1408), a prominent halakhist and talmudist, criticized Maimonides for using Greek "wisdom" to explain certain miracles, among them the Sinaitic revelation. Yitz<u>h</u>aq b. Sheshet, *Sheelot u-Teshuvot*, responsum 45, 26b-27b. I am indebted to Marc Shapiro for this reference.

112. In place of the *SE*'s "to know," the *ShM* uses the more nuanced Arabic term, *itikad*, which semantically lies somewhere between knowledge and belief, perhaps best translated as "firm conviction." See Hilman, "Tsiyunim," *Sefer ha-Mitsvot*, ed. Frankel, *ad loc.*, s. v. "*le-ha'amin*," 207. Also see Rawidowicz, "On Maimonides' Sefer ha-Madda'," 317. Moshe ibn Tibbon, one of the translators of the *ShM*, rendered *itikad* as "to believe" (*le-ha'amin*). Unfortunately, there is no Hebrew word that conveys the nuanced meaning of *itikad*, and translators have had to choose between translating it as "knowledge" and

the Divinity;[113] that is, to believe that there is a cause of causes who is the efficient cause[114] of everything in existence." According to this formulation, the existence of God is assumed; it is only the *nature* of this deity that we must consider when we affirm His existence.[115] Technically,

as "belief." Hilman points out that the title of Sa'adiah's theological treatise, *al-Amanat ve-al-Itikad*, was translated by Yehudah ibn Tibbon as *Emunot ve-De'ot*, showing that *itikad* ought to be translated as *de'ot*, "opinions." Hilman also notes the use of *itikad* in the opening line of *GP* I:50 as referring to knowledge, as does Kafih, in his note there. But see Schwarz's comments in *Moreh Nevukhim*, ed. Schwartz, vol. 1, 10n15, who acknowledges Ibn Tibbon's correct translation of Sa'adiah's title but believes that the *GP* uses it to mean "belief." Septimus notes: "*itikad* refers to any firm belief or conviction: true, false or heretical, rationally derived or otherwise." He observes further that this true conviction, however, implies nothing with respect to its truth and rationality. Septimus draws his conclusions from the use that Maimonides makes of the term in the *GP*. It follows that Maimonides in the *ShM* would require one to believe in God even if such belief was not fully demonstrable. This reading is a bit difficult to entertain in the *ShM*, though perhaps Maimonides' use of the term changed over time, and earlier on, he had indeed used the term to refer to knowledge that is rationally demonstrable. A not-fully-demonstrable belief in God, however, might fit with the more skeptical tone of the *GP*. Septimus, "What Did Maimonides Mean by *Madd'a*?" 91n42.

113. More precisely "Lordship," a term denoting power and mastery. Haggai ben-Shammai indicated to me in a private communication that the Arabic term, *al-rububiyya,* is extremely rare in Maimonides' writings, neither appearing in Maimonides' Arabic text of the thirteen principles nor even once in the *GP*. Based on a number of Islamic sources, he suggested that the term can perhaps be rendered "Lordship" or "divine Lordship." For stylistic purposes, I adopted the term "Divinity," a close parallel to *ha-eloqut*, which is how the traditional translators have rendered this term.

114. The efficient cause of a house, for example, is the builder, or more exactly, the idealized form of the house in the builder's soul. Chavel has "creator" instead of "cause" (Arabic *alpaal*, Hebrew *po'el*). According to Efros (*Philosophical Terms,* s. v. "*po'el*"), the word either means "efficient cause" or "doer." Efros notes that "doer" "was chosen by the Mutakallimum with reference to the Creator rather than First Cause, which is the Aristotelian name, because of their belief in the constant coexistence of the Cause and the caused." Both here and throughout the writing of the *MT,* Maimonides deliberately avoids using the simpler and more forthright term "the Creator." He confirms this usage in *GP* I:71 and in a late gloss to the fourth article of the Thirteen Articles of Faith. The surprising implication of this formulation is that one can fulfill this commandment without necessarily believing that God created the world.

115. This is also how Abarbanel explained it in his rebuttal of Crescas, who thought that in the *ShM*, Maimonides was simply saying that one must affirm that God caused the world to come into existence. Don Hasdai Crescas (d.1412?) was a critic of Aristotle's philosophy and one of Maimonides' strongest medieval critics. See Crescas, *Or Adonai,* 3; and Abarbanel, *Rosh Amanah*, 71-72. For an analysis of Crescas' critique of Maimonides on this and related matters, see Ben Porat, "Emunot ve-De'ot le-Mitsvot le-Da'at ha-RaMBaM ve-R. Hasdai Crescas," 216-229.

it is therefore more correct to say that Maimonides believes the first commandment to be the obligation to affirm the nature of the existence of God. The phrase "the efficient cause of everything in existence" likely refers to God in His capacity as Prime Mover. In Aristotelian terms, God is thus defined as First Cause and Prime Mover. In the second commandment, Maimonides explicitly unifies these two qualities.

Proof: Maimonides' proof text is the verse from Exodus 20:2-3, "I am YHWH your God." In his explication of the commandment, he goes on to say that the proof that this statement represents a commandment comes from R. Simlai's aggadah (which he cites verbatim): it reckons this verse and the subsequent one, "Thou shalt have no other gods before Me" (Exod. 20:3), as part of the *TaRYaG* count.

Maimonides learns two aspects of the deity from the biblical phrase "I am YHWH your God [*Elohekha*]": First Cause and Prime Mover.[116] Yet he does not show how the phrase itself connects to these two qualities. Which name of God would epitomize the quality of being the First Cause, and which the Prime Mover?[117] Not only the exegesis but also the definition appears to be incomplete in the *ShM*, the gloss appearing to represent perhaps only Maimonides' first attempt to define this important dogma in a philosophically rigorous and complete form.

As it is stated here, the commandment offers very imprecise guidelines for action. What actions should one take to acquire this belief? In the *MT*, and certainly in the *GP*, Maimonides urges one to study metaphysics in order to learn truths about the universe. If one studies but fails to believe in God, would one have fulfilled the

116. This reading represents philosophic eisegesis. More plausibly, the author of the aggadah likely viewed "I am the Lord, your God" as a commandment to believe in the God that took the Israelites out of Egypt, the God of History rather than the First Cause. For an interesting discussion on this point, see Harvey, "The First Commandment and the God of History," 203-216.

117. Harvey reads Maimonides as parsing this verse to account for both terms: *YHWH* is the name that refers to God as the Supreme Cause, and *Elohekha* refers to His being "the cause of everything in existence." Harvey, "The First Commandment and the God of History," 209. Though his interpretation is entirely plausible, there is no textual support for it. I believe that Harvey was simply inserting the *Halakhot*'s exposition into the *ShM*, as I will discuss later.

commandment?[118] Is one obligated to acquire this strong belief under any circumstances? Additionally, Maimonides does not define what he means by "cause." Hanna Kasher has observed that throughout his works, Maimonides uses this term in various ways, all consonant with the multiple meanings that the term came to possess in Aristotle's works. In this particular case, the term could indicate final cause as well as efficient cause.[119]

These questions and others are fundamental to a proper understanding of the commandment. Since Maimonides warned in the introduction of the *ShM* that the *ShM* was not going to be absolutely precise nor necessarily complete in its formulations, one is tempted to resort to the *Halakhot* for help in elaborating on and complementing some of these inchoate formulations. Unfortunately, this strategy is methodologically flawed: one must consider the possibility that Maimonides had altered his views by the time he wrote the *Halakhot*. It cannot thus be assumed that the *Halakhot* reflects his earlier thinking.[120]

---

118. Abarbanel grapples with Crescas' objection that commands imply choice, while logically demonstrated truths leave no room for choice. If one knows, one *must* believe—and therefore, genuine beliefs cannot be commanded. Abarbanel responds by arguing that the command to believe should be understood as a command to prepare oneself through studies that will (or might?) eventually lead to belief. One is thus commanded to prepare oneself to believe. But does Abarbanel think that Maimonides maintains that studies will inevitably lead to believing in the nature of His existence? And if his studies do not succeed in producing belief, has the faithful fulfilled the commandment? Abarbanel does not say. See Abarbanel, *Rosh Amana*, 118-119.

119. Kasher, "Does 'Ought' Imply 'Can' in Maimonides?" 17-18. See also note 114 above. The final cause of a house, for example, is its purpose or end (*telos*): the provision of shelter. God may be the final cause of the universe in the sense that the universe is moving toward actualization, living completely according to the will of God.

120. Two small examples will suffice to make this point. First, on close reading, one notes that the definition in the *Halakhot* varies slightly but meaningfully from the one offered in the *ShM*: "The basic principle of all basic principles ...is that *there is* a First Existent who brought every existing thing into being" (emphasis added). In the *Halakhot*, Maimonides seems here to posit God's existence rather than to presuppose it. Crescas also thought that there was a difference between the *ShM*'s formulation and the *Halakhot*'s. Abarbanel did not accept this distinction and attempted to harmonize both pronouncements. Abarbanel, *Rosh Amanah*, 70-72. Second, the *Halakhot* differs from the *ShM* in the way it parses the phrase "I am YHWH your Lord": "*YHWH* stands for Necessary Being" (*Hilkhot Yesode ha-Torah* 1:1-4), while "*Elohekha* stands for God of the universe and Lord of the earth, the one who controls the sphere of the universe, the Mover" (ibid., 1:5).

> P2. To acknowledge His Unity,[121] as it is said, "The Lord our God, the Lord is One" (Deut. 6:4).

This is the second of the two beliefs that Maimonides innovatively introduces in the enumeration of commandments. More specifically, the *ShM* reads, "We are commanded in the belief of unity,[122] that is to say, to believe that the cause of all things in existence and their first cause is one." What was stated only in passing in P1 is now stated explicitly: God, the First Cause, is also the Prime Mover.[123]

Proof: Maimonides maintains that the injunction is contained in the phrase "Hear O Israel: the Lord our God, the Lord is One" (Deut. 6:4). In support of this claim, he writes:

> In most midrashim you will find this explained as meaning that we are to declare the unity of God's name, or the unity of God, or something of that kind. The intention of the Sages was to teach that God brought us out of Egypt and heaped kindness upon us only on condition that we

121. Literally, "to unify Him" (*le-yah̲ado*). The Arabic equivalent of unification, *tawhid*, "is a term applied to the belief, or the profession of faith, in one God" (*GP*, ed. Pines, I:35, 81 n. 4). I used Hyamson's translation of *yih̲ud* as "unity" because it matches Efros, *Philosophical Terms*, 57, s. v. "*yih̲ud*," although "oneness" may convey a slightly more precise philosophical understanding. In general, I have used the words "oneness" and "unity" interchangeably in this work.

122. Hebrew, *be-emunat ha-yih̲ud*. Arabic, *b-itikad al-tuh̲id*. I have already discussed the Arabic term *itikad* in connection with P1, showing that it represents firm conviction. Chavel translated the sentence as "to believe in the unity of God," but the added words are not in the original text.

123. As he did with respect to P1, Maimonides changes this definition in the *Halakhot* (see above, note 122) in this case rather dramatically. In *Hilkhot Yesode ha-Torah* 1:7, he writes: "This God is One ... so that none of the things existing in the universe to which the term one is applied is like unto His unity; neither such a unit as a species which comprises many units, nor such a unit as a physical body which consists of parts and dimensions. His unity is such that there is no other Unity like it in the world." He does not mention the unity of the First Cause and the Prime Mover. Harvey asserts that while *Hilkhot Yesode ha-Torah* 1:5 and 1:7 identify the Prime Mover with God, 2:3 and 3:1 disprove this identification (and so, he notes, does *GP* II:4). He claims that ultimately, Maimonides does not identify the Prime Mover with God. This position is supported by the different definitions of "unity" in the *ShM* and in the *Halakhot*. Harvey, "The *Mishneh Torah* as a Key to the Secrets of the Guide," 17-19. I am indebted to Marc Shapiro for helping me refine this point and for referring me to Harvey's article.

> believe in His unity, which is our bounden duty. The commandment to believe in God's unity [*mitsvat yiḥud*] is mentioned in many places, and the Sages also call this commandment "Kingdom" [*malkhut*], for they speak of the obligation "to take upon oneself the yoke of the Kingdom of Heaven [*le-qabbel 'alav ol malkhut shamayim*]," that is to say, to declare God's unity and to believe in Him.

Maimonides struggles to find a source for this independent commandment. He introduces the term *mitsvat yiḥud*,[124] stating that the commandment is "mentioned in many places," and that this commandment is the equivalent of taking upon oneself the yoke of the Kingdom of Heaven. Perla points out that the referenced midrashim relate to the declaration of unity made while reciting the Shema—a commandment separately enumerated as P10. Furthermore, Perla notes that neither of the cited expressions, *mitsvat yiḥud* or *mitsvat malkhut*, which could have been read as commandment markers, are in evidence in the midrashim.[125]

The expression "to take upon oneself the yoke of the Kingdom of Heaven" comes from *M Berakhot* 2:2, where it serves as justification for reciting the Shema before reciting the section "And it shall come to pass if ye shall hearken" (Deut. 11:13-21). One must accept the yoke of Heaven, symbolized by the first paragraph of the Shema, before one accepts the performance of the commandments (*meqabbel 'alav 'ol mitsvot*), symbolized by the second paragraph. However we understand the idea of accepting the yoke of Heaven—and it is often read as offering one's life and possessions for God's sake (martyrdom, *qiddush ha-Shem*)[126]—it is difficult to equate such a pious expression of acceptance with a mandate to believe in His unity. Kafih's explanation,

124. We see here again that Maimonides uses the term *mitsvat-X* to prove a commandment claim. See the discussion of this marker in chapter 2.

125. Perla, *Sefer ha-Mitsvot le-RaSaG*, vol. 1, 141-142. See also *Sefer ha-Mitsvot*, ed. Kafih, ad loc., n. 11, regarding *mitsvat yiḥud*. Confirming their observations, I conducted a quick search of rabbinic literature and did not encounter a single use of the term *mitsvat yiḥud* in the extant literature. While it may have existed in lost texts, it is hard to square an occasional mention with the statement that it is found in "many places."

126. Note that the acceptance of the yoke is qualified by the phrase "with all your heart, with all your soul and with all your resources." In *BT Berakhot* 61b, a tanna interprets "with all your soul" to mean "even if he takes your soul."

"one cannot adequately accept the yoke of Heaven without first recognizing the truth of His unity" does no more than beg the question.

The talmudic dictum to which Maimonides refers states that the order of the Shema's sections allows one to "first accept the yoke of Heaven and then one can accept the yoke of commandments." In *Hilkhot Qeriyat Shema* 1:2, Maimonides reformulates this dictum, stating that one recites the first section of the Shema first "because there is in [the section] the unity of God, the love for Him, and the study [*talmudo*] of Him. This is the great and essential matter on which all depends."[127] This reformulation matches his statement in the *ShM* that to accept the yoke of Heaven is to believe in His unity. Regardless which formulation of the dictum we use, Maimonides clearly maintains that the scriptural commandment consists of internalizing the belief in His unity, rather than proclaiming it (as the rabbinic sources imply).[128]

Conspicuously absent from this commandment's argumentative apparatus is the aggadah about the 613 commandments. As we saw earlier, Maimonides interprets this aggadah to indicate that the words spoken directly by God, "I" and "Thou shalt not have," conveyed two principles: the existence and the unity of God. Perhaps he fails to quote "Thou shalt not have" as a proof text for this commandment because that injunction is negatively phrased. Since positive commandments must be phrased in the positive, "Thou shalt not have" cannot be used as a proof text. Nevertheless, Maimonides certainly relies on this aggadah to define his commandment, which otherwise finds no echo in rabbinic sources.

Maimonides' ethico-philosophical approach informs the concept of God's unity and compels him to find a place for it in the *TaRYaG* constellation. The goal of the commandment "to unify Him" is to acquire

127. At least two commentators struggled to understand Maimonides' reformulation: Isaac Almosonino, *'Edut BiYehosef*, and David Luria, *Yad David*, both cited by Kafih in his commentary. *Mishneh Torah*, ed. Kafih, *Hilkhot Qeriyat Shema* 1:2.

128. Neither Qayyara nor any of the other geonic enumerators understood the commandment to declare the unity of God as entailing anything other than the recitation of the Shema. See Qayyara, Pq1; Elijah ha-Zaqen in *Sefer Mitsvot he-Arukh*, 184, P29; al-Bargeloni in *Sefer Mitsvot he-Arukh*, 228, P1-P2; Sa'adiah Gaon, *Sefer ha-Mitsvot*, Ps3-Ps4; Ibn Gabirol, *Zohar ha-Raqia*, 5, P1, Also see the discussion of the commandment to recite the Shema below, in chapter 8.

the basic beliefs for attaining intellectual virtue and "through which the ultimate perfection may be obtained." In his efforts to add this commandment to his list, Maimonides subtly reinterprets a tannaitic statement that more literally concerns *praxis*, the recitation of the Shema, rather than *doxa*, the belief in His unity. He transforms the monotheistic affirmation into an obligatory dogma and then moves to add a second and related commandment, that of reciting the Shema twice daily (P10). Would Scripture, on Maimonides' reading, have mandated an obligation to recite the unity of God, even as it has already mandated the faithful to apprehend His unity? In chapter 8, we will resolve this apparent superfluity by positing the existence of two distinct legal sources.

* * *

Perhaps here is the place to take a small detour and reflect on what it means to introduce dogma as a religious duty. When reviewing these two commandments of belief, one is struck by how difficult they are to understand and thus how impractical they are for the average religious practitioner. While the *ShM* may not be a fully formed halakhic work, as we noted earlier and as Maimonides had himself admitted, the same cannot be said with respect to the *MT*, which was intended to be not only a comprehensive but also a practical legal code. And yet, even after reading the *MT*, one is left wondering how the faithful reader is to go about fulfilling these highly sophisticated commandments of belief. If one cannot understand the philosophic definitions attached to these dogmas, can one still fulfill these two commandments? Should one conclude that Maimonides was an elitist who only addressed the *cognoscenti*? In his introduction to the *MT*, Maimonides states that his intention is to make the law accessible to all—"the young and the old."[129]

129. M. M. Schneerson notes that Maimonides presents in the *Halakhot* general foundational principles that nevertheless fall short of what the talmudic rabbis called "the heads of the topics" (*BT Hagigah* 13a), since the latter can be communicated only to an individual who is "wise and able to draw conclusions independently" (as per *Hilkhot Yesode ha-Torah* 2:12, 4:10-11). At the beginning of studying Torah, everyone must know these principles. See Schneerson, "Mitsvat Yedi'at ha-Shem," vol. 2, *siman* 22 (5745), 136 and 145.

If this statement of intention is only remotely true, one would have to conclude that the religious person need not be a philosopher to affirm these two theological propositions and consider him or herself to have satisfied these commandments.

Kellner suggests that Maimonides writes for a variety of audiences simultaneously "without drawing explicit attention to that fact." He writes for talmudists with no background in philosophy, for talmudists who aspire to become philosophers, and for philosophers, all at once. When talmudists read Maimonides' works, because of the context, vocabulary and style, they think "they are reading a wholly traditional text, totally unobjectionable, and fully consistent with conventional religion as popularly understood." The more philosophically sophisticated reader, however, can read the same passage and find in it "statements consistent with some of the more daring Maimonidean theses expressed (later) in the *Guide of the Perplexed*."[130] The faithful, uninitiated in philosophical matters, would gain the basic ideas that the belief in God is a foundational belief, that God is characterized as the creator of all things, and that everything derives its existence from God and cannot exist without Him.[131] They would also learn that God's unity is unlike any other kind of unity, and that it necessarily precludes His being corporeal. Finally, they would learn that the belief in God's unity is also foundational, that "God brought us out of Egypt and heaped kindness upon us only on condition that we believe in His unity."[132]

In the previous section, I referred to a passage in *GP* II:33 in which Maimonides reveals the deep secret hidden in the aggadah of R. Simlai and what it tells us about the revelation at Sinai. Embedded in the content of the philosophical revelation, however, is a key pedagogical

130. Kellner, "The Literary Character of the Mishneh Torah," 30-31. This in no way implies that Maimonides intended to deceive his unsophisticated audience. Rather, as a master pedagogue, he allowed the reader to climb the ladder of religious sophistication. Maimonides does demand a minimum understanding of the foundational beliefs. For example, he insists that "children, women, stupid ones, and those of a defective natural disposition" be taught basic principles such as the incorporeity of God, despite their inability to prove these doctrines (*GP* I:35, 81).

131. Kellner, "The Literary Character of the Mishneh Torah," 33.

132. *ShM*, P2.

approach. Maimonides comments that while all Israel heard the "voice of words" (Deut. 4:12) at Sinai—that same voice through which Moses and Israel learned the doctrines of "I" and "Thou shalt not have"—not everyone understood the message equally. "Know," he says, "that with regard to that voice too, their rank was not equal to the rank of Moses our Master." Each member of the Israelite nation heard the principles as befitted his or her level of philosophical sophistication. Everyone, even those totally uninitiated in philosophical matters, heard the two principles, and understood them in their own ways.[133]

The varying levels of understanding of the heterogeneous crowd at Sinai offers a working model for the pedagogic presentation of the two foundational credos. Despite their physical and intellectual constraints, with proper training and effort, the philosophically uneducated can reach higher levels of understanding of the divine, eventually coming to love and fear God. In the *MT*, Maimonides offers a minimum definition of what one must believe and affirm to fulfill these two commandments.[134] As Kellner has shown, however, these definitions can be heard and understood in many different, even non-philosophical ways. Still, as the Sinaitic model teaches, the unenlightened faithful will no doubt have satisfied the religious obligation. Maimonides would nevertheless recommend that the person who wishes to fulfill these commandments in an optimal manner should read and re-read these definitions, while getting a deeper appreciation through a systematic study of the sciences of logic and metaphysics.

---

133. Maimonides states in the *GP* (III:27, 510) that the welfare of the soul "consists in the multitude's acquiring correct opinions *corresponding to their respective capacity*" (emphasis added). These pedagogic tendencies were not always appreciated. Samuel ibn Tibbon, his main translator and student, attacked Maimonides for presuming that the masses could rise to the philosophical heights of attaining a proper understanding of divine matters, suggesting instead that they be taught to believe in the God who took them out of Egypt, the God of History. See Frankel, "Ma'avar le-Talmid Ne'eman," 61-82

134. In this respect, Maimonides, the pedagogue, imitated the Law, which had presented these notions in "a summary way" (*GP* III:28, 512). See the discussion of the commandment to love God in chapter 9. As we shall see there, the commandments to love and fear God are but extensions of the first two commandments, rather than separate commandments.

SOME CLOSING REFLECTIONS ON *SEFER HA-MITSVOT*

Before we move to the second half of this book, which will deal almost exclusively with the *MT*, it might be in order to make a few concluding remarks about the focus of our work to this point, the *Sefer Ha-Mitsvot*. The *ShM* represents Maimonides' first attempt to unravel, identify, and interpret the complete corpus of scriptural law.[135] This hermeneutic interest continued to engage his attention for at least another 25 years, during which time he composed the *MT*, the *GP*, and the Essay on Resurrection, among other minor essays and letters. As befits a great thinker, Maimonides frequently brought new interpretative insights to old material, and so we find, for example, that many of the *ShM*'s initial claims were tweaked, changed, or even omitted in the *MT* and the *GP*. At the same time, he never ceased to make revisions to all his literary creations even after he had completed them, witnessed by the existence of a number of extant versions of some of his works. Nevertheless, it can be said that each of the stages of Maimonides' literary activity, always infused with original and creative ideas, represents a finality of sorts, each reveals a possibility persuasively dressed in conclusive garb, and yet none give the impression of being truly conclusive, if only because one senses that Maimonides continues to find new ways to read texts. That is why the *ShM* can stand on its own, despite later revisions.

The *ShM* has a character all of its own. It is distinctively a rhetorical work, making bold claims and briefly supporting these claims with scriptural and rabbinic texts. It is uniquely a methodological work, synthesizing and fitting a vast body of rabbinic material into a number of taxonomic principles. And it is a uniquely popular work, written in the Judeo-Arabic vernacular, favoring broad and general definitions and stating them in a simple and uncomplicated form.[136]

---

135. I use the phrase "Scriptural Law" here to contrast with the Oral Law, to which Maimonides dedicated the commentary to the Mishnah.

136. We already saw that while the *MT* may also be directed to a popular audience, it contains language and hints that operate on a highly sophisticated level, often intended to accommodate more than one meaning. See Kellner, "The Literary Character," 29-45. For more on this manner of writing, see Henshke, "On the Question of Unity in

By Maimonides' own admission, the *ShM* is often imprecise, as if in a hurry to be completed, but for that reason it tends towards valuable first impressions, raw ideas that lack the full complexity and casuistry of talmudic discussions or the rigours and detainment required for harmonizing disparate passages, but which reveal the author's immediate and favorite concerns. In common with some of his other works, and despite its avowed brevity, the *ShM* is didactic, presenting a fair number of important and original theological, juridical, historiographical, and politico-philosophical ideas. Because the *ShM* is a popular work, it addresses a wide audience. It sets out to instruct Rabbanites, to edify readers of Scripture unfamiliar with rabbinic midrash,[137] to polemicize against Karaite sympathizers and committed Karaites,[138] and to impress enlightened Muslims and Muslim colleagues.[139]

The *ShM* is not only an important work of *halakhah*, but it is also an important work in the history of Jewish thought. In composing the *MT*, Maimonides both builds on the *TaRYaG* framework he had developed and revisits many of the views he held in the *ShM*. In the chapters that follow, I shall explore how he reinterprets, redefines and reorders much of the earlier material, offering a much more nuanced view of the Law. I will also analyze a dichotomy that has lain dormant for centuries in the subtle crevices of Maimonides' exquisite language: Maimonides the jurist versus Maimonides the legal philosopher.

Maimonides' Thought," 37-52. For a philosophical appreciation of the *MT*, see Twersky, *Introduction to the Code of Maimonides,* 356-507; Pines, "The Philosophical Purport," 1-14; and Harvey, "The *Mishneh Torah* as a Key to the Secrets of the Guide," 11-28.

137. Replying to a correspondent who questioned Maimonides' interpretation of Scripture in the matter of one of his commandment claims (P8), Abraham Maimonides writes: "in this regard, we, the congregation of Rabbanites differ from the way of the Karaites." While the inquirer may or may not have been a Karaite, he was certainly a close reader of Scripture who appreciated the Rules of the *ShM* but may have been unfamiliar with rabbinic midrash. See Abraham Maimonides, "Teshuvot Rabbenu Abraham ben ha-RaMBaM," *siman* 63.

138. For example, see Maimonides' lengthy disquisition at P153, discussed below in chapter 7. Also see Maimonides' comments at P109 and his reference to the "true book."

139. Friedberg, "Cross-Cultural Influences and the Possible Role of Competition in the Selection of Some Commandments," 410-414.

APPENDIX:

The TaRYaG Count as an Outline of Legal Themes in Scripture: Evidence from N194

In chapters 3 and 5 of this work, I give examples of my thesis that Maimonides' enumeration of commandments in the *ShM* might be more accurately viewed as a classified outline of the legal themes to be covered in the upcoming *MT* than as a precise enumeration of scriptural commandments. In this appendix, I wander outside of my self-imposed universe of positive commandments and examine the claim that prohibits the drinking of libation wine (N194). I shall argue that this commandment supports my thesis that the enumeration of the commandments is first and foremost an outline of scriptural themes. I find implicit support for this view from no less than one of the most prominent medieval authorities on matters of enumeration, Simeon b. Tsemah Duran, author of the *Zohar ha-Raqia*.

The *SE* version of N194 reads as follows: "Not to drink libation wine [*yein nesekh*] [of idolaters], as it is said, 'Which did eat the fat of their sacrifices, and drank the wine of their drink-offering' [Deut. 32:38]." In the *ShM*, Maimonides, following *BT 'Avodah Zarah* 29b, glosses: "this shows that the prohibition which applies to sacrifices offered to an idol applies likewise to libation-wine." Maimonides' unusually long evidentiary discussion following this gloss evinces a certain degree of discomfort with the proposed argument.

Nahmanides' critique of the argument deals primarily with Maimonides' interpretation of the sources he cites. For the most part, the critique is not immediately relevant to our concerns. What draws our attention, however, is Nahmanides' remark that this prohibition is already included in N25. That prohibition, as formulated in the *SE*, reads as follows: "Not to make use of an idol, or its accessory objects, or its offerings, or its libations, as it is said, 'Neither shalt thou bring an abomination into thy house' [Deut. 7:26]." Nahmanides notes:

> It is surprising that he, may his memory be blessed, takes the trouble to demonstrate in this gloss that the prohibition to drink libation wine

> is scriptural, even though, according to him, libation wine is already included in the rubric of offerings to an idol, from which even benefit is prohibited by scriptural dint.[140]

In other words, N194 is redundant.

Nahmanides also rejects the possibility that the claim might be justified on the basis of its punishment, namely, that drinking libation wine is punishable with a third set of lashes in addition to the two sets of lashes for deriving benefit from idolatrous offerings. He argues that even if we were to grant that drinking libation wine is prohibited separately from deriving benefit from it, and thus punishable with additional lashes, Maimonides does not provide an adequate scriptural proof text for this new prohibition. This is because Maimonides disqualified laws derived from Scripture through the use of hermeneutic rules.[141] It is true that the Talmud makes an analogy (*heqesh*) between libation wine and sacrifices offered to an idol on the basis of Deuteronomy 32:38, but such analogies are not valid evidence on which to base a scriptural commandment claim, despite Maimonides' quoting it.[142]

---

140. *Hasagot*, 352. Note that, at N25, the *ShM* mentions the prohibition against deriving benefit from "anything attributed to idolatry," but does not mention the prohibition on libation wine. Nahmanides identified "anything attributed to idolatry" with offerings to idols and then assumed that libation wine was included in the general prohibition of offerings. Nevertheless, Nahmanides is aware of and actually cites the *SE*, which mentions libation wine explicitly.

141. See the discussion of Rule 2 in chapter 7.

142. While Isaac de Leon (in *Megillat Esther*, ad loc.) argues, contra Nahmanides, that he who drinks libation wine incurs an additional set of lashes because the new prohibition is unrelated to the prohibition against deriving benefit from idolatrous practices, his thesis runs afoul of a serious problem. Maimonides never produces a proof text for this commandment in the form of an admonition (as Nahmanides argues). Even if we follow Rule 14 and grant that one can use a hermeneutically-derived prohibitive admonition to justify a commandment when there is evidence that Scripture intends to punish the transgressor (see applications in N9, N26, N60, N195, N318, N319)—as suggested by de Leon—this does not appear to be the case here. No punishment is prescribed in Deuteronomy 32:38 for one who drinks libation wine. The passage merely describes the activity attributed to these foreign gods: "they did eat the fat of their sacrifices and drank the wine of their drink-offerings." The absence of an explicit punishment for those who drink libation wine as well as the absence of a properly formulated admonition leaves us with only one possibility: the passage cited by Maimonides compares libation wine to idolatrous sacrifices merely to teach that just as it is prohibited to derive benefit from the latter (under N25), so too it is prohibited

To complement the above argument, Nahmanides takes aim at Maimonides from yet another direction. He points out that one would not escape the charges of redundancy by positing that N194 comes to teach that an additional set of lashes is due to one who drinks libation wine, even if one could find another admonishing text. This is because Maimonides had made it clear in a number of cases that no more than one set of lashes may be administered, even where Scripture enjoins one repeatedly from committing the same act.[143] Since drinking libation wine is included in the prohibition against deriving benefit from the wine, only one set of lashes can be prescribed, even if we were to find a new prohibitive admonition. The redundancy of N194 is once again exposed.

The simplest answer to this crux is that the prohibition against deriving benefit from libation wine, as a sacrifice offered to an idol, should be first mentioned in, and traced to, the laws of idolatry. A full discussion of it *as a forbidden food*, however, should be reserved for the treatise on forbidden foods.[144] If a topical outline is to be useful in helping organize a code of law, it would have to deal with the prohibition against drinking libation wine *separate and apart* from the

---

to derive benefit from libation wine. But this conclusion itself is problematic: why would we need a special analogy to prohibit the use of libation wine if it is no different from sacrifices offered to an idol? And if the latter is prohibited under N25, why would libation wine not be included in the same admonition? Moreover, Maimonides also includes libation wine in that prohibition, as we saw.

Drawing on the language of the *Halakhot*, Isaac Gatinio (*Bet Ishaq* [Salonika, 1792], 36), offers a more plausible suggestion: it is prohibited to derive any benefit from all types of sacrifices offered to idols, including libation wine, under penalty of lashes (*Hilkhot 'Avodah Zarah* 7:2). If and when these sacrifices are edible, however, benefit is only derived when one eats (or drinks) them (*Maakhalot Asurot* 11:1, based on *Maakhalot Asurot* 8:16). Any other form of benefit is not liable for lashes. While this explanation has the benefit of a reasonable fit with the language of the *Halakhot*, it still leaves unanswered the ultimate question: why was it necessary for Maimonides to enumerate the special prohibition of N194? Why was it not a detail of N25?

143. "Furthermore, according to the Master, multiplicity of prohibitions does not translate into multiple lashes." *Hasagot*, 352. For this principle, see Rule 9, and his discussion on pages 157-159. For one of the applications of this principle, see N179 (last paragraph on page 346) where Maimonides counts the prohibition against eating swarming creatures as a single negative commandment, despite there being many ("even [if He warned as many as] one thousand times") injunctions against eating these creatures.

144. The importance of libation wine and its derivatives as a forbidden food cannot be gainsaid; its laws cover three full chapters in the *MT*.

laws that discuss the basis for its prohibition. Through this lens, N194 is not a redundant claim.

Simeon b. Tsemah Duran appears to concur with this conclusion. After pointing out that Maimonides does not offer a scripturally-based admonition for this commandment, but merely gives a cryptic analogy to sacrifices, he suggests that:

> It was not the intention of Maimonides to count this prohibition as an independent prohibition among the 613 commandments; for when he counted the commandments [in his *Short Enumeration*], he included [this prohibition] among the rest of the prohibitions related to idolatry, under "and there shall cleave naught (of the accurse thing) to thine hand" [N24] and "neither shalt thou bring an abomination into thy house" [N25]. Rather, he wanted to include this prohibition among the special laws of forbidden foods, and [or but] this prohibition is the same prohibition that includes all the rest of the prohibitions related to idolatry. Note that he did not offer a new proof-text.[145]

In the arch-conservative world of rabbinic *halakhah*, the implications of what Duran suggests are nothing less than revolutionary: not all of the 613 enumerated commandment advanced by Maimonides are intended as independent commandments. Some may simply represent organizational notations to help outline his later work.

---

145. That is, Duran continues to maintain that the Deuteronomy 32:38 passage does not qualify as a genuine prohibition, given its form. The quote is from *Zohar ha-Raqia*, *siman* 29, negative commandment 74, 121.

CHAPTER VI

REVISITING THE TERM *MITSVAT 'ASEH*

In moving from the *Sefer HaMitsvot* and the accompanying "Short Enumeration of the Commandments" (*SE*) to the *Halakhot*[1] of the *Mishneh Torah,* we note the deliberate boldness with which Maimonides designates a *mitsvat 'aseh*. The declaration usually appears at the start of his discussion of the commandment, using the formula "it is a positive commandment to [do] X," or sometimes, "it is a positive commandment of [or from] the Torah to [do] X." It is thus surprising that so many Maimonidean scholars neglect to note the absence of such a formula on a significant number of occasions. In this chapter, I explore the nature of this formula in greater detail, explaining its relevance and compiling a list of commandments in which this formula is absent. I offer an explanation of why most commentators do not comment on this phenomenon, present the explanations advanced by those who do notice it, and thus begin to present a systematic approach to this puzzle.

THE ENUMERATION ACCORDING TO THE *HALAKHOT*

In the *Halakhot,* Maimonides' topical discussions typically begin with a simple and clear statement that the obligation being discussed is a positive (or a negative) commandment. These statements almost invariably take the form of "it is a positive commandment to [do] X." Here are a few examples, taken from the first two books of the *MT*, *Sefer ha-Madda'*

1. A reminder to the reader: I use the term "*Halakhot*" instead of the more common and general appellation "*Mishneh Torah*" because I deliberately refer only to the specific sections of *Halakhot*, not to the entire *Mishneh Torah*. The latter includes the "Headings to the Treatises," which I consider a separate composition.

(Book of Knowledge) and *Sefer Ahavah* (Book of Love): "It is a positive commandment [*mitsvat 'aseh*] to adhere to the Sages" (*Hilkhot De'ot* 6:2); "It is a positive commandment to destroy idolatry and its appurtenances" (*Hilkhot 'Avodah Zarah* 7:1); "It is a positive commandment to pray daily" (*Hilkhot Tefillah* 1:1); "It is a positive commandment on every Israelite male to write a scroll of Law for himself" (*Hilkhot Tefillin u-Mezuzah ve-Sefer Torah* 7:1); and "It is a positive commandment from the Torah[2] to recite grace after the meal" (*Hilkhot Berakhot* 1:1).

We also find slight variations on this formula, such as: "Circumcision is a positive commandment for which one incurs excision, as it says..." (*Hilkhot Milah* 1:1); "Abstention from work on the seventh [day] is a positive commandment, for Scripture says..." (*Hilkhot Shabbat* 1:1); and "The Nazirite is bound by a positive commandment to let the head of his hair grow long, for Scripture says..." (*Hilkhot Nazir* 1:1).

Where the commandment requires an added explanation or where it is too complex or subtle to be explained with a simple definition, Maimonides digresses briefly and then returns to designate the commandment as a *mitsvat 'aseh*. For example, in *Hilkhot Teshuvah* 1:1, Maimonides states that confession is a positive commandment only after stating that confession is conditional on the decision to repent. In other words, confession can be designated as a positive commandment only if and when one is ready to repent. (It falls in the category of contingent commandments discussed in chapter 3.) A somewhat lengthier digression takes place at the beginning of *Hilkhot Yesode ha-Torah*:

> (1.1) The basic principle of all basic principles ... is to realize that there is a First Being.... All existing beings ... exist only through His true existence....(1:2) If it could be supposed that He did not exist....(1:3) If, however, it were supposed that all other things were non-existent.... Hence, His real essence....(1:4) This is what the prophet means....(1:5) This being is the God of the Universe ... a power that is without end or limit. (1:6) To acknowledge this truth is a positive commandment.[3]

---

2. The additional phrase "from the Torah" appears on a number of other occasions. I believe that the more common expression is a short form of this longer formula. It is also possible that the extra emphasis may have been polemically motivated, as I will suggest on a number of instances. For an example, see chapter 7, note 56.
3. These complex formulations can lead to numerous other problems. For example, in this

As discussed in the previous chapter, this digression is absolutely necessary for a proper understanding of the commandment. A similar approach is used with respect to the commandment to know God's unity, where Maimonides offers a robust and lengthy definition of the meaning of unity and then ends the presentation by adding: "to realize this truth is a positive commandment" (1:7).

All of these declarative designations begin by identifying the commandment, presenting the relevant scriptural proof text, and reiterating at the end that it is a commandment. I argue that all deviations from this pattern are significant and may signal a change in Maimonides' paradigm of categorizing positive commandments. In my analysis, I call these deviations from the formula "failures to designate," to emphasize that the omissions did not occur by chance but were rather the product of design. Specifically, by a "failure to designate," I mean a failure to designate a commandment (one previously identified as such in the *ShM*) at the topic's first introduction in the *Halakhot*. While some deviations from this formula later refer to the commandment as a *mitsvat 'aseh*, these offhand designations cannot substitute for the omitted formula in the commandment's introduction.

Using this metric, I found in the *Halakhot* 109 instances of failures to designate commandments that were previously claimed in the *ShM*—a surprisingly large number. Many of the omissions can be explained by reassessing Maimonides' criteria for what constitutes a *mitsvah* or by reassessing the specific individuations. While those two types of explanations do not carry exegetical or theological implications, the remainder of these 109 failures to designate does carry, as I see it, significant jurisprudential significance.

Table 1, below, identifies the 109 failures to designate commandments.

---

particular case, the clause "to acknowledge this truth" does not have a clear antecedent. Faur understands that *halakhot* 1-4 are not part of the commandment; they simply represent theological doctrines. The commandment is only defined in *halakhah* 5, the acceptance of His Lordship as a power that ceaselessly causes the sphere to revolve. Incidentally, this ambiguity also connects to the concerns regarding the exact definition of the belief, as discussed in chapter 5. Faur, "Maimonides' Starting Precept," 15-16. For a contrary view, see Kasher, "Does 'Ought' Imply 'Can' in Maimonides?" 18.

Table 1

P3. To love Him.
P4. To fear Him.
P8. To imitate His good and upright ways.
P9. To hallow His name.
P10. To read the Shema twice daily.
P11. To learn Torah and to teach it.
P12. To bind the phylactery on the head.
P13. To bind the phylactery on the arm.
P14. To make fringes.
P15. To affix a mezuzah.
P18. That the King shall write a scroll of the Torah for himself, besides the one which every individual should write, so that he shall possess two scrolls of the Torah.
P26. That the priests shall bless Israel.
P34. That, when the ark is carried, it should be carried on the shoulder.
P41. To offer an additional sacrifice every Sabbath.
P42. To offer an additional sacrifice every new moon.
P43. To offer an additional sacrifice on Passover.
P44. To offer the meal offering of the Omer[4] on the morrow after the first day of Passover, together with one lamb.
P45. To offer an additional sacrifice on Shavu'ot.
P46. To bring on Shavu'ot loaves of bread together with the sacrifices which are then offered up in connection with the loaves.
P47. To offer an additional sacrifice on Rosh ha-Shanah.
P48. To offer an additional sacrifice on the Day of the Fast [Yom Kippur].
P49. To observe, on the Day of the Fast, the service appointed for that day.
P50. To offer an additional sacrifice on Sukkot.
P51. To offer an additional sacrifice on Shemini 'Atseret, which is a feast by itself.
P68. That the court of judgment shall bring an offering if it has erred in a judicial pronouncement.
P70. That an individual shall bring an offering if he is in doubt as to whether he has committed a sin for which one has to bring a sin offering.
P71. That an offering shall be brought by one who has in error committed a trespass against sacred things, or robbed, or lain carnally with a bondsmaid betrothed to a man, or denied what was deposited with him and swore falsely to support his denial.This is called a trespass offering for a known trespass.

4. First fruits of barley harvest.

P72. To offer a sacrifice of varying value in accordance with one's means.
P74. That a man having an issue shall bring a sacrifice, after he is cleansed of his issue.
P75. That a woman having an issue shall bring a sacrifice, after she is cleansed of her issue.
P76. That a woman after childbirth shall bring an offering when she is clean.
P77. That the leper shall bring a sacrifice, after he is cleansed.
P87. That an exchanged beast [a beast that is exchanged for one that had been set apart as an offering] is sacred.
P95. To decide in cases of annulment of vows, according to the rules set forth in the Torah.
P96. That anyone who touches the carcass of a beast that died of itself shall be unclean.
P97. That eight species of creeping things defile by contact.
P98. That foods become defiled (by contact with unclean things).
P99. That a menstruating woman is unclean and defiles others.
P100. That a new mother in confinement is unclean like a menstruating woman.
P101. That a leper is unclean and defiles.
P102. That a leprous garment is unclean and defiles.
P103. That a leprous house defiles.
P104. That a man, having a running issue, defiles.
P105. That the seed of copulation defiles.
P106. That a woman, having a running issue, defiles.
P107. That a corpse defiles.
P108. That the waters of sprinkling defile one who is clean, and cleanse [the unclean] from pollution by a dead body.
P109. That purification from all kinds of defilement shall be effected by immersion in the waters of a *miqveh.*
P113. To carry out the ordinance of the red heifer so that its ashes shall be always available.
P114. That one who vows to the Lord the monetary value of a person shall pay the amount appointed in the scriptural passage.
P115. That one who vows to the Lord the monetary value of an unclean beast shall pay its value.
P116. That one who vows the value of his house shall pay according to the appraisal of the priest.
P117. That one who sanctifies to the Lord a portion of his field shall pay according to the estimation appointed in the scriptural passage.
P119. That the fruit of fruit-bearing trees in the fourth year of their planting shall be sacred.

P127. To set apart the tithe of the corn for the Levites.
P128. To set apart the second tithe to be eaten by its owner in Jerusalem.
P129. That the Levites shall set apart a tithe of the tithes, which they had received from the Israelites, and give it to the priests.
P130. To set apart in the third and sixth year the tithe for the poor, instead of the second tithe.
P139. That houses sold within a walled city may be redeemed within a year.
P145. To decide, in regard to dedicated property, which is sacred to the Lord, and which belongs to the priest.
P148. To set the mother bird free when taking the nest.
P149. To examine the marks in cattle.
P150. To examine the marks in fowl, so as to distinguish between the unclean and the clean.
P151. To examine the marks in locusts, so as to distinguish the clean from the unclean.
P152. To examine the marks in fish.
P159. To rest on the first day of Passover.
P160. To rest on the seventh day of that feast [Passover].
P162. To rest on the fiftieth day (from the time of cutting the Omer).
P163. To rest on the first day of the seventh month.
P166. To rest on the first day of Sukkot.
P167. To rest on the eighth day of that feast [Sukkot].
P168. To dwell in booths seven days.
P169. To take on that feast a palm branch and the other three plants.
P172. To heed the call of every prophet in each generation, provided that he neither adds to, nor takes away from, the Torah.
P173. To appoint a king.
P178. That one who possesses evidence shall testify in court.
P181. To decapitate the heifer in the manner prescribed.
P183. To give the Levites cities to dwell in that also serve as cities of refuge.
P190. In an optional war, to observe the procedure prescribed in the Torah.
P191. To anoint a special priest [to address the soldiers] in a war.
P199. To return a pledge to its owner.
P201. That the hired laborer shall be permitted to eat [of the produce which he is reaping].
P205. To rebuke the sinner.
P209. To honor the wise.
P214. That the newly-married husband shall give happiness to his wife.
P221. To deal with a beautiful woman taken captive in war in the manner prescribed in the Torah.
P222. To divorce by a formal written document.

P223. That the woman suspected of adultery be dealt with as prescribed in the Torah.
P226. That the court shall execute [sentences of death] by decapitation with the sword.
P227. That the court shall execute [sentences of death] by strangulation.
P228. That the court shall execute [sentences of death] by burning with fire.
P229. That the court shall execute [sentences of death] by stoning.
P232. To deal judicially with the Hebrew bondsman, in accordance with the laws pertaining to him.
P233. To espouse a Hebrew maidservant.
P234. To redeem her [the Hebrew maidservant].
P235. To keep the Canaanite slave forever.
P236. That he who inflicts a bodily injury shall pay monetary compensation.
P237. To judge cases of injuries caused by beasts.
P238. To judge cases of damage caused by an uncovered pit.
P239. To adjudge a thief to pay compensation, or [in certain cases] suffer death.
P240. To adjudicate cases of damage caused by trespass of cattle.
P241. To adjudicate cases of damage caused by fire.
P242. To adjudicate cases of damage by a gratuitous depositary.
P243. To judge cases of damage of a paid depositary and a hirer.
P244. To adjudicate cases of damage of a gratuitous borrower.
P245. To adjudicate cases of purchase and sale.
P246. To adjudicate other cases between a plaintiff and a defendant.
P247. To save the pursued even at the cost of the life of the pursuer.
P248. To adjudicate cases of inheritances.

There are various ways to account for this surprisingly large number of failures to designate laws as positive commandments which had been designated thus in the *ShM*. One could posit that Maimonides was careless in drafting the *Halakhot*, and that he erred in failing to indicate that certain commandments were *mitsvot 'aseh*. Less dramatically, perhaps he decided that it was not necessary to state in every case that the command was a positive commandment. If we assume that Maimonides did change his mind about whether these laws should be considered *mitsvot 'aseh*, we could posit that he used the Rules from the *ShM* to revisit his analyses, concluding that only 139 of the commandments were defensible. Finally, we might posit that Maimonides changed the criteria for defining a *mitsvat 'aseh*, modifying or rejecting the Rules of the *ShM*.

Can Maimonides be accused of slipshod writing? Medieval and modern rabbis praise the language of his rulings for its precision and nuance, as capable of shouldering inferences as is talmudic language.[5] Rabbinic literature teems with observations, indications, and rulings that are derived from the nuances of Maimonides' formulations—from his commissions as well as from his omissions. As Twersky posits in a lengthy discussion, modern Jewish law has been built on the back of the *MT*.[6] On the basis of the subjective appreciation of hundreds of scholars, one might be tempted to conclude that the failure to designate commandments with a standard form cannot be seen as mere oversight.

But there are two additional factors that make this conclusion a near certainty, factors intimately related to the very essence of Maimonides' project. First, he displays an extraordinary interest—one might call it an

5. See Malachi ben Yaaqov ha-Kohen, *Yad Malachi,* "Kelale ha-Rambam," 182, para. 3, citing *Mishpete Shmuel*, no. 120, and *Migdal Oz* "in many places." Levinger (in *Darkhe ha-Mahshavah*, ch 1, 13-33) attempts to demonstrate that this reputation for extreme precision is somewhat overstated. He attributes this imprecision to the popular nature of the work—the *MT*, as Maimonides writes in the introduction, is addressed to "young and old." Words and phrases are sometimes used that lack precise values, and one can conclude that they are to be read synonymously. Examples include the side-by-side use of the words *matar* and *geshamim* throughout *Hilkhot Ta'anit*, *yom ha-kippurim* and *yom ha-tsom* in *Hilkhot Kele ha-Miqdash* 8:3-5, and *qibbets* and *tsiref* in *Hilkhot Maakhalot Asurot* 4:17. Levinger also discusses other types of imprecision, such as internal contradictions. I would add other oddities to his list. For example, new terms appear suddenly in discussions without prior definition (such as *iggeret* in *Hilkhot Sotah* 4:8); often, cases that are cited almost verbatim from talmudic passages fail to provide necessary context, making it difficult if not impossible to understand the ruling; inconsistent classification for identical indications (such as in *Hilkhot Ishut* 15:17, "*ẖovah*" vs. *Hilkhot Sotah* 4:18, "*mitsvat ẖakhamim*"); and others. For an extremely interesting and well-documented monograph arguing that Maimonides was indeed "all too human"—he made errors, forgot things, contradicted himself, and used imprecise language—see Shapiro, *Principles of Interpretation in Maimonidean Halakhah*. I do not dispute these criticisms. Rather, I argue that the very nature of this massive project, to organize, categorize, and clearly present the totality of the Jewish Law, required standard and unambiguous statements formulating the scope and nature of each commandment. To say that Maimonides forgot to provide such statements on many occasions impugns the character of the work. To put Maimonides' errors in his own philosophic language, one could say that the many mistakes that he made were all of an "accidental" nature. Failures to designate, on the other hand, would represent errors of an "essential" nature.

6. See Twersky, *Introduction to the Code of Maimonides*, 517.

obsession—in clearly demarcating between commandments of scriptural origin and those of rabbinic origin. This is as true in his commentary to the Mishnah as it is in the *MT* and the *ShM*.[7] In all these writings, Maimonides continuously reminds the reader of the sources of the law: which commandments are scriptural and which are not. Scriptural laws must be identified because they are more strictly enforced than rabbinic ones and can never be repealed, unlike rabbinic laws.[8] Scriptural laws occupy a privileged position not only in Maimonides' jurisprudence but also in his theology. He dedicates an important part of the *GP* to justifying the great majority of the Mosaic laws, since in his opinion, unlike man-made laws (*nomos*), these laws are deemed to be perfect.[9] The statement "it is a positive commandment to do X"—usually accompanied and supported by a scriptural proof text—is as simple as it is unequivocal, and functions well as an effective demarcation of such laws. Maimonides has good reason to consistently use this formula to designate commandments.

Second, the formula "it is a positive commandment to do X" is not only a rhetorically powerful and dramatic statement; it also bespeaks authority. Maimonides identifies more than 140 positive commandments throughout the entire *MT* with this formula, or with a slight variant. It is unlikely that an author so attuned to rhetorical effect and so intent on establishing authority would have forgotten to use this formula on as many as 109 occasions.[10]

---

7. Other scholars also note this interest. For example, Feldblum states that "Maimonides is unique among the codifiers of Jewish law in his careful and systematic assignment of laws to ... specific categories.... Such categories are significant both halakhically and historically." Feldblum, "Criteria for Designating Laws: Derivations from Biblical Exegesis, and Legislative Enactments," 45.
8. On the immutability of scriptural law, see *Hilkhot Yesode ha-Torah* 9:1 and *Hilkhot Mamrim* 2:9. On the difference in the strictness of their enforcement, see *Hilkhot Mamrim* 1:5.
9. *GP* II:39, 40.
10. On the author's high self-evaluation of his work and on his expectations that "in coming days...all of Israel will fill all its needs with this [the *MT*]," see Maimonides' letter to his disciple Yosef b. Yehudah, in *Iggerot ha-RaMBaM,* ed. Shailat, vol. 1, 300-301. Maimonides' high expectations were realized quickly because of the quality and authoritativeness of the work. On the rapid dissemination of the *MT*, even during Maimonides' lifetime, see Twersky, *Introduction to the Code of Maimonides*, 518. On the nature of his expectations for the *MT*, see Halbertal, "What is *Mishneh Torah*?" 81-111.

On a handful of occasions, Maimonides does apply the label *mitsvat ʿaseh* to a particular command, but he does so outside of the main discussion of the commandment (its *locus classicus*), which I do not see as equivalent to designating the commandment as a *mitsvat ʿaseh* in its section. It is highly unlikely that the failure to designate these commandments in their proper places is a *lapsus calami*, given Maimonides' organizational skills and the routine nature of the formulation. Indeed, naming these commands *mitsvot ʿaseh* outside of their *loci classici* also requires analysis and explanation.

A clarifying example: Maimonides does not designate the wearing of phylacteries (tefillin), the dwelling in booths (sukkah) and the taking of a branch (*lulav*) as *mitsvot ʿaseh* when he introduces these commandments in their sections of the *Halakhot*. However, when he discusses these commandments in *Hilkhot Berakhot* 11:2, he does refer to them as *mitsvot ʿaseh*. Can these out-of-place designations compensate for the lack of designation in the main treatments of these commandments, perhaps making up for the earlier omission? And despite Maimonides' failure to designate in the introduction to these commandments, does the later usage of the term *mitsvat ʿaseh* indicate that they are nevertheless obligatory and enjoy scriptural force?

I answer both of these questions with a categorical no. First, the primary sections for two of the named commandments (the dwelling in booths and the taking of a branch) are placed after *Hilkhot Berakhot*. There was no need for Maimonides to compensate in *Berakhot* for an earlier slip; he could have named these commandments *mitsvot ʿaseh* in their proper place.

Second, I argue that the imprecision actually occurred in *Hilkhot Berakhot*, where the scriptural nature of the commands was not the main concern, rather than in the sections that discuss those commandments in detail. The key focus of *Hilkhot Berakhot* 11:2, which discusses blessing formulas, is not whether a particular commandment is of scriptural or rabbinic authority, but rather whether or not the injunction is a *ẖovah,* a commandment that "one must strain to do and run after them to fulfill them." Depending on its degree of obligation, Maimonides assigns a specific blessing formula to each commandment. In this *halakhah*, Maimonides contrasts obligatory commandments, like tefillin, sukkah and *lulav*, with non-obligatory commandments, like building a parapet on the roof and affixing a mezuzah to the door of a house. The first group is called *mitsvot 'aseh*, and the second group is simply called *mitsvot*, which Maimonides describes as "akin to the permissible [optional]" (*domeh le-reshut*). The term *mitsvat 'aseh* is here used as equivalent to the term *h̲ovah*, obligatory, in much the same sense as the latter term is generally used—it does not indicate that these commandments are commanded explicitly in the Torah.[11] Thus the question still remains: why does Maimonides fail to designate tefillin, sukkah, and *lulav* as *mitsvot 'aseh* in their main sections?

I posit that Maimonides' failure to designate these 109 commandment claims previously identified in the *ShM* is deliberate, and that analyzing the omissions can provide useful information. In attempting to resolve the problem, I will avoid providing 109 ad hoc, fit-to-order solutions, which lack an underlying coherence. My approach will be guided by Ockham's Razor, the rule that the most likely philosophical theory is the one that accounts for the most variables.[12] All else being equal, I will accept the principle that is likely to explain the greatest number of failures to designate, even at the risk of overturning long-running conventions. I ask the reader to judge my effort on its logic and not on its radical implications. At the very least, my explanations can be read as a first attempt at a better understanding of Maimonides' complex exegetical, legal, and theological creation.

---

11. Note that Maimonides here calls the parapet commandment a *mitsvah* rather than a *mitsvat 'aseh*, even though he designates it as a *mitsvat 'aseh* in its *locus classicus*, *Hilkhot Rotseah̲* 11:1. Clearly, in *Hilkhot Berakhot*, he is not being precise with his terms: the difference between *mitsvat 'aseh* and *mitsvah* here is the level of obligation. One can counter that Maimonides used these two terms interchangeably. I discuss this issue in later chapters, where I will posit that these terms stand for different categories of commandments.

12. The exact formulation, attributed to William of Occam (c. 1285-1349), reads: *Entia non sunt multiplicanda praeter necessitatem*, meaning "entities are not to be multiplied beyond what is necessary." Martin Mosse notes that Aristotle already had written that "other things being equal, that proof is the better which proceeds from the fewer postulates," and Euclid evidently subscribed to the same principle. Mosse, *The Three Gospels*, xxi.

THE ROLE OF THE HEADINGS TO THE *MISHNEH TORAH*

As noted at the beginning of this chapter, one might have expected Maimonides' failure to designate positive commandments to have attracted considerable attention from scores of commentators over the past eight hundred years. That this is not the case is nothing less than astonishing. What may have misled commentators is the fact that Maimonides headed each treatise of the *MT* with a list of the positive and negative commandments that he was about to explicate, a list that parallels the *SE* (in theme, though not in formulation). This seemed to confirm not only the enumerative scheme but also the definitional work done previously in the *ShM* and *SE,* even when he failed to designate the commandments as such in the *Halakhot*. This argument falters, however, when we note that, in over 140 cases, Maimonides *did* explicitly designate positive commandments in the text of the *Halakhot*, despite the fact that their Headings described them as such. Either the Headings serve as sufficient evidence that the commandments are *mitsvot 'aseh*, in which case he need not have designated them explicitly in the text, or the Headings should not be considered sufficient evidence, in which case he should have designated every commandment explicitly in the body of the *Halakhot*.

The notion that there is a seamless continuity between the *SE/ShM*, the Headings, and the *Halakhot* is demonstrably false. The *Halakhot* do not always reflect the thinking of the Headings, and the Headings do not always reflect the thinking of the *SE/ShM*, as evidenced by their differences in formulation.[13] But the discontinuity and incongruence

13. We find several examples of such incongruence in the *MT*. The Heading to *Hilkhot Talmud Torah* lists two positive commandments. The first, "to study the Torah," is formulated significantly differently from how it is formulated in both the *SE* and the *ShM* ("to study the Torah and to teach it"). More importantly, the opening lines of the *Halakhot* omit any reference to studying Torah and simply discuss teaching Torah (without stating that it is a positive commandment—see chapter 8). A more subtle difference exists in the second entry of the Heading: "to honor its [Torah's] teachers and those versed in it." This law is formulated in the *Halakhot* as "it is a duty to glorify (*le-hadro*) every scholar (*talmid ḫakhamim*)" (*Hilkhot Talmud Torah* 6:1). If "scholar" is a term equivalent to "teachers and those versed in the Torah," then the Heading is unnecessarily wordy. If it is not equivalent, then a substantive difference exists between the formulations.

is more significant than mere differences in formulations for the same commandments. On occasion, a commandment posited in the earlier works and clearly signaled in the Headings cannot even be found in the *Halakhot*. At the end of this chapter, we examine extreme examples of such incongruence: two commandments mentioned in the Headings but omitted in the *Halakhot*. These examples should persuade the still-skeptical reader that the Headings do not necessarily represent the thinking of the *Halakhot*.

A more likely answer to why commentators did not notice Maimonides' failure to designate positive commandments is that they were subject to a form of cognitive dissonance. Maimonides' *TarYaG* count was and still is viewed as the definitive count of Torah-legislated commandments. In a sense, he was too successful in persuading generations of scholars that this count produced the unique and incontrovertible list of commandments. It was inconceivable to the vast majority of Maimonides' students that the master would have changed his mind on such a canonical belief. If, however, we view the enumeration project in the light in which it ought to be seen, we can begin to understand the divergences between the Headings and the *Halakhot*. As I argue in the first half of this book, Maimonides' enumeration was intended to function primarily as an outline for the *Mishneh Torah*. There is then no reason why the commandments defined in the *Halakhot* should match the outline of the work, the simple list of topics and themes that may or may not represent specific commandments. Therefore, the Headings should not be seen as proxy for what does and does not constitute a positive commandment.

Moreover, one wonders why the Heading (composed in Hebrew, I might add) uses the word "respect" (*kabed*) instead of the scripturally-indicated "glorify" (*hadar*) used by the *Halakhot*. Similarly, the Heading to *Hilkhot 'Avodah Zarah* lists "not to make use of an idol or of an article subsidiary to it" but omits the two categories that follow in the text of the *Halakhot*: "sacrifices offered to it, and anything made for its sake" (*Hilkhot 'Avodah Zarah* 7:2). We also find that the Heading to *Hilkhot Teshuvah* lists one positive commandment: "that the sinner shall repent of his sin before the Lord and make confession." The text of the *Halakhot* is substantively different: "if a person transgressed ...either willfully or in error, and repents and turns away from his sin, he is under a duty to confess before God" (*Hilkhot Teshuvah* 1:1), implying that repentance may be optional. There are many examples of such divergences throughout the *MT*.

HAI-RAQAH AND KAFIH'S THESIS

At least two commentators did notice this problem of the failure to designate positive commandments in the *Halakhot*.[14] The first to notice it was Masud b. Aaron Hai-Raqah (1690-1768), the author of the commentary *Ma'aseh Roqeah̲*. Unfortunately, Hai-Raqah did not pursue this anomaly systematically and, as a result, came to the wrong conclusions. In his opening comment to *Hilkhot Tefillah*, Hai-Raqah notes:

> One needs to investigate the holy ways of our master, his memory be blessed, in this composition, the reason why, with regard to some commandments, he wrote "it is a *mitsvat 'aseh* to do so-and-so" and at other times he totally failed to mention it, as in the case of the recitation of the Shema and others similar, and sometimes he says "this thing [*davar zeh*] is a *mitsvat 'aseh*," as with respect to Sabbath where he writes "rest from work on the seventh is a *mitsvat 'aseh*, etc."

Hai-Raqah then offers an explanation that fits only a limited number of observations, asking the reader to apply the explanation throughout. Joseph Kafih revisits Hai-Raqah's observation and suggestion, applying them to a larger (but still limited) number of instances, all of them occurring in *Sefer Ahavah* (Book of Love) and *Sefer Zemanim* (Book of Seasons). He concludes by acknowledging that "the *Ma'aseh Roqeah̲* wrote something similar to [what I have offered]."[15]

These two commentators argue that Maimonides felt no need to designate a commandment as a *mitsvat 'aseh* if it was absolutely explicit in Scripture (*mefureshet le-gamre ba-torah*). This criterion explains why Maimonides did not immediately designate as positive commandments the obligation to dwell in booths (sukkah) on the fifteenth of Tishre, the obligation to take a palm branch (*lulav*) on Sukkot, and the obligation to study Torah. Conversely, they argued, Maimonides felt compelled to offer the designation *mitsvat 'aseh* when

---

14. David ibn Zimra (RaDBaZ) examines every one of these introductory formulations, searching for variants and trying to explain them. While RaDBaZ's solutions are ingenious (though at times unintelligible), they are *ad hoc* and offer little of relevance to our inquiry. David ibn Zimra, *Sheelot u-Teshuvot ha-RaDVaZ*, vol. 8, *Orah̲ H̲ayyim*, no. 1.

15. Comments on *Mishneh Torah*, ed. Kafih, *Hilkhot Qeriyat Shema* 1:1, 13-14.

the commandment was not explicitly stated in Scripture, as with the obligations to pray (*tefillah*) and to consecrate the lunar month (*qiddush ha-ẖodesh*). While he only analyzes a handful of cases, Hai-Raqah suggests that the student may want to apply this method to other cases "if it is possible." To Hai-Raqah's first category—those commandments explicitly formulated in Scripture—Kafih adds the priestly blessings, phylacteries (tefillin), mezuzah, *tsitsit* and *milah*. To the second category—those commandments not explicitly formulated and thus requiring a designation—he adds the obligations to write a book of Law and to blow a horn on the New Year.

This thesis runs into difficulty almost immediately. The *Halakhot* designates several commandments as positive commandments, despite the fact that they are all explicitly mandated by Scripture: to recite grace after a meal (*Hilkhot Berakhot* 1:1); to rest from work on the Sabbath (*Hilkhot Shabbat* 1:1); to rest from work on Yom Kippur (*Hilkhot Shevitat 'Asor* 1:1); to eat matzah on the fifteenth of Nisan (*Hilkhot Ḫamets u-Matsah* 6:1); to discuss the departure from Egypt on the first night of the feast of Passover (ibid. 7:1); to give half a sheqel every year (*Hilkhot Sheqalim* 1:1); and to sound the trumpets in times of trouble (*Hilkhot Ta'anit* 1:1). Faced with counterexamples, Kafih applies talmudic casuistry to dismiss each case on an ad hoc basis.

But the counterfactual evidence does not end there. Moving beyond *Sefer Ahavah* and *Sefer Zemanim*, we find more commandments explicitly mandated in Scripture and yet designated as positive commandments. A few examples from *Sefer 'Avodah* (The Book of Temple Service): the commandments to build the sanctuary (*Hilkhot Bet ha-Beẖirah* 1:1); to revere the sanctuary (ibid., 7:1); to make the oil of anointment (*Hilkhot Kele ha-Miqdash* 1:1); to send the unclean out of the sanctuary (*Hilkhot Biat ha-Miqdash* 3:1); to offer the regular daily sacrifices (*Hilkhot Temidin u-Musafin* 1:1); to keep fire always burning on the altar (ibid., 2:1); to offer incense twice a day (ibid., 3:1); that the High Priest shall give a meal offering daily (ibid., 3:18); and to count 49 days from the time of cutting the Omer (ibid., 7:22). I have chosen these examples because they are counted by other enumerators and can therefore be deemed to be uncontroversial. This list of counterexamples could be expanded greatly.

It is more difficult to test their complementary hypothesis, namely, that commandments that Scripture does not explicitly mandate are *always* designated as positive commandments. This is because in some way, most commandments are midrashic interpretations of scriptural texts. The line between what is absolutely explicit and what is an interpretation is not always clear. Indeed, this distinction may be too subjective to confidently test the hypothesis.

With this caveat, I have found two counterexamples to the second criterion, commandments that seem to be products of interpretation which Maimonides does not refer to as *mitsvot 'aseh*. The first counterexample is the commandment that when the ark is carried, it should be carried on the priests' shoulders (P34 in the *SE/ShM*; *Hilkhot Kele ha-Miqdash* 2:12). In the *ShM*, Maimonides cites Numbers 7:9 as a proof text for this commandment. That verse, as we saw in chapter 5, does not indicate a clear commandment, and it is only through midrashic interpretation that Maimonides can craft it into a commandment claim. According to the reasoning of Hai-Raqah and Kafih, Maimonides should have designated this midrashically-supported claim as a positive commandment—yet he does not. The second counterexample is the commandment to honor the wise (P209 in the *SE/ShM*; *Hilkhot Talmud Torah* 6:1). The scriptural verse (Lev. 19:32) mandates honoring an old man (*zaqen*); building on this language, a rabbinic midrash uses the letters of *zaqen* as an acronym, standing for someone who has acquired wisdom (*zeh she-qanah ḫokhmah*), a sage. Since the command to honor the wise is only based on this midrash, Maimonides should have designated this claim a positive commandment if Hai-Raqah and Kafih were right; yet he did not.

In sum, Maimonides' deliberate omissions of a significant number of declarative statements in his main legal work continue to beg for a consistent and more systematic explanation. The Hai-Raqah/Kafih hypothesis advanced to account for these omissions does not withstand close scrutiny. While one might be able to explain every counterfactual piece of evidence, as Kafih did with the counterexamples in *Sefer Ahavah* and *Sefer Zemanim*, presenting numerous and thin justifications greatly weakens their case. More generally, the convoluted explanations run counter to Maimonides' stated objectives in writing the *MT*—to make the layout of the law clear to everyone, "young and old," the learned and the ignorant. On this basis, it is inconceivable that Maimonides would have left the reader to determine the origin, force, and status of each of the commandments.

I offer below an explanation that I hope is as parsimonious as it is consistent. It consists of a redefinition of the term *mitsvat 'aseh* as understood in the *ShM* and a tightening of the individuation criteria utilized there. I also posit that a more mature and restrained analysis led Maimonides to change his mind on a small number of previous claims, in keeping with the more conservative and sophisticated nature of the full code of law.

A REDEFINITION OF *MITSVAT 'ASEH*

In chapter 3, I discuss the various definitions of *mitsvat 'aseh* used in the *ShM*. I conclude that some of the commandment types, specifically the procedural commandments and the descriptive commandments, would be better characterized as laws than as formal *mitsvot*, since they are not consistent with the literal meaning of the term *mitsvat 'aseh*, literally the "commandment of 'do,'" much less with the equivalent term, *qum 'aseh*, literally, "arise, do!" Because procedural commandments and descriptive commandments lack the properties of being performative and absolute obligations, it is hard to categorize them as *mitsvot 'aseh*. Maimonides was aware of this problem, and, in an excursus at the end of the section on positive commandments, he acknowledges that "it is possible for a man to go through life without doing or experiencing" many commandments, such as those relating to the offering of special sacrifices. He also acknowledges that many laws, such as those regarding a Hebrew bondsman, a Canaanite bondsman, or an unpaid bailee, "may never be applicable to a particular man, and which he may never be liable to carry out, throughout the whole of his life." After these acknowledgements, Maimonides presents the reader with a new type of *mitsvat 'aseh*, the compulsory commandments (*mitsvot hekhre<u>h</u>iyot*), and states that there are only sixty of this type. As discussed earlier, compulsory commandments, often referred to by the term *<u>h</u>ovah*, better fit the literal meaning of *mitsvot 'aseh*. In rabbinic semantics, a *hovah* is an absolute and unconditional obligation that one must strive assiduously to fulfill.[16]

Maimonides structures this list of compulsory commandments around a number of lifestyle conditions, assuming that "the man whom we regard as bound by these 60 unconditional commandments is living in normal conditions." When a commanded man lives under "normal conditions," owning a house and eating meat, for example, he becomes necessarily obligated to perform commandments that are otherwise contingent, such as mezuzah, ritual slaughter, and building a parapet to his roof. As a contrasting example, the law that governs the revocation of vows (P95) is not enumerated here because a husband is not obligated to revoke his wife's vows when she utters a vow.[17] Finally, Maimonides does not include commandments applicable to a particular caste, such as priests and Levites, nor does he include commandments binding only when the Temple stands, such as the commandments of the assembly during Sukkot (*haqhel*, P16) and the tithing of cattle (P78).

I submit that this list of sixty compulsory commandments is critical to a correct understanding of the term *mitsvat 'aseh* in the *Halakhot*. As I discuss in the first half of this book, to achieve the self-imposed target of 248 positive commandments in the *ShM*, Maimonides had to resort to some imaginative but questionable interpretations of what constitutes a positive commandment. This category includes a wide and varied array of so-called commandments: some obligatory, some contingent, some prescriptive procedures, some descriptive laws. Once he turned his attention to writing a full-fledged code of law, the *MT*, Maimonides no longer felt compelled to preserve this artificial delineation of 613 biblical commandments. Henceforth, he tacitly redefined the term *mitsvat 'aseh* to refer to compulsory or unconditional obligations.

A word of caution: because the list of sixty is a subset of the 248 positive commandments that Maimonides already enumerated, it follows that the shorter list also reflects Maimonides' early exegetical

16. Cf. *Hilkhot Berakhot* 11:2.
17. Maimonides calls this commandment a *din* or "law," counting it as a commandment because we are obligated to act according to this law. See above, chapter 3, note 4.

thinking.[18] As I will demonstrate later, Maimonides reversed his thinking on some of these designations. Nevertheless, the *conceptual* basis upon which this list is constructed still serves as a useful paradigm for understanding the definition of *mitsvat 'aseh* used in the *Halakhot*.

We are now in a position to explain a substantial portion of the failures to designate appearing in Table 1. The following commandments are either contingent and do not occur under "normal conditions," or are not obligatory if one does not wish to change one's status, as when one wishes to remain unclean or does not want to obtain atonement. As a result, they fail to meet the revised criteria of *mitsvat 'aseh* as an absolute, unconditional, obligation:

P70. That an individual shall bring an offering, if he is in doubt as to whether he has committed a sin for which one has to bring a sin offering.

P71. That an offering shall be brought by one who has in error committed a trespass against sacred things, or robbed, or lain carnally with a bondsmaid betrothed to a man, or denied what was deposited with him and swore falsely to support his denial. This is called a trespass offering for a known trespass.

P72. To offer a sacrifice of varying value in accordance with one's means.

P74. That a man having an issue shall bring a sacrifice, after he is cleansed of his issue.

P75. That a woman having an issue shall bring a sacrifice, after she is cleansed of her issue.

P76. That a woman after childbirth shall bring an offering when she is clean.

P77. That the leper shall bring a sacrifice, after he is cleansed.

---

18. For example, the list of 60 does not make the finer distinction between *mitsvot de-oraita* and *mitsvot mi-divre sofrim* that I believe Maimonides ultimately makes in the *Halakhot*. Additionally, the list does not distinguish between commandments that constitute absolute obligations and those better placed in the category of counsels. I will argue that this second distinction is a late innovation of the *Halakhot*. The popular nature of this list is evident by the playful manner by which Maimonides explains the numbers 60 (commandments incumbent on all males) and 46 (incumbent on all females): "A mnemonic for the number of unconditional commandments is: 'There are threescore queens' (Song 6:8), and the mnemonic for the 14 of those [commandments] taken away for women may be remembered by the expression 'their stay (*yad*) is gone' (Deut. 32:36) [the numerical value of *yad* being 14]."

P95. To decide in cases of annulment of vows, according to the rules set forth in the Torah.
P148. To set the mother bird free when taking the nest.
P199. To return a pledge to its owner.
P247. To save the pursued even at the cost of the life of the pursuer.[19]

Also omitted from the list of unconditional commandments are the few descriptive commandments, commandments that define or stipulate legal consequences but do not entail action, such as:

P87. That an exchanged beast [a beast that is exchanged for one that had been set apart as an offering] is sacred.
P96. That anyone who touches the carcass of a beast that died of itself shall be unclean.
P97. That eight species of creeping things defile by contact.
P98. That foods become defiled (by contact with unclean things).
P99. That a menstruating woman is unclean and defiles others.
P100. That a new mother in confinement is unclean like a menstruating woman.
P101. That a leper is unclean and defiles.
P102. That a leprous garment is unclean and defiles.
P103. That a leprous house defiles.
P104. That a man, having a running issue, defiles.
P105. That the seed of copulation defiles.

---

19. Here is an example of how Maimonides treats a contingent commandment. He begins discussing the laws of saving the pursued in *Hilkhot Rotseah̲* 1:6.Yet it is not until *Halakhah* 15 that he posits that saving the pursued is a positive commandment: "If one sees someone pursuing another in order to kill him, or sees someone pursuing a woman forbidden to him in order to ravish her, and although able to save them does not do so, he thereby disregards [*bitel*] the positive commandment *Then thou shalt cut off her hand* and transgresses two negative commandments." Having avoided at the outset the outright declaration that saving the pursued is a positive commandment, Maimonides carefully returns to the topic, affirming that under certain specific circumstances, saving the pursued is an unconditional obligation. By this artifice, he avoids positing an outright obligation to save a pursued person, which might lead to the ingenuous belief that a person is obligated to live in an area where crime is common, for example. I submit that Maimonides did not include this commandment in the list of the sixty unconditional obligations for precisely the same reason: there is no obligation to find a rapist or murderer so that one can save the pursued. In effect, to save the pursued is a contingent obligation, when and if such a circumstance occurs, rather than an unconditional obligation.

P106. That a woman, having a running issue, defiles.
P107. That a corpse defiles.
P108. That the waters of sprinkling defile one who is clean, and cleanse [the unclean] from pollution by a dead body.
P119. That the fruit of fruit-bearing trees in the fourth year of their planting shall be sacred.

Recall that most of these commandment claims caused Nahmanides to vehemently declare that "they are optional [*reshut*] from every angle, they have no connection to *mitsvah* [*ein ba-hem inyan mitsvah*] that they should deserve to be counted."

Finally, Maimonides fails to designate as positive commandments the types of commandments that are technical laws and procedures, because they do not imply active obligation. In this group we find:

P109. That purification from all kinds of defilement shall be effected by immersion in the waters of a *miqveh*.
P139. That houses sold within a walled city may be redeemed within a year.
P145. To decide, in regard to dedicated property, which is sacred to the Lord, and which belongs to the priest.
P181. To decapitate the heifer in the manner prescribed.
P190. In an optional war, to observe the procedure prescribed in the Torah.
P221. To deal with a beautiful woman taken captive in war in the manner prescribed in the Torah.
P222. To divorce by a formal written document.
P223. That the woman suspected of adultery be dealt with as prescribed in the Torah.
P232. To deal judicially with the Hebrew bondsman, in accordance with the laws appertaining to him.
P233. To espouse a Hebrew maidservant.
P234. To redeem her [the Hebrew maidservant].
P235. To keep the Canaanite slave forever.[20]

---

20. I assume that the commandment claim should be understood as expressed in the *ShM*: "We are commanded concerning the law of a Canaanite bondman; that he is to remain a bondman forever," which parallels the *ShM*'s formula in P232: "We are commanded concerning the law of a Hebrew bondman." See also *Yad ha-Levi*, 165n5. This way of formulating the commandment turns P235 into a law rather than a command.

P236. That he who inflicts a bodily injury shall pay monetary compensation.
P237. To judge cases of injuries caused by beasts.
P238. To judge cases of damage caused by an uncovered pit.
P239. To adjudge a thief to pay compensation, or [in certain cases] suffer death.
P240. To adjudicate cases of damage caused by trespass of cattle.
P241. To adjudicate cases of damage caused by fire.
P242. To adjudicate cases of damage by a gratuitous depositary.
P243. To judge cases of damage of a paid depositary and a hirer.
P244. To adjudicate cases of damage of a gratuitous borrower.
P245. To adjudicate cases of purchase and sale.
P246. To adjudicate other cases between a plaintiff and a defendant.
P248. To adjudicate cases of inheritances.

In sum, none of the above claims meet the *Halakhot*'s revised criteria for positive commandments when we define them as unconditional obligations. Thus have we explained 50 of the 109 failures to designate that were listed in Table 1.

The full implications of the thesis—that the *Halakhot* used criteria narrower and more conventional than the ones assumed in the *ShM*—now become clear: when writing the *MT*, Maimonides did not genuinely subscribe to the notion that there were 248 positive commandments.[21] By this point in my analysis, this implication should not be surprising. In fact, it is fully consistent with the conclusions

Note that in the *Halakhot*, Maimonides retracts the claim made in the *SE* that there is an unconditional obligation to keep the Canaanite slave forever. In *Hilkhot 'Avadim* 9:6, Maimonides states: "It is not permitted (*assur*) for a person to free a Canaanite slave; whoever frees him, transgresses (*'over*) an *'aseh*, as it says, *Of them may ye take your bondmen forever* (Lev. 25:46)." Both the injunction itself, couched as a prohibition, and the use of the verb "transgress" (*'over*) instead of "abrogate" (*bitel*) indicate that this is a prohibition derived from a positive statement (*issur 'aseh*), rather than a true positive commandment. See above for the discussion of *issur 'aseh* in chapter 2. On the distinction between *'over* and *bitel*, see Perla, *Sefer ha-Mitsvot le-RaSaG*, vol.1, 693-694. In sum, this failure to designate is well justified: either the command should be considered a law, or it is a prohibition inferred from a positive statement rather than a positive commandment.

21. While the same is almost certainly true with respect to the 365 negative commandments, given the logical problems that one would encounter in composing such a list, analyzing this claim would require a separate investigation.

reached in chapter 4: there is no conceivable way to defend a single, logically compelling, fixed number of commandments.

THREE REVERSALS FROM THE LIST OF 60 UNCONDITIONAL OBLIGATIONS

Our current revised theory of how the *Halakhot* defines a *mitsvat 'aseh* follows the one proposed as the basis for the *ShM*'s list of sixty compulsory commandments: unconditional obligations, operative under a specific set of circumstances. These circumstances are that "the man ... is living in normal conditions, that is to say, that he lives in a house in a community, eats ordinary food, namely bread and meat, pursues a normal occupation, marries and has a family." Maimonides fails to define three of the commandments included on this list as positive commandments in their respective sections of the *Halakhot*: P9, "To hallow His name"; P14, "Fringes"; and P26, "That the priests shall bless Israel." I argue that when he wrote the *Halakhot,* Maimonides did indeed reverse himself; because he had reclassified these commandments as contingent rather than unconditional obligations, he deliberately avoided designating them as *mitsvot 'aseh.* I examine these three commandment claims below.

P9. To hallow His name, as it is said, "And I will be sanctified in the midst of the children of Israel" (Lev. 22:32).

While Qayyara enumerates "sanctifying the Name" (*qiddush ha-Shem*) in his list of *qum 'aseh* (Pq28), Maimonides may not have agreed with this definition. In Rule 4, Maimonides stipulates that charges that cover the whole of the Torah and do not contain specific actions ought not to be counted as commandments. One might argue that "And I will be sanctified in the midst of the children of Israel" describes the result of the Israelites fulfilling all the commandments, rather than commanding a specific action. Perhaps this concern drives Maimonides to find a rabbinic justification for the positive commandment of sanctifying the name. As he quotes *BT Sanhedrin* 74b: "Is a Noahide commanded to sanctify His Name or not? Listen to this: 'The Noahides were commanded to observe seven commandments; but if they were

[also] commanded to sanctify His Name, there are eight.'" "Thus," Maimonides concludes,

> it has been made clear to you that this is one of the commandments that are obligatory upon Israel, the Sages having deduced this commandment from the words *I will be hallowed among the children of Israel* [Lev. 22:32].[22]

But while Maimonides demonstrates that the verse points to a positive commandment, the requirements of the commandment itself are not defined in this talmudic passage. Specifically, what must one do to sanctify God's name? In the opening lines of his gloss to the *ShM*, Maimonides is bold and poetic:

> The purport of this commandment is that we are duty-bound to proclaim this true religion to the world, undeterred by fear of injury from any source. Even if a tyrant tries to compel us by force to deny Him, we must not obey, but must positively rather submit to death; and we must not even mislead the tyrant into supposing that we have denied Him while in our hearts we continue to believe in Him.

The primary requirement of this commandment is the unconditional obligation to proclaim monotheism to the world. Moreover, this obligation must be carried out even in the face of danger.[23]

Maimonides' accompanying exegesis does not quite support the missionary aspect of this claim. He cites an incident in the book of Daniel,

---

22. In the talmudic text, Rava responds to this argument by stating that the obligation to sanctify the Divine Name by observing the seven Noahide laws is included in those seven laws. This argument would nullify the proof upon which Maimonides' argument rests, as observed by the commentary *Mishneh le-Melekh* (on *Hilkhot Melakhim* 10:2). Ultimately, it may well be the case that the difference between these amoraic opinions rests on the same matter that concerned Maimonides: is *qiddush ha-Shem* an independent commandment or merely an outcome of performing all the commandments?

23. Because Levinger did not realize that the *qiddush ha-Shem* mentioned in the list of 60 unconditional commandments followed the *ShM*'s definition of *qiddush ha-Shem* (the unconditional obligation to proclaim the true religion), rather than the multiple definitions given in the *Halakhot*, he was forced to offer an unsatisfactory answer to how *qiddush ha-Shem* could be an unconditional obligation. Levinger, *Ha-RaMBaM ke-Filosof*, 81-83.

which describes how Hananiah, Mishael, and Azariah were ready to die by Nebuchadnezzar's hand, "when he forced people to prostrate themselves before the idol, and all did so, the Israelites included and there was none there to sanctify the Name of Heaven, all being in terror." Note, however, that we are never told that these three martyrs proclaimed the "true religion" of their own volition. Rather, the three martyrs were forced to proclaim God's greatness as a direct result of Nebuchadnezzar's decree. Maimonides confirms this nuanced understanding: "This commandment applies only in circumstances such as those of that great occasion when the whole world was in terror, and it was a duty to declare His Unity publicly at that time." In other words, these martyrs sanctified God's name only after being pressed to do so. This scenario differs slightly from the idea that "we are in duty bound to proclaim this true religion to the world," implying that this commandment is carried out on one's own initiative and as an unconditional obligation.

In the space of a few sentences, Maimonides wavers between the conflicting claims that the commandment requires one to go to all lengths to proclaim the true religion and that one is only obligated to sanctify God's Name during a "great occasion" when the world is forced to deny God's existence. Even within the *ShM* itself, this commandment changes from representing an unconditional obligation fit for the list of 60 unconditional commandments to representing a contingent commandment—which should not be designated as a *mitsvat 'aseh* in the *Halakhot*.[24]

Maimonides continues in support of the public aspect of this commandment by quoting a revealing midrash from the *Sifra*: "On this condition I brought you out of the land of Egypt, that *ye sanctify My name publicly*" (emphasis added).[25] Maimonides' statement that "this commandment applies *only in circumstances such as those of that great*

24. The subtle contradiction that we noted may be the result of an unintended conflation of two literary layers. Likely the older layer is the one that defines this as an unconditional commandment, which may be why it is included in the list of sixty unconditional obligations.

25. *Sifra Emor* 9:6 (99d). The critical word *be-rabbim* (publicly) is missing in our edition of the midrash. In his edition of the *ShM*, Heller quotes the midrash in full as we have it in our editions, showing that he is aware of the fact that Maimonides' version contained the critical extra word *be-rabbim*. Yet, he does not comment on the extraordinary significance that this extra word has for the definition of the commandment.

occasion" (emphasis added) is highly innovative, as it stipulates that *qiddush ha-Shem* can only be fulfilled under very special and unique circumstances: when the entire world is being forced to abandon monotheism. The implication is that anything less public or less dramatic than the worldwide rejection of monotheism would not constitute grounds for *qiddush ha-Shem*.[26] It is this latter thread that the *Halakhot* explores.

Maimonides discusses the positive commandment of *qiddush ha-Shem* and the correlating prohibition against *ḥillul ha-Shem* (desecration of God's name) in the *Mishneh Torah*, in *Hilkhot Yesode ha-Torah* 5. As I noted in Table 1, he does not declare in the opening lines of that passage that *qiddush ha-Shem* is a positive commandment. In *Halakhot* 5:1-4, Maimonides stipulates the conditions under which one should transgress rather than be killed, and the converse conditions under which one must die rather than transgress. In 5:4, he differentiates between a private and a public act of sanctification:

> When one is enjoined to die rather than transgress, and suffers death so as to not transgress, he sanctifies the name of God. If he does so in the presence of ten Israelites, he sanctifies the name of God publicly, like Daniel, Hananiah, Mishael and Azariah, Rabbi Akiva and his colleagues. These are martyrs, than whom none ranks higher.

While the *ShM* only focuses on the public sanctification of God's name, in the *Halakhot*, Maimonides explicitly discusses two types of sanctification, a private act and a public one. But as he writes in the *ShM*, public sanctification is the only type that can fulfill the positive commandment. He makes this clear in the continuation of the same *halakhah*:

26. Heller's edition of the *ShM*, which reads "this commandment was only commanded for that great occasion" instead of "this commandment applies only in circumstances such as those of that great occasion," clearly has a different meaning. In note 9, Heller offers, instead, three supporting witnesses for our reading, including the text of the first edition of the *ShM* (Constantinople 1516), Ibn Ayub's translation, and one of his Arabic manuscripts (which, incidentally, reads the same as Kafih's manuscript). Hurewitz, *Sefer ha-Mitsvot im Perush Yad ha-Levi, ad loc.*, glosses that there was no better opportunity to publicly sanctify God's name than at the time of Hananiah, Mishael, and Azariah. This comment is surprising, given that his edition is based on the Constantinople edition and reads as I have quoted above.

> When one is enjoined to suffer death rather than transgress, and commits a transgression and so escapes death, he has profaned the name of God. If the transgression was committed in the presence of ten Israelites, he has profaned the name of God in public, failed [*bitel*] to observe a positive commandment—to sanctify the name of God—and violated a negative commandment—not to profane His name.

According to this technical definition, *qiddush ha-Shem* can be considered a *mitsvat 'aseh* only when one is coerced to transgress a serious injunction in the presence of ten Israelites and chooses martyrdom instead.[27] Whether one can define *qiddush ha-Shem* as an unconditional obligation depends on whether one uses the definition from the *ShM* or from the *Halakhot*. If *qiddush ha-Shem* translates into an obligation to "proclaim this true religion to the world, undeterred by fear of injury from any source," as is formulated in the *ShM*, then it can be considered an unconditional obligation. If, on the other hand, *qiddush ha-Shem* is defined only as the obligation to accept martyrdom were one to be forced to transgress one of the few fundamental sins as defined by the *Halakhot*, then it should be considered a contingent obligation. In such a case, the *Halakhot* can justifiably omit the declaratory statement that *qiddush ha-Shem* is a positive commandment.

27. In the *Halakhot*, Maimonides handles the dichotomy between public and private acts with a certain amount of ambivalence. On the one hand, he treats private acts of sanctification/profanation with the utmost gravity. For example, in *halakhah* 3, Maimonides rules that in a time of religious persecution (*sha'at ha-shemad*) when the authorities attempt to abolish the Israelites' religion or any of its precepts, the Israelite is obligated to die rather than profane God's name, even if the coercion takes place in the private domain. His source for this is the uncontested statement of R. Dimi in the name of R. Yoẖanan (*BT Sanhedrin* 74a), who asserted that in a time of persecution, one must suffer death rather than transgress even a minor commandment. When one couples this statement with the one that follows, it appears that this severity applies even in the private domain. On the other hand, Maimonides rules that one only deems a transgression to be a scriptural violation if the action is publicly performed in the presence of ten Israelites. In *halakhah* 4, it seems that the violations of these commandments apply only in the public domain, not in the private one. Maimonides appears to be emphasizing the essential message of the scriptural verse, as the *Sifra* articulates it: "ye sanctify my name in public." While it might be hard to read the severe stance of *halakhah* 3 as intending a rabbinic ordinance, the scriptural commandment clearly intends to refer to public acts.

P14. To make fringes.

In the *SE*, the *ShM*, and the Heading to *Hilkhot Tsitsit*, Maimonides states that there exists a positive commandment to make fringes (*tsitsit*),[28] stemming from the scriptural command "that they make them ... fringes in the corners of their garments" (Num. 15:38). In the *Halakhot*, however, there is no introductory statement that "it is a *mitvsat 'aseh* to make *tsitsit*," merely a statement that "one who wears a cloak [*tallit*] having white or azure or both together has fulfilled one positive commandment" (*Hilkhot Tsitsit* 1:5).[29] The delayed positioning of the declaration and its soft, almost incidental tone alert us to the subtle change in the nature of the commandment and confirms the care with which Maimonides crafts introductory declarations to his *Halakhot*.

In fact, there is no obligation to affix fringes to a cloak—as the formulation "to make *tsitsit*" implies—or even to wear a cloak with fringes attached, but only the instruction that if one were to wear a cloak with such fringes attached, one would fulfill a positive commandment. As formulated by the *Halakhot*, this is a contingent commandment: if one wears a four-cornered garment, one must put *tsitsit* on it. This revised view is confirmed in *Hilkhot Tsitsit* 3:10:

> When is one obligated to fulfill the commandment of fringes? Anyone obligated by this commandment[30] who covers himself with a garment fit[31] for fringes must first affix fringes to it, and only then cover himself with it. If he has covered himself with it without fringes, he has nullified a positive commandment.

As noted earlier, the list of sixty compulsory commandments comes from the *ShM* and *SE*. In both of these compositions, Maimonides formulates the commandment to imply that there is an unconditional obligation

---

28. Kafih reads the *ShM* as "we are commanded in the work (Arab., *b'ml*; Heb., *be-maaseh*) of the *tsitsit*."
29. This follows the thesis already developed in the *ShM* that the white tassel and the azure thread are to be considered one commandment, not two, despite the fact that the absence of either the white tassel or the azure thread does not invalidate the other.
30. See *Hilkhot Tsitsit* 3:9 for those who are exempt from this commandment.
31. See *Hilkhot Tsitsit* 3:1-2 for a discussion of the type of garment to which one must attach fringes.

to affix fringes on every garment in one's possession.[32] In the *Halakhot*, however, Maimonides follows the normative rabbinic opinion that "the point of the commandment is to wrap oneself with them [fringed garments]," as he rules in *Hilkhot Tsitsit* 3:8,[33] rather than to affix the fringes on one's garments. According to this rabbinic interpretation, the commandment to attach fringes is only applicable when one wears a four-cornered garment—in essence, a contingent commandment.

Even in light of this revision, we might still ask why Maimonides did not formulate his commandment more strongly in the *Halakhot*: he could have stated that it is a positive commandment to affix fringes to a garment that requires it. The simple answer may be that wrapping oneself in such a garment is not part of the "normal condition" that Maimonides views as transforming a contingent commandment into an obligation. He may have had a subtler reason for deliberately omitting such a formulation, however: declaring that "it is a positive commandment to affix fringes to a garment that requires it" could have misled his readers into thinking that they are required to own a tallit to fulfill the commandment. Rather:

> Even though one is not obligated to purchase a tallit and wrap himself in it, so that he has to affix fringes to it, it is not fitting for a person who is pious [*ḥasid*] to exempt himself from this commandment; rather, such a one should always endeavor to be wrapped in a garment which requires fringes so that he fulfills this commandment. (3:11)

While one is not obligated to wear a garment with fringes, it is a point of piety for one to own such a garment and thus fulfill the commandment to attach fringes.

P 26. That the priests shall bless Israel.

In the previous two examples, we saw that in the *Halakhot*, Maimonides characterizes the commandments differently from the way he had

32. This is the opinion of one of the amoraim in *BT Menaḥot* 42b. See chapter 7 for a discussion of Maimonides' views on the plain sense of the scriptural text (*peshateh di-qera*).

33. This is the reason why one does not pronounce a blessing over the affixing of the fringes.

characterized them in the *ShM* and *SE*. These new definitions affect how he categorizes these commandments in the *Halakhot*. While such a redefinition of the commandment for the priests to bless Israel may be one of the reasons this commandment is not designated as a *mitsvat 'aseh* in the *Halakhot*, this rationale may not be a sufficient explanation.

The laws of the priestly blessings (*Hilkhot Nesiyat Kapayim*) are appended to the end of *Hilkhot Tefillah* (ch. 14 -15), because the priestly blessings form an organic part of the *'Amidah* prayer. Maimonides introduces *Hilkhot Nesiyat Kapayim* as follows: "The priests bless the congregation [*ha-kohanim nosim et kapehem*, lit., "the priests raise their hands"] during the morning, additional [*musaf*], and *ne'ilah* prayers" (14:1). Notably absent from the introductory statement is a declaration that the priestly blessings are a positive commandment. Other unusual features include the absence of a scriptural proof text for the obligation and the use of the participial rather than the infinitival form to describe the commandment. While we might infer that Maimonides no longer believes that this is a *mitsvat 'aseh*, he elaborates his position in the next chapter. He writes that no priest should be prevented from blessing the community,

> even if he is neither wise nor punctilious in the observance of the commandments, or even if people speak slightingly of him, or even if his business dealings are not just...since it is a positive commandment [*mitsvat 'aseh*] incumbent on every single priest to bless the community, and we do not tell a wicked man to be more wicked, and refrain from fulfilling commandments. (*Hilkhot Nesiyat Kapayim* 15:6)

Furthermore, at the very end of chapter 15, Maimonides writes: "Even though a priest who fails to ascend the platform has violated only one positive commandment [*bitel mitsvat 'aseh*], it is as if he had transgressed three positive commandments."[34] These rulings make it

34. The source for the statement that a priest who fails to ascend to the platform transgresses three positive commandments is *BT Menaḥot* 44a. For Maimonides, this statement does not appear to carry legal force; it serves as a way for the rabbis to emphasize the importance of this duty. See Rule 9, *ShM*, ed. Frankel, 161. On the other hand, the expression *bitel*, translated as "cancelled," "abrogated," or "nullified," applies to genuine positive commandments, as opposed to inferred prohibitions. See above, note 20.

clear that Maimonides continues to maintain that the priestly blessing constitutes a positive commandment.

So how can we account for the *Halakhot*'s failure to designate this commandment as a *mitsvat 'aseh* in its opening lines? The simplest explanation holds that Maimonides had changed his mind on whether this was an absolute or contingent obligation. While in the *ShM*, he defines this commandment as an absolute obligation, he now maintains that the obligation is only contingent:[35] the priest transgresses a positive commandment only if and when he fails to bless the congregation during communal services when asked to do so.[36] While this explanation is consistent with my earlier thesis, it is still not entirely satisfactory. Maimonides could have begun the exposition noting that this is a contingent commandment: he could have stated that "it is a *mitsvat 'aseh* to bless the congregation whenever the priest is called upon to do so," similar to his formulation of repentance at the start of *Hilkhot Teshuvah*.[37] Why does Maimonides wait until nearly the end of the exposition to state that blessing the congregation is a *mitsvat 'aseh*?

I wish to suggest here a highly speculative solution, one for which I cannot offer talmudic or midrashic support. I argue that the literary ambiguity of the *Halakhot* is a product of Maimonides' doubt as to whether the commandment, as performed in daily prayer, meets the exacting strictures of Scripture and the interpretations of the Oral Law.[38] In *Hilkhot Nesiyat Kapayim* 14:11, Maimonides offers an exegetical basis for the commandment:

---

35. The biblical verse only discusses the form and manner by which the priests must bless the congregation: "On this wise ye shall bless the children of Israel." The text does not *require* such a blessing.

36. This sense may be inferred from *Hilkhot Nesiyat Kapayim*, 15:11-12. See *JT Berakhot* 5:4 and *Arba'ah Turim, Orah Hayyim*, sec. 128 on his reading of *Tg. Onqelos*.

37. "With regard to all the precepts of the Torah ... if a person transgressed ... when he decides to repent he has a duty to confess" (*Hilkhot Teshuvah* 1:1).

38. In chapter 9, I propose other examples of literary ambiguity in Maimonides' legal writings. Maimonides' ambiguities can be detected in subtle changes in formulations. They may incorporate two contradictory opinions, omit a talmudic source, or quote a source without an explanation, leaving the reader to make assumptions about the circumstances of the case. This phenomenon was noted by early commentators. See Shapiro, *Studies in Maimonides and His Interpreters*, 8-9 and n. 37.

> The priestly blessing is never recited in any language but Hebrew, as it says, And the Lord spoke unto Moses, saying: *Speak unto Aaron and unto his sons, saying: On this wise* [in this way] *ye shall bless the children of Israel* [Num. 6:22-3], and thus they learned from the oral tradition [*kakh lamdu mi-pi ha-shemu'ah*] from Moses: *On this wise ye shall bless*—standing; *On this wise ye shall bless*—with raised hands; *On this wise ye shall bless*—in Hebrew; *On this wise ye shall bless*—face to face; *On this wise ye shall bless*—aloud; *On this wise ye shall bless*—with the explicit Name, if they are in the Temple, as we said.[39]

The oral tradition defined the priestly blessings as invoking the explicit or articulated Name. This could only be done in the Temple, as Maimonides explains:

> They recite the divine name as it is written, that is the letters *yod*, *heh*, *vav*, and *heh* are pronounced. This is what is universally called "the explicit name." Outside the Temple, they use its appellation, that is, *alef dalet*, since the name is expressed as it is written only in the Temple.... The early Sages taught it to their worthy students and sons only once every seven years. All this out of esteem for the great and awesome name.[40] (*Hilkhot Nesiyat Kapayim* 14:10)

Because of the oral tradition's insistence that the priestly blessings use the explicit name, which could only be done in the Temple, Maimonides may have inferred that the priestly blessings conducted outside of the Temple do not conform to the dictates of the scriptural commandment.[41] He may have conjectured that these blessings were the product of a formal

39. Maimonides here summarizes a lengthier exposition found in *BT Sotah* 38a. Mishnaic sages deduce each interpretation of "On this wise ye shall bless" independently by various textual and analogical means. He likely viewed these *halakhot* as the product of an oral tradition "from Moses" rather than implausible textual and analogical derivations.

40. In the *GP*, Maimonides discusses this topic at length, arguing that the articulated name alone, the tetragrammaton, "is indicative of the essence without associating any other notion with it." *GP* I:61, 149. See also I:62, 150-151.

41. The blessings conducted in the Temple were clearly of a different order of gravitas than the ones conducted outside of it. Compare *BT Hagigah* 16a, discussing those who lose their sight: "(he who looks on) the priests when the Temple stood, as they rose to bless the people." RaSHI, s. v. "*u-mevarhin et ha-'am*," explains "because the Shekhinah rested on their fingers." Apparently, the Shekhinah does not rest on the fingers of the priests when they bless the people outside of the Temple.

rabbinical enactment (*taqanah*) or an informal popular practice sanctioned by the rabbis. If the scripturally-commanded priestly blessing were only applicable in the Temple, Maimonides would have had to further qualify his opening statement. Since he was uncertain of the commandment's bounds, he simply stated that "the priests bless the congregation during the morning, additional, and *ne'ilah* prayers" (14:1). As I will discuss in chapter 8, the use of the participle ("the priests bless") to describe a commandment conveys a weak sense of obligation. Such obligations can often be traced to rabbinic ordinance or custom. With this language, Maimonides may have wished to convey his tentative opinion to the careful reader: the priestly blessing, as practiced outside of the Temple, is non-scriptural. Towards the end of his exposition, however, he implies that the blessing outside the Temple is scriptural, stating: "even though a priest who fails to ascend the platform has violated only one positive commandment [*bitel mitsvat 'aseh*], it is as if he had transgressed three positive commandments."[42] Still, to defend this interpretation, one could argue that the *mitsvat 'aseh* designation here applies solely to the scriptural paradigm, the priestly blessing conducted in the Temple.

In sum, I submit that the unusual literary presentation of this commandment in the *Halakhot* reflects Maimonides' ambivalence regarding the exact status of the commandment. By using a participle to describe the commandment in the introduction, and by moving the expected designation and the proof text to the end of the exposition, the *Halakhot* allows for two possible readings. The priestly blessings are a scriptural obligation when practiced in the Temple, but only a custom when practiced in a synagogue. Alternately, the priestly blessings are always a scriptural obligation; outside of the Temple, however, the priests may not use the articulated Name.

REVISITING INDIVIDUATION

As I discussed in chapter 4, many of the individuations in the *ShM* do not seem to be logically unique commandments. In the *Halakhot,* many of these less-logical individuations are either subsumed under

42. *BT Sotah* 38b, in the name of R. Joshua b. Levi.

larger headings or no longer designated as *mitsvot 'aseh*. I revisit those problematic cases here.

Moving from the simpler to the more complex cases, P68 (sacrifices brought by the court) is now subsumed in the *Halakhot* under P69 (sacrifices brought by individuals), while P114-P117, the laws of valuations (*'arakhin*), are now condensed into one commandment: "It is a positive commandment to adjudge the laws of *'arakhin* as stipulated in the Torah" (*Hilkhot 'Arakhin* 1:2).[43] Commandments P149-152 are subsumed in *Hilkhot Maakhalot Asurot* 1:1 under one positive commandment: "Concerning the tokens with which one can differentiate between those domesticated and wild animals, owls, fishes and grasshoppers, that may be eaten and those that may not be eaten."[44]

Another individuation scheme that is revisited is the series of commandments about resting from work on the festival days (P159-60, P162-63, P166-67). In the *Halakhot*, Maimonides collapses these six commandments into one, stating:

> Anyone who rests from work [*melekhet 'avodah*, a term that the rabbis understood as referring to the kind of work unrelated to the preparation of food] on any of these [six festival days] has fulfilled a positive commandment.[45] (*Hilkhot Shevitat Yom Tov* 1:2)

43. The reader may object that the law of *'arakhin* should not be designated a positive commandment because it does not command one to perform a certain act; it merely describes the financial consequences of undertaking certain types of vows. It is best defined as a "law" rather than as a "commandment." I do not have a satisfactory answer to this objection, and I believe that this case represents an exception to the rule. This odd formulation also caught the attention of a commentator who wondered why Maimonides did not designate the adjudication of personal vows (*nedarim*) as a positive commandment in the same way as he had designated the adjudication of *'arakhin* as a positive commandment: see Epstein, *Arukh ha-Shulhan he-Atid*, sec. 33, no. 8.

44. Maimonides created four positive commandments in the *SE/ShM* based on positive statements that make up four individual inferred prohibitions (*lav ha-ba-mikhlal 'aseh*). See the earlier discussion of P149-152 in chapter 5.

45. Here Maimonides invokes their common requirement to rest from "the kind of work unrelated to the preparation of food" as criteria for grouping all the festivals under one roof. Maimonides did not follow the same logical scheme regarding the obligation of absolute rest prescribed for the Sabbath and the Day of Atonement because these two days of rest require separate treatises to deal with their particular sets of scriptural and rabbinic commandments and ordinances. In other words, the rest-from-work

In the *Halakhot*, Maimonides omits the positive commandment to appoint a special priest to address the soldiers in war (P191). In chapter 4, I question the justification for individuating this claim, since it represents a single element of the laws of waging war.[46]

In chapter 2, I note Maimonides' unconvincing individuation of the four modes of capital punishment. In the *Halakhot*, he resolves this issue in an elegant fashion. After describing the four modes of capital punishment, he states: "[With reference to] each one of these deaths [*kol mitah me-hen*], it is a positive commandment for the court to execute, by means of it, those who are liable to it" (*Hilkhot Sanhedrin* 14:1-2). Maimonides' formulation is ambiguous. He could mean that all four forms of execution collectively count as one positive commandment; alternately, he could mean that each one of them singly is its own positive commandment. The ambiguous formulation allows us either to claim that Maimonides indeed designated the four types of executions individually and explicitly, or that he changed his mind and posited that all four executions should be individuated as one commandment.

To summarize: in this section, I found that certain groups of related commandments were subsumed under one of their own group of commandments or under a different commandment claim, to yield a more generic formulation. This was the case with:

---

individuation was dictated by topical considerations, particular to the drafting of a code of law, rather than by theoretical considerations. Note, too, that the punishment for transgressing the prohibition to work is different for the Sabbath (stoning) than for the Day of Atonement (excision). See *Hilkhot Shevitat 'Asor* 1:2.

46. In chapter 4, I suggest that didactic considerations may have influenced Maimonides' decision. Despite the commandment's omission in the *Halakhot*, the special educational message that he wishes to convey does make its appearance. In *Hilkhot Melakhim* 7:2-3, he details the preparations for war and cites the particulars of the address of the special priest as recounted in the scriptural passage. In a special and seemingly redundant peroration at 7:15, Maimonides tells us that once "the man who is fearful and fainthearted" (Deut. 20:8) has "joined the ranks of battle, he should put his reliance upon Him who is the hope of Israel, their Savior in time of trouble. He should note that he is fighting for the oneness of God, risk his life, and neither fear nor be affrighted. Nor should he think of his wife or children, but forgetting them and all else, concentrate on the war." This addition appears to be gratuitous but it is not: These eloquent and stirring words are designed to instill in the faithful a special zeal to combat heresy, the very same objective that I suspect led Maimonides to individuate P191.

P68. That the court of judgment shall bring an offering if it has erred in a judicial pronouncement
(now subsumed under the general positive commandment to bring a sin offering for sinning in error by committing a transgression, as per *Hilkhot Shegagot* 1:1);[47]

P114. That one who vows to the Lord the monetary value of a person shall pay the amount appointed in the scriptural passage;

P115. That one who vows to the Lord the monetary value of an unclean beast shall pay its value;

P116. That one who vows the value of his house shall pay according to the appraisal of the priest;

P117. That one who sanctifies to the Lord a portion of his field shall pay according to the estimation appointed in the scriptural passage
(now subsumed under a general law of valuations, as per *Hilkhot 'Arakhin va-Haramin* 1:2);

P149. To examine the marks in cattle;

P150. To examine the marks in fowl, so as to distinguish between the unclean and the clean;

P151. To examine the marks in locusts, so as to distinguish the clean from the unclean;

P152. To examine the marks in fish
(now subsumed under a general law to differentiate all edible animals, as per *Hilkhot Maakhalot Asurot* 1:1);

P159. To rest on the first day of Passover;

P160. To rest on the seventh day of that feast [Passover];

P162. To rest on the fiftieth day (from the time of cutting the Omer);

P163. To rest on the first day of the seventh month;

P166. To rest on the first day of Sukkot;

P167. To rest on the eighth day of that feast [Sukkot]
(now subsumed under a general rule to rest on festivals, as per *Hilkhot Shevitat Yom Tov* 1:2);

P191. To anoint a special priest (to address the soldiers) in a war
(now subsumed under the commandment that governs the conduct of obligatory and permissible wars, as per *Hilkhot Melakhim* 7:1);

P226. That the court shall execute [sentences of death] by decapitation with the sword;

P227. That the court shall execute [sentences of death] by strangulation;

P228. That the court shall execute [sentences of death] by burning with fire;

---

47. See comments to P68-69 in chapter 4.

P229. That the court shall execute [sentences of death] by stoning (now subsumed under a general rule mandating the great court to execute all those liable by various methods, as per *Hilkhot Sanhedrin* 14:1-2).

The above list totals sixteen redundant individuations. The overall number of claims is not reduced precisely by sixteen, since the *Halakhot* re-categorizes rather than eliminates some of them. These revised individuations present few conceptual difficulties. For the next group of failures to designate, however, I take a somewhat more speculative approach.

P41-51. Musafin (additional offerings)

In chapter 4, we saw that Maimonides listed separate positive commandments for each of the additional offerings (*musafin*) brought on festivals. I note there that Maimonides' individuation was not logically definitive; he could easily have followed Qayyara's scheme of categorizing all the *musafin* under one commandment.

Surprisingly, we find no mention anywhere in the *Halakhot* that any of the *musafin* are positive commandments. Maimonides opens *Hilkhot Temidin u-Musafin* with a characteristically bold statement: "It is a positive commandment to offer two lambs as burnt offerings every day. They are called daily offerings [*temidin*]." This designation corresponds to P39, the commandment to offer a burnt offering twice a day. One would expect a similar statement with respect to the additional offerings but none is found. The additional offering for the Sabbath (P41) is mentioned only in passing—tucked away in a mundane chapter that deals with the priestly method of arbitration. In a discussion of how the various Sabbath sacrifices are brought, Maimonides explains that the priests cast a special lot (*payis*) to choose which priest offers the sacrifices, and that the priest who brings the daily offering also brings the additional offering. In this understated way, Maimonides introduces us to the additional offering of the Sabbath (*Hilkhot Temidin u-Musafin* 4:9).

Section 7:1 discusses the *musaf* of the new moon, detailing the time of sacrifice, the number and types of animals to be offered and the types of offering (burnt offerings, sin offering). No mention is made of it being a *mitsvat 'aseh*. The Passover *musaf* (7:3), the *musaf* of Shavu'ot (8:1), the *musaf* of the first day of Tishre (9:1), the *musaf* of Yom Kippur (10:1), the *musaf* of Sukkot (10:3) and the *musaf* of Shemini 'Atseret (10:5) are all handled in similar fashions. Maimonides does not designate any of these as positive commandments.

In similar fashion, Maimonides describes the meal offering of barley (Omer) that is brought on the second day of Passover together with the *musaf* (7:3), as well as the loaves of bread that are brought with the *musafin* on Shavu'ot (8:1), without designating any of them as *mitsvot 'aseh*. Finally, Maimonides dedicates an entire treatise to the rituals of Yom Kippur, *Hilkhot Yom ha-Kippurim*, without once stating that the entire ritual of the day—considered one commandment in the *ShM* (P49)—is a *mitsvat 'aseh*.

To justify these extraordinary failures to designate, I propose that Maimonides came to see all the services and sacrifices of each day, bounded by the twice-daily burnt offering (*temidin*), as representing one overarching commandment. This position follows the manner in which Scripture introduces *temidin* and *musafin*: "Command the children of Israel, and say unto them: My food which is presented unto Me for offerings made by fire, of a sweet savour unto Me, shall ye observe to offer unto Me in its due season" (Num. 28:2). The verses continue to describe the *musafin* applicable to each festival, each with its own *temidin*. In each mention of *musafin*, the verses remind the officiating priests: "Ye shall offer these [the *musafin*] beside the burnt offering of the morning, which is for a continual burnt offering ... it shall be offered beside the continual burnt offering" (Num. 28:23-24).

In P49, the *ShM* offers an important clue in support of this hypothesis: the elements of a ritual that follow a certain order are to be considered as one commandment.[48] Maimonides writes: "We are commanded to

48. It should not be surprising that Maimonides does not make use of this individuating criterion in the *ShM* to define the *musafin*. As I discussed in chapter 4, no particular individuating criterion is logically compelling. When composing the *ShM*, Maimonides likely juggled a number of different criteria. We also recall that in the *ShM*, Maimonides needed to hit a fixed numerical target, and he may have subordinated criteria to this objective.

perform the service of the day, that is to say, *all the sacrifices and the confessions* ordained by Scripture for Yom Kippur, to atone for all our sins" (emphasis added). Immediately thereafter, he adds:

> The proof that the whole of this service in its totality constitutes only one commandment is found at the end of the fifth chapter of *Yoma*: "Concerning every ministration of the Day of Atonement mentioned in the prescribed order, if one service is done out of order before another one, it is as if it had not been done at all."

By analogy, since the order of the day's service is bound by the morning and evening *temidin*, it suffices for Maimonides to designate the *temidin* as a positive commandment and ignore the *musafin*.[49]

P169. Lulav

In *Hilkhot Shofar, Sukkah ve-Lulav*, Maimonides discusses at length the details of the taking of the four species (ch. 7-8). In 7:5, he states that the four species are "one *mitsvah*...and together [lit., "all of them"] they are called *mitsvat lulav*." In 7:13, when describing the obligation, Maimonides employs a rare passive voice: "*mitsvat lulav* [the combination of the four species] is to be taken [*le-hinatel*] on the first day of the festival only—anywhere and at any time, even if this happens to be a Sabbath." The use of the active verb "to take" (*li-tol*, as in the *SE*) would certainly have forced Maimonides into the standard introductory formula—"it is a positive commandment to take"—something I surmise he wished to avoid. The omission of the declarative statement is patently obvious. I contrast this formulation with the way he introduces the commandment to blow the shofar: "It is a positive commandment of the Torah to listen to the sound of the shofar on Rosh Hashanah" (*Hilkhot Shofar, Sukkah ve-Lulav* 1:1).

49. The correct order of sacrifices: *temidin* first, followed by *musafin* and other offerings, and *temidin* again to end the day's service. While the order of the *temidin* and *musafin* is stipulated, the service is valid even if the *musafin* are brought first (*Hilkhot Temidin u-Musafin* 8:20). Indeed, the fact that an improper order does not invalidate the sacrifices and that the lambs can be consecrated for either sacrifices supports my reasoning that these offerings essentially fulfill one purpose.

In Rule 11, Maimonides specifies that in situations where the Torah requires an assemblage of elements to fulfill a single goal, the commandment is defined as the unitary *telos* behind the individual activities. No single element of the assemblage is to be considered its own commandment. By way of example, Maimonides states that "we have been commanded to rejoice before the Lord on the first day of Tabernacles,[50] and then He explains that the rejoicing be by taking [unto the hand] certain objects." In other words, the "taking of the four kinds" is an aspect of the commandment to rejoice before the Lord. In short, instead of individuating *mitsvat lulav*, Maimonides may have thought it more appropriate to subsume the action under the commandment to rejoice on the festivals (P54).[51]

P113. Red Heifer

In the *ShM*, this commandment is formulated as follows: "To prepare the red heifer, so that [its ashes] will be available for what has to be done in order to remove impurity [contracted because of] a dead body." By defining these acts as "the law of the red heifer" (*din parah addumah*), the Heading to *Hilkhot Parah Addumah* avoids the active formulation of the *SE/ShM*. In the main text, the *Halakhot* also fails to designate the preparation of the red heifer as a positive commandment.

The claim of the *SE/ShM* appears to contradict Rule 10, which states that one does not count acts that are preparatory to a final goal. Since making the ashes from the red heifer is only a preparation to making water for sprinkling (*mey niddah*), Maimonides' logic of individuation should subsume this commandment under P108,

50. The verse (Lev. 23:40) commands one to take the four kinds on the first day and to rejoice before the Lord seven days. The Sages interpreted this to mean that the taking of the four kinds for seven days was obligatory only in the sanctuary; outside of the sanctuary, the taking of the four kinds was obligatory only for one day. At P169, Maimonides states: "we are commanded to take a palm-branch, and rejoice with it before the Lord seven days."

51. *JT Sukkah* 3:11 reports a dispute regarding the command to rejoice: does it refer to peace offerings (*shelamim*) or to *lulav*? See also *BT Sukkah* 43b, RaSHi, s. v. "*lulav nami*." According to one opinion, *mitsvat lulav* was a way to fulfill the commandment to rejoice during the festival.

which discusses the purifying and defiling properties of the waters of sprinkling. Furthermore, the text on which Maimonides based the positive commandment in the *SE/ShM*, namely "it shall be kept for the congregation of the children of Israel [for a water of sprinkling]" (Num. 19:9), becomes the proof text for a detail of the overall preparation of the ashes of the red heifer (*Hilkhot Parah* 3:4). One-third of the ashes was to be used to consecrate high priests who worked on other heifers, one-third was to be used to purify those who became defiled through contact with a corpse, and the final third was to be set aside. Maimonides grounds the disposition of the final third on the above proof text, although it seems that the practice of dividing the ashes into thirds is non-scriptural.[52]

While the surface meaning of the verse may have given Maimonides justification for individuating the preparation of the ashes as a commandment in the *SE/ShM*, the talmudic rabbis attached no independent meaning to the act. Instead, they used it to support a detail of the overall preparation.[53] As a result, the *Halakhot* reclassifies the verse "[the ashes] shall be kept for the congregation" from being an injunction deserving of individuation to being a detail of the greater law of the waters of sprinkling (P108). The Heading to *Hilkhot Parah Addumah* already moves in this direction by calling this rubric "the law of the red heifer" (*din parah addumah*), a law rather than a commandment. P108 itself is not individuated in the *Halakhot*, as I discussed earlier, because it is a law rather than a *mitsvat 'aseh*.

52. So noted Mizrahi in his super-commentary on RaSHi, Numbers 19:9. *MParah*, at the end of third chapter, discusses the tripartite division without adducing any proof-texts; *TParah* also discusses the tripartite division but adduces support only for the third that was set aside, from our verse (19:9). The lack of proof-texts for the other two-thirds strengthens the view that the verse at 19:9 was merely an *asmakhta*, and that the three-way division was only a rabbinic practice.

53. *Sifre Numbers*, *Hukkat* 124 (158), expounds on the words "shall be kept [*ve-haytah ... le-mishmeret*] for the congregation," teaching that the waters, while still not mixed with the ashes, can be disqualified by distraction. Maimonides adopted the legal ruling of the *Sifre* (see *Hilkhot Parah* 7:1) but resisted the far-fetched exegesis, preferring instead to treat this conclusion as a tradition (*u-devarim elu divre qabbalah hen*) rather than a reading of the verse.

Two commandments that go missing: P183 and P214

In this section, I examine two positive commandments that appear on the *SE*, *ShM*, and Headings lists, and yet are not discussed in the *Halakhot* at all. I offer some suggestions to explain why Maimonides may have reclassified these commandments.

P183. To give the Levites cities to dwell in

In the *SE*, Maimonides states that particular cities in the Land of Israel are to serve as cities of refuge. The *ShM* adds that the Levites are to receive these cities "because they received no portion in the land." This rationale for receiving cities of refuge as compensation for not receiving a portion of the land is stated explicitly in the Heading to *Hilkhot Shemitah ve-Yovel*: "That the entire tribe of Levites must not take possession in the Land of Israel; instead, they are granted cities that they may dwell in them in the form of gifts."[54]

One problem exists with individuating this commandment: the biblical directive to give the Levites these cities is only binding during the time of the conquest of the land, and under Rule 3, commandments that are not binding for all time must not be enumerated.[55] In the *Halakhot*, Maimonides seems to have come to this conclusion. He writes in *Hilkhot Shemitah ve-Yovel* 13:1: "Even though the tribe of Levi has no portion in the Land, *the Israelites were already commanded* [*kvar nitstavu*] to give them cities to dwell" (emphasis added). Besides the lack of a declarative statement, I also note the use of the past tense in the brief historical explanation. The giving of these cities of refuge clearly represents a one-time historical event; it does not

54. Note that Deuteronomy 18:1-3 prohibits the Levitical priests from owning territory in the Land of Israel but makes no mention of their being given cities of refuge. The compensatory aspect of the gift is Maimonides' original insight.

55. In an attempt to circumvent this problem, Hurewitz (in *Sefer ha-Mitsvot im Perush Yad ha-Levi,* ad loc.) speculates that cities other than the cities of refuge would also be given to the Levites as their population increased. I could find no indication of this in any of Maimonides' writings. Perla (in *Sefer ha-Mitsvot le-RaSaG*, vol. 3, 423) suggests that neither Ibn Gabirol nor Eliyahu ha-Zaqen counted this commandment because they did not see it as binding for all time.

constitute a commandment binding for all time. This explains the lack of a declarative statement.[56]

P214. That the newly married husband shall give happiness to his wife

The claim in the *ShM* is "that a bridegroom is to devote himself to his wife for a full year, in the course of which he is not to go on a journey,[57] or on a war abroad, or to undertake any obligation of a like nature." The commandment undergoes a substantial revision in the Headings to *Hilkhot Melakhim*, where it appears as follows: "That those who betroth a woman, or build a house, or plant a vineyard be happy with their acquisition a full year and they are returned from the war [front]."

To appreciate this change, one needs to look more closely at two scriptural sections: Deuteronomy 20:1-9, which discusses the anointed priest (P191), and Deuteronomy 24:5, which discusses the new husband's deferral from military service. In the anointed priest section, we are told that a man is sent back from the battlefront under any one of three circumstances: he has built a house but not yet dedicated it, he has planted a vineyard but not yet gleaned it, or he has

---

56. Maimonides' revisions do not always consist of erasures from the original *TaRYaG* list. At least once, Maimonides' revision consisted of adding a new positive commandment: in *Hilkhot Rotseah̲* 11:4, he writes: "Similarly, regarding any obstacle which is dangerous to life, there is a positive commandment (*mitsvat 'aseh*) to remove it and to be beware of it, and to be particularly careful in this matter, for Scripture says, *Take heed unto thyself and take care of thy life* [Deut. 4:9]." This commandment seems to stand independently of "Then thou shalt make a parapet for thy roof" (Deut. 22:8), enumerated in the SE/ *ShM* as P184 and presented in *Hilkhot Rotseah̲* 11:1. I hesitatingly suggest that the *ShM* could have accommodated this injunction under a broader and more figurative understanding of "Then thou shalt make a parapet for thy roof." In the current version, P184 is narrowly defined as an injunction related only to physical structures. It is not so clear, however, that Maimonides is adding a new positive commandment here. He may have intended to include the more general injunction of 11:4 under the positive commandment "Then thou shalt make a parapet for thy roof" already described in *Hilkhot Rotseah̲* 11:1. Supporting this position is the fact that he does not cite a proper proof text for the more general injunction—"take heed" and "take care" indicate negative commandments! While Babad (*Minhat Hinnukh, mitsvah* 546, para. 11) struggles to find Maimonides' source, he does believe that "take heed" is an independent commandment. For another possible exception, see *Hilkhot Avel* 2:6.

57. *MnT* reads here "not to go outside the city."

betrothed a woman but not yet married her. The text does not discuss any timeframe for the commandment. Deuteronomy 24:5, however, stipulates that a new husband is exempt from military service for one full year: "and [he] shall give happiness [instead of cheer; Heb. *ve-simah̲*] to his wife whom he hath taken."

In the *SE/ShM*, Maimonides treats these two verses separately. The commandment to send particular individuals home from the battlefront is subsumed under P191, and the commandment to exempt a new husband from military service to "give happiness to his wife" for one year becomes P214. In the Heading to *Hilkhot Melakhim*, however, Maimonides conflates these two sections. On the basis of tradition, he expands the one-year timeframe to include those who have built a house and/or have planted a vineyard, and he reiterates the three categories of returnees from the battlefront. This formulation is not entirely precise[58] and can probably be attributed to considerations of brevity and the strains of the conflation. The Heading is noncommittal with respect to the command to actively entertain the new wife; it is content with stating that he who betroths a woman, builds a house, or plants a vineyard "be happy with [his] acquisition a full year."

In the *Halakhot*, Maimonides introduces two correctives to the Heading's formula and omits any reference to a positive commandment to give happiness to the new wife. *Hilkhot Melakhim* 7:3 discusses the battlefield return of men in the three above-noted categories. Maimonides quotes verbatim the speech that Scripture puts in the mouth of the specially-anointed priest: a house that has "not [yet] been dedicated," a vineyard that has "not [yet] been eaten [lit., "not been treated as non-sacred"]," a woman whom a man has betrothed "but not married." The *halakhah* is silent about these men taking one year to rest and rejoice at home, as the Heading claims that they should do. On the contrary, when they leave the battlefield, they return to logistical support, providing water and food for the troops and repairing the roads (ibid. 7:9).

---

58. While it is true that the bridegroom (*arus*) is sent home from the battlefront, only married men are enjoined to make their wives happy for the first year (*ha-nose et arusato*) according to *M Sotah* 8:3. The *Halakhot* corrects this imprecision.

Halakhah 10 discusses the responsibilities of those who do not go out to the battlefield "at all and are not inconvenienced for anything in the world." This category includes one who, within the past year, has built a house and "dedicated it," one who has "married the woman whom he had betrothed," or one who "has eaten from his vineyard." Note that the one-year reprieve is not for he who has betrothed a woman, as stated in the Heading, but for "one who *married* the woman whom he had betrothed" (emphasis added). *Halakhah* 11 fleshes out this exemption, which runs for an entire year:

> He neither provides water and food [to the troops], nor does he repair the roads, guard the walls of the city or contribute to the pillars of the city, nor is he charged with any business at all anywhere, as it says, *He shall not go out in the host, neither shall he be charged with any business* [Deut. 24:5], [this teaches that he may] transgress on two prohibitions, regarding the needs of the city and regarding the needs of the troops [lit., "not the needs of the city and not the needs of the troops"].

This law, or rather this exemption, is stated in the negative, "and these men do not go out...they are not inconvenienced...he neither provides water," in keeping with the adduced proof-text. In 7:10-11, Maimonides only discusses the prohibition formulated as N311 in the *ShM* (N310 in the *SE*). Crucially, the positive commandment of "he shall give happiness to his wife" is never articulated.

There is another interesting difference between the *ShM* and the *Halakhot*. While the former clearly states, as part of the positive commandment (P214), that the new husband shall not undertake any type of obligation but "shall rejoice with his wife for a full year," the latter only orders that he shall be "free [*naqi*] to deal with his new house, his new wife and his new vineyard." No mention is made of him having to rejoice with his wife, even though the adduced proof text states quite clearly that "he shall be free at home one year and shall give happiness to his wife."[59] While it is assumed that he will rejoice with his wife, the obligation is not explicitly stated.

59. As noted, the proof text "he shall be free at home one year and shall give happiness to his wife" is adduced in 7:10. However, it is only cited to undergird the traditional exposition, which parses this text to show that the one-year exemption also applies to one who has bought a house and one who has eaten from a new vineyard.

The commandments obligating certain soldiers to return from the battlefront and the newly married man to give happiness to his wife underwent complex development and revision through Maimonides' various compositions. In the commandment's final iteration, the *Halakhot* has no reference or allusion to an obligation to make a newly married wife happy or any implication of impropriety in the new husband's traveling. I note that in the *ShM*, Maimonides' only support for the commandment is the scriptural proof text itself, which could be read merely as stating a fact: husbands make their new wives happy in their first year of marriage. Alternatively, "and [he] shall give happiness to his wife" could be read as granting the husband the opportunity to gratify his wife, rather than obligating him to do so. Regardless of the reason for Maimonides' reversal, it remains significant that P214 is not discussed in the *Halakhot*, neither as a *mitsvat 'aseh* nor as a non-scriptural obligation.[60]

These two discontinuities between the Headings and the *Halakhot* are further evidence that the Headings were not intended to represent a comprehensive or precise count of commandments. Rather, the Headings were simply an initial draft of an outline that helped Maimonides organize the enormous mass of material that was to be included in the *MT*.

In this chapter, I have offered explanations for 82 out of a total of 109 failures to designate. Fifty-three commandments are re-categorized

60. In a recent article, Henshke also concludes that the *Halakhot* omits the supposed commandment. Henshke ascribes the reason for this change to a number of technical factors, among them Alfasi's silence on the matter and the municipal tax exemptions stipulated in the Tosefta and in the Jerusalem Talmud. These exemptions imply that the one-year holiday cannot be for the purpose of giving happiness to the wife since the need to pay taxes would not force the new husband to absent himself from the home. As an aside, Henshke notes that the *ShM* follows Qayyara's lead in claiming that there is a positive commandment to give happiness to a new wife. Qayyara's entry reads: "to cheer a bride" (*le-sameah kallah*; Pq149). In note 26, Henshke explains that this interpretation of Qayyara's entry is not definitive, referring the reader to Perla and to Hildesheimer (*Haqdamat Sefer Halakhot Gedolot*, n. 387). Although Henshke acknowledges those who disagree with his interpretation of Pq149, he maintains his position. Alternately, it is possible that "*le-sameaẖ kallah*" indicates the rabbinic obligation imposed on the public to entertain a bride on her wedding day, supported by Qayyara's use of the word "bride" (*kallah*) instead of "his wife" (*ishto*) (Henshke, "Ve-Simaẖ et Ishto," 22-30).

as claims that did not meet the new definition of *mitsvat ʿaseh* as an unconditional obligation. Instead, they function as contingent obligations, procedures, and laws. Three of the commandments are reformulated in the *Halakhot* and can no longer be categorized as unconditional obligations. Twenty-seven other commandments are re-individuated in the *Halakhot*, subsumed under broader themes. Finally, in two instances, Maimonides reversed himself in the *Halakhot* by eliminating two commandment claims made in the earlier works.

To explain the remainder of the failures to designate, we shall need to examine Maimonides' approach to reading legal material in Scripture and the implications that it holds for categorizing the law according to its various biblical and rabbinic sources.

CHAPTER VII

PESHATEH DI-QERA[*]

In the preceding chapters, we saw how Maimonides built his *TaRYaG* enumeration following a systematic and original set of rules, which we called rules of individuation (Rules 4, 6-7, and 9-14). While these rules are sensible and do not appear to violate rabbinic tenets, they do not always accord with talmudic notions of what constitutes a *mitsvah*. One might say that for the most part, these rules run *parallel* to theories of rabbinic jurisprudence. These rules did generate disagreement among other enumerators. However, such disagreement should not be entirely unexpected, since one can always individuate commandments in a somewhat different manner, just as one can formulate different purposes and rationales for commandments.

Rules 1, 2, and 3, the rules of identification, were far more controversial, however: they challenged a nearly unanimous geonic consensus. I paraphrase these rules here for clarity:

Rule 1: It is not proper to enumerate commandments resting only on rabbinic authority.

Rule 2: It is not proper to enumerate every exegetical derivation known through one of the thirteen *middot* by which the Torah is expounded or through the rule of inclusion (*ribbuy*).[1]

---

* Please see Postscript on page 337.

1. My own translation. The inference is that *some* derivations may be included. In *Responsa*, ed. Blau, no. 355, 631-633, Maimonides alludes to "three or four" such instances. Chavel's translation leaves no room for exceptions: "We are not to include in this enumeration [laws] derived from Scripture by *any* of the thirteen exegetical principles by which the Torah is expounded, or by [the principle of] inclusion" (emphasis added). Neither Nahmanides nor the other translations interpret this rule so absolutely.

Rule 3: It is not proper to enumerate commandments that are not binding for all time.

Rule 1 eliminates rabbinic laws, since they postdate the giving of the written law at Sinai. Conceptually, this rule did not present a major challenge to rabbinic understanding. The Talmud was very aware of the difference in status and force between Torah law and rabbinic law,[2] despite the occasional self-serving admonitions regarding the *gravitas* of rabbinic law.[3] Rule 3 eliminated temporal commandments, i.e. commandments given for specific occasions, as they were generally associated with the Israelites' sojourn through the wilderness. Geonim are found on both sides of the divide regarding the counting of temporal commandments.[4]

Rule 2, on the other hand, shook the very grounds of rabbinic tradition. Traditionally, legislation derived from scribal hermeneutics was seen as equivalent to what the Torah explicitly orders. Maimonides

2. For example, doubts concerning the applicability of a particular rabbinic enactment were treated leniently, favoring the easier practice. The opposite was true with regard to scriptural law. See e.g. *BT Betsah* 3b.

3. Such rare statements of rabbinic law's superiority over biblical law can be seen in *BT 'Eruvin* 21b: "Raba made the following exposition: What is the purport of the Scriptural text: *And, furthermore my son, be admonished: Of making many books* etc.? My son, be more careful in [the observance of] the words of the Scribes than in the words of the Torah, for in the laws of the Torah there are positive and negative precepts; but, as to the laws of the Scribes, whoever transgresses any of the enactments of the Scribes incurs the penalty of death. In case you should object: If they are of real value why were they not recorded [in the Torah]? Scripture stated: *Of making many books there is no end.*" See also Song of Songs Rabbah 1:2, s. v. "*ki tovim dodekhah mi-yayin*": "[It was said in the name of the] friends of Rabbi Yohanan: the words of the Scribes are more desirable than the words of the Torah."

4. Ibn Balaam argues that temporal commandments should not be included in the *TaRYaG*. According to Ibn Balaam, H̲efets did count temporal commandments (as we discussed in chapter 1). Ibn Ezra sharply questions the value of enumerating temporal commandments, although some of the commandments that he lists as examples of temporal commandments are surprising and were not considered as such by Maimonides (and others). See Ibn Ezra, *Yesod Mora, sha'ar* 2, para. 7, 95-96, editors' notes. Though Maimonides accuses Qayyara of counting temporal commandments, Nahmanides (*Hasagot*, 106) defends Qayyara's position by redefining those commandments as not of a temporal nature. His apology, however, runs into some difficulties when he tries to explain away *terumat ha-mekhes* (dues offered from the spoils of war) and *tah̲anunim* (special pleadings in time of anguish), which Qayyara included in his *parashiyyot*.

distinguishes sharply between interpretations of the scriptural text (including divinely revealed interpretations) and legal inferences or derivations from the text.[5] Borrowing terms from Arabic jurisprudence, Maimonides called the former "roots" (Arab., *usul*) and the latter "branches" (Arab., *furu'*), arguing that hermeneutically-derived laws should not be counted because they were mere "branches from the root."[6] In the more familiar rabbinic terms, the "roots" are called *de-oraita* laws (the Aramaic word for Torah) and the branches *divre sofrim* laws (the words of the scribes). What exactly constitutes *de-oraita* and *divre sofrim* laws and how they are to be identified is the subject of most of this chapter.

Maimonides' rule was so foreign to the rabbinic mindset that it managed to mislead even one of his sharpest critics. Daniel ha-Bavli could not imagine that Maimonides intended to disqualify hermeneutic derivations from the category of *de-oraita*. He interprets Maimonides as suggesting that hermeneutic derivations should only be counted as *mitsvot 'aseh* if the rabbis had designated them as coming from the Torah, but that the derivations should still be considered *de-oraita*, even without such designation.[7]

Unlike Daniel ha-Bavli, Nahmanides fully understands this rule—and criticizes it harshly. In multiple examples, Nahmanides argues that talmudic tradition does not draw such a demarcation and that it treats hermeneutic derivations with the same deference and force as the explicit injunctions of the Torah. Nahmanides ends his critique of Rule 2 with a fulminating indictment:

> [F]or this book of the master, its content is *delightful, full of love* [based on Song 5:16] except for this principle, which uproots great mountains of the Talmud and throws down fortified walls of the Gemara. For the students of the Gemara, this notion is evil and bitter. Let it be forgotten and not said.

---

5. For a good discussion of this distinction, see Halbertal, "Maimonides' Book of Commandments," 457-480.
6. *ShM*, Rule 2, 56.
7. Abraham Maimonides, "Teshuvot Rabbenu Abraham ben ha-RaMBaM," question 1, 541. Perla is correct to say that Daniel ha-Bavli anticipates Duran in this respect. See below.

This is not the place to review the complexities and ramifications of Maimonides' position, and how it can be reconciled with the numerous talmudic passages that contradict it. Maimonides' apologists and interlocutors explore these concerns in their commentaries to the *ShM*. I do believe, however, that the full implications of this powerful salvo have not been totally appreciated. In this chapter, I will argue that reasonable explanations can be found for a number of failures to designate commandments as *mitsvot 'aseh* if one follows Rule 2 to its ultimate and radical conclusions.

RULE 2 AND THE BROAD MEANING OF *DIVRE SOFRIM*

With its circuitous wording—"it is not proper to enumerate *every* exegetical derivation" (emphasis added)—Rule 2 allows an opening for some rabbinically derived laws to enter the scripturally based count. In addressing these exceptions at the outset of the discussion of this rule, Maimonides argues that certain hermeneutically derived laws only *appear* to be derived rabbinically; in such cases, the hermeneutic derivation represents an act of discovery rather than of creation. These laws, Maimonides claims, are known to have originated at Sinai, a fact communicated by the tradition's tradents (transmitters), who label the derivations "itself Torah" (*guf torah*) or "from the Torah" (*mi-de-oraita*). Thus he permits the enumeration of some commandments whose derivation appears to stem from the thirteen hermeneutic rules.

Later in his analysis, Maimonides discusses another sort of scriptural analysis employed in identifying commandments, showing where such analysis can lead to error. In his words:

> Their [i.e. Qayyara and his followers'] lack of knowledge has already brought them to this more serious mistake: If they found [in the Talmud] an interpretation of a certain verse, the interpretation requiring the performance or the prohibition of a certain act—duties which are no doubt of rabbinic authority—they count them among the commandments, even though the plain meaning of the verse [*peshateh di-qera*] indicates in no way any of these things. This is contrary to the principle which [the Sages] of blessed memory, teach us: "A scriptural verse never loses its literal sense" [*ein miqra yotse mi-yede peshuto*]. It is also contrary to the process of

> reasoning throughout the Talmud, as is evidenced from the fact that when the Sages speak of a verse from which many topics are derived by way of interpretation and various proofs—they ask [in conclusion]: "But what is the verse itself about [*gufe di-qera be-mai qa-medabber*]?"
>
> These [authors], however, depending as they do upon baseless comparisons, count among the Positive Commandments visiting the sick, consoling mourners, and the burying of the dead—all because of the following interpretation mentioned in connection with His words, exalted be He: *And thou shalt show them the way wherein they must walk, and the deeds they must do* [Exod. 18:20]—*the way* refers to deeds of loving kindness; *they must walk* refers to visiting the sick; *wherein* has reference to the burying of the dead; *and the deeds*, this refers to the laws; *they must do*, this has reference to more than the strict requirement of the law. On the basis of this text, these authors thought that each and every duty mentioned constituted a commandment in itself, but they were unaware that all these and similar duties are embraced within the terms of one of the Commandments explicitly stated in the Torah, as contained in His words, exalted be He, *And thou shalt love thy neighbour as thyself.*[8]

Maimonides attacks his geonic predecessors for grounding commandments on a type of reading that bore little relation to the true import of the text, a sort of playful exegesis. Maimonides sets off *gufe di-qera* ("the text itself") from this type of playful exegesis where "many topics are derived by way of interpretation and various proofs." Although he does not use the term here, I infer that he considered the scriptural text underlying this type of exposition to be no more than a mnemonic device, a type of para-textual support that the rabbis called an *asmakhta* (discussed below).

A brief digression to explain this critique: In his "Introduction to the Mishnah," in discussing laws transmitted through tradition without a difference of opinion, Maimonides writes: "It is possible for us to derive these explanations from the wisdom of the Torah given to us, through one of the types of deductive reasoning [Arab. *Qyas*, Heb. *heqesh*, referring to the 13 hermeneutic rules] or through supports [*asmakhtot*], or from allusions or suggestions that may be found in the

8. *ShM*, 53-55.

scriptural text."[9] This second type of textual "supports" comes in two forms. Some provide a weak but nonetheless supportive basis for an exegesis, while others provide nothing but a memory hook, a playful connection to the text that does not stand up to analysis. Maimonides writes that the Talmud calls the latter kind of proof a "mere support" (*asmakhta be-'alma*). As he puts it, these "mere supports" are a literary device to help one "observe and remember" the law in question: "they are not the meaning intended by the text." The text serves as a mnemonic device, rather than as a genuine proof text. For Maimonides, an important difference between the oral traditions that are textually-based (those using substantive supports, allusions, and suggestions) and those mnemonically linked to a text is that only the latter type of support can serve as justification for a *halakhah le-Moshe mi-Sinai.* Indeed, the term *halakhot le-Moshe mi-Sinai* refers to oral traditions that enjoy no substantive textual grounding.[10]

9. *Haqdamot Ha-Rambam la-Mishnah*, ed. Shailat, 39.

10. This is not to say that every *halakhah le-Moshe mi-Sinai* is linked to a text, even if only mnemonically; some are not linked to any text. While on the subject of *asmakhtot*, I note that Jay Harris makes an observation relevant to our later discussion. By claiming that in the Talmud, "an *asmakhta* represents an exegesis marshaled in support of a rabbinic law," Harris may be explicating Maimonides' rationale for believing that para-textual or weak textual indications underlying traditions indicate rabbinic or scribal laws (*divre sofrim* legislation). Some caution is in order, however, since we do not know exactly to what type of *asmakhtot* Harris (and the Talmud) was referring: the more substantive textual ones, the mnemonic ones, or both (see Harris, *How Do We Know This?* 78). Medieval rabbinic authorities frequently consider certain exegeses *asmakhtot*, even without specific talmudic statements to that effect, to support their contentions that the particular law was rabbinic. A good example can be found in Nahmanides' *Hasagot* to P5. After citing a number of talmudic passages supporting the rabbinic origin of prayer, Nahmanides questions the nature of Maimonides' midrashic exegesis that supports his commandment claim, suggesting that it is merely an *asmakhta*, "and thus a rabbinic ordinance. In Maimonides' defense, at least one commentator (de Leon, "Megillat Esther," 211) notes that characterizing the nature of a midrash is a difficult enterprise and that one can infer that a given midrash stems from a tradition from Sinai, as long as it is not contradicted by the final authority of the Talmud. According to such commentators, the determination that a certain exegesis is an *asmakhta* is based on factors extraneous to the midrash itself, such as its agreement with talmudic conclusions, rather than on the ability of the midrash to correctly convey the meaning of the biblical text. In general, Nahmanides reads *midreshe halakhah* as *asmakhtot* if they do not agree with talmudic exegesis. This has more to do with his epistemological views than with his reading strategies. For a similar difference, see *Hasagot* to P36, N353.

Maimonides considered counting commandments based on *asmakhtot* to be an even graver error than counting commandments that were derived via the use of the 13 hermeneutic rules (analogical derivations), for he writes:

> Now if they had counted matters which are even clearer than that [*asmakhtot*], and more conceivable that they be enumerated [among the commandments]—these being, namely, the laws which are derived through one of the Thirteen [Exegetical] Principles by which the Torah is expounded—the number of the commandments would then reach many thousands!

The inference is that *asmakhtot* are even further removed from genuinely representing the biblical text than hermeneutic derivations.

Implicit in Maimonides' critique of his geonic predecessors is that, for him, only philologically grounded readings, what he calls the "plain readings of the verse," can yield the scriptural laws that he enumerates. We shall explore this category in the next section. Analogical derivations and *asmakhtot*, however, only yield non-scriptural laws, commandments that Maimonides would designate as *mitsvot mi-divre sofrim*. With regard to the last two categories, Maimonides writes, more generally: "Whatever they did not explicitly hear at Sinai is considered as coming from the 'words of the scribes' [*mi-divre sofrim*]."

In contrast, Maimonides seems to characterize interpretations on the basis of their internal exegetical logic. That is, if the interpretation stems from the plain sense of the text, it can be considered a genuine *derashah*; otherwise, it is considered an allusion or an intimation. For the purpose of this determination, it mattered little if the source of the interpretation was one of the *midreshe halakah* or the Talmud. For general criteria for the divergence of views in the matter of *asmakhta*, see Hurewitz, *Sefer ha-Mitsvot im Perush Yad ha-Levi*, comments to Rule 2. For a brief but excellent discussion on *asmakhtot* and their place in rabbinic exegesis, see Elon, *Jewish Law*, 300-305. Quoting Guttmann's comprehensive study on *asmakhtot*, Elon concludes that "the term *asmakhta* does not imply ... that the law in question cannot be connected with the verse in a logical and rational manner. It indicates rather that the halakhic authorities knew that the creative source of the particular law was not interpretation but one of the other legal sources, such as tradition or legislation." As a fitting conclusion to this complex issue of *asmakhtot*, I quote a wise remark made by Harris with which I wholeheartedly agree: "No matter what is said here, there will be many scholars, possessing far greater expertise than I, who will disagree. Stepping into this issue is to step into a raging controversy" (47).

Scholars are divided on how to understand the status of *mitsvot mi-divre sofrim* in Maimonides' jurisprudence. It should be noted that in the *ShM*, Maimonides refers to these laws as *de-rabbanan*, a technical term that represents rabbinic laws in talmudic literature, standing in opposition to *de-oraita* laws. According to this interpretation, *mitsvot mi-divre sofrim* are rabbinic in status. Others have argued that Maimonides had designated these laws as *de-rabbanan* not because of their legal status, but simply because they represent the product of rabbinic exegetical activity. Therefore, these commandments could still command a scriptural status of sorts.[11] No consensus has emerged among scholars.[12] The maximalist interpretation, espoused by Nahmanides, maintains that Maimonides effectively gives *divre sofrim* legislation a status equivalent to rabbinic enactments. At the other extreme, scholars such as Simeon b. Tsemah̲ Duran take the view that while Maimonides excludes hermeneutically derived *divre sofrim* from his enumeration, he agrees that they all carry the weight of Torah law.[13]

As I noted earlier, Maimonides stipulates that whatever was not heard explicitly on Sinai is considered as coming from the "words of the scribes" (*mi-divre sofrim*). This includes rabbinic decrees and ordinances[14] and oral

---

11. The term "*divre sofrim*" can refer to two distinct types of rabbinic laws. In my analysis, I use the term to refer only to the type of legislation deeply rooted in scriptural law, in the spirit of "*'iqqaro min ha-torah ve-shiuro mi-divre sofrim*" ("its essence is from the Torah and its boundaries are from the scribes"). See Maimonides' comments to *M Kelim* 17:12. There are other cases where the term "*divre sofrim*" refers to pure rabbinic laws, like ordinances. The status of the latter legislation is never in doubt: it is always rabbinic. When I discuss *mitsvot mi-divre sofrim*, I refer to the former category, "*'iqqaro min ha-torah ve-shiuro mi-divre sofrim.*" See below, note 13.
12. See Neubauer, *Ha-RaMBaM al Divre Sofrim*, for an extensive survey.
13. Duran, *Zohar ha-Raqia*, 11. This is also the position of Daniel ha-Bavli (as we have seen) as well as that of the two most prominent commentators on the *MT*, Joseph Karo and Vidal di Tolosa, who believed that *divre sofrim* enjoyed the status of scriptural law; see their comments to *Hilkhot Ishut*, 1:2. As I have noted, modern scholars have also not reached a consensus. Levinger (*Darkhe ha-Mahshavah*, 46-50) concludes with a fair degree of confidence that *mitsvot mi-divre sofrim* should be considered of rabbinic force and Henshke argues strenuously for this view (Henshke, "Le-Havhanat ha-RaMBaM bein de-Oraita le-de-Rabbanan, " 205n2). Contrarily, Shailat concludes that they have scriptural force (*Iggerot ha-RaMBaM*, ed. Shailat, vol. 2, 451-452). See also, more recently, Rabinovitch, "Al Divre Sofrim she-Toqfam de-Oraita," 93-111.
14. This is, in fact, the typical usage of the term in the Mishnah. See, for example, *M Teharot* 4:7, 11 and *M Yadayim* 3:2, where *divre sofrim* refer to rabbinic ordinances. See also note 11 above.

traditions,[15] some of which are lightly attached to verses by hints and allusions, and some of which bear no explicit connections to the text, such as *halakhot le-Moshe mi-Sinai*. It should be noted that this latter group of laws carry special significance in the rabbinic tradition because they were viewed as laws given orally to Moses at Sinai. Many jurists conferred on them a special status, equal in force to scriptural law.

Confirming what Maimonides says in the *ShM*, we find the following statement in his commentary (*PhM*) to *M Miqva'ot* 6:7:

> I already explained that this expression ["measurements are *mi-divre sofrim*"] does not contradict what they said, namely, that measurements are a *halakhah le-Moshe mi-Sinai*, because everything that is not explicitly stated in Scripture is called "the words of scribes" [*divre sofrim*].[16]

And again in *PhM*, *M Kelim* 17:12:

> Don't let their dictum "measures are from the words of the scribes" [*shiurim mi-divre sofrim*] confuse you when you consider their principle that all measures are *halakhah le-Moshe mi-Sinai*, because in effect anything that is not explicitly stated in Scripture is called *mi-divre sofrim*, even things that are *halakhah le-Moshe mi-Sinai*. When they said *mi-divre sofrim,* they meant to say that the matter is a tradition from the scribes, like all explanations and authoritative *halakhot* from Moses, or the "reforms of the scribes" (*tiqqun sofrim*), like all enactments and ordinances. Remember this.[17]

Maimonides' views with respect to *halakhah le-Moshe mi-Sinai* also engendered a great deal of controversy—a controversy second only to

---

15. See note 16 below.
16. Some caution is in order, however. Henshke (in "Le-Havhanat ha-RaMBaM", 205n2) has suggested that in the *PhM*, Maimonides may have been referring to the way the Mishnah and Talmud understood that term, not necessarily to the way he himself understood it.
17. The word "explanations" is puzzling in this context, because Maimonides often interprets scriptural texts with the aid of these explanations and yet considers them *de-oraita*. In the *ShM*, he calls these traditional explanations *perushim mequbbalim*, and in the *Halakhot* he refers to these interpretations with the phrase "as it was learned from tradition" (*lamdu mi-pi ha-shemu'ah*). For an example, see P198 and the corresponding *Hilkhot Malveh ve-Loveh* 5:1. Also see my discussion of the phrase *mi-pi ha-shemu'ah* later in the chapter.

the one aroused by his theory on analogically derived commandments. Nahmanides seems to have understood Maimonides as maintaining that *halakhot le-Moshe mi-Sinai* are *mitsvot mi-divre sofrim*. Since Nahmanides held that, in Maimonides' legal system, *mitsvot mi-divre sofrim* were of rabbinic force only, then *halakhot le-Moshe mi-Sinai* would equally have the legal status of rabbinic laws.[18]

Maimonides uses a number of terms in addition to *halakhah le-Moshe mi-Sinai* to describe the variety of oral traditions, terms such as *mi-pi ha-qabbalah*, *halakhah mi-pi ha-qabbalah*, *mi-pi ha-shemu'ah*, and *halakhah mi-pi ha-shemu'ah*. While the terms "*qabbalah*" and "*shemu'ah*" stand loosely for "reception" and "teaching," Maimonides never defines these terms. Their approximate meanings can only be inferred from the context in which they are found. It should be noted that previous scholars' attempts to achieve some semantic precision have not been extremely successful. With this caveat, we must nonetheless attempt to define these terms before we can categorize these traditions as *de-oraita* or as *divre sofrim*. In general, and as a good approximation, we can say that Maimonides categorizes the oral traditions that elucidate how we read certain scriptural words, phrases, or passages as *de-oraita*, while scribal traditions that innovate laws, such as hermeneutical derivations or *halakhot le-Moshe mi-Sinai*, he categorizes as *divre sofrim*. In the next section, I examine the tools Maimonides uses to determine what can be categorized as scriptural law.

"*EIN MIQRA YOTSE MI-YEDE PESHUTO*": A SCRIPTURAL VERSE NEVER LOSES ITS *PESHAT* SENSE

We saw earlier that Maimonides approvingly cites the talmudic principle: "A scriptural verse never loses its literal sense" (*ein miqra yotse mi-yede peshuto*). What is the meaning of the term *peshat*, and how does Maimonides use it?

---

18. Nahmanides disagrees forcefully with that categorization. Nahmanides, *Hasagot* to Rule 2, 78. He bases his understanding of Maimonides' position on a responsum written to Pinhas ha-Dayan (*Responsa*, ed. Blau, no. 355, pp. 631-632). For an inquiry into the status of *halakhah le-Moshe mi-Sinai* in Maimonides' legal system, see Levinger, *Darkhe ha-Mahshavah*, 50-65 and 190-205; Kahana, *Heqer ve-'Iyyun*, 9-18; and Henshke, "Le-Yesode Tefisat ha-Halakhah shel ha-RaMBaM," 144.

The Aramaic *peshateh* and the Hebrew *peshuto* derive from the same root, *p.sh.t*. In biblical Hebrew, this root means "to strip off" or "to flatten" a garment, later evolving to encompass "extend" and "stretch out." Over time, *peshat* became an exegetical term understood as representing the plain or literal sense; it is often contrasted with the term *derash*, representing fanciful homiletics.

In recent years, scholars have examined the role of this term in talmudic literature. In his classic study on *peshat* in talmudic literature, Raphael Loewe notes that the word *peshat* means different things to different amoraim. In at least one instance (attributed to the third-century amora Rava), the expression "*ein miqra yotse mi-yede peshuto*" means "the natural and explicit meaning of the text, at any rate within the context of this formula."[19] He concludes that, on the whole, *peshat* does not represent a particular way of reading a text; it rather seems to be shorthand for saying that a given reading has achieved authoritative status.[20]

In another classic study of exegetical terms, M. Gertner finds that in the Talmud, the Hebrew form of the noun (*peshut*) occurs only in the phrase "*ein miqra yotse mi-yede peshuto*," and that phrase, only three times. Each time, the term correlates with the idea that "the ordinary sense of the phrase in question should not be ignored." Gertner concludes that the Hebrew noun *peshut* represents "the simple straightforward explanation, i.e. 'unfolding' of the text (explanation)."[21] He emphasizes that the ordinary meaning should not be confused with an extreme literal interpretation; sometimes, an allegorical interpretation better reflects context than an overly literalist reading. He finds, however, that while the Aramaic term *peshat* has the same dictionary meaning as Hebrew *peshut*, it is not used in the same way. Studying the context in which *peshateh di-qera* appears, Gertner concludes that this term designates a midrashic interpretation; rather than "simple" or "plain," the Aramaic term *peshat* meant "widespread" and "widely accepted" by custom or tradition. This parallels Loewe's conclusion.

19. Loewe, "The 'Plain' Meaning of Scripture in Early Jewish Exegesis," 165.
20. Ibid., 181-182.
21. Gertner, "Terms of Scriptural Interpretation," 20.

Sarah Kamin is not satisfied with the conclusions of the scholarly studies that she reviews, including Loewe's and Gertner's. Instead, she suggests that the terms *peshateh di-qera* and *peshuto shel miqra* parallel the terms "verse" or "text"; they are simply another way of referring to the words of the text under consideration. In contrast, the question "in what is it written?" (*be-mai ketiv*) seeks to find the literal meaning of the text. Since the terms *peshateh di-qera* and *peshuto shel miqra* do not imply a specific method of interpretation, but rather the object of interpretation, the responses to queries with these terms can accommodate any number of interpretations, including literary and homiletic ones. While we can diagram their functional use in a sentence, these terms derived from the root *peshat* do not reflect a well-defined concept that fits into a discernable hermeneutic category.[22]

A few years after Kamin's work, David Weiss Halivni made a valiant attempt to find a uniform meaning for terms related to *peshat* throughout the rabbinic corpus. Examining the different iterations of *peshuto* and *peshateh*, he concludes, contra Gertner, that there is no semantic distinction between the Hebrew and the Aramaic nouns. Instead, he concludes that the word *peshat* continually yields a uniform meaning of "extension, continuation, and derivatively, context."[23]

Weiss Halivni resorts to a great deal of tortured logic (*pilpul*) to prove his point. He works under the assumption that the principle of contextual reading has always been acknowledged and rejects any suggestion that some talmudic rabbis did not use this reading strategy, even when the passage implies otherwise.[24] Nevertheless, Weiss Halivni

---

22. She does acknowledge that, with respect to the expression "*ein miqra yotse mi-yede peshuto,*" the talmudic exegetes were referring to a literal reading. Kamin, *RaSHi's Exegetical Categorization in Respect to the Distinction Between Peshat and Derash*, 31-48.

23. Weiss Halivni, *Peshat and Derash*, 54.

24. For example, "*ein miqra yotse mi-yede peshuto*" in *BT Shabbat* 63a means that the verse must also have a simple, plain meaning. There is no reason for one to read the exchange between Mar bar R. Huna and R. Kahana in any other manner. Weiss Halivni creates a difficulty—for which he then has to offer a complicated and stretched answer—by saying that "it is extremely unlikely that R. Kahana had not heard of the many *derashot* where biblical verses (or words) were metaphorically or allegorically exposited while at the same time retained their simple meaning" (59). In other words, he creates a difficulty by assuming that Rav Kahana must have known that texts can be read for their plain sense. But it is quite clear that R. Kahana did not know that verses can be

acknowledges in the end that the dictum "no text can be deprived of its context" only emerges clearly by the third century, and that even by then it was not universally accepted. He concludes: "the dictum was either not too well known or not honored by all scholars."[25] I note that if the formal rabbinic exegetical tool of *peshat* was neither uniformly understood nor even widely known, one gathers that it could not have played a major role in rabbinic interpretation. This theory is corroborated by the relatively sporadic appearance of terms derived from *peshat* in the talmudic and midrashic literature.

None of the proposed definitions for the talmudic usage of the term *peshat* that I reviewed—plain or literal sense, straightforward sense, or contextual sense—seem to fit the totality of the talmudic data consistently, however sparse the data may be. I thus return to Kamin's assessment that *peshat* simply refers to the words of the text in their context, to the object of the inquiry rather than to a method of interpretation. While this understanding seems to be the best objective interpretation of how the term was used in the Talmud, it is not necessarily the way that medieval scholars, including Maimonides, understood the term.

Pre-twelfth-century Andalusian scholars likely understood the term *peshat* as Weiss Halivni explicated it: the sense of a word or phrase in its context. These scholars, which include the grammarians Menaḫem b. Saruq, Hayyuj, and Ibn Janaḫ, as well as the exegetes Moses b. Chiquitilla, Judah Ibn Balaam, and Abraham ibn Ezra, adopt this contextual method and marry it with grammatical and philological insights. As M. Cohen has noted: "The use of the term *peshat* in the medieval tradition as the basis of the philological-contextual method ... represents an appropriation of talmudic terminology, recast to support an essentially novel exegetical approach."[26] Maimonides appears to

interpreted according to their plain sense, as he says: "I was eighteen years old and I had already studied the entire Talmud, *yet I did not know that a text cannot be deprived of its peshat*" (emphasis added). It is only after the exchange with Mar bar Rav Huna that he was able to acknowledge this fact.

25. Weiss Halivni, *Peshat and Derash*, 63.

26. A few months after I had completed my dissertation, Mordechai Z. Cohen presented a paper on Maimonides' hermeneutics at the 2008 Association of Jewish Studies

have drawn from this rich exegetical heritage. It is only within this Andalusian context that one can understand his sharp criticism of his adversaries' exegetical methods as well as his appeal to follow the dictates of *peshat*:

> This is contrary to the principle which [the Sages] of blessed memory, teach us: "A scriptural verse never loses its literal sense" [*ein miqra yotse mi-yede peshuto*]. It is also contrary to the process of reasoning throughout the Talmud.

Despite his protestation that we find this "reasoning throughout the Talmud," Maimonides reads Scripture with a method that was relatively foreign to the early amoraic rabbis. His reading strategy, which he terms *peshateh di-qera*, is an adaptation of the Andalusian theory of *peshat*. In the next section, I explore Maimonides' particular understanding of this category of terms.[27]

MAIMONIDES' UNDERSTANDING OF *PESHATEH DI-QERA*

From the way Maimonides groups them together in Rule 2, *peshateh di-qera* and *gufe di-qera* appear to be interchangeable terms. Moreover, Maimonides references the hermeneutic *peshateh di-qera* in the explication of Rule 8[28] and *gufe di-qera* in the explication to N45, both times to justify his exhortation against reading the verse "That he be

convention. The paper discussed many of the same issues that I discuss in this chapter. At my request, he was very gracious and sent me a much longer version of this presentation in an 83-page draft (dated December 13, 2008) titled "A Talmudist's Halakhic Hermeneutics: Maimonides on 'Scripture Does not Leave the Hand of its *Peshat*.'" As he notes in the draft: "This essay is one part of a series of studies of mine ...that aim to reveal and assess Maimonides' contributions to the so-called "*peshat* school" of Jewish exegesis. This subject will be addressed comprehensively in my forthcoming monograph, *Opening the Gates of Interpretation: Maimonides' Biblical Exegesis in Light of His Geonic-Andalusian Heritage and Muslim Milieu*" (5). Cohen's mastery of the subject, in both breadth and depth, is quite impressive. To my great pleasure and relief, I found that we arrived at essentially the same conclusion.

27. On the Andalusian *peshat* school, see Cohen, "The Best of Poetry," 15-57, and literature cited there.

28. Rule 8 states: "A mere negative statement excluding a particular case from the scope of a commandment is not to be included among the negative commandments."

not [*ve-lo*] as Korah and as his company" (Num. 17:5) as a prohibition (despite the presence of the negative particle *lo*), thus further demonstrating that these two hermeneutical strategies are identical.

Since Maimonides never explains what he means by *peshateh di-qera/gufe di-qera*, one must deduce the terms' meaning by examining how they are used throughout the *ShM*. I begin by noting that words described by these terms must convey a discrete idea. As a counterexample, the midrashic exposition on the verse "And thou shalt show them the way wherein they must walk, and the deeds they must do" (Exod. 18:20), cited in the discussion of Rule 2, states:

> *The way,* refers to deeds of loving kindness; *they must walk,* refers to visiting the sick; *wherein,* has reference to the burying of the dead; *and the deeds,* this refers to the laws; *they must do,* this has reference to more than the strict requirement of the law.

Maimonides describes this as an exposition that does not satisfy the principle of *peshateh di-qera*. The referenced words and phrases do not convey the specific and discrete ideas that the midrash infers.

A more subtle deviation from *peshateh di-qera* is noted in P94. While the underlying text does provide support for the exegesis, the text is unnaturally split to accommodate additional legal implications. In *BT Rosh Hashanah* 6a, the Sages parse the verse "That which is gone out of thy lips thou shalt observe and do" (Deut. 23:24) as follows: "*That which is gone out of thy lips*: this is an affirmative precept. *Thou shalt observe*: this is a negative precept. *And do*: this is an injunction to the Bet Din to make thee do." Maimonides comments:

> Although the Sages have minutely analyzed this verse, and explained each word in it separately, the general purport of all that they say amounts to this: that it is a positive commandment to fulfill any obligation which a man has taken upon himself.

After quoting the midrash, he adds:

> Now you know that no [commandment] can be derived from the mere words *That which is gone out of thy lips* and hence the sense of it must be

> what I have mentioned as the plain meaning of Scripture [*peshateh di-qera*], namely that a man is obliged to carry out whatever his lips have uttered.

In other words, the text must literally unfold its meaning, as in the original definition of the term *peshat*.

Context helps us understand the plain sense of the text. The rabbis derive a prohibition to eat and/or drink filthy things from the words "Ye shall not make yourselves detestable" in the verse "Ye shall not make yourselves detestable with any swarming thing that swarmeth" (Lev.11:43). Maimonides notes, however, in N179, that "one is not liable to whipping for [these violations] since the plain sense of the text [*peshateh di-qera*] refers solely to creeping things."[29]

Much the same can be understood from what he says in N45, the admonition against self-mutilation. In support of the claim, Maimonides cites the verse "ye shall not cut yourselves [*lo titgodedu*], nor make any baldness between your eyes for the dead" (Deut. 14:1). He continues by saying that the Sages (*BT Yevamot* 13b) interpret this verse "to [also] forbid dividing the people and causing faction and strife, understanding *lo titgodedu* as 'you shall not form yourselves into factions [*agudot*].'" This interpretation is the product of wordplay that solely uses the first two words of the verse and ignores the context. Maimonides rejects this interpretation by invoking his *peshateh di-qera* reading strategy. He writes: "The *gemara* in *Yevamot* [13b] explains that *lo titgodedu* is required for its own context [*gufe di-qera*], the All-Merciful having said, 'You shall not inflict upon yourselves any bruises for the dead.'" In other words, the intention of the text (*gufe di-qera*)

29. At first glance, Maimonides' scripturalism appears to resemble the reading strategies employed by the Karaites. On closer examination, however, the differences are much greater than the similarities. Maimonides' exegeses were bound by the dictates of the Oral Law. For example, he quotes this verse as evidence for the claim that one is forbidden to eat a creature that swarms in the *water*, even though there is no mention of water-borne creeping things in the verse (though they are included in the general prohibition). Most probably, Maimonides' warrant is a midrash. For a possible source, see Kasher, *Torah Shelemah*, ad loc., n. 269. On Karaite scripturalism, see, inter alia, Polliack, "Major Trends in Karaite Biblical Exegesis in the Tenth and Eleventh Centuries," 363-413. On how tradition caught up with some plain sense readings, however, see Frank, *Search Scripture Well,* 33-94.

must be discovered from its context; any other reading results in a non-legally binding interpretation—in essence, a homily. While the Talmud accommodates both interpretations, Maimonides argues that only the plain sense of the text can convey a scriptural commandment.

In his discussion of Rule 3, Maimonides contrasts an intimation or allusion (*remez*) with *peshateh di-qera*. He writes:

> Again has a certain other scholar [Qayyara] erred in respect of this principle [i.e. not to count laws that are not binding for all time] and counted [among the commandments the injunctions applying to the Levites:] *And they shall not go in to see the holy things as they are being covered* [*ke-vala'*] [Num. 4:20]....Now although [the Sages] do say: "An intimation [*remez*] against stealing a holy vessel [is found in the verse], *And they shall not go in to see*, etc."—the term "an intimation" is sufficient evidence that this is not the plain sense [Chavel: "literal sense"] [*peshateh di-qera*] of the verse.

The verb *vala'* is a *pi'el* infinitive in the construct state meaning "to swallow up" or "to cover." The unusual expression prompts the Sages to suggest that the verse alludes to one who steals a holy vessel from the Sanctuary. Neither the grammar of the verse nor its context (the dismantling and transport of the holy vessels in the wilderness) supports such an interpretation. Thus Maimonides observes that this interpretation is merely an intimation (*remez*), rather than the *peshat* meaning.

Maimonides' identification of *peshat* with contextual reading is also demonstrated in N165, where he reads the verse "Ye shall not go out from the door of the Tent of Meeting" (Lev.10:7) in its context as conveying a prohibition against the priests' taking leave from the Temple services while ministering. He labels this interpretation *gufeh di-qera*, and by doing so, he draws a distinction between *gufeh di-qera* and a more basic *peshat* reading (Ar. *zahir al-nass*) advanced in the early part of the gloss to this negative commandment, one that yielded a prohibition against the high priest's following the funeral bier of a relative.[30]

30. As Cohen notes, *zahir al-nass* can also connote the obvious and correct sense of the biblical text; however, "in many cases, it has a very different connotation, namely the apparent sense, which is ultimately incorrect." Cohen, "A Talmudist's Halakhic Hermeneutics," 69. See note 26 in this chapter. I now harbor some doubts about Cohen's distinction. I hope to address the nature of *zahir al-nass* more fully at a future time.

In this next example, Maimonides criticizes Qayyara and his followers for not reading a verse in its context. Maimonides notes in Rule 2 that they (Qayyara and his followers) base the obligation to reckon seasons on the verse: "For this is your wisdom and understanding in the sight of the peoples" (Deut. 4:6), taking the "sight of the peoples" as literally referring to the activity of studying the heavenly bodies. "Wisdom and understanding" would therefore represent the calendrical sciences. Maimonides assumes that their warrant is the rabbinic homily: "Which branch of wisdom and understanding is *in the sight of the peoples*? I must say, this is the reckoning of seasons and constellations" (*BT Shabbat* 75a). While he does not explain here how one should understand the words "wisdom and understanding," we know from his other writings that he reads this verse as referring to *all* statutes and ordinances (*huqim u-mishpatim*), in accord with the opening line of the paragraph, "Behold I have taught you statutes and ordinances."[31]

For Maimonides, context is the natural arbiter of *peshat*, even if the text must be stretched a bit. This is what he does in N4 with the verse "Ye shall not make with Me gods of silver, or gods of gold, ye shall not make unto you" (Exod. 20:20), where he uses the syntactically awkward sentence to support the claim that one is forbidden to craft representative figures of living things out of any substance, even when not for purposes of worship. This last unexpected condition is inferred from the second half of the verse. Maimonides quotes the words of the *Mekhilta*: "Lest you should say: I am going to make them merely for ornaments, as others do in various countries, Scripture says: *ye shall*

31. See the immediately preceding verse, Deuteronomy 4:5. In *GP* III:31:*524*, Maimonides cites this earlier verse to buttress the idea that both laws and statutes have reasons that support them: "And it says *Which shall hear all these statutes [huqim] and say: surely this great community is a wise and understanding people* [end of verse 6]. Thus it states explicitly that even all the statutes [*huqim*] will show to all the nations that they have been given with wisdom and understanding." Interestingly, Ibn Ezra uses this verse in a similar way: "And Moses our lord said with reference to all the commandments *surely this great community is a wise and understanding people* [Deut. 4:6]. If they [the commandments] do not have reasons that we could comprehend, how would the nations say that these are *righteous statutes* [Deut. 4:8] and we, who adhere to them, *wise*?" Ibn Ezra, *Yesod Mora, sha'ar* 8, 150.

not make unto you."[32] The midrash understands the phrase "unto you" as referring to one's personal use rather than for worship, a stretch of the plain meaning. Maimonides makes reference to other exegetical derivations from this verse, noting that the verse also contains "other matters that go beyond the scope of this commandment, but the plain sense of the text [*peshateh di-qera*] is what we have set out, as explained in the *Mekhilta*." Maimonides adopts the *Mekhilta*'s reading, despite the fact that the *Mekhilta*'s reading is only one of several philologically acceptable possibilities, and certainly not the most compelling one.[33]

In a similar vein, Maimonides uses *peshateh di-qera* in N299 to claim that the verse "Nor shalt thou put a stumbling-block before the blind" (Lev. 19:14) prohibits one from offering misleading advice. He bases this reading on the *Sifra*, which comments: "If one is 'blind' in a [certain] matter, and asks you for advice, do not give him advice which is not suitable for him."[34] Maimonides contrasts this interpretation with other rabbinic interpretations, concluding that: "the *peshateh di-qera* is as we have stated above [the *Sifra*'s reading]." He makes no mention of the possibility of an alternative literal reading, even though the context does not eliminate such a possibility.[35] As in the previous case, Maimonides gives priority to the *midrash halakhah*, although in this instance, he may have thought that the midrashic interpretation also represents the best plain reading of the verse.[36]

32. *Mekhilta Yitro* 10 (241).

33. Among rabbinic commentaries, the most plausible reading is given by Sa'adiah Gaon (also offered by Ibn Ezra and cited by Abraham Maimonides), who argues that the two halves of the verse convey two separate ideas: the prohibition against imagining a second deity and the prohibition against making physical representations of the divinity. Maimonides' adoption of the *Mekhilta*'s reading recalls an expression used by the medieval *parshanim* with respect to rabbinic midrash: "Their understanding is deeper [lit., wider] than ours" (*da'atam rehavah mi-da'atenu*). See Ibn Ezra's commentary on the Pentateuch, *passim*. See also David Qimhi's commentaries on Joshua 4:11 and 2 Chronicles 5:9. Perhaps Maimonides prefers to defer to rabbinic interpretations—so long as context is respected—because he sees their authors, being closer in time and mindset to the text, as showing a superior understanding.

34. *Sifra Qedoshim, parshah* 2:14 (88d).

35. By contrast, Ibn Ezra appears to read the verse as prohibiting the literal placing of a stumbling block in the way of a blind man. See his comments to the Pentateuch, ad loc., and in Ibn Ezra, *Yesod Mora, sha'ar* 9, 161, and the helpful note on line 30.

36. The fact that Maimonides neither labeled this interpretation an accepted tradition (*perush*

An emphasis on contextual reading coupled with a fine historical perspective allows Maimonides to offer a remarkably daring and likely original interpretation of the verse "An altar of earth thou shalt make unto Me" (Exod. 20:21). Not only does this command stand apart from the general commandment to build a sanctuary and its vessels, appurtenances, and parts that begins at Exodus 25:8, but it also flagrantly contradicts an explicit commandment to build an altar made of stone.[37] Maimonides resolves the contradiction by giving us a *peshateh di-qera* reading at P20 that places the verse in an historical context. He writes: "The *peshateh di-qera* refers to the time when outside altars (*bamot*) were permitted to us, and we were allowed to make an altar of earth in any place." Following this explanation, however, Maimonides notes that the Sages read the words "an altar of earth thou shalt make unto Me" to mean "an altar *attached* to earth." Thus the verse no longer requires that the altar be made of earth, contradicting other scriptural indications, but rather that the altar will need to be attached to the (earthly) ground. In this way, the rabbis manage to harmonize the verse with the traditional view that the altar is to be made of stone.[38]

---

ha-mequbbal) in the *ShM*, in the *SE*, nor in the *MT* suggests that he thought that the figurative interpretation of the midrash was actually the more valid of the readings. Cohen finds the omission "surprising," especially in view of the fact that Maimonides interpreted the first half of the verse, "Thou shalt not curse the deaf," literally. Consequently, he argues that the context would have justified a literal interpretation. Cohen, "A Talmudist's Halakhic Hermeneutics," n. 267. However, the negative commandment based on this verse (N317) indicates that Maimonides also did not interpret the first half of the verse literally, since he read it as a prohibition against cursing "any Israelite," not just the deaf. See the intricate rationale used by Maimonides in his gloss to N317.

37. Deut. 27:6. Paradoxically, the oral tradition derives this teaching from the words "And if thou make me an altar of stone" (Exod. 20:22), reading the word "if" as meaning *ḥovah* (obligation) rather than *reshut* (optional). *Mekhilta de Rabbi Ishmael*, *ad loc.*

38. Interestingly, in the *MT*, *Hilkhot Bet ha-Beḥirah* 1:13, Maimonides takes what appears to be a more conservative position and labels this rabbinic exposition a teaching *mi-pi ha-shemu'ah*. This is an interpretation suggested by the oral tradition from Sinai; it has some textual plausibility but clearly does not represent the best contextual reading. Note that while this particular exegesis may not quite be "philologically defensible," in Meyer Feldblum's words, it still represents Torah law. In his otherwise excellent article, Feldblum clumps together philologically defensible laws and laws derived by the 13 hermeneutic principles for interpreting the Torah. This conglomeration is inexact. According to Maimonides, the hermeneutical

In sum, according to Maimonides, the term *peshat* refers to a reading of Scripture that adheres to the rules of grammar and language, that reads a verse contextually within a longer passage, and that is consistent with the historical reality. It is important to note that this strategy does not assume either a literal or a figurative reading: sometimes one and sometimes the other will offer the sought-after plain sense. In this respect, Maimonides' term *peshateh di-qera* comes quite close to our modern conception of the plain sense of the text. When re-reading Rule 2 in light of this conclusion, we understand that scriptural commandments must be grounded in the plain sense of Scripture, as opposed to the type of fanciful homiletic readings that one most commonly finds in the aggadic midrashim. When more than one interpretation is offered, Maimonides gives precedence to the reading that comes closest to reading the verse in context. In some cases where multiple contextual interpretations are possible, Maimonides defers to rabbinic midrash. If we were to assume that he does so because he genuinely believes in the early rabbis' superior linguistic skills and their familiarity with the *sitz im leben* of the period, we are still able to affirm that Maimonides values contextual interpretations above all else.[39]

As an aside, I note that Maimonides' interest in reading contextually spawned two Rules, the discussion of which I do not see as relevant to our present inquiry—specifically, Rule 5 ("The reason given for a commandment is not to be counted as a separate commandment") and

activity of the Scribes is analytical and inferential rather than philological, as I argued earlier. I agree wholeheartedly with Feldblum's conclusion: "I wish to emphasize that Maimonides' care in assigning laws to their respective categories is uniquely intertwined with his philosophy and perception of the halakhic process. Maimonides' criteria for classification are based on a careful philological and literary analysis of the underlying sources in each given case." Feldblum, "Criteria for Designating Laws," 45-49.

39. On the superior linguistic skills of the earlier scholars, see Maimonides' interesting comments to *M Orlah* 3:2. Navigating close to the surface of the text, eschewing fanciful midrashic interpretations and analytic derivations, Maimonides can declare in the *GP* that his purpose "is to give reasons for the [biblical] texts and not for the pronouncements of the legal science" (*GP* III:41:*558*). The intent of the divine lawgiver can only be properly understood by attuning oneself to the "plainness" of the text.

Rule 8 ("A mere negative statement excluding a particular case from the scope of a commandment is not to be included among the negative commandments").[40]

"THEY LEARNED IT FROM THE ORAL TRADITION" (*MI-PI HA-SHEMU'AH LAMDU*)

In Maimonides' works, the overwhelming majority of positive commandments (as well as negative commandments) are identified and interpreted according to the plain sense of the scriptural text (*peshateh di-qera*). In a handful of cases, Maimonides adopts a traditional reading, which he believes to carry a unique force of authority in cases where the tradition is not impugned by rabbinic objections or alternative views. By the very absence of dispute, incontrovertible traditions reflect consensus, a powerful source of legal authority in talmudic, pre-Islamic and Islamic jurisprudence.[41] The consensus surrounding this type of tradition, he argues in the introduction to his commentary to the Mishnah, guarantees its Sinaitic origin.[42]

40. Nahmanides, *Hasagot*, Rules 5 and 8, shows that the talmudic rabbis did not always make these distinctions. These Rules are good examples of the type of "Greek" logic (linguistic logic in this case) that Maimonides tried to impose on the creative but unsystematic and unyielding corpus of rabbinic exegeses. Herbert Davidson (in *Moses Maimonides*, 98n124) notes that in Rule 8, Maimonides quotes the "words" of the "students of the art of logic" with a quotation taken *verbatim* from Al-Farabi's epitome of Aristotle's *De Intepretatione*.

41. In talmudic literature, *divre ha-kol* (the opinion of all scholars) is a phrase that denotes legal finality. A computer search reveals that this term occurs 402 times in the Babylonian Talmud and 279 times in the Jerusalem Talmud. Maimonides' commentators often corroborate his rulings by citing a talmudic use of *divre ha-kol*. See, e.g., *Migdal Oz* on *Hilkhot Shofar, Sukkah, ve-Lulav* 4:11, s.v. "*ve-ani omer*," last line; *Maggid Mishneh, Hilkhot 'Eruvin* 7:2 and passim. For the principle of consensus (*ijma*) in Islamic jurisprudence, see note 42 below.

42. *Haqdamot ha-Rambam*, ed. Shailat, 38: "and, lo, this principle must be known, that is, that the explanations received from Moses are without controversy whatsoever." See also 40, where Maimonides discusses the five epistemological bases for the oral law, in particular the first two. Besides the oral interpretation that accompanied the commandments, the received explanations include the famous textually ungrounded traditions called *halakhot le-Moshe mi-Sinai*. Scholarly analysis has shown that not all *halakhot le-Moshe mi-Sinai* are incontrovertible. See Bacharach, *Sheelot u-Teshuvot Havvot Yair*, no. 192. For an example from the enumeration of the commandments,

We find occasional divergences from this rule, instances in which Maimonides interprets according to the "incontrovertible" tradition while leaving behind evidence that he upholds the plain sense of the text (or at least upheld it at one time). I offer a number of possible explanations for these rare occurrences, including that Maimonides forgot to erase the earlier view; he is deliberately ambiguous, because he does not know which meaning is correct; or he continues to maintain somehow that "a text cannot be deprived of its *peshat* meaning," even when tradition says otherwise. The following example, found at *Hilkhot 'Edut* 13:1, is consistent with the third explanation. After citing the verse "Parents shall not be put to death for children nor children be put to death for parents" (Deut. 24:16), Maimonides comments: "It is taught by the oral tradition that included in this negative commandment is the exhortation not to condemn fathers to death on the testimony of their sons, nor sons on the testimony of their fathers." This oral tradition contradicts the plain sense of the verse, namely, that of vicarious punishment—parents cannot be put to death for their children's crimes and vice-versa—an idea reinforced by the second half of the verse: "a person shall be put to death only for his own crime." No allusion to testimony is present in the verse. Note Maimonides' subtle hint, however, to the secondary nature of the tradition in the words "included in this negative commandment."[43]

---

see P5, where Maimonides disregards that a cited rabbinic source gives two mutually exclusive definitions for "worship of the heart," defining it both as prayer and as study. Not only is the tradition under dispute, but Maimonides presents the tradition as if it is consensual! Also see P173, P198, P199, N198, and N199, none of which represents unanimous views. At very least, we can say that with respect to commandments, Maimonides only resorts to this principle occasionally. He appears to have enunciated this principle more as a polemic against the Karaites than as an authentic epistemological principle. Maimonides was presumably also taking issue with Sa'adiah, "one who thought that even laws that are disputed are part of the tradition from Moses," because Sa'adiah had left the Rabbanite side exposed to the Karaite attack on tradition. On Sa'adiah's view, see Zucker, *Perush Rav Sa'adiah Gaon le-Bereshit*, 187-188. The principle of consensus (*ijma*)—in its many forms—as an authoritative source of the law, was a well-known principle of Islamic (and even pre-Islamic) jurisprudence. See Schacht, *Origins of Muslim Jurisprudence*, 82-97, and more recently Hallaq, *History of Islamic Legal Theories*, 75-81.

43. This literal understanding is also how Amatsiah, king of Judah, understood the verse, as we find in a rare piece of inter-textual interpretation (2 Kgs 14:5-6). Amatsiah puts

This reading of Maimonides' intentions is consistent with the rabbinic dictum of Rule 2: "a text cannot be deprived of its plain sense (*ein miqra yotse mi-yede peshuto*)." The traditional interpretation does not uproot the plain sense of the text.

In the following example, we see the degree to which *peshateh di-qera* is ingrained in Maimonides' exegesis and how he struggles to maintain these readings even when accepting the traditional interpretation. Leviticus 25:32-34 teaches that the Levites' city dwellings may be sold and redeemed in perpetuity, but never the unenclosed lands (*migrash*) around their assigned cities. In *Hilkhot Shemitah ve-Yovel* 13:5, Maimonides writes: "The Sages have learnt by tradition that [*the fields of the open lands about their cities*] *may not be sold* [Lev. 25:34] means 'may not be changed'—the field, the open space, and the city space, each one of the three must remain as it is forever after." The non-philological reading that *lo yimakher* means "may not be able to change" rather than "may not be able to sell" forms the basis of N228 in the *ShM* and in the *SE*, prefaced there by the words "it was taught by the oral tradition." Yet, in the Heading to *Hilkhot Shemitah ve-Yovel,* Maimonides defines the law as follows: "That one may not make a permanent sale of the open lands about their cities; these open lands can be redeemed at any time, before the Jubilee or after," which is exactly in line with the plain sense of the text. We see here traces of Maimonides' current or former attachment to *peshateh di-qera.*

The traditional readings that Maimonides invokes when interpreting certain verses in support of commandment claims do not represent the text's best or plainest sense. In these admittedly few cases, Maimonides makes a highly visible effort to keep these traditional readings within acceptable grammatical, syntactical, contextual and logical bounds.

Maimonides does not appear as insistent on applying plain sense canons and justifying traditional readings when it comes to details and particulars of commandments. In fact, in some of these cases, tradition can offer an interpretation contrary to plain sense.[44]

---

to death the courtiers who had assassinated his father, "but he did not put to death the children of the assassins, in accordance with what is written in the Book of Teaching of Moses, where the Lord commanded, *Parents shall not be put to death for children nor children be put to death for parents; a person shall be put to death only for his own crime.*"

44. Here are three egregious examples of interpretations that are not contextually,

Maimonides employs many terms to denote the presence of an oral tradition, but only one term to indicate its use in support of a scriptural commandment claim. The term is "*mi-pi ha-shemu'ah lamdu*," which can loosely be rendered as "they learned it from the oral tradition." It is only found in the *SE* and in the *Halakhot*.[45] According to Maimonides, these uncontroverted traditions, which bear some semblance to the plain sense of the text but which may not be identical with the *peshateh di-qera*,[46] enjoy a Sinaitic status. By this measure, Maimonides considered these traditions authentic interpretations of the text and infused them with scriptural authority. Because the *SE* only comprises a list of commandments, when this phrase makes its appearance in this list, it is intimately and exclusively associated with delineating a particular commandment. In the *Halakhot*, by contrast, the term is also associated with particulars of the law.[47] As a result, in such cases, I am less confident in asserting that when Maimonides used the expression *mi-pi ha-shemu'ah lamdu* when accompanying a verse, he intended to signal that these particulars also enjoy scriptural authority (*de-oraita*).[48]

---

syntactically or logically plausible: *Hilkhot Yibbum* 2:6, "If a man dies and is survived by several brothers, it is the eldest brother's religious duty to marry the widow, as it says, *And it shall be that the first-born that she beareth* [*shall succeed in the name of his brother that is dead*]. The oral tradition taught that here *first-born* signifies the first-born of the brothers," offers an interpretation contrary to the plain sense of the verse. Similarly, in *Hilkhot Na'arah Betulah* 3:6, tradition reads the claims and counter-claims about a maiden's virginity as being proffered by witnesses rather than on physical evidence (i.e. blood stains), which contradicts the sense of the text. Finally, in *Hilkhot Isure Biah* 16:10, "Even though it is said, *Neither shall ye do thus in your land* [Lev. 22:24], the oral tradition taught that this prohibition [against castrating a male of any species] applies everywhere, the purport of Scripture here being, 'This shall not be done among the people of Israel whether upon their own bodies or upon the body of others.'" The plain-sense meaning of the verse forbids castration only in the Land of Israel, while tradition extends this prohibition anywhere Jews live. Note Maimonides' (weak) attempt to reconcile tradition with plain sense. In *Hilkhot Sanhedrin* 3:3 and 3:8, Maimonides allows tradition to read the texts totally out of context.

45. In the Arabic *PhM* and *ShM*, Maimonides refers to this notion in a less precise and inconsistent fashion, using expressions such as "it came via tradition" and "the received interpretation."

46. See my discussion of Meyer Feldblum's work in note 38, above.

47. For example, in *Hilkhot Talmud Torah* 1:2, *Hilkhot Qiddush ha-Hodesh* 8:1, *Hilkhot Hovel u-Maziq* 1:2, *Hilkhot Sanhedrin* 3:3, 3:8.

48. *Hilkhot Yibbum* 2:6 is an interesting case in point. Maimonides uses the expression *mi-*

Matters become confusing when Maimonides uses *mi-pi ha-shemu'ah lamdu* without an accompanying scriptural proof text. In such cases, the term may simply be referring to an ancient tradition; most likely, no scriptural authority is ascribed to it.[49] The situation is further confused by the fact that in the *Halakhot*, Maimonides uses other terms associated with the oral law, such as *mi-pi ha-qabbalah, halakhah mi-pi ha-qabbalah, halakhah mi-pi ha-shemu'ah*, and a few other variants of these expressions. Scholars have conducted systematic terminological investigations into these terms for at least a century, starting with Adolf Schwarz in 1905[50] and continuing to this day. Recently, Joseph Kafih surveyed all the instances where these terms appeared in the *MT* without coming to a consistent conclusion.[51] While *mi-pi ha-shemu'ah* can signify particulars

pi ha-shemu'ah lamdu in connection with the verse "And it shall be that the first-born that she beareth" (Deut. 25:5) to indicate that the verse is referring to the first-born of the *mother* of the brothers, and thus that the commandment requires the elder of the brothers to perform the levirate marriage, a problematic reading (as I noted above in note 44). Later, in *Hilkhot Yibbum* 6:8, Maimonides quotes the very same verse to teach that a barren woman (*aylonit*) is exempt from levirate marriage, since the verse teaches that the widow shall bear a child. The two exegeses reflect diametrically opposed conceptions of the verse—it can either refer to the mother or to the wife, but not to both. Which exegesis did Maimonides believe conveyed a scriptural law, and which merely a *divre sofrim* law? Y. Horowitz (in "Le-Mishneh Torah u-le-Perush ha-Mishnayot shel ha-RaMBaM," Sinai 15, 279-288) thinks that the former exegesis is an *asmakhta* (and thus *divre sofrim*) and the latter a genuine scriptural reading (and thus a scriptural law). I am not convinced that the former exegesis should be considered *divre sofrim*, even though it seems stretched. Maimonides' philological attempt to justify the exegesis, both here and in the *PhM* (*M Yevamot* 2:6), shows that he considered this implausible exegesis to be within the range of acceptable readings according to the plain sense.

49. See, for example, *Hilkhot Sotah* 2:12, *Hilkhot Isure Biah* 4:1, and *Hilkhot Maakhalot Asurot* 1:10 and *passim*.

50. Schwarz, *Der Mischneh Thorah*.

51. See Kafih's commentary to the *MT, Sefer Mishpatim*, end of vol. 21. While on the surface, his attempt appears to be systematic, it is actually far from being so. Kafih offers individual, ad hoc explanations for each entry without summarizing his findings. His reasoning throughout is vague and inconsistent. In example no. 19 and referring to *Hilkhot Hamets u-Matsah* 1:8, he points out that Maimonides signals that the transgressor is liable for lashes because we are in the presence of an interpretation of the verse (*lamdu mi-pi ha-shemu'ah*) rather than of the norm itself (*etsem din*), leaving the reader wondering what he meant by that distinction. In speaking about the term *mi-pi ha-qabbalah*, he infers, at no.18 (p. 277), that the expression *divre qabbalah* means that the tradition comes from Moses himself, as opposed to the term *mi-pi ha-shemu'ah*. But *divre qabbalah* is unlikely to mean the same thing as *mi-pi ha-qabbalah*;

of laws that are not of scriptural authority, and while Maimonides uses a number of hard-to-define terms to convey the manner and form of diverse oral traditions, this much is certain: *mi-pi ha-shemu'ah* is the only expression of the oral tradition that introduces an interpretation of the scriptural text in the presentation of a commandment.[52]

In total, the number of positive commandments that draw their authority from a traditional interpretation (rather than from a reading that is informed by the plain sense of the verse) is very small—five in the *SE* and 10 in the *Halakhot*—out of a total of 248 commandments. The *Halakhot* repeats the *SE*'s hermeneutic in four places: P85 is paralleled at *Hilkhot Ma'aseh ha-Qorbanot* 18:1, P86 at *Hilkhot Isure Mizbeah̲* 1:10, P109 at *Hilkhot Miqvaot* 1:2, and P198 at *Hilkhot Malveh ve-Loveh* 5:1. There is

more likely, it means that it is derived from the non-Pentateuchal sections. Nor does he explain how he comes to that particular distinction. At no. 17 (p. 256), Kafih points out that by citing *mi-pi ha-shemu'ah* to elucidate the meaning of affliction (*'inuy*) used in connection with the Day of Atonement, Maimonides signifies that it is a *halakhah* accepted by the people (*halakhah she-nitqablah be-ummah*), and, for that reason, it is intrinsically a Torah law (*guf torah*). Its authority comes from the people's acceptance of this law (which, I presume, has no linguistic basis), rather than the fact that Moses informed the meaning of the term "affliction." While this interpretation is interesting, it is unclear how Kafih substantiates this hypothesis, and how consistently he uses that explanation. Note the contrast with what he proposes at no. 12 (p. 256). There, Kafih states that *mi-pi ha-shemu'ah* is not the equivalent of inferences arrived via the use of the 13 hermeneutic rules, nor does it represent a tradition from Moses at Sinai. Rather, it indicates linguistic inferences that the Sages have drawn from the text and that have been accepted by succeeding generations of Sages. Kafih does make a few interesting comments, however, as in nos. 140 and 144, where he indicates that while *mi-pi ha-shemu'ah* may not necessarily be the best interpretation, it does not contradict the plain sense of the text. More recently, Henshke revisited this issue and convincingly demonstrated that the expression *mi-pi ha-shemu'ah* is a marker of Sinaitic authority if and only if it is accompanied by a proof text. Cf. Henshke, "Le-Yesode Tefisat ha-Halakhah," in particular the appendix, 138-144. See also the systematic and careful analysis of these special terms by Shohetman, "Halakhah mi-Pi ha-Qabbalah ve-Halakhah le-Moshe mi-Sinai." Shohetman notes that when citing a proof text, Maimonides uses the term "as it says" to signify that the plain reading supports the claim, and uses *mi-pi ha-shemu'ah* or *hen mi-pi ha-qabbalah* to signify a rabbinic interpretation that is not in accordance with the plain meaning. I would add only that Maimonides tolerates such rabbinic interpretations because the scriptural text is ambiguous and the rabbinic interpretations do not conflict with the context.

52. The expression *mi-pi ha-qabbalah* is sometimes used in connection with a scriptural text to explain a *detail* of the commandment. See, for example, *Hilkhot 'Edut* 20:2, *Hilkhot Melakhim* 7:10.

no parallel in the *Halakhot* for the reliance on tradition as the source for the commandment to set aside the second tithe (P128); I will comment later on the implications of this apparent reversal. The *Halakhot* references tradition as the interpretive authority for six additional commandment claims: *Hilkhot Tefillah* 1:1, *Hilkhot H̲amets u-Matsah* 2:1, *Hilkhot Shofar* 1:1, *Hilkhot Shevitat 'Asor* 1:4, *Hilkhot Malveh ve-Loveh* 1:2, and *Hilkhot Melakhim* 5:5.

Let us examine the 10 instances from the *Halakhot* in more detail:

1) *Hilkhot Tefillah* 1:1:

> It is a positive commandment to pray every day, as it is said, *Ye shall serve the Lord your God* [Exodus 23:25]. The oral tradition said [*mi-pi ha-shemu'ah amru*] that this "service" is prayer. And it is written, *serving Him with all your heart and soul* [Deut. 11:13], about which the Sages said, "What is service of the heart? Prayer."

Maimonides clearly struggles with this commandment claim. The unique expression *mi-pi ha-shemu'ah amru*, which appears in the good manuscripts[53] (instead of the common expression from the printed editions, *lamdu mi-pi ha-shemu'ah*) and its immediate linguistic and hermeneutic link with the Sages' comment (*amru hakhamim*), shows that Maimonides does not have a firm authority for this tradition.[54] The interpretation that Maimonides offers is both plausible and reasonable in view of the Sages' comments but certainly not as authoritative as it had seemed in the *ShM*.[55] By marshalling a rabbinic tradition, Maimonides attempts to strengthen the idea that prayer is the

---

53. See *Rambam Meduyaq*, ed. Shailat, *Hilkhot Tefillah*, 20n2. Note that the base of Shailat's text is the version of the *MT* carrying Maimonides' own signature, attesting that the book was proofread against his own copy, and which contains also some of Maimonides' own corrections, MS Oxford 577 (Huntington 80).

54. A similar though not identical deviation from the standard formula *mi-pi ha-shemu'ah lamdu* takes place in *Hilkhot Lulav*. See my comments regarding the commandment to take the four species, chapter 8, note 47.

55. In the *ShM* (P5), however, his argument turns confusing, after he cites a second opinion of the *Sifre* that equates service with the study of the law. This is further evidence that Maimonides lacked a clear authoritative tradition that prayer was a scriptural obligation. See also Nahmanides' powerful critique, *Hasagot*, ad loc., 210.

authoritative interpretation of a vague and very general formulation.

2) *Hilkhot Hamets u-Matsah* 2:1:

> It is a positive commandment from Scripture[56] to put away leaven before the time when one is forbidden to eat it, as it says, *Howbeit the first day ye shall put away leaven out of your houses* [Exod. 12:15]; they learned from the oral tradition [*u-mi-pi ha-shemu'ah lamdu*] that this first day is the fourteenth of Nissan. This is corroborated by the verse, *Thou shalt not offer the blood of My sacrifice with leavened bread* [Exod. 23:18; 34:25], which means: "Thou shalt not slaughter the Paschal lamb while leavened bread is still in existence," and the time for slaughtering the Paschal lamb is after midday on the fourteenth of Nissan.

Counter-intuitively, the oral tradition identifies "the first day" with the fourteenth day of Nissan, rather than with the more logical first day of the festival of Passover, the fifteenth of Nissan. Here is a good example of what we had suggested earlier: Maimonides goes out of his way to defend traditional readings that do not seem to reflect the plainest sense.

3) *Hilkhot Shofar* 1:1:

> It is a positive commandment from Scripture[57] to hear the blast of a horn [*shofar*] at New Year, as it is said: *It is a day of blowing unto you* [Num. 29:1]....Although Scripture does not expressly stipulate the blast of a horn in the case of New Year, it does say of the Jubilee year: *Then shalt thou make proclamation with the blast of the horn on the tenth day of the seventh month; in the Day of Atonement shall ye make proclamation with the horn* [Lev. 25:9], and they learned from the oral tradition [*u-mi-pi ha-shemu'ah lamdu*] that just as the blast of a Jubilee year must be blown on a horn, so must the blast of New Year be blown on a horn.

56. Did Maimonides purposefully add the phrase "from Scripture" (*min ha-torah*), a rare addition, as a polemic directed at his Karaite adversaries who held that leaven could be kept until the beginning of the first day of the festival? For the Karaite interpretation, see the commentary of Aaron ben Elijah of Nicomedia, *Sefer Keter Torah*, 62, who wrote in the first half of the fourteenth century.

57. See note 56 above. Here, too, the Karaites rejected the rabbinic law and taught that the word *teru'ah* commands shouting, not blowing a horn. See Miller, "Karaite Perspectives in Yom Teru'ah," 537-541.

The oral tradition explains that "a day of blowing" refers to a day when a horn is blown. A *baraita* in *BT Rosh Hashanah* 33b-34a derives this point from an analogy (*heqesh*): the verse mentions blowing the horn on Yom Kippur (of the Jubilee year) "in the seventh month." Since we already know that Yom Kippur is in the seventh month, the mention of the seventh month is redundant. The redundancy comes to inform that *all* the blowings of the seventh month should be on the same horn—which includes the blowing of Rosh Hashanah. While Maimonides does appear to adopt this analogy, he does not make the hermeneutic explicit, leaving the reader in doubt as to whether he had really intended the somewhat convoluted analogy offered by the *baraita*.[58] By adding the analogizing phrase, "just as...so must," Maimonides attempts to bring the traditional interpretation closer to a plain reading of the text.

4) *Hilkhot Ma'aseh ha-Qorbanot* 18:1:

> Likewise, it is a positive commandment that every person take care of and bring from outside the Land [of Israel] to the Holy Temple the animal sacrifices that he was obliged to offer. For it is said: *Only thy holy things which thou hast, and thy vows, thou shalt take and go unto the place which the Lord shall choose* [Deut. 12:26]; they learned from the oral tradition [*mi-*

58. The *baraita*'s exegetical presentation is equivocal. While it begins by using a *heqesh*, it switches to using a *gezerah shavah*, a different form of analogy. The Talmud notes the equivocation and concludes that the ruling could have been derived from the *heqesh*; once a *gezerah shavah* is found, however, the *baraita* preferred to use the latter method of interpretation. *Kesef Mishneh* (ad loc.) argues that Maimonides adopted the *gezerah shavah*, and this is the reason Maimonides used the term *mi-pi ha-shemu'ah*, since according to Karo's understanding of Maimonides' position, a *gezerah shavah* signals a Sinaitic tradition and not a *divre sofrim* derivation. This analysis contradicts Rule 2, where Maimonides groups together all 13 hermeneutic rules, a group that includes the *gezerah shavah*. Had Maimonides believed that the linchpin of this tradition was a *gezerah shavah*, he would have considered blowing a horn to be a *divre sofrim* commandment, and would not have used the term *mi-pi ha-shemu'ah*. More likely, the very ambiguity (and insufficiency) of the *baraita*'s complex hermeneutic led Maimonides to believe that an authentic Sinaitic tradition was at work, rather than a full-fledged scribal derivation. For the unusual way the term *heqesh* is used in the *baraita*, see Ayyash, *Lehem Yehudah*, *ad loc.* It should be noted that a *heqesh* analogy is not one of the 13 hermeneutic rules, thus allowing Maimonides to label this obligation a scriptural *mitsvat 'aseh*. The Talmud, however, appears to give primacy to the *gezerah shava*, as noted above, and that would indeed present a problem for Maimonides.

> *pi ha-shemu'ah lamdu*] that this verse speaks only with reference to the hallowed offerings of outside the Land; that they were to be taken care of until they were brought up to the Holy Temple.

The verse could be read as only requiring one to bring one's domestic offerings to the Temple, rather than those offerings from outside of the Land of Israel. The oral tradition reads the verse as imposing a further requirement to look after and bring offerings to the Holy Temple from outside the Land of Israel.

5) *Hilkhot Miqvaot* 1:2:

> Wherever "washing of the flesh" or "cleansing of the garments" from uncleanness is spoken of in Scripture, it means nothing else but the immersion of the whole person or object in an immersion pool....And although all these things are learned only from the oral tradition [*she-hem mi-pi ha-shemu'ah*], it is nevertheless said, *It must be put into water and it shall be unclean until the even; then shall it be clean* [Lev. 11:32]—a basic principle applying to all that are unclean, that they should enter into water.

The oral tradition understands that the words "washing of the flesh" refer to a full body immersion in water. Here again, to defend this reading and uphold the oral tradition, Maimonides resorts to new textual support, introduced by the words "it is nevertheless said."

6) *Hilkhot Isure Mizbeaḫ* 1:10:

> It is a positive commandment to redeem an offering which had incurred a blemish, so that it would become profane and be eaten. For it is said: *Notwithstanding thou mayest kill and eat flesh after all the desire of thy soul* [Deut. 12:15]; they learned from the oral tradition [*mi-pi ha-shemu'ah lamdu*] that Scripture speaks here of hallowed offerings that became unfit and were redeemed.

The oral tradition understands this verse as referring to a hallowed animal that became ritually unfit, commanding[59] one to redeem it so

59. It seems odd for Maimonides to designate the redemption of offerings that have

that its flesh can become available to eat. In this case, Maimonides makes no attempt to justify the oral tradition.[60]

7) *Hilkhot Malveh ve-Loveh* 1:2:

> It is a positive commandment to exact payment from a heathen debtor. For it is written *Of a foreigner thou mayest exact it* [*but that which is thine with thy brother, thine hand shall release*] [Deut. 15:3]. They have learned from the oral tradition [*mi-pi ha-shemu'ah lamdu*] that this is a positive commandment.

The oral tradition eschews the more plausible reading that Scripture *permits* one to press the foreigner for repayment of a loan in favor of a less plausible reading that *obligates* one to exact that repayment. No attempt is made here to justify this reading.[61]

8) *Hilkhot Malveh ve-Loveh* 5:1:

> It is a positive commandment to lend money at interest to a heathen. For it is written, *Of a foreigner thou mayest exact it* [*but that which is thine with thy brother, thine hand shall release*] [Deut. 23:21]. They learned from the oral tradition [*mi-pi ha-shemu'ah lamdu*] that this is to be construed as a positive commandment and this is scriptural law.

The oral tradition makes it a positive commandment to lend at interest to a heathen. A more plausible reading is that one *may* lend money at interest to a heathen but one may not lend with interest to an Israelite—in effect, an implicit prohibition. This prohibition is explicitly

---

incurred a blemish as a positive commandment, meaning an obligation. Perla raises serious and important objections to this view. Perla, *Sefer ha-Mitsvot le-RaSaG*, vol.1, Ps 131, s. v. "*ve-nirah*," 380-383.

60. The scriptural context suggests the possibility that this passage concerns offerings, in contrast to the sections that immediately follow (vv. 20-22), which appear to discuss non-sacrificial meat. (Cf. RaSHI *ad loc.*) The word "notwithstanding" implies that some event had just occurred to block the animal from being offered on the altar. The "notwithstanding" clause thus comes to offer a remedy: that the animal be redeemed. Once it is redeemed, it can then be consumed.

61. See my comments to P142 in chapter 5.

stated at the end of the verse.[62] Still, the text can easily accommodate the oral tradition, and no justification is necessary.

9) *Hilkhot Melakhim* 5:5:

> It is a positive commandment always to bear in mind ['Amaleq's] evil deeds, the waylaying [he resorted to], so that we keep fresh in others [*kede le-orer evato*] the memory of the hatred manifested by him, as it is said: *Remember what 'Amaleq did unto thee* [Deut. 25:17]. They learned from the oral tradition [*mi-pi ha-shemu'ah*], *Remember*, by way of mouth; *do not forget*, out of mind, because it is forbidden to forget his hatred and enmity.[63]

In what might seem like no more than an emphatic exhortation, the oral tradition sees a positive commandment: that one must remember 'Amaleq with words. The traditional interpretation is plausible and requires little justification.

10) *Hilkhot Shevitat 'Asor* 1:4:

> Another positive commandment concerning the Day of Atonement requires abstention from eating and drinking on that day. For Scripture says, *Ye shall afflict your souls* [Lev. 16:29]. They learned from the oral tradition [*mi-pi ha-shemu'ah lamdu*] that the term "affliction" when applied to the soul means "fasting."

The oral tradition understands "affliction" to mean fasting from foods. None of the standard exegetes disagree with the notion that the term "affliction of the soul" refers to fasting. It is possible the term may have once enjoyed a broader meaning, and Maimonides may have resorted to tradition to restrict the punishment of excision exclusively to one who does not fast.[64]

---

62. See my comments to P198 in chapter 5.
63. I read the claim as follows: "Remember 'Amaleq's hatred for the purpose of keeping it fresh in the minds of other members of the nation." "Remember" here is used in the sense of "remind," which is why the activity of remembering is carried out "by way of mouth." See my earlier comments to P189 in chapter 5.
64. The next *halakhah*, 1:5, states: "it is similarly known by tradition [*mi-pi ha-shemu'ah*] that one is forbidden to wash, anoint himself, wear shoes, or have sexual

In summary: in order to identify and frame commandment claims, Maimonides follows a *peshateh di-qera* hermeneutic, a plain-sense reading of Scripture that considers phrases and clauses in their grammatical, linguistic, literary, and historical context. In as few as five and up to ten cases (out of 248), Maimonides relies on certain interpretative traditions that appear to enjoy unanimous consent and are thus held to be of Sinaitic origin, even when these interpretations fail to offer the most contextual, and therefore plainest, readings. These traditions are grouped under the rubric *mi-pi ha-shemu'ah lamdu.* Despite the undisputed authority of these interpretations, Maimonides nonetheless attempts in almost every case to justify exegetically the bona fides of the tradition.

THE PRESENTATION OF A POSITIVE COMMANDMENT IN THE *HALAKHOT*

One notable aspect of Maimonides' rhetorical presentation of commandments in the *Halakhot* is the basic sentence that forcefully and unequivocally designates the commandment to be discussed: "It is a positive commandment to do X." I refer to these introductory presentations as declaratory statements. After declaring the commandment's presence, Maimonides cites the relevant scriptural proof text, as he does in the *ShM* and the *SE*. By citing a proof text, Maimonides follows the basic tenets of rhetorical argument, as well as adhering to the format of the *midreshe halakhah*, the fundamental cornerstones of the Oral Law.[65]

For the overwhelming majority of commandments, the scriptural

intercourse on that day." Maimonides then adds: "Nevertheless, one becomes liable for excision or a sin offering only for eating or drinking; if one washes, anoints himself, wears shoes, or has sexual intercourse, he is liable to a disciplinary flogging [*makkat mardut*]." Only fasting is scripturally enjoined and only eating and drinking are scripturally prohibited, not the broader activities possibly implied by the phrase "affliction of the soul." As we saw earlier, when not accompanied by a proof text, *mi-pi ha-shemu'ah* may simply represent an ancient tradition of rabbinic authority; thus, the law prescribes "disciplinary flogging," a rabbinic punishment, rather than the scriptural flogging.

65. I am indebted to Tirzah Meacham for this insight.

proof text itself is sufficient evidence of the claim's validity. Maimonides had already demonstrated in the *ShM* that the evidence was well warranted, a work familiar to most readers of the *MT*. Additionally, even a casual reader who had not studied the *ShM* would recognize the natural relation of the claim to the scriptural verse being cited. The *peshateh di-qera*, the contextual, plain reading of the verse, assures this recognition. In the few cases where Maimonides allows tradition to override the plain sense, he cites the verse and follows it with the traditional interpretation. It is critical that the proof text be an integral part of the initial presentation of the commandment.

Where neither a designation nor a proof text is found in the presentation of what the *ShM/SE* had already identified as a positive commandment, one wonders whether Maimonides had changed his mind. I argue that he did indeed change his mind: the *peshateh di-qera* does not validate the claim, and no rabbinic warrant can convincingly connect a verse to the claim. The commandment thus passes from the category of *de-oraita* to *divre sofrim*, revealing the unsuspected significance and ramifications of Rule 2. In the next section, I discuss the literary artifice that Maimonides uses to convey this changed perception.

CHAPTER VIII

THE PARTICIPIAL FORM AND OTHER PECULIARITIES

In many places in the *Halakhot*, Maimonides deviates from his standard formula. He neglects to declare that a given commandment is a *mitsvat 'aseh* and fails to produce a scriptural proof text. In some of these cases, he uses the participial form to describe the commandment, a formula such as "the Shema is recited" rather than "it is a positive commandment to recite the Shema." While the participle is a common mishnaic grammatical form, it is not one particularly well suited to articulating imperatives.[1] What is the significance of this grammatical form, and why does Maimonides use it?

In an article curiously entitled "Haustafeln,"[2] David Daube points out that a large majority of tannaitic rulings use this form, and suggests that perhaps it reflects the less categorical or less authoritative standing of rabbinic legislation. Daube notes that the Hebrew participle "stands for our present tense as referring to a habitual event, action or omission.... it is in this function, as an expression of the course to be taken in accordance with proper interpretation and custom, that the participle became the typically rabbinic form of legislation." He concludes: "[i]f we want to give it a name, we should call it, not imperatival participle or participial imperative, but rather advisory, didactic participle or perhaps best, participle stating the correct practice."[3]

---

1. The standard imperative form that Maimonides uses to indicate commandments is the infinitive of the verb, preceded by the preposition *lamed*. See, e.g., *Hilkhot Hamets u-Matsah* 2:1, 6:1, 7:1, and passim.
2. Daube, "Haustafeln," 295-306. The term *haustafeln* literally means "house panels," and it commonly refers to the domestic code of the first century C.E., as discussed in the New Testament. It centers on how the various members of the family (wife, children, slaves) were to relate to the dominating male (husband/father/master) of the household.
3. Ibid., 295-296.

I raised this issue in chapter 6 in discussing the commandment of the priestly blessings, where Maimonides uses this odd participial form. In this chapter, I will show that the use of the participial form is more frequent than an isolated instance. I now suggest that Maimonides deliberately utilizes these participles to describe what Daube called "habitual events" or "correct practices" in places where we may have expected scriptural commandments. While not explicitly commanded by Scripture, those rituals are ancient and generally accepted, and would logically be categorized as scribal interpretations, *divre sofrim,* rather than as scriptural commandments.

At this point, a clarification is in order. In the next few pages, I will argue that a number of commandments that are commonly thought to be scriptural, and which the *ShM* deems to be scriptural, are not categorized as scriptural (*de-oraita*) in the *Halakhot*. In effect, I will ascribe to Maimonides notions that some might be inclined to label scandalous, if not downright heretical. But one need not view these notions in such an extreme fashion. I am not arguing that these commandments are not obligatory—they most clearly are. Nor do I even imply that these commandments lack scriptural force. Indeed, some of Maimonides' most prominent commentators maintain that Maimonides viewed certain *divre sofrim* enablements as enjoying the force of scriptural law.[4] What is at issue here is not praxis but *doxa,* theory. Specifically, we see here how Maimonides (*qua* legal theorist rather than *qua* decisor) categorizes certain commandments that he did not find present in the plain sense of Scripture.

4. One such law categorized as *divre sofrim* but ostensibly enjoying the force of scriptural law is *qiddushe kesef* (betrothal by means of money); a marriage effected by money grants the woman the full legal status of a married woman, making her, for example, liable for the death penalty in case of adultery. See both Karo, *Kesef Mishneh*, and di Tolosa, *Maggid Mishneh*, on *Hilkhot Ishut*, 1:2, s.v. "*u-be-eḫad*." Analyzing a well known responsum of Maimonides' on the legal status of *qiddushe kesef*, Duran interprets him as saying that anything not explicitly written in Scripture—such as *qiddushe kesef*—"is not scriptural but rabbinic (*mi-de-rabbanan*)." Duran interprets this statement as excluding hermeneutically derived laws from the enumeration of the commandments. He concludes, however, that Maimonides would certainly agree that such laws carry scriptural force. Duran, *Zohar ha-Raqia,* 11. Our version of the responsum does not contain the word *mi-de-rabbanan* and instead contrasts scriptural laws with *divre sofrim* laws. *Responsa*, ed. Blau, no. 355, 631-633.

In chapter 7, I argued that Maimonides used the tool of *peshateh di-qera* to examine Scripture for commandments, interpreting the text plainly and contextually. I analyzed a few exceptional places where Maimonides deferred to traditional readings—when those readings could be said to lie within the limits of the plain sense of the text. For Maimonides, exegetical readings that deviate from context could not serve as bases for identifying scriptural commandments. In this chapter, I shall explore how the participial form functions in lieu of a declarative statement, informing us in a subtle but precise way that the specific commandment may not quite follow the canons of *peshateh di-qera*. This ambiguity is reinforced by the lack of a quoted proof text, effectively disconnecting the practice from the text. While most of the examples include use of the participial form, some of them reveal, if ever so subtly, an ambivalent stance through different sorts of literary artifices. These, too, we shall explore.

Following is an analysis of commandments in the *Halakhot* that, for the most part, use the participial form in their definition while also showing other deviations from the usual declarative introductory formula. I argue that these anomalies point to a subtle re-assignment of the commandment to another legal category, following the exigencies and implications of the *peshateh di-qera* hermeneutic.

P10. THE RECITATION OF THE SHEMA

In the *Halakhot,* Maimonides opens discussion of this commandment thus:

> The Shema is recited [*qorim*] twice every day, once in the evening and once in the morning, as it is said: *when thou sittest in thy house, and when thou walkest by the way, and when thou liest down, and when thou risest up* [Deut. 6:7]. The time when people customarily lie down is evening and the time when people customarily get up is morning. (*Hilkhot Qeriyat Shema* 1:1)

Note, first and foremost, that Maimonides does not explicitly designate the recitation of the Shema a positive commandment, neither here nor anywhere else in this section. He does not say, "[it is a positive commandment] to read the Shema," as he does with regard to prayer, for example: "It is a positive commandment to pray every day" (*Hilkhot Tefillah* 1:1). Instead, he uses the participle *qorim*, idiomatically translated as "is recited" (literally, "we/you/they recite").

In the *SE/ShM*, the words "*and thou shalt talk of them* [when thou sittest in thy house, and when thou walkest by the way, and when thou liest down, and when thou risest up]" (Deut. 6:7, emphasis added) are cited as evidence for the obligation to recite the Shema. Surprisingly, this proof text is entirely omitted in the *Halakhot*. It appears that in the *Halakhot*, Maimonides is only concerned with proving that the Shema is recited twice daily—night and morning, as the expression "when thou liest down, and when thou risest up" implies—rather than proving that there exists a scriptural requirement to recite it. While such a literalist reading is plausible, it does not meet the criterion of plain sense. As Tigay observes, "these pairs of contrasting phrases are merisms. Accordingly, our verse means: speak of these words wherever you are, and at all times."[5] What makes the metaphorical interpretation more philologically compelling is that a very similar expression is used in Proverbs 6:21-22[6] in a wisdom, non-legal, context, where the expressions "lying down" and "rising up" are clearly not intended to signify day and night. Rather, they are intended to signify continuous, round-the-clock, engagement. This may explain the reason Maimonides fails to adduce a proof text in the *Halakhot* for the recitation of the Shema and employs the participial form to express the obligation to recite it.

What type of obligation, then, is the recitation of the Shema? Note that the enumerative works (*SE/ShM*) contain one commandment to "unify Him" (*le-ya<u>h</u>ado*), listed as P2, and a second commandment, to recite the Shema, listed as P10, making it appear as if there are two independent scriptural commandments. A noticeably different path is taken by the *Halakhot*. After describing God's particular type of oneness in *Hilkhot Yesode ha-Torah* 1:7, Maimonides concludes: "to

5. *The JPS Torah Commentary,* Deut. 6:7. See also the medieval commentator Joseph Bekhor Shor, *Perushe R. Yosef Bekhor Shor*, ad loc.
6. Referring to "your father's commandment" and "your mother's teaching," Proverbs (6:21-22) says: "Tie them over your heart always; bind them around your throat. When you walk it will lead you; when you lie down it will watch over you; and when you are awake it will talk to you."

know this truth is a positive commandment, as it says, *Hear, O Israel: The Lord our God, the Lord is One*." The formulation is as forceful as it is unequivocal; the intellectual act of cognizing God's oneness is a positive commandment. This clarity is sorely missing when it comes to the recitation of the Shema. Here, the Shema "is recited," and no proof text is offered. I submit that Maimonides no longer puts the recitation of the Shema on a par with the cognitive act, as he had ostensibly done in the *ShM/SE*. Instead, the recitation is simply a "correct practice," in Daube's words. This formulation places the recitation of the Shema in the category of *mitsvot divre sofrim* rather than in the category of *mitsvot de-oraita*. For the legal theorist and philosopher, the oneness of God is not something that is recited but rather something that is acknowledged and understood; it is not a formula to be recited twice a day, but rather a fundamental truth that must be assimilated and affirmed at all times.

I believe that this ambivalence with respect to the recitation of the Shema can already be detected in the *ShM*. The argument there, which I review immediately below, proceeds confusedly to discuss times rather than recitation and digresses unnecessarily and excessively beyond *qeriyat shema*. As mentioned above, Maimonides' evidence for the obligation to recite the Shema twice daily comes from the verse: "and thou shalt talk of them when thou sittest in thy house, and when thou walkest by the way, and when thou liest down, and when thou risest up." In the *ShM*, Maimonides adduces two rabbinic warrants, the first from *BT Berakhot* 21a, "where it is shown that the reading of the Shema is ordained by the Torah," and the second from *T Berakhot* 3:1. In context, the talmudic passage is not as definitive as Maimonides implies, for it also contains an amoraic opinion maintaining that the recitation of Shema is rabbinic. Moreover, the passage reaches no firm conclusion on this question.

The Tosefta reads: "Just as the Torah has ordained an appointed time [*qeva'*][7] for the reading of Shema, even so have the Sages appointed a

7. Our edition of the Tosefta (ed. Zuckermandel) has here "just as an appointed time has been ordained," omitting the reference to the Torah. This omission bears on the question of whether the daily reading of Shema is a scriptural or a rabbinic precept.

time [*zeman*] for prayer."[8] The ostensible value of the passage is to show by inference that appointing times for reading Shema is a scriptural requirement, while appointing times for other prayers is a rabbinic ordinance. Oddly, Maimonides does not make this inference explicit; instead, he proceeds to discuss prayer in more general terms. In effect, he uses this warrant to show that it is the rabbis who appointed times for prayers, although the activity of prayer itself is scripturally prescribed. This distinction appears unnecessary, since Maimonides already explained in P5 that prayer is scripturally mandated. It is surprising that Maimonides does not use this text to emphasize the scriptural character of the recitation of the Shema, perhaps implying that while he accepted the second half of the dictum (that times for prayer are rabbinically ordained), he was not convinced of the first (that times for the Shema are biblically ordained). He may have, for example, thought it possible to read the Tosefta passage as indicating that the Torah merely *hinted* at the appropriate times for the Shema—thus reading the verse as an *asmakhta* rather than as a genuine proof. As I have noted on a number of previous occasions, *asmakhtot* are not valid hermeneutics on which to base scriptural claims. By way of contrast, the Tosefta suggests that when it came to appointing times for prayers, the Rabbis were left to their own ingenuity.

This interpretation dovetails well with what appears to be another seemingly redundant statement immediately following Maimonides' interpretation of the second half of the dictum:

> This is what the Sages mean when they say: "[The Men of the Great Assembly] appointed prayers to correspond with the daily burnt offerings"; that is to say, they fixed the times of prayer to correspond with the times at which [the daily burnt offerings] were brought.

Note that in this text, the term *qeva'* is set in apposition to *zeman* (time), perhaps bearing the meaning of "fixed form" rather than "appointed time." The phrase could thus mean that just as the Torah has set a fixed *form*, the Shema, for the affirmation of God's unity, so too have the Sages appointed a *time* for prayer. But see following note.

8. The Zuckermandel edition of the Tosefta has the word *zeman* here. However, the Tosefta appended to the standard editions of the Babylonian Talmud uses the term *qeva'* again instead of *zeman*. See *Sefer ha-Mitsvot*, ed. Heller, ad loc., n. 22.

Consistent with the above thesis, Maimonides explains that the Rabbis appointed times for prayers to correspond with the daily burnt offerings. This was an entirely original contribution and one that, unlike the *asmakhta* of the Shema, could not be traced to an allusion in the text. The Tosefta thus offers a comparison and a contrast. While both the recitation of the Shema and daily prayers are rabbinic commandments, the former is based on an *asmakhta* and the latter is based on a reasoned argument. In short, this rambling presentation gives us a window onto Maimonides' own doubts with respect to the legal status of the Shema recitation.

The use of the participial form in the *Halakhot* may reflect Maimonides' continued ambivalence regarding the scriptural status of this commandment. Alternatively, it may reflect a fully settled position that *qeriyat shema* is not a *mitsvat 'aseh* but simply a *divre sofrim* obligation. Regardless of how one understands the obligation, no change in praxis is implied. Towards the end of this chapter, I will attempt to demonstrate that there is indeed a difference between the views that *qeriyat shema* is *de-oraita* or *mi-divre sofrim* even according to those jurists who saw the latter as enjoying scriptural force.

P11. TO LEARN TORAH AND TO TEACH IT

What is noteworthy about the presentation of this commandment is not that it uses the participial form, which it does not, but rather that it lacks the typical declarative statement that accompanies positive commandments. In its place we find the following roundabout and atypically worded introduction:

> Women and slaves are exempt from the obligation of studying Torah. But a father is obligated [*aviv hayav le-lamdo*] to teach his young son Torah, as it is said, *And ye shall teach them to your children, talking of them* (Deut. 11:19). (*Hilkhot Talmud Torah* 1:1)

Maimonides begins by identifying everyone who is *exempt* from the obligation to study Torah, and then goes on to list those who are obligated to teach Torah and to whom: father to son, grandfather to grandson and, lastly, teacher to disciples. Notably, neither teaching nor studying Torah is ever designated as a positive commandment.[9] Note, too, that to convey the sense of obligation, Maimonides chooses the term *ḥayav*, a commonly used rabbinic expression, instead of a verbal form of *mitsvah*, the scriptural designation for obligation.

Finally, it should be noted that the introductory section only discusses *teaching* Torah—to one's children, one's grandchildren and one's disciples—and supports this obligation with Torah passages. No mention is made of the obligation to *study* Torah until *halakhah* 8, where it is supported by a non-Torah passage: "But thou shalt meditate therein day and night" (Josh. 1:8).[10] By way of contrast, in the enumerative works, both obligations are derived from the same proof text: "and ye shall teach them to your children, talking of them" (Deut. 11:19).[11]

All the peculiar features noted above suggest that in the *Halakhot*, Maimonides does not subscribe to the idea that there is a scriptural basis for the commandments to study and teach Torah. And I would submit that the *peshateh di-qera* supports this thesis. Indeed, the context of Deuteronomy 11:19, urging one to teach one's children, does not appear to refer to the study of Torah, but rather to the proclamation of God's unity and to the love that we must show for Him (vv. 5-6).

Further support for this conjecture can be found in a statement that Maimonides makes in *Hilkhot Qeriyat Shema*. After ruling that one must recite the Shema twice each day, Maimonides explains why one recites the passage beginning "Hear O Israel" (Deut. 6:4-9) before those beginning

---

9. The failure to make a declaratory statement and the peculiar and absolutely atypical opening prompts the commentator RaDBaZ to offer a justification: Maimonides wanted to emphasize the fact that women and slaves are exempt from the obligation even though they are generally obligated to perform all positive commandments that have a fixed time. In any case, one can see that Maimonides succeeded in diverting attention from the critical issue, namely, that he has not designated the study and teaching of Torah as a positive commandment. See RaDBaZ, *Sheelot u-Teshuvot ha-RaDBaZ*, vol. 8, *siman* 1.

10. By definition, prophetic passages cannot serve as valid proof texts for scriptural commandments.

11. The *Sifre* comments that the Hebrew word *ve-shinantam*, here translated as "you shall teach them," can also be understood as coming from the *pi'el* form of the verb *shinen*, "sharp." The words of Torah shall be "sharp" in the mouth of the teacher, a fluency that implies prior study and familiarity.

"And it shall come to pass" (Deut. 11:13-21) and "The Lord spoke" (Num. 15:37-41). He writes: "The section beginning *Hear O Israel* is recited first, because it contains the unity of God, the [duty to] love Him [*ve-ahavato*] and [the duty to teach about] Him [*ve-talmudo*], because this is the great principle on which everything depends."[12] As Maimonides details elsewhere, Scripture commands the believer to cognize intellectually God's oneness (P2; *Hilkhot Yesode ha-Torah* 1:7). Therefore, one may conclude that the passage "and thou shalt teach them diligently unto thy children" exhorts one to impart *this* knowledge to others.

Maimonides may have viewed the commandments to study and teach Torah as merely a rabbinic appropriation of scriptural advice, a classic example of *divre sofrim*.[13] At least to Maimonides' way of thinking, this appropriation may have been justified by practical considerations: only the study of the Law can lead to the proper performance of commandments.[14] As we saw, the introductory presentations of each of the commandments in the *Halakhot* contain a great deal of information about Maimonides' legal philosophy and classification. Given the revered standing that the study of Torah enjoyed among rabbinic students and the general public, it is not surprising that Maimonides came to use subtle literary devices, such as formulaic variants, to hide his true opinion.

P12, P13. TO BIND PHYLACTERIES ON THE HEAD AND ON THE ARM

Maimonides opens *Hilkhot Tefillin* in the following manner:

12. My translation. I take *ahavato* and *talmudo* as referring to God, while the words "because this is the great principle" (*ki hu ha-iqqar ha-gadol*), refer back to God's unity. Hyamson translates the phrase as "studying His words," an interpretative statement that follows the approach of most rabbinic commentators.
13. In *Hilkhot Talmud Torah* 1:2, Maimonides states: "on traditional authority (*mi-pi ha-shemu'ah lamdu*), the term 'thy children' includes disciples." This tradition does not say that one ought to teach one's children Torah; it simply says that Scripture uses the word "children" to include disciples.
14. See *Hilkhot Talmud Torah* 1:3 on the importance of study for the performance of commandments. Alternatively, the study of the Law settles a person's mind (*meyashvim da'atam shel adam teẖillah*) and allows him to embark on the true goal of the scriptural commandment: metaphysical contemplation. *See Hilkhot Yesode ha-Torah* 4:13.

> The following four passages...are the ones that are written by themselves [or "individually," *bi-fne 'atsmam*]; they are wrapped in leather and are called tefillin. They are to be placed [*u-manihin otam*] on the head and they are tied [*ve-qoshrin otam*] on the arm.[15] (*Hilkhot Tefillin* 1:1)

Because tefillin are not explicitly defined (or mentioned by that name) in Scripture,[16] Maimonides logically chooses to describe the objects with which one is to perform the commandment before he declares and explains the nature of the commandment. It is only immediately after this description that the difficulties become apparent: "They are to be placed [*u-manihin otam*] on the head and they are tied [*ve-qoshrin otam*] on the arm." Why does Maimonides use the participial form, rather than declaring clearly and unequivocally that it is a positive commandment to place these tefillin on the head and tie them on the arm? And why does he fail to support this practice with the appropriate scriptural citation, as he did in the *SE/ShM*—and as he does in the presentation of nearly every commandment?

Similarly, in *Hilkhot Tefillin* 4:1-2, Maimonides discusses the exact spot on which one should place these tefillin. Yet he not only omits the scriptural verse that supports this identification, but he adds: "We learned the positioning of the tefillin on the arm and on the head from the oral tradition [*mi-pi ha-shemu'ah lamdu*]." His resorting to tradition for this point implies that he does not think that the scriptural verse "And thou shalt bind them for a sign upon thy hand and they shall be for frontlets between thy eyes" is sufficiently revealing. Moreover, as discussed in chapter 7, the expression *mi-pi ha-shemu'ah* without an accompanying proof text generally signifies that we are in the presence of an ancient tradition rather than a scriptural law. Lastly, nowhere does Maimonides

---

15. In the continuation, Maimonides states further that "according to the Torah, a mistake in the tip of only one of the letters in the four passages renders the whole unfit; they must be written perfectly as they are supposed to be." He then rules that the same is true for passages written for the mezuzah and for the Torah scroll. These are laws that pertain to scribing any passages or sections of the Torah; they do not confer a scriptural status on the commandments of placing tefillin on the head and arm and mezuzot on doorposts.

16. "And thou shalt bind them for a sign upon thy hand, and they shall be for frontlets between thy eyes" (Deut. 6:8).

cite the midrashic play on the scriptural word *totafot* used to substantiate the idea that the phylacteries contain four passages.[17] The impression we get is that Maimonides was both troubled by the correspondence between the praxis and the plain meaning of the commands to place a "sign" (*ot*) and a "remembrance" (*zikaron/totafot*)[18] on one's arm and head and by the philological genuineness of the midrash on the word *totafot*.[19]

Throughout history, several interpreters have suggested that these verses should be understood in a metaphoric sense. Aqila, Theodotion, and some manuscripts of the Septuagint read the verses as exhorting one to be aware constantly of God's teachings. In the Middle Ages, the Karaites also stressed the metaphoric view. In his long commentary to Exodus 13:9, Ibn Ezra, repeating the familiar refrain *ein miqra yotse mi-yede peshuto* ("a scriptural verse never loses its *peshat* sense") rejects the metaphoric views of *totafot* offered by the Karaites because the literal interpretation is plausible in context.[20] By even citing and engaging such a view, he seems to show a certain degree of sympathy for the figurative interpretation. RaSHBaM also writes that according to the "depth of the plain interpretation" (*omeq peshuto*), these words should be taken metaphorically.[21] These disagreements among Maimonides' predecessors and contemporaries highlight the exegetical difficulties encountered with Deuteronomy 6:8 and the so-called commandment

17. Cf. RaSHI on Deut. 6:8, based on *BT Sanhedrin* 4b.

18. *Zikaron* in Exod. 13:9; *totafot* in Exod. 13:16, Deut. 6:8, 11:18.

19. Cf. *BT Menaẖot* 34b. R. Ishmael and R. Aqiba both parse the *tris legomenon* "*totafot*" to signal the quantity four, referring to the four sections inscribed on the parchments, but without explicating the term. The far-fetched etymological explanations in the Talmud all imply that *totafot* is only an allusion (*remez*) to tefillin, which is another way of saying that tefillin are not explicitly discussed in Scripture. Accordingly, at least part of the commandment of tefillin should be seen as *mi-divre sofrim*, like all precepts informed by tradition and only tenuously linked to the text. See chapter 7, note 10 above.

20. After equating *peshat* with literalism, Ibn Ezra says that one should be willing to accept literalism as long as it makes good sense. Interestingly, he rejects a philological interpretation based on the way similar expressions are used in Proverbs (1:9, 6:21), because Proverbs, unlike the Torah, is a book of parables. Clearly, his appreciation of *peshat* is quite different than the one I ascribe to Maimonides, as is his belief that the Torah contains no parables. In his short commentary, Ibn Ezra also offers the metaphoric interpretation—before going on to reject it—but does not ascribe it to the Karaites.

21. RaSHBaM, *Perush ha-Torah* on Deut. 13:9. See *The JPS Torah Commentary, Deuteronomy*, Excursus 11.

of tefillin. The view that the commandment of tefillin is not a *mitsvah de-oraita* would have surely shocked the Jewish community. The use of the participial hid this opinion from the masses by simply not having to state explicitly that the obligation to wear them is *mi-divre sofrim*. It is also possible, however, that the participial form may have genuinely expressed a more ambivalent stand on the matter.

P15. TO AFFIX A MEZUZAH

Much of what was said about tefillin can be said about the commandment to affix a mezuzah. Maimonides opens *Hilkhot Mezuzah* (*Hilkhot Tefillin u-Mezuzah ve-Sefer Torah* 5:1) by describing the mezuzah and the process of its production: "How is the mezuzah to be written [*ketsad kotvin*, lit., "how do they write the mezuzah"]? One writes two passages ... in a single column on a piece of parchment."[22] Most of the first chapter is devoted to explaining how to write the mezuzah. In 5:10, Maimonides rules that "all are obligated [*ha-kol h̠ayavin*] to affix mezuzot, even women and slaves," without designating this obligation a positive commandment. Instead, we note here too, as with the study of Torah, the use of the common rabbinic term for obligation, *h̠ayav* (here *h̠ayavin*). Maimonides misses the last opportunity to designate the writing and placing of a mezuzah as a positive commandment in 6:12, when he explains where the mezuzah is to be affixed. Once again, he makes use of the participial form: "Where is the mezuzah to be affixed [*ve-hekhan qovin et ha-mezuzah*]?" Furthermore, nowhere in *Hilkhot Mezuzah* does Maimonides cite the traditional evidence for this commandment claim, as he did in the enumerative works: "And thou shalt write them upon the doorposts of thy house, and upon thy gates" (Deut. 6:9).[23]

I suggest that, here again, Maimonides reads the scriptural pericope in a manner consistent with the context, in this case giving

22. Note that the verse speaks about writing the words "upon the doorposts of thy house," and that it is only via an inference from similar words (*gezerah shavah*) that the rabbis interpreted the passage to say that the pentateuchal sections should be written on parchment. See *BT Menah̠ot* 34a. As we saw earlier, Maimonides deems derivations using hermeneutic rules like *gezerah shavah* to be *mi-divre sofrim*.

23. He does cite part of this verse in connection with a detail of the law: "Granaries, barns, lumber rooms, and storehouses are exempt from mezuzah, since it says, *of thy house* [Deut. 6:9]."

it a figurative meaning. Since the subject of the larger passage is God's unity, this knowledge is what should always envelop each person; the doorposts are as much a sign of constancy, immediacy and nearness as one's forehead and arms.[24] Maimonides' formulaic deviation, the lack of a declaratory statement[25] and the failure to adduce textual evidence for the commandment to write or affix a mezuzah, as well as his use of the participial form and the rabbinic term for obligation, suggest, at the very least, an extraordinary ambivalence about the scriptural status of this commandment. I posit that Maimonides' exegetical sense would not allow him to accept the Sages' traditional reading of Deuteronomy 6:4-9, a passage that contains the fundaments of the religion. Through various literary means and through the use of the participial form, Maimonides either hinted that the commandment to affix a mezuzah is a *mitsvah mi-divre sofrim* or simply expressed doubt regarding the scriptural status of the commandment. Regardless, there would be no impact on praxis; Maimonides made sure to uphold every detail of the traditional rabbinic interpretation when explicating the practice in the *Halakhot*.

P17/P18. THAT THE KING SHALL WRITE A SCROLL OF THE TORAH FOR HIMSELF (P18 IN THE SE AND P17 IN THE SHM ENUMERATION)

While the command that the king shall write a scroll of the Torah for himself has a scriptural basis, Maimonides does not designate it as a

---

24. Maimonides does not approve of the objectification of the "great duty" to affirm God's unity, love, and worship. The commandment of belief is condensed into an object that could become an amulet for personal interests, in the hands of fools. Writing about those who inscribe the mezuzah with the names of angels, holy names, or other such protective mantras, Maimonides says: "For these fools not only fail to fulfill the duty [*bittlu ha-mitsvah*] but made a great duty [*mitsvah gedolah*], namely the unity of the Name of God, His love and His worship, as it were an amulet to promote their own personal interests" (*Hilkhot Mezuzah* 5:4). Note the expression *bittlu ha-mitsvah* instead of the phrase that one might expect, *bittlu mitsvat 'aseh*.

25. Maimonides also fails to designate the commandment as a *mitsvat 'aseh* in the rest of *Hilkhot Mezuzah*, even when he points out how one is liable if one fails to fulfill the command. We note that at 5:4, he uses the expression *bittlu ha-mitsvah* instead of the expected *bittlu mitsvat 'aseh*. See the note 24 above.

positive commandment in the *Halakhot*.[26] Oddly enough, although Maimonides discusses the king's obligation to write a *sefer torah* in two separate places, *Hilkhot Sefer Torah* (7:2) and *Hilkhot Melakhim* (3:1), the obligation is listed only under the Headings to *Hilkhot Sefer Torah* and not under the Headings to *Hilkhot Melakhim*.

The two formulations are substantively similar, with one exception: in *Hilkhot Sefer Torah*, Maimonides writes: "The king is obligated [*metsuveh*][27] to write one scroll of Law for himself, for the sake of the king, *an additional scroll to the one he had while still a commoner*" [emphasis added]. Maimonides here refers to the commandment that everyone is obligated to write a scroll of the Torah (P17). In *Hilkhot Melakhim*, on the other hand, Maimonides writes that "the king writes for himself a scroll of Law in addition to the scroll *that his forefathers had left him*" [emphasis added]. This is based on a *baraita* quoted in *BT Sanhedrin* 21b: "And he must not take credit [lit. "adorn himself"] for the one belonging to his ancestors." A few sentences later, Maimonides acknowledges the obligation on each person to write a scroll of the Torah, when he says that "one [of the scrolls], the writing of which is obligatory upon every Jew, he places in his treasure-house."[28] In neither of these sections, however, does Maimonides designate this royal obligation a positive commandment, despite the clear proof text: "And it shall be, when he sitteth upon the throne of the kingdom, that he shall write him a copy of this law in a book, out of which is before the priests the Levites " (Deut. 17:18).

I argue here that Maimonides' failure to declare a positive commandment is supported by a *peshateh di-qera* reading of the scriptural passage. The idea that the king must write two scrolls of law, one as a commoner and one as a king, comes from reading *mishneh* as "double" and then abstracting the phrase from its context, so it is interpreted that he must write to himself a double torah, that is, two *torot*.[29] Taking the context into account, however, the plain sense of

26. Not so with regard to the average man's obligation to write a *sefer torah*. There he clearly states that it is a positive commandment to write one. See *Hilkhot Sefer Torah* 7:1.
27. See *RaMBaM Meduyaq*, ed. Shailat, *Hilkhot Sefer Torah* 7:2, n. 7.
28. The phrase used is "*bet genazav*." Compare Ezra 5:17; 6:1.
29. The talmudic exegesis (*BT Sanhedrin* 21b), "he writes for his own sake [*lishmo*] two *torot*" likely means that he writes two scrolls when he accedes to the throne, not that

the text calls for a different reading; namely, the king must write a double, i.e., a copy, of *this* torah, which is in the hands of the Levites ("from in front of the Levite priests). In the *Halakhot*, Maimonides renders "*mishneh*" in a manner to reflect this plain sense (and as the targumic interpreter did), specifically, a copy of the Torah.

The king must copy for himself the Torah (probably working from the one lodged in the Temple), which he shall keep about him at all times. It does not mean that he has to write for himself a second scroll.[30] Thus the king is only obligated to write one scroll of the Torah, the same obligation incumbent on every Jew. Furthermore, the requirement that the king store one scroll in his treasure house is rabbinic: Scripture refers only to the one he must write, saying, "and it shall be with him, and he shall read therein all the days of his life" (Deut. 17:19). Yet, to uphold an ancient tradition that the king must place a scroll in his treasure house, Maimonides has the king write an *extra* scroll of law while placing the one that he wrote as a commoner in the treasure-house ("one, the writing of which is obligatory upon every Jew, he places in his treasure house").[31] Thus all of the regulations requiring a king to write a second scroll are rabbinic, not scriptural.

To reiterate: the *Halakhot* adopts the plain sense of the verse that the king must write one copy of the Torah for himself—the very same obligation incumbent upon every commoner, as stated in *Hilkhot Sefer Torah* 7:1. In light of this, it is the king's obligation to write a scroll of the law is not a separate positive commandment. This also explains why Maimonides officially positioned this detail of the commandment in *Hilkhot Sefer Torah,* rather than in *Hilkhot*

---

he writes one upon accession to complement a previously inherited scroll. See *PhM*, *M Sanhedrin* 2:5. Note that this reading differs from the ones presented in the *Halakhot* and would constitute a third position.

30. See Onqelos, ad loc.

31. Karo (*Kesef Mishneh*, *Hilkhot Melakhim* 3:1) correctly sensed that Maimonides obligates the king to write only one scroll, noting that this contradicts the plain sense of the passage in *BT Sanhedrin* 21b. Karo acknowledged that his attempt to reconcile Maimonides' ruling with the passage is forced. According to my interpretation, Maimonides' philological understanding of the term *mishneh* does indeed reject the talmudic passage; even this one extra scroll is a concession to a rabbinic ordinance.

Melakhim:[32] the commandment to the king is only a detail of the general commandment that every Jew must write a scroll of law. Maimonides labels the general commandment a *mitsvat 'aseh,* but omits such a designation for the command that the king write a scroll of law, since, from a scriptural point of view, no such special commandment exists.[33]

P127-P130. TO SET ASIDE VARIOUS TITHES

As interpreted by the Oral Law, Leviticus 27, Numbers 18, and Deuteronomy 14 describe the tithes that were incumbent on the Israelites upon entering the Land of Israel, three of which were to rest on the Israelites and the fourth on the Levites. The first tithe was to be given to the Levites, and the oral law stipulates that everything growing from the land would be subject to the tithe. The second tithe prescribed by Scripture was to be consumed by the owner in Jerusalem, while a third tithe would be levied for the benefit of the poor. In the *Halakhot*, Maimonides fails to designate any of these tithes as positive commandments. Additionally, he makes heavy use of the participial form—in this case, the terms "*mafrish*" and "*mafrishin*," from the root "to set aside" or "to separate"—throughout his discussion of the tithes, both in *Hilkhot Matnot 'Aniyim* and *Hilkhot Ma'aser*.

Maimonides introduces the first tithe (*ma'aser rishon*) in the following manner: "After one has set aside the great heave offering [*terumah gedolah*], he sets aside [*mafrish*] one-tenth of what is left. This is what is called first tithe" (*Hilkhot Ma'aser* 1:1). Contrast this with the way he presents the commandment (P126 in the *ShM*) to separate the great heave offering (*terumah gedolah*) for the priest: "All human food

32. One might well ask: according to Maimonides, what is the novelty of the king's command? I suggest that the novelty lies in the king's obligation to carry the scroll with him wherever he goes, reading from it all the days of his life, as per the proof text: "And it shall be with him, and he shall read therein all the days of his life" (Deut. 17:19), an obligation not required of a commoner.

33. From a hermeneutic point of view, however, the commandment that the king must write a scroll for himself provides the basis for the general commandment that every Jew must write his own scroll. This is the reason that the *ShM* enumerated the king's commandment before the general one, following *BT Sanhedrin* 21b. See the earlier discussion of P17 in chapter 5, note 52.

that is watched over and that grows out of the soil is subject to the heave offering. It is a positive commandment to separate from it the first fruits for the priest" (*Hilkhot Terumot* 2:1).

The second tithe (*ma'aser sheni*) follows the form of the first:

> After the first tithe has been set aside each year, one must set aside [*mafrishin*] also the second tithe ... In the third and sixth years of each septennate, the poor man's tithe [*ma'aser 'ani*] must be set aside [*mafrishin*] instead of the second tithe as we have explained. (*Hilkhot Ma'aser Sheni* 1:1)

The briefly-mentioned third tithe, *ma'aser 'ani,* is described in greater detail in the sixth chapter of *Hilkhot Matnot 'Aniyim*, which also details five types of gifts that one gives to the poor from the produce of the land: *peah* (lit., "corner of the field"), gleanings of grapes, gleanings of olives, the forgotten sheaf, and the defective grape clusters. *Ma'aser 'ani* is introduced there as "a sixth gift." The fourth tithe, incumbent on the Levites and given to the priest (*terumat ma'aser*), is discussed in *Hilkhot Terumot* (3:12) because of its affinity to the great heave offering.[34] Maimonides refers to this requirement as *mitsvat terumat ma'aser*, though he still fails to designate it a *mitsvat 'aseh.*[35]

I have not yet found a totally satisfactory solution to this unusual presentation. Perla offers a promising approach, observing that scriptural evidence for the obligatory nature of the tithe commandments is ambiguous. He suggests that the exegeses underpinning the tithe of cattle (which I have not analyzed here), the first tithe, and the poor man's tithe are merely *asmakhta be-alma* and *derashot be-alma*,[36]

34. Since this tithe is particular to the Levites, it does not form part of the ordinary order of tithes.

35. The expression *mitsvat terumat ma'aser* should be rendered as "the proper way to perform *terumat ma'aser*" and it is used deliberately as a contrast with a second and less desirable way to fulfill this requirement. The *halakhah* reads as follows: "The commandment of heave offering of the tithe applies to the Levite, who must set it aside out of his tithe.... An Israelite, however, may set it aside and give it to the priest, and then give the balance of the tithe to the Levite, after he has set aside the latter's heave offering, which is the tithe from the tithe" (*Hilkhot Terumot* 3:12).

36. In these formulations, *be-alma* means "merely" or "only," and the expressions may be translated as "merely an *asmakhta*" and "merely a *derashah*." These creative exegeses

rabbinic ordinances supported by scriptural verses. As a result, Perla argues that Sa'adiah was correct to list these three tithes in the indicative rather than the imperative mode.[37] Through a *peshateh di-qera* lens, one could argue that these tithing commandments, or at least some of them, could be classified as *mitsvot mi-divre sofrim,* thus justifying Maimonides' use of the participial form when describing these commandments.

Scripture's indeterminacy may even extend to the second tithe. In the *ShM*, Maimonides quotes the *Sifre,* which, commenting on the words "Thou shalt surely tithe all the increase of thy seed" (Deut. 14:22) writes: "I would only know this about the second tithe, *regarding which Scripture speaks*" (emphasis added).[38] This comment helps Maimonides prove that the second tithe represents a scriptural obligation. Maimonides' reliance on the oral tradition is confirmed in the *SE*: "To set apart the second tithe to be eaten by its owner in Jerusalem, as it is said, *Thou shalt surely tithe* [Deut. 14:22]. They learnt from tradition [*mi-pi ha-shemu'ah lamdu*] that this refers to the second tithe." This is one of the five instances occurring in the *SE* (noted earlier in chapter 7) in which Maimonides resorts to the oral tradition rather than relying directly on the text to substantiate a commandment claim. Yet, it appears that he harbored some doubts after all with respect to this reading, because he does not cite it in the *Halakhot*. While reversals from previously held opinions are not rare in Maimonides' works, I could find no other instance in the *Halakhot* in which Maimonides fails to make use of a traditional reading on which he had previously depended for the elucidation of the same scriptural proof text.[39] Perhaps by the

---

do not represent veritable sources of the law; rather, they constitute supports or mnemonics for an existing law that was already known from tradition.

37. Perla, *Sefer ha-Mitsvot le-RaSaG*, vol. 1, 612b-c. With respect to at least one of these three tithes, the tithe of cattle, we find that Maimonides upholds the scriptural basis of the commandment and designates it as such.

38. *Sifre Deuteronomy* 105 (164). For an explanation of the rabbinic exegesis that underpins this tradition, see Epstein, *Torah Temimah*, Deut. 14:22, n. 38. Ibn Ezra, Deut. 14:28, s. v. "*miqtseh*," cites an opinion of the "heretics" (i.e., Karaites), stating that the passage commencing with "Thou shalt surely tithe" refers to the first tithe, not the second. Does he believe that their interpretation is plausible according to the peshat?

39. See the discussion of "*mi-pi ha-shemu'ah lamdu*" in chapter 7.

time he wrote the *Halakhot,* Maimonides had come to question the authoritativeness of the tradition, which in turn forced him to change his opinion about the scriptural status of the second tithe.

There is even some evidence that Maimonides equivocated regarding the exegetical basis for the first and second tithes. In the various versions of the *ShM*, we find three separate probatory texts substantiating the first tithe (P127): two of the explanations use their own proof texts, while a third one conflates both proof texts.[40] Contrary to Maimonides' assertion, the Leviticus 27:30 proof text used in one version is contradicted by rabbinic opinion, which maintains that it refers to the second tithe, rather than to the first.[41] This or perhaps some other reason may have led Maimonides to offer a second proof text, found in a second version preserved by one of the Arabic manuscripts: "For the tithe of the children of Israel, which they set apart as a gift unto the Lord" (Num. 18:24). The Numbers proof text does not denote an obligation, however, nor can it easily be identified with the first tithe (*ma'aser rishon*) of the tithing cycle.[42]

In sum, the participial form may well reflect Maimonides' ambivalent stance on the scriptural status of tithes, a stance that can be attributed to the lack of exegetical clarity found in talmudic and midrashic sources. It is also possible that Maimonides had not been ambivalent after all, and the use of the participial may reflect a view that tithing laws represent only correct practices—and therefore ought to be categorized as *mitsvot mi-divre sofrim* and not as *mitsvot de-oraita*.

---

40. In the Arabic manuscript (and in the *Halakhot*), Maimonides quotes the verse "for it is the tithes set aside by the Israelites as a gift to the Lord [that I give to the Levites as their share]" (Num. 18:24) to indicate "that this tithe belongs to the Levites." In Nahmanides' version of the *ShM*, Ibn Ayub's translation, and the *SE,* however, Maimonides instead quotes the verse "And all the tithe of the land, whether of the seed of the land or of the fruit of the tree [shall be the Lord's]" (Lev. 27:30). *MnT*'s translation presents both proof texts, conflating the two versions. It is reasonable to conclude that the Numbers 18:24 proof text forms part of the latest version, since it is the proof text ultimately quoted in the *Halakhot*.
41. See RaSHI's commentary to the Pentateuch, ad loc.; Nahmanides, *Hasagot* to Rule 12, 190.
42. Cf. *Sefer ha-Mitsvot*, ed. Heller, ad loc., n. 5, who alerts the reader to the textual confusion. See also Henshke, "Le-Toldot Parshanutan shel Parashiyyot Ma'aser," 97-101, who arrives at a similar conclusion.

P168. TO DWELL IN BOOTHS SEVEN DAYS

The presentation of this commandment in the *Halakhot* exhibits a number of peculiar elements. First, the chapter that discusses the duty to dwell in a booth (sukkah), chapter 6 of *Hilkhot Sukkah*, begins by listing those who are exempted from dwelling in the booth—"women, slaves, and minors"—rather than declaring that there is a positive commandment for men to dwell in a sukkah. Note that the form of this opening presentation parallels almost exactly the one used in *Hilkhot Talmud Torah* for the commandment to study and teach Torah. In my discussion of that commandment, I demonstrated that, at a minimum, Maimonides was ambivalent about its scriptural status. Accordingly, this presentation might suggest a similar concern.

Additional peculiarities may be cited. The proof text does not appear until *halakhah* 5, and then only to describe the manner in which the duty should be performed—not to substantiate the basic obligation to dwell in booths during those seven days:

> How is the commandment to dwell in a booth [*mitsvat ha-yeshivah ba-sukkah*] to be observed? One should eat, drink, and reside in the booth day and night throughout the whole of the seven days of the festival, exactly as one resides in his house during the rest of the year. During these seven days one should regard his house as a temporary home and the booth as his permanent home, in accordance with the verse, *Ye shall dwell* [*teshvu*, lit., "sit"] *in booths seven days* [Lev. 23:42].

The imperative form is notably absent from *halakhah* 6, and in its stead, the participial is used heavily: "Both by day and by night, one eats, drinks and sleeps [*okhlin ve-shotin ve-yeshenim*, lit., "they are eating, drinking, and sleeping"] in the booth throughout the whole of the seven days." Finally, in *halakhah* 7, when Maimonides at last declares that there is an obligation to eat in the sukkah on the first night of the festival, he states:

> It is obligatory [*ẖovah*] to eat in the booth on the first night of the festival. Even if one eats as little as an olive's bulk of bread, he has fulfilled his duty. Thereafter the matter is optional: If one wishes to eat a regular

> meal, he must eat it in the booth, but if he prefers to eat only fruit or parched ears outside of the booth during the remainder of the seven days he may do so. This is thus analogous to the law concerning the eating of unleavened bread during Passover.

For "obligation," Maimonides uses the rabbinic term h̲ovah, not the expected phrase *mitsvat 'aseh*. Contrast this formulation with the way he describes the obligation to observe the Passover festival: "It is a positive commandment from the Torah to eat unleavened bread on the night of the fifteenth of Nissan, as it says, *At even ye shall eat unleavened bread* [Exod. 12:18]."

These general literary considerations suggest that Maimonides may have viewed the commandment to dwell in a sukkah as non-scriptural. Moreover, Maimonides' use of the more neutral participial form that I hypothesize indicates correct practices, strengthens my suspicion that he categorizes this commandment as a *mitsvah mi-divre sofrim*. I suggest that the rituals of Sukkot are not based in scriptural law—they appear to be purely a construct of the oral law. My demonstration rests on three separate but complementary arguments: the historical analogue; the h̲ovah, or obligation to eat in the sukkah the first night of the festival; and the laws of the sukkah.

The historical analogue

Scripture declares: "Ye shall dwell in sukkot seven days.... that your generation may know that I made the children of Israel to dwell in sukkot, when I brought them out of the land of Egypt" (Lev. 23:42-43).

Despite this explanation, the scriptural narrative of the Israelites does not recount their dwelling in sukkot anytime during their journey in the wilderness. What, then, were these sukkot in which "the children of Israel dwelt when they were brought out of Egypt"? Tannaim are divided on this question. R. Eliezer[43] maintains that sukkot were booths,

---

43. Based on *Sifra Emor* 17:11 (103b). The printed editions of the Babylonian Talmud, *BT Sukkah* 11b, reverse the attributions. Jeffrey L. Rubenstein offers persuasive arguments for considering the Sifra's version of the attributions to be the more reliable one. See Rubenstein, *The History of Sukkot in the Second Temple and Rabbinic*

dwellings used by the sojourners to protect them from the inhospitable desert climate. R. Akiva maintains that the word "sukkot" alludes to the "clouds of the glory" (*anane ha-kavod*) that surrounded the Israelites during their travels through the desert, providing them with multiple types of protection, including shade against the searing sun. If, as is the norm in legal matters, one follows R. Akiva's opinion, then the word "sukkot" refers to heavenly clouds rather than manmade booths. We might then wish to interpret the injunction "Ye shall dwell in sukkot seven days" figuratively: you shall live under My protection for seven days, as you did in the days of old. We are left with the question: how does one live under God's protection for seven days? It would appear then that only the oral law can resolve this question.

The hovah or obligation to eat in a sukkah the first night of the festival

The practice of eating the minimum equivalent of an olive's bulk of bread in a sukkah on the night of the fifteenth of Tishre appears to be a *mitsvah mi-divre sofrim* and not a *mitsvah de-oraita*. While eating unleavened bread on the night of the fifteenth of Nissan is scripturally prescribed, the Torah does not mention eating in the sukkah on the night of the fifteenth day of Tishre. The talmudic sages (*BT Sukkah* 27a) derive this obligation through a *gezerah shavah*, a hermeneutic method based on linguistic analogies. The common term that connects the two festivals is "fifteenth." Just as one is obligated to eat (unleavened) bread on the fifteenth day of Nissan, so must one eat bread on the fifteenth of Tishre. Since the *gezerah shavah* is one of the thirteen hermeneutic rules, the resultant obligation can only be *mi-divre sofrim* according to Maimonides (as per his Rule 2). This understanding would readily explain Maimonides' use of the rabbinic term *ẖovah* to convey that night's obligation.

The laws of sukkah

The details of who must dwell in a sukkah and who is exempted from it, as well as all the physical details of the sukkah—its roof, walls, and

---

Periods, 239n1.

materials—are dictated by tradition. Maimonides uses this series of laws in his introduction to the *PhM*, illustrating the authoritative role of oral law in the interpretation of written law and the inextricable relationship between the two. This analysis corroborates our suspicion that Maimonides considered the scriptural sukkah commandment to be a textual riddle. As he writes:

> An example. God said to him [Moses]: *Ye shall dwell in sukkot seven days*. He, the exalted one, also informed him that the *sukkah* obligation is incumbent on males and not on females, and that the sick and the traveler are exempted from this obligation. One must roof the *sukkah* only with material that grows from the land; one may not roof it with wool, silk or utensils [*kelim*], even those that grow from the land, like mats and clothes. Eating, drinking and sleeping must take place in it all seven days. Its living space must not be smaller than seven by seven *tefahim*, and it must not be lower than ten *tefahim*.

The specifics of the laws of sukkah are thoroughly a construct of oral law. At best, the scriptural reference to sukkot is an *asmakhta* for the immensely complex set of rules that define all aspects of the sukkah's construction and the holiday's obligation.

I conclude that Maimonides lacked sufficient evidence to treat the laws of dwelling in a sukkah as a *mitsvat 'aseh de-oraita*. From a *peshateh di-qera* perspective, the obligation to dwell in a specially constructed booth for seven days did not seem to be scripturally commanded. Maimonides indicates this doubt through the use of a number of literary artifices, among them (but not limited to) the peculiar opening statement and the use of the participial form in which he couched the obligation.

P169. LULAV

In chapter 6, I noted the lack of a declarative statement in the commandment of taking the four species on Sukkot. I suggested that Maimonides may have thought it more appropriate to subsume this obligation under the commandment to rejoice on the festivals (P54). In other words, I treated his unusual presentation as a case of revised individuation. I also noted his use of a passive infinitive to describe the command to take the *lulav*:

"*mitsvat lulav* [that is, the combination of the four species] is to be taken [*le-hinatel*] on the first day of the festival only—anywhere and at any time, even if this happens to be a Sabbath" (*Hilkhot Lulav* 7:13).

I now offer an alternative solution, based on the analysis of Maimonides' *peshateh di-qera* hermeneutics. The scriptural text does not specify the types of species (*minim*) that one must take on the festival of Sukkot. The verse "And ye shall take you on the first day the fruit of goodly trees, branches of palm trees, and boughs of thick trees, and willows of the brook" (Lev. 23:40) forms the basis of the commandment to take branches of a palm tree, a citron (*etrog*), branches of myrtle, and branches of willows of the brook. While tradition interprets the "fruit of goodly trees" and the "boughs of thick trees" as citrons and myrtle branches, respectively, the identification of these particular species cannot be derived from the text alone.[44] Various midrashim attempt to justify the traditional identification of the four species,[45] but, as Maimonides describes these midrashim, "they are not meant to bring out the meaning of the text in question."[46] Maimonides posits that taking these four species commemorates the "joy and gladness" that the Israelites felt when leaving the barren desert "for places in which there were fruit-bearing trees and rivers." He suggests that the choice of the four specific species was discretionary; the traditional interpretation satisfies a number of criteria, such as the availability of the species in the land of Israel, special fragrance, and guaranteed freshness for seven days.[47]

---

44. Translating *peri ets hadar* as the "boughs of majestic trees" allows the generalization of the three species that follow in the text and eliminates the notion of a single species. Similarly, *anaf ets avot*, the branches of a leafy tree, is also a non-specific category, difficult to reconcile with the myrtle. See Milgrom, *Leviticus,* 2065. In fact, the *anaf ets avot* and the leaves of the myrtle (*hadas*) are listed as two separate species in Nehemiah 8:15. See the comments of Ibn Ezra on Leviticus 23:40 and his defense of the rabbinic tradition against Karaite attacks.

45. See Maimonides' discussion of this point in his introduction to the Mishnah (*Haqdamot ha-RaMBaM la-Mishnah,* ed. Shailat, 38-39). Maimonides notes that while the identification of "fruit of goodly trees" with an etrog comes from the oral tradition, it is not considered a *halakhah le-Moshe mi-Sinai,* because hints in the verse allude to the etrog. See our discussion of *halakhah le-Moshe mi-Sinai* in chapter 7, note 10.

46. *GP* III:43: 573.

47. Ibid., 574. An element of practical discretion may also be detected in the words that Maimonides uses in *Hilkhot Lulav* 7:4 to support the identification of the four species:

The laws of the four species parallel those of *tefillin*: observances for which the rabbis find creative but philologically untenable links between the underlying text and traditional practice. Because the *peshateh di-qera* does not indicate particular species, Maimonides does not classify the commandments as scriptural. In this instance, however, because Maimonides does not use the participial form indicating customary practice, my conclusions are more tentative. Nevertheless, the rare passive infinitive form coupled with the lack of a declarative statement suggests that Maimonides is alerting the careful reader to a change in the commandment's classification: the taking of the four species is not, properly speaking, a *mitsvat 'aseh de-oraita*.

In this analysis, I have shown how Maimonides reclassified some of the most colorful and idiosyncratic practices of the Jewish faith from scriptural to non-scriptural status. This reclassification proceeds from the ultimate implications of Maimonides' hermeneutics of *peshateh di-qera*, which he dramatically postulates in the second Rule of the *ShM*. Certain subtle rhetorical hints signal this change: the *lack* of a declarative statement that the practice is a positive commandment; the *absence* of scriptural proof texts supporting the commandment; and the use of the *participial form* to describe the obligation.

To close this chapter, I offer a final point of clarification on the distinction between *mitsvot de-oraita* and *mitsvot mi-divre sofrim*. I noted above that Maimonides uses a participial form to indicate the level of obligation of several ostensibly scriptural commandments. Maimonides views these commandments as removed from the plain sense of Scripture; the practices associated with these commandments appear to originate in rabbinically-sanctioned customs and traditions, rooted in some unspecified past. By implication, these practices ought to be classified as *mitsvot mi-divre sofrim* instead of *mitsvot de-oraita*.

The very absurdity of such a proposition, which runs contrary both to centuries-old commonplace notions and to a substantial body of legal

---

"all these things [the identification of the four species] come down by tradition [*mi-pi ha-shemuah*] and were so explained [*nitparshu*] by Moses." This formulation deviates from the more usual "taught by tradition" [*mi-pi ha-shemuah lamdu*]. The difference between "taught" and "explained" may carry some significance.

scholarship, throws doubt on such a radical proposition. For example, to call tefillin or sukkah a *mitsvah mi-divre sofrim* instead of a *mitsvah de-oraita* would certainly be dismissed without any further consideration in any respected *bet midrash*. Yet this counterintuitive notion does seem to flow naturally from the *peshateh di-qera* doctrine of Rule 2. Moreover, in the *Halakhot* themselves, one finds support for the idea that commandments based on tradition, rabbinic interpretations, or analogic derivations from scriptural passages do not share the legal standing of explicit scriptural commandments, even if they impose the same practical sense of unconditional obligation as *de-oraita* commandments.

In chapter 7, I made brief reference to the ongoing controversy regarding the nature of *mitsvot divre sofrim*: should they be considered rabbinic both in origin and in force, or should they be considered rabbinic in origin but scriptural in force? Proponents for each of these views can be found among the most prominent medieval and modern scholars; the matter remains open. I have noted that I am not prepared to take a stand on this controversy.[48] Nevertheless, I do not think that it is unrealistic to suggest that resistance to viewing mitsvot like tefillin as *mitsvot mi-divre sofrim* begins to diminish when one assumes that *mitsvot mi-divre sofrim* carry the force of *mitsvot de-oraita*. Nevertheless, a larger question remains: if *mitsvot mi-divre sofrim* do carry the force of Torah law, why would Maimonides bother to make this distinction—even using the language of customary practice?

Following *Hilkhot Mamrim* 2:1, one might want to posit that a significant distinction between a *mitsvah de-oraita* and a *mitsvah mi-divre sofrim* is that only the latter type could be annulled by a court. On closer reading, however, one notes that Maimonides only applies this rule to laws derived hermeneutically through the thirteen principles, not to any *mitsvah mi-divre sofrim*. This legal distinction would not hold for cases of correct practices, since the latter appear to stem from traditions, perhaps *halakhot mi-pi ha-qabbalah*. Maimonides posits no mechanism for setting such types of laws aside.

The question stands: if these types of *mitsvot mi-divre sofrim* possess the same immutable characteristics as *mitsvot de-oraita*, what is the

---

48. See in particular chapter 7, notes 11-13.

difference between these two categories? In what follows, I point to a small number of meaningful differences. A more thorough study may find additional examples.

In the treatise discussing transgressions incurred in error (*Hilkhot Shegagot*), Maimonides draws a distinction between scriptural laws explicitly found in the text and those that are not (though they still enjoy scriptural force). In the case of "the bullock offered for the unconscious transgression of the congregation," Maimonides rules that:

> If the court erred and gave a ruling such as would uproot some main principle of the Law [*guf mi-gufe torah*], and all the people acted on their authority, the court are exempt and everyone who so acted is liable to a fixed sin offering ... The court never becomes liable unless they so rule as partly to annul and partly to sustain matters *not explicit and plainly stated in the Law*, whereupon the court becomes liable for the offering and they who act on their authority are not liable. (*Hilkhot Shegagot* 14:1-2, emphasis added)

Explicitly stated laws are laws that even the Sadducees, a prominent sectarian group who rejected the Oral Law, accepted; the Talmud (*BT Horayot* 4b) describes them as laws that any child would recognize. Erring with regard to such laws indicates forgetfulness rather than errors in judgment. Because the court was only liable for errors in judgment, they would not be liable for uprooting such laws.

In this analysis, Maimonides clearly distinguishes between explicitly formulated commandments and laws that derive their authority from tradition. The continuation of the *halakhah* makes this distinction clear: it contrasts carrying "a burden on the Sabbath from one domain to another" (an explicit scriptural law) with throwing or passing a burden from one domain to another (learned by tradition). Similarly, if the court uproots "one of the primary acts of work" on Shabbat, the court is liable because the laws relating to the primary acts of work are not stated explicitly in Scripture. Maimonides provides other examples of the distinct status of explicitly formulated laws in connection with the determination of the court's culpability when it has committed errors in judgment.

A similar distinction can be found in *Hilkhot Biat ha-Miqdash* 1:3, where Maimonides forbids an intoxicated individual from offering a legal decision unless the decision relates to "matters that are so explicit in the Torah that even the Sadducees know them." Once again, we see that explicitly stated laws, those recognizable by a fundamentalist literalist sect, enjoy a different standing than those not explicitly stated, which come under the heading of "teachings." The distinction between *mitsvot de-oraita* and *mitsvot mi-divre sofrim* that I am attempting to make would only work, of course, if we can assume that "teachings" are the functional equivalents of *mitsvot mi-divre sofrim*.

In this section, I have argued that in his rulings, Maimonides does consider explicitly-stated scriptural laws to be more authentically "scriptural" than the law derived from tradition, although I recognize that this pair of contrasting categories may not represent an exact parallel to the *mitsvah de-oraita/mitsvah mi-divre sofrim* pair. Moreover, I have assumed that the term "explicitly-stated" is equivalent to "the plain sense of Scripture," though I admit that "literal" might be a closer synonym. This distinction is evident in *Hilkhot Shehitah* 5:3, where Maimonides discusses the eight classes of *trefot*, animals unfit to eat, categorizing them as *halakhot le-Moshe mi-Sinai*. As we pointed out in chapter 7, laws of this type are considered by Maimonides to be *mitsvot mi-divre sofrim*. Crucially, Maimonides draws a legal distinction between the unfitness of the "torn" (*derusah*) animal and the seven other types of unfit animals, on the basis that the former is explicitly stipulated while the latter are only known by tradition.[49]

While I do not claim to have exhausted this complex subject, I believe that I have shown that there are meaningful differences between *mitsvot de-oraita* and *mitsvot mi-divre sofrim*, even on the assumption that the latter have the force of Torah law. Juristic precision would thus demand that Maimonides demarcate clearly between correct practices, or *mitsvot mi-divre sofrim*, and *mitsvot de-oraita* (in this case, *mitsvot 'aseh*).

We can only speculate as to why Maimonides *qua* legal theorist chose not to state explicitly that the given commandments were *mitsvot mi-divre sofrim*. One reason may be a fear of appearing to espouse

49. The distinction is applicable to punishments in the presence of a doubtful infringement of the prohibition to eat such *trefot*. For an interesting take on this matter, see the comments of Kelz, *Maggid Mishneh*, ad loc.

heretical, Karaite views by prioritizing scriptural readings. A second, perhaps less likely reason may have to do with genuine doubts that he may have harbored about the full ramifications of his *peshateh di-qera* hermeneutics. Recall that in Rule 2, Maimonides eliminates derivations obtained via the thirteen rules of interpretation. We inferred from his discussion that *all* traditional interpretations, not just hermeneutic derivations, that do not stand textually on their own would also fall outside of the category of scriptural law. On this particular point, he may not have been all that certain. The use of the participial form would therefore reflect this ambivalent stance. With it, Maimonides neither acknowledges the commandment's scriptural status nor its non-scriptural one. He simply records the obligation without having to take a definitive stand.

CHAPTER IX

WHEN *MITSVAH* STANDS ALONE

In chapter 8, I presented a group of claims that had been enumerated as *mitsvot 'aseh* in the *SE* and *ShM* and yet had not been designated as positive commandments in the *Halakhot*. I noted that they lacked supporting proof texts and that they were formulated in the participial form, rather than with the standard *lamed*-infinitive. This led me to characterize them as "correct practices" (in Daube's words) rather than as scriptural commandments, and, consequently, to posit that Maimonides had categorized them as *mitsvot mi-divre sofrim*. I allowed for the possibility that Maimonides avoided the *de-oraita* designation because of interpretative misgivings; without confidence in their scriptural roots, he affirmed their obligatory character by using language that implied correct practice.

I now look at another group of claims in the *MT* that also do not follow the characteristic declarative formula. They differ from the first group, however, in that Maimonides calls their performance simply a *mitsvah* (rather than a *mitsvat 'aseh*). To complicate matters, in these instances, he does quote the proof texts that had supported the original claims in the *ShM*. In this chapter, I attempt to explain the meaning and use of the solo term *mitsvah* in connection with this special group of commandments. I begin by investigating how the term *mitsvah* is used throughout the *Halakhot* outside of the small number of instances in which it is used in connection with commandments proper.

THE TERM *MITSVAH* IN THE *HALAKHOT*

It is worth noting that in the introduction to the *MT*, Maimonides defines *mitsvah* as being a *perush,* or explanation of the written law. He says:

> All the precepts which Moses received on Sinai were given together with their interpretation, as it is said, *And I will give unto thee the tables of stone, and the law, and the commandment* [Exod. 24:12]. *The law* [*ha-torah*] refers to the written law; *and the commandment* [*ha-mitsvah*] to its interpretation.

Maimonides refers to this explanation in *Hilkhot Sheḫitah* (1:4) when discussing the laws of ritual slaughter. The numerous and complex details that regulate ritual slaughter are not stated explicitly in Scripture. Instead, Scripture states, "as then shalt thou kill of thy herd and thy flock as I have commanded thee [*ka-asher tsivitikha*]" (Deut. 12:21), which Maimonides understands as an allusion to the oral law's interpretations (as per *BT Ḫullin* 28a). He interprets the phrase "as I have commanded thee" to mean "that Moses was commanded concerning all these matters orally, as in the case of the rest of the oral law, which is referred to as a commandment." In this verse, Scripture seemingly alludes to an earlier instance in which the slaughtering rituals had been explicated to Moses. Since such explications cannot be found in Scripture, Maimonides, following the Talmud, assumes that these explications were given orally. As a result, he concludes that the root "command" (*ts.v.h*) and thus the word "commandment" (*mitsvah*) refer to the oral explications of the written law.

Since the term *mitsvah* is also used in the *Halakhot* in connection with rabbinic laws, I posit that Maimonides' definition of *mitsvah* was included here to make a theological point: the written law—which of course includes the 613 commandments—must be parsed in light of the oral tradition. While this passage illuminates Maimonides' theology, we still need to understand how Maimonides used the term *mitsvah* in a purely juristic context.

In the *Halakhot*, the term *mitsvah* is highly nuanced, its meaning generally referring to shades of "recommended" or "commendable"—certainly lacking the force of obligation. I note in chapter 2 that in talmudic literature, *mitsvah* could loosely mean "preferred," "commendable," "praiseworthy," or simply "a good deed." These usages were not systematized; a reader would generally recognize the particular meaning by its context. Nevertheless, in rabbinic literature, *h̲ovah* and *mitsvah* were clearly differentiated, *h̲ovah* representing an absolute obligation and *mitsvah* a desideratum. It is interesting to note that Islamic legal theory after Shāfi'ī (d. 820), itself likely under the influence of rabbinic law, recognized five values or categories with which all legal acts must be designated. These were: the obligatory (*wajib*), the recommended (*mandub*), the permissible (*mubah*), the prohibited (*haram*), and the reprehensible or repugnant (*makrub*). They correspond to the rabbinic designations *h̲ovah, mitsvah, reshut, asur,* and *meguneh*. Maimonides appears to be under the influence of this system of classification in some areas of law, as one understands from his comments to *M Avot* 1:16. On that occasion, Maimonides uses five terms—*ha-metsuveh bo, u-muzhar 'alav, u-meruh̲aq, ve-ratsui, u-reshut*—with the third and fourth terms clearly representing softer forms of prohibitions and obligations.[1]

A better way to understand the lone term *mitsvah* is to contrast it with the familiar term *mitsvat 'aseh*. Whereas a *mitsvat 'aseh* is a commandment that one must strive to fulfill, a *mitsvah* carries less weight: one *ought* to fulfill a *mitsvah* but one is not obligated to do so. Another way of viewing this contrast is to think of the former as representing an obligation and the latter as merely a suggestion. Alternatively, while a *mitsvat 'aseh* represents an absolute obligation, a *mitsvah* represents a non-absolute obligation. Note that a *divre sofrim* law can also be categorized as a *mitsvat 'aseh*, a rabbinic commandment that one must strive to fulfill. There are some rabbinic commandments that Maimonides describes as *mitsvot 'aseh mi-divre sofrim*, as, for example, the reading of the Megillah (*Hilkhot Megillah ve-H̲anukah* 1:1).[2]

1. Note that these terms are translations from the Arabic; while they do not quite match the rabbinic designations given earlier, they are synonymous with the rabbinic ones. I have used Kafih's translation of *M Avot* 1:16. Kafih slightly changes the rendition of these terms when he translates Maimonides' commentary to *M Sanhedrin* 7:4. There, Maimonides uses only four legal categories, this time with respect to sexual behavior: *asur*, *meguneh*, *ratsui/ahuv*,and *mutar*, the exact equivalents of the last four terms given in *M Avot*. On rabbinic influence, see Romney-Wegner, "Islamic and Talmudic Jurisprudence." On the halakhic categories, see DeVreis, "Ha-Categoriyot ha-Hilkhatiyot."
2. Similarly, *mitsvat 'aseh shel divrehem*, as in *Hilkhot Avel*, in connection with the duties of *gemilut hasadim*. In *Hilkhot Megillah ve-Hanukah* 3:3, in connection with the lighting

In many locations, Maimonides uses the term *mitsvah* to indicate a preference or recommendation rather than an obligation. *Hilkhot Sefer Torah* 10:10 uses the term *mitsvah* to describe the advisability of singling out a place to keep a scroll of law; *Hilkhot Milah* 1:8, to describe the advisability of performing circumcision early in the day, following the rabbinic principle that the zealous fulfill their religious obligations at the earliest possible time; *Hilkhot Ishut* 3:19, to characterize the advisability of betrothing a woman in person (instead of through an agent), also in line with a rabbinic principle that personal effort is to be commended. None of these advisories have the force of a scriptural command: failure to perform as recommended does not abrogate any positive commandment. One could find many more examples that fall largely or totally into this category: a non-scriptural obligation that one need not strive to fulfill and that consequently carries a connotation of desirability and praiseworthiness.

A closely-related usage of the term *mitsvah* is as a worthy deed, such as attending a rabbinic sermon, teaching a profession to a son (*Hilkhot Shabbat* 24:5), or welcoming a teacher or friend who has just come from a journey (*Hilkhot 'Eruvin* 6:6). Another example can be found in *Hilkhot Melakhim* 2:5, where Maimonides stipulates that while the High Priest neither needs to come to the king nor rise for him, it is a *mitsvah* for the High Priest to show respect to the king when the king comes to him, to stand when he enters and to help him sit. *Mitsvah* here is understood as something desirable although clearly beyond the strictly legal requirement. Note that in none of these examples does Maimonides use a scriptural proof text, clearly indicating that these recommendations are rabbinic in nature. They are generally grounded on some rabbinic principle or may have as their object the attainment of a particular desirable goal. On certain occasions, however, we do note that the term *mitsvah* is linked with a scriptural proof text. I posit that on *those* occasions, Maimonides wishes to signal the presence of a scriptural recommendation rather than a commandment. In those cases, the use of the solo term *mitsvah*, when

of the Hanukah candles, he is just slightly less than precise and uses the expression *mitsvah mi-divre sofrim*, leaving out the second half of the compound term. Nevertheless, we note that Maimonides also adds to the Hanukah formulation the words "like the reading of the Megillah," leaving no doubt with regard to its obligatory nature.

accompanied by a scriptural proof text, is a clue to read those particular Torah passages much as one might read the book of Proverbs: as wise and useful instructions rather than as commandments, suggestions rather than as obligations. I further posit that behind this determination lies some particular hermeneutic difficulty that precludes the interpreter from characterizing the scriptural passage as a commandment. The scriptural verse may lack the formal characteristics typical of commandments: it may not be specific enough, it may not convey the desired message in an explicit manner, it may need to be read out of context to yield the desired message, and so on.

The contrasting usage of *mitsvat 'aseh* and *mitsvah* can be quite informative, as for example in *Hilkhot Hamets u-Matsah* 7:1-2. In 7:1, Maimonides writes that it is an absolute obligation (*mitsvat 'aseh*) to "recount on the night preceding the fifteenth day of Nissan the great miracles and wonders that were performed for our forefathers in Egypt." The proof text is "Remember this day in which ye came out of Egypt, out of the house of bondage," (Exod. 13:3) to which Maimonides adds: "even though he has no son." In 7:2, he writes: "it is a *mitsvah* to inform his children, even though they did not ask, as it says *And thou shalt tell thy son in that day* [Exod. 13:8]." While one can fulfill the scriptural obligation by telling one's son about the events of the exodus, it is clear that it is not a requirement to tell one's child in particular. The proof text supports the absolute and unconditional obligation to recount those miraculous events, regardless of whether one has a son. Once one has fulfilled the basic obligation to recount the events, one has no deeper responsibility to teach about the events of the fifteenth of Nissan—even to one's own son. There is a secondary *mitsvah*, however, which we might understand as a recommendation rather than as an absolute obligation. As per 7:2, the father performs a *mitsvah* (not a *mitsvat 'aseh*), a commendable deed, when he instructs his son. As Maimonides sees it, this is what Scripture means by "and thou shalt tell thy son in that day": it recommends that a father should engage his son to explain to him, on the son's own terms, the miraculous events of the night of Passover.[3]

3. I cannot determine whether, on Maimonides' account, this *mitsvah*, this scriptural recommendation, is categorized as a rabbinic obligation, or whether it stays in a

For the sake of completeness, I add that on occasion, *mitsvah* refers to a positive commandment, but only after the commandment has already been identified as a *mitsvat ʿaseh*, as in *Hilkhot Deʿot* 6:2[4] and *Hilkhot Hamets u-Matsah* 6:1.[5] And finally, as we have seen a number of times, the term *mitsvah* in the construct form, as in *mitsvat terumat maʿaser* (*Hilkhot Terumot* 3:12), simply represents a correct or proper form of performing a duty, presumably in accordance with the dictates of oral law. In sum, I contend that for Maimonides, the solo term *mitsvah,* when accompanied by a scriptural proof text, points to a recommendation, or perhaps even to a goal. Just as the rabbis, in their own legal system, drew a clear differentiation between mitsvah and hovah, one describing a recommendation and the other an obligation, so too, I argue, and in the same manner, the Halakhot draw a clear differentiation between *mitsvah* and *mitsvat ʿaseh.*

Even if we understand a *mitsvat ʿaseh* as an absolute obligation and *mitsvah* as a non-absolute obligation, we still need to fully understand the legal consequences of this differentiation. I submit that there is one important difference: absolute scriptural obligations are legally enforceable, while non-absolute scriptural obligations (or, for that matter, absolute rabbinic obligations) are not. We find in the Talmud the principle that the courts can whip a person to force him to fulfill a *mitsvat ʿaseh.*[6] Maimonides finds this principle important enough

separate category of scriptural recommendations that Maimonides crafted into a law. I lean towards the latter interpretation. This is the same question at play in P3, P4, and P8, as I discuss later in this chapter. It is in fact possible that Maimonides viewed himself as an independent exegete-jurist with the authority to mine scriptural passages for commandments, a task that was normally assumed by the Talmudic rabbis. In fact, hundreds of rabbinic laws are based on such scriptural indications, as I showed earlier.

4. In *Hilkhot De'ot* 6:3, Maimonides appears to commit an error, calling the duty to love one's neighbor a *mitsvah* instead of a *mitsvat ʿaseh.* Note, however, that he corrects himself in 6:4, when discussing the commandment to love the stranger, and says that one who loves the stranger fulfills two *mitsvot ʿaseh*, to love one's neighbor and to love a stranger.

5. In *Hilkhot Berakhot* 11:2, the context makes the commandment's identity obvious. But see my comments in chapter 6 regarding the impropriety of examining these particular *halakhot* for the purposes of drawing terminologically valid conclusions.

6. "But in the case of positive commandments, as for instance, if a man is told 'Make a sukkah' and he does not make it [or, 'Perform the commandment of] *lulav*, and he does not perform it, he is whipped until his soul leaves him" (*BT Ketubbot* 86b and *BT Hullin*

to mention it in the *ShM*, which he does towards the end of Rule 14, after noting that he will mention the pertinent punishment for violating each commandment along with its explanation. With only a few exceptions, these punishments are associated with violations of negative commandments:

> but, as regards all positive commandments, if the time of the performance is still applicable, we are to whip with a strap he who refuses to do it until he dies or performs [the commandment], or until such time as the obligation [*mitsvah*] passes, for he who violates the positive commandment of dwelling in a tabernacle is not to be whipped for his sin after [the passing of the festival of] Tabernacles. Know this principle.

While the principle has a number of qualifications—for example, it is not applicable where the Torah provides for an explicit reward[7]—its import is clear: the law means to enforce positive commandments, absolute obligations. Nothing of this sort is said or implied with respect to non-absolute *mitsvot*, and I would suggest that therein lies the legal difference between the two types of commandments.[8]

132b). In the post-talmudic literature, the principle is referred to as *kofin al ha-mitsvah*, literally, "they coerce one to perform a *mitsvah*."

7. See *BT Hullin* 110b. See also *Hilkhot Matnot 'Aniyim* 7:10 and the extensive bibliography cited by *Sefer ha-Mafteah*, ad loc. Note that in this passage, Maimonides betrays the variegated typologies with which he characterized positive commandments in the *ShM*. The reason is simple: the courts cannot force one to perform any of the procedure-commandments, such as "to decide in cases of annulment of vows according to the rules set forth by the Torah" (P95), or, more problematically, any of the descriptive positive commandments, such as "that anyone who touches the carcass of a beast that died of itself shall be unclean" (P96). It is clear that the Sages only intended the class of positive commandments that are absolutely obligatory, such as the ones they gave as examples. Note also that Maimonides changed the example given in the Talmud: instead of the positive commandment to *build* a sukkah, which he did not enumerate in the *ShM*, Maimonides offered the positive commandment of *dwelling* in a sukkah. The latter commandment (P168) is one of the 60 unconditional obligations. Also see the discussion of the commandment to dwell in a sukkah in chapter 8.

8. There is a punishment for violating rabbinic prohibitions (*makkat mardut*), but I am not aware of courts enforcing rabbinic precepts. Nevertheless, even if we group the *mitsvot 'aseh mi-divre sofrim* like megillah and Hanukah into the category of enforceable obligations, non-absolute obligations—which also constitute the great majority of rabbinic law—remain unenforceable. Indeed, megillah and Hanukah are unusual commandments in that they were made absolutely obligatory.

One final point: in the previous chapter, I proposed that Maimonides treats "correct practices" as *mitsvot mi-divre sofrim*. I am not quite as certain, however, about the legal category for commands described solely as *mitsvot*. I lean toward the view that Maimonides maintains that these commands are genuinely *mi-de-oraita*, unlike "correct practices," but that they differ from *mitsvot 'aseh* with regard to the force of the command, as we extensively discussed. Implicit in this tentative distinction between "correct practices" and *mitsvot* is that the former can be annulled or reinterpreted by a qualified court,[9] while the latter may not. However, *mitsvot* do not enjoy legal force and are not enforceable, while "correct practices" may be, as we saw earlier.

We now move to examine the handful of commandments that Maimonides determined should be labeled *mitsvot* rather than *mitsvot 'aseh*. Earlier on we had summarily suggested a number of reasons for his determination. We now hope to discuss these reasons in some greater detail.

P3. TO LOVE GOD

The scriptural source for this commandment in all of Maimonides' legal works is the verse "And thou shalt love the Lord thy God" (Deut. 6:5). Although the verse makes it clear that one is enjoined to love God, we are left wondering: what specifically must one do to perform this duty? Furthermore, how is love dependent on one's conscious will? Finally, to quote one of the classical super-commentators on RaSHI: "how can the command to love God apply to something a man has not seen or never recognized?"[10]

One way to infuse meaning into the command is to assume that what is meant is not love in the literal sense but rather total and absolute devotion and loyalty. Thus the continuation of this verse, "with all thy heart, and with all thy soul, and with all thy might," indeed demands an action: the sacrifice of one's life and possessions for God, what the rabbis

9. See *Hilkhot Mamrim* 2:1-2.

10. Eliyahu Mizrahi, super-commentary on RaSHi, *Parashat Va-Et-hanan*, ad loc., in *Otsar Pirushim al ha-Torah–Mizrahi*.

call *qiddush ha-Shem*. Such sacrifice would be necessitated if one were to be asked to transgress one of the most stringent commandments, such as the prohibition against worshipping other gods.[11]

Maimonides, however, appears to insist on the more literal meaning of love, citing a fascinating rabbinic midrash that relates to above rhetorical questions. The *Sifre*, commenting on this verse, asks: "how does one love the Omnipresent?"[12] and answers: "Scripture therefore says: *And these words that I command thee this day, shall be upon thy heart* [Deut. 6:6]; for through this [i.e. the acceptance of God's words] you will learn to discern He who spoke[13] and the Universe came into existence."[14] The authors of the *Sifre* believe that one can indeed come to love God, specifically by studying and accepting God's words, the words of Torah. The implication of this midrash is that the command to love God is not a new commandment, but simply another way of saying that one ought to contemplate and accept upon oneself the words of Torah, and that love will ensue from this contemplation.

Though the *Sifre* does not explain how this love comes about, the presumption is that the authors of the midrash believe that the words of Torah, which exude wisdom and purpose, will move the faithful to admire and love the divine lawgiver.[15] Maimonides quotes this midrash in the *ShM* with an unusual and highly original twist:

---

11. Perla speculates that Sa'adiah must have understood it thus. See Perla, *Sefer ha-Mitsvot le-RaSaG,* vol. 1, 65. It is interesting to note that comparative Ancient Near Eastern studies have suggested that, rather than being used to denote an emotion, the term "love" was often used as a technical term of ancient vassal treaties in which the vassal is urged to "love"—to be absolutely loyal to—his overlord. The technical term would then convey the idea that the Israelites must be absolutely loyal to God by worshipping only Him. See Moran, "The Ancient Near Eastern Background of the Love of God in Deuteronomy," 77-87.
12. «*Ketzad ohev et ha-Maqom*»? Chavel's translation, "how is one to manifest his love for the Lord?" may not capture the sense of what is intended, i.e. what one needs to do to love the Omnipresent.
13. *Amar*, "said." See *M Avot* 5:1, "By ten sayings was the world created." There are ten instances of "*and God said*" in the creation story: Gen. 1:3, 6, 9, 11, 14, 20, 24, 26, 29, and 2:18.
14. Our version of the *Sifre* reads, "for through this you recognize the Holy One Blessed be He and become attached to His Ways." But see note 22 below.
15. It is worth noting that RaSHi's ad loc. paraphrase of the midrash, "you will recognize the Holy One Blessed be He," entirely misses this potential allusion.

> We are commanded to love God; that is to say, to dwell upon and contemplate His commandments, His decrees[16] and His works, so that we may obtain a conception of Him, and in conceiving Him attain ultimate joy. This is the love that is commanded.[17]

Love of God will come about not only if "we dwell upon and contemplate" His commandments and His decrees,[18] but also, and crucially, if we do so with regard to His works. Maimonides' interpretation may have been inspired by the words of the midrash, "He who spoke and the Universe came into existence," which draw one's attention to the words spoken at the time of Creation. Those words represent the mechanics and the works of the created universe. Maimonides notes that proper contemplation will enable us to attain an undefined "ultimate joy," which he says is equivalent to the love that is commanded. A little further on in his gloss to the commandment, Maimonides nuances the joy-love relation slightly differently and explains that one will attain "that stage of joy *in which love of Him will follow of necessity*" (emphasis added).[19] To summarize the view of the *ShM*: knowledge of God's laws and works leads to a conception of God that yields ultimate joy, which, in turn, inevitably leads to love.

This reading of the midrash takes a further turn in the *Halakhot*. No longer do "these words" refer to commandments and decrees; now they refer exclusively to the study of the natural and divine sciences (physics and metaphysics). In *Hilkhot Yesode ha-Torah* 2:2, Maimonides writes:

---

16. *Maamarav*, lit., "sayings." These words are found in Ibn Ayub's and in the Arabic manuscripts in Heller's possession. *MnT* has "His commandments and His works (*mitsvotav u-pe'ulotav*)." See Heller, ad loc., n. 16. Chavel: "His injunctions," based on Kafih's *tsivuyav*.

17. So *MnT*, and so too Bloch's Arabic MS. On the other hand, Kafih has "This is the ultimate [Ar. *ghaya*; Heb. *takhlit*] love that is commanded." Chavel incorrectly translates "This is the goal of the love that is commanded," taking *takhlit* to mean "goal" instead of "ultimate" and distorting the meaning. I am indebted to Haggai ben-Shammai for his kind help in showing me the various nuances of the Arabic term *ghaya*.

18. Note that the *Sefer ha-Hinukh*, no. 411, which elaborates on the *ShM*, goes so far as to say that the *Sifre*'s words "with this act of contemplation" really stand for "upon reflecting on the Torah."

19. Slightly but noticeably reformulated in the *Halakhot*, where the initial step, that of the attainment of ultimate joy, is omitted. See below.

> And what is the way that will lead to the love of Him and the fear of Him? When a person contemplates His great and wondrous works [*ma'asav*] and creatures [*beru'av*] and from them obtains a glimpse of His wisdom which is incomparable and infinite, he will straightaway love Him, praise Him, glorify Him, and long with an exceeding longing to know His great name.... In harmony with these sentiments, I shall explain some large, general aspects of the Works of the Sovereign of the Universe,[20] that they may serve the intelligent individual as a door to the love of God, even as our Sages have remarked in connection with the theme of love of God: "For through this [*she-mitokh kakh*] you will realize He who spoke and the Universe came into existence."

Clearly, the intended objects of contemplation are not His commandments but rather His works—which include the heavenly spheres, stars, planets, and the sub-lunar elements—and His creatures—which include the intelligences that guide the spheres and the sub-lunar elements and inhabitants. Maimonides describes these works and creatures in the balance of chapter 2 and in chapters 3 and 4 of *Hilkhot Yesode ha-Torah*. The descriptions of creatures and works, respectively, constitute the highly esoteric "Account of the Divine Chariot" (*ma'aseh merkavah*)—metaphysics—and the slightly less esoteric "Works of Creation" (*ma'aseh bereshit*)—physics and natural sciences.[21] The last allusion leaves little doubt that Maimonides was basing his remarks on the earlier-referenced *Sifre*.[22]

---

20. The first four chapters of *Hilkhot Yesode ha-Torah* offer a brief survey of the science and metaphysics of the day, the "Works of the Sovereign of the Universe."
21. See *Hilkhot Yesode ha-Torah* 2:11 and 4:10-11.
22. I note that Maimonides cites what appears to be another rabbinic proof text in his *Responsa* (no. 150), where it is said in the name of Rabbi Meir: "Look at His works, because through this you will learn to discern He who spoke and the Universe came into existence." In note 2, Blau indicates that the source of this dictum, in particular the words "look at His works," has not been located. The responsum seems to have been signed in the year 1177, very close to the time Maimonides completed the *MT* (*Iggerot*, ed. Shailat, vol. 1, 198) and probably 10 years or more after he completed the *ShM*, since the *ShM* was written before he commenced writing of the *MT*, as he himself acknowledges (see responsum to Tsur on the matter of the enumeration of the commandments, *Iggerot*, ed. Shailat, vol. 1, 223). The significance of this is that Maimonides may have found a version of the *Sifre* that did explicitly state the object of the contemplation. However, there also remains the possibility that Maimonides was paraphrasing the midrash according to his interpretation.

While it is not absolutely clear that the midrash did not intend the phrase "these words" to imply contemplation of metaphysical and physical beings and works, it does seem quite clear that the midrash understood "these words" to refer to the Torah, as indicated by the proof text. By eliminating the words of Torah from the category of objects of contemplation, Maimonides has radically altered the midrash.[23]

We also see that in the *Halakhot*, Maimonides introduces another significant change from what he had posited in the *ShM*, this time with reference to the nature of the love demanded. In the *Halakhot*, the ultimate objective of contemplation is passionate longing; the search for undefined ultimate joy is abandoned, with love now becoming both the first consequence of proper contemplation and the first step towards a powerful, mystical-intellectual experience of longing. A well-known *halakhah* in *Hilkhot Teshuvah* 10:5 corroborates Maimonides' new emphasis on passionate love:

> What is the love of God that is befitting? It is to love the Eternal with a great and exceeding love, so strong that one's soul shall be knit up with the love of God, and one should be continually enraptured by it, like a love-sick individual, whose mind is at no time free from his passion

23. Basing himself on a comment by R. Eliyahu Mizrahi, Hananiah Kazis (in "Qinat Sofrim," ad loc.) offers to read the *ShM*'s definition sequentially. He suggests that the faithful are inspired to contemplate nature and God's wondrous acts by the performance of the commandments. The reading is unconvincing, and this sequence is totally lacking from the *Halakhot*, which mentions only works and creatures. More recently, in an attempt to reconcile the *ShM* and the *Halakhot*, A. Feintuch (in *Sefer ha-Mitsvot im Perush Pequde Yesharim*, 126-128) has argued that in the *Halakhot*, the two types of contemplations are discussed in two separate sections. In *Hilkhot Yesode ha-Torah* 2:2, Maimonides discusses the contemplation of His works, while in *Hilkhot Talmud Torah*, Maimonides discusses the study of Torah, which includes *pardes*, the natural and divine sciences (also covered in the first four chapters of *Hilkhot Yesode ha-Torah*, as per 4:13) as he states in *Hilkhot Talmud Torah* 1:12. Moreover, in *Hilkhot Yesode ha-Torah* 4:13, Maimonides makes it clear that *pardes* must be preceded by the study of the commandments. Thus, argues Feintuch, the two aspects covered by the *ShM* are also covered by the *Halakhot*. In a second attempt to reconcile the *ShM* and the *Halakhot*, Feintuch argues that by the term "His commandments," the *ShM* refers only to the first two commandments (His existence and His oneness), which are included in divine science, while the term "His works" refers to natural science. Thus, in Feintuch's opinion, the *ShM* covers essentially the same topics as the *Halakhot*. I believe that these attempts do not capture the true philosophical spirit of Maimonides' appropriation of the midrash.

> for a particular woman, the thought of her filling his heart at all times, when sitting down or rising up, when he is eating or drinking. Even more intense should be the love of God in the hearts of those who love Him.

We must not, however, believe that this love is beyond the reach of plain human beings. At the very end of *Sefer ha-Madda'* (*Hilkhot Teshuvah* 10:10), Maimonides writes:

> A person ought therefore to devote himself to the understanding and comprehension of those sciences and studies which will inform him concerning his Master, *as far as it lies in human faculties to understand and comprehend*—as indeed we have explained in *Hilkhot Yesode ha-Torah* [emphasis added].

The quality of the *mitsvah* stands in direct relation to the depth of intellectual effort.

To sum up what we have seen so far: in the *Halakhot*, the command to love God is seen as too vague to be accorded the status of a commandment. In effect, one does not know how to love Him, one is not capable of manipulating one's emotions to love Him, and one does not understand the object of this love sufficiently to be able to say that one has fallen in love. The *midrash halakhah* confirms this sentiment and offers Maimonides a solution: the command to love God is not a direct command to love Him, but a call to learn about Him so that one may come to love Him. In fact, the command to love God may not be a commandment, but rather a consequence of doing what is demanded of every faithful believer: to study the commandments and to take them to heart. In many respects, the command to love God may be compared to the exhortations that Maimonides cites in the discussion of Rule 4 and which he disqualifies from making the grade of commandment, statements such as "Ye shall keep My statutes" (Lev. 19:19), "Mine ordinances ye shall do" (Lev. 18:4), "Ye shall be holy" (Lev. 19:2), and others. As he argues there, these statements represent general charges: they do not relate to any specific duty.

Maimonides accepts the basic tenor of the midrash that the verse to love God does not directly mandate love and thus cannot be a commandment. As we have seen, different commentators view the verse as an exhortation to contemplation, each with his own idea of what type of contemplation can lead to love of God. The *Sifre* maintains that the commandments will lead to love, either through developing an admiration for their wise legislator or simply through obeying. In the *Halakhot*, by contrast, Maimonides states that man will come to love God through acquiring a deepening knowledge of Him. This can only come via the study of physics and metaphysics. To love God cannot qualify as a *mitsvat 'aseh* because the command to love entails no specific action. We do not know what specifically is being commanded. Yet loving God does appear to be the pinnacle of all religious activity—clearly a worthy and desirable goal.

We are finally in a position to understand Maimonides' puzzling presentation of this commandment in the *Halakhot*:

> This God, honored and revered, it is a *mitsvah* to love Him and to fear Him, as it says, *And thou shalt love the Lord thy God* [Deut. 6:5] and it says *Thou shalt fear the Lord, thy God* [Deut. 10:20].

The obvious problem is that there is no mention of these two commands being positive commandments.[24] The answer is that to love God (and to fear Him, as I will discuss next), are not positive commandments in the formal sense of absolute obligations, but simply suggested goals. These commandments cannot be mandated, given their esoteric nature and the particular degree of preparation required to fulfilling them. To love God is first and foremost a call to study the sciences. Consequently,

24. As discussed in chapter 6, few scholars throughout history have noticed the general problem of Maimonides' failure to designate. One exception was Tsvi Elimelekh Shapira (in *Sifre me-HaRTSa mi-Dinov*, vol. 2, 52), who noticed that Maimonides calls the love of God (and the fear of Him) a *mitsvah*, rather than a *mitsvat 'aseh*, which he uses for the commandments to recognize God's existence (*Hilkhot Yesode ha-Torah*, 1:6) and His unity (1:7). Unfortunately, Shapira's failure to systematically investigate Maimonides' use of the term *mitsvat 'aseh* led him to the wrong conclusion. His answer attempts to justify the use of the term *mitsvat 'aseh* with respect to these last two commandments, rather than the use of the term *mitsvah* for the former. His explanation, that Maimonides was prompted to write *mitsvat 'aseh* for the commandments to recognize His existence and unity because Scripture does not formulate them in the imperative (unlike *And thou shalt love the Lord thy God*), misses the scores of commandments that Maimonides designates as *mitsvot 'aseh* even though they are formulated in the imperative.

Maimonides understood that Scripture cannot impose this obligation on everyone. In no way then does the statement "it is a *mitsvah* to love Him and to fear Him" represent a failure to designate. Rather, it should be seen as a delicate attempt to guide, instruct and motivate the faithful to achieve these ambitious and noble goals. No command is thereby implied.

* * *

It is worth noting that the *Halakhot* entirely omit an aspect of this commandment to which the *ShM* gives considerable space and thought. After explaining that intellectual contemplation brings joy, which in turn brings love of God, the *ShM* continues:

> The Sages say that this commandment also includes an obligation to call upon all mankind to serve Him, and to have faith in Him. For just as you praise and extol anybody whom you love, and call upon others also to love him, so, if you love the Lord to the extent of the conception of His true nature to which you have attained, you will undoubtedly call upon the foolish and ignorant to seek knowledge of the Truth which you have already acquired.

Maimonides bases this understanding on the *Sifre*: "*And thou shalt love the Lord thy God*: this means that you should make Him beloved of man as Abraham your father did, as it is said, *And the souls they had gotten in Haran* [Gen. 12:5]."[25]

In this passage, Maimonides does not discuss how one attains this feeling of love, but rather discusses the outcome of this love. To "call upon mankind to serve Him and to have faith in Him" is the natural result of loving God, in much the same way as one would "extol and praise" anybody whom one loves. This desire to exhort others to follow Him is thus included in the obligation to love God. Why then does Maimonides omit this complementary aspect from the *Halakhot*? The type of exhortation proposed might itself suggest a solution. Maimonides explains that the one who has attained this degree of

25. *Sifre Deuteronomy* 32 (54).

love must not only exhort mankind, more specifically, the "foolish and ignorant," to serve Him and to have faith in Him, but he must also exhort them to seek His love. On Maimonides' account, this implies that the foolish and ignorant must be directed to study the sciences. It occurs to me that this is a seriously impractical undertaking.

I suggest, therefore, that the practical difficulties, even the futility, that would be faced by the one who attempted to arouse the foolish and the ignorant to study the sciences and attain contemplative bliss is what caused Maimonides to omit the requirement to "call upon all mankind" from the *Halakhot*. This impracticality would not have deterred the Maimonides of the *ShM* from mentioning this aspect, however, since the *ShM* is a rhetorical composition, which uses every opportunity to offer noble didactic messages and bold political views, and not a practical work.[26]

P4. TO FEAR GOD

The verse "Thou shalt fear the Lord thy God" (Deut. 6:13) also appears to be a non-specific injunction, a simple exhortation to perform all His commandments. As Maimonides stated in Rule 4, the words "Ye shall be holy" (Lev. 19:2) and other similar expressions cannot constitute a separate commandment "since there is nothing specific in them outside of what we know already." As Ibn Ezra comments on this verse:

> And I found one verse that embodies all the commandments, namely, *Thou shalt fear the Lord thy God, and Him thou shalt serve* [Deut. 6:13]. Now, *Thou shalt fear* includes all negative commandments, carried out with the heart, lips and deeds. It is the first step that one takes in the ascent to the service of the Glorious God.[27]

---

26. Howard Kreisel (in *Maimonides' Political Thought*, 230) has argued that the absence of this public aspect from the *Halakhot* stems from "pedagogical concerns. There he attempts to underscore the notion that love itself follows from intellectual apprehension. No additional idea that may blur this point is included in his formulation of the commandment." I do not disagree with this last point, but I do disagree with his larger point that Maimonides omitted it in the *Halakhot* because of pedagogical concerns. While a code of law always risks blurring the main point, it still cannot shy away from providing even potentially blurring minute details.
27. Ibn Ezra, *Yesod Mora, sha'ar* 7, 144.

Notwithstanding the seeming generality of this command, Maimonides finds a rabbinic indication to provide specific content to the verse. Using this indication, he substantiates a commandment claim ostensibly grounded on this verse.[28] The proof that is offered in the *ShM* is more important for what it does *not* establish than for what it does.

Maimonides bases his discussion on an analysis of a talmudic passage. Proceeding in dialectic fashion, *BT Sanhedrin* 56a hypothesizes that the verse "he that blasphemeth the name of the Lord, he shall surely be put to death" (Lev. 24:16) does not refer to a blasphemer, but simply to a person who pronounces the name of the Lord (*noqev* may also mean pronounce), and for such a crime, he is to be executed. Because of the well-known talmudic maxim that one does not punish unless one first admonishes, the Sages seek to find an explicit admonition for this crime. The talmudic redactor of the passage first suggests and then rejects a number of potential scriptural proof texts. His final suggestion is the verse "Thou shalt fear the Lord thy God," arguing that he who pronounces the name of the Lord has abandoned the fear of the Lord, an offense that merits death. In rejecting the proof text, the Talmud states:

> The admonition that you cite is in the form of a positive admonition [*azharat 'aseh*] and it is a principle that positive admonitions are not valid admonitions.

The redactor's argument for rejecting this possibility provides Maimonides with his proof. He explains:

> That is to say, your suggestion that a prohibition against the mere pronouncing of the name of God can be derived from the verse *Thou shalt fear the Lord thy God* is inadmissible because the verse is a positive commandment, and a prohibition cannot be based upon a positive commandment.

28. Maimonides is reticent about drawing halakhic inferences from the "give and take" dialectics of the Talmud. See, for example, *Responsa* (ed. Blau) no. 345, where he repeats three times that, in adjudicating law, he would not abandon the apodictic statements of the Talmud and decide on the basis of inferences drawn from dialectics. It is surprising that he is willing to do so here.

Maimonides leads us to believe here that the Talmud considers the verse "Thou shalt fear the Lord thy God" to be a positive commandment. I note, in contrast, that the Talmud does not state that the verse represents a *mitsvat 'aseh*; it merely states that the prohibition is derived from an *'aseh*, a positive statement. Since rabbinic convention is that admonitions follow the form "do not do X" or "you shall not do X," the Talmud argues that this positively-phrased statement cannot be used as an admonition. However, Maimonides' claim that "Thou shalt fear the Lord thy God" is a positive commandment seems unwarranted.[29]

Equally problematic is how Maimonides uses this talmudic passage. In the passage, the Talmud is interested in finding an explicit prohibition against blasphemy. It posits that the positively-worded verse that admonishes one not to take God's name in vain can be used as such a proof text. Maimonides wants to use this verse to prove the commandment to *fear* God—to fear His prompt and fulminating punishment. However, the Talmud rejects this understanding when it considers the word *yirah* to mean reverence; one avoids taking God's name in vain because doing so is irreverent, not because one fears punishment. The Talmud looks for ways that one could actively express

29. *Azharat 'aseh* is an extremely rare expression in talmudic literature. A search of the Bar-Ilan database reveals that this expression appears only twice throughout the Talmud, *BT Sanhedrin* 56a and *BT Temurah* 4a. In both instances, the expression is used for the same purpose, that of refuting the validity of the verse "Thou shalt fear the Lord thy God" from serving as an admonition, since it is an *azharat 'aseh.* Note, however, that the term *azharat 'aseh* signifies the same thing as *lav ha-ba mikhlal 'aseh*, an admonition inferred from a positive statement (discussed in ch. 2). Perla (*Sefer ha-Mitsvot,* vol. 1, 700) points out that this hermeneutic can yield either a positive commandment or a negative commandment—but not both. If our verse were to yield a positive commandment to fear God, as Maimonides claims, then one should not be able to derive from the verse an additional prohibition against not fearing God (which one might transgress by pronouncing His name in vain, for example). The most that one could say is that by pronouncing His name in vain, one fails to uphold the positive commandment. Furthermore, *lav ha-ba mikhlal 'aseh* is used throughout the Talmud as a hermeneutic formula to derive a prohibition: it thus should not be adduced to establish a positive commandment. I presume that this was the reason Maimonides abandoned this hermeneutic formula for supporting positive commandment claims. See chapter 2, note 11. For those who tried to justify Maimonides' use of the *lav ha-ba mikhlal 'aseh* formula in his hermeneutics, see Kazis, "Qinat Sofrim," comments to P38, 231, and Bacher, *Divre Emet*, sixth *quntrus.*

this reverence, determining that one way to do so is to use God's name sparingly and effectively.

This is how Maimonides describes the commandment to fear God in the *ShM*: "We are commanded to believe[30] in the fear and awe of God, and not to be at ease and self-confident but to anticipate His punishment at all times." Though the sentence is awkward (how does one believe in fear?), the meaning is clear. One must believe in the inevitability of divine punishment as retribution for transgressing His commandments: the fear of God follows from this belief.[31] I note that elsewhere in the *Halakhot*, Maimonides criticizes those who perform *mitsvot* because of fear of retribution. As he writes in *Hilkhot Teshuvah* 10:1:

> Let not a man say: "I ... will abstain from transgressions against which the Torah warns, so that I may be saved from the curses written in the Torah, or that I may not be cut off from life in the world to come." It is not right to serve God after this fashion for whoever does so, serves Him out of fear. This is not the standard set by the prophets and Sages. Only those who are illiterate, women or children whom one trains to serve out of fear, serve God in this way, till their knowledge shall have increased when they will serve out of love.

If Maimonides still held that fear of punishment was a positive commandment when he wrote the *Halakhot,* it is strange that he would relegate the practice of the commandment only to those "who are illiterate, women, or children."

A close reading of the discussion of this commandment in the *Halakhot* supports our suspicions that Maimonides had either changed his mind or, at the very least, added a new dimension to this exhortation. As I quoted above, *Hilkhot Yesode ha-Torah* 2:1 opens:

30. Arab., *itikad*. Kafih translates "to establish in our mind." See chapter 5, note 112.

31. One may be inclined to contrast this commandment with Maimonides' comment in the *Guide* (III:28:*512*) that God's anger is only a necessary belief "for the sake of political welfare" with the corollary that believing in God acting to punish misdeeds is also part of this necessary belief. In an oral exchange, Marc Shapiro quite correctly pointed out that one would be overreaching in drawing this conclusion. Maimonides was not here discussing the issue of punishment but rather the issue of God's anger. God does not get angry because of His unchanging essence; punishment may indeed follow, although not out of anger.

"This God, honored and revered, it is a *mitsvah* to love Him and to fear Him, as it says *And thou shalt love the Lord thy God* [Deut. 6:5] and it says *Thou shalt fear the Lord, thy God* [Deut. 10:20]." Calling it a *mitsvah* rather than a *mitsvat 'aseh*, Maimonides uses the shortened language to indicate that the fear of God is not an obligation but rather a worthy goal. He explains the way to achieve this goal:

> And what is the way that will lead to the love of Him and the fear of Him? When a person contemplates His great and wondrous works and creatures and from them obtains a glimpse of His wisdom which is incomparable and infinite, he will straightaway love Him, praise Him, glorify Him, and long with an exceeding longing to know His great Name.... And when he ponders these matters, *he will recoil affrighted,* and realize that he is a small creature, lowly and obscure, endowed with slight and slender intelligence, standing in the presence of Him who is perfect in knowledge. (*Hilkhot Yesode ha-Torah* 2:1-2; emphasis added)

The term "fear" here does not refer to fear of punishment, as we saw in the *ShM*, but rather to the fear that comes from feeling small and insignificant in the presence of an awesome Being. Rather than being part of the legal material, the verse lends itself to a philosophic interpretation.

Some commentators[32] have noticed this change and suggested that Maimonides is redefining the commandment as *yirat ha-romemut*, fear of His exalted presence or fear of His majesty, idiomatically referred to

32. This is a relatively popular view. See, among others, Krakovsky, *'Avodat ha-Melekh*, on *Hilkhot Yesode ha-Torah* 2:2; Babad, *Minhat Hinnukh*, on *mitsvah* 432; and Kazis, "Qinat Sofrim," on P4. Insisting that Maimonides maintained his views from the *ShM* (that fear of God was equivalent to fear of punishment), see Kafih, *MT*, Hilkhot *Yesode ha-Torah*, chapter 2, note 2, and *Hilkhot Teshuvah*, chapter 10, note 5. These comments reverse his earlier view that in the *Halakhot*, Maimonides believes that fear is the equivalent of *yirat ha-romemut* (see Kafih's notes to the *ShM*, 60n25). Eliyahu Nagar (in "Fear of God in Maimonides' Teaching") sees two definitions of fear in the *ShM*: the popular one, the simple fear of punishment, and the philosophic one, where the enlightened individual fears the loss of divine providence and his consequent exposure to the vagaries of chance through the "estrangement" of sin. I fail to see, however, how one can read this into the *ShM*. Nagar cannot find *yirat ha-romemut* in the *ShM* (which I believe is correct), but then derives from this absence that Maimonides never meant to describe this type of fear/ reverence, *even in the MT*. This derivation is methodologically flawed; the *MT* reversed and changed the nature of the claims and definitions of the *ShM* on scores of occasions.

as "awe," as distinguished from *yirat ha-onesh*, the fear of punishment. Unlike love, which leads to an intense desire to acquire wisdom in divine matters, this cosmic fear or "awe" does not appear to lead to any greater goal; yet Maimonides seems to allude to some sort of connection by juxtaposing these two exhortations.[33] It is therefore reasonable to suppose that love and fear complement each other. Perhaps it may be said that fear acts to restrain love, to place bounds on the infinite longing to know the ineffable. As Kreisel puts it:

> the fear that Maimonides describes in [*Hilkhot Yesode ha-Torah*] designates a type of humbleness of spirit that belongs to the intellect.... Despite the fact that Maimonides treats love and fear of God as two sides of the same coin, it is important to note the essential distinction between these commands. The former focuses directly on God. The latter command too focuses on God, but involves self-focus. Love always seeks union. The ultimate desire of the lover is to unite with the beloved, to become one. Love of God, if left unchecked, leads to the pursuit of *unio mystica*, which is an impossibility for Maimonides. Fear serves to preserve the gap between the individual and the object of fear.[34]

The goal of feeling worthless in the "presence of He who is perfect" is to force restraint on the headlong dive to achieve union with God, "to preserve," as Kreisel so delicately puts it, "the gap between the individual and the object of fear."

Support for this view can be found in *GP* I:5. Maimonides ascribes to "the chief of the philosophers" (i.e. Aristotle)[35] the idea that man

---

33. The anonymous commentary (*perush*) to the *MT* interprets Maimonides' remarks in light of the pedagogic remarks he makes in *Hilkhot Teshuvah* 10:1, cited above, arguing that "love can only come after fear." Yet by explicitly placing love ahead of fear in his formulation, Maimonides clearly rejects this type of interpretation. The curious but meaningful syntax has already been noted by a number of *aharonim*. See *Sefer ha-Mafteah* on *Yesode ha-Torah* 2:2. Kreisel notes: "It is clear from Maimonides' approach in the *Mishneh Torah* that he posits different types of fear...For the most part he treats fear as antithetical to love. At best it serves as a means to attain love." Kreisel, *Maimonides' Political Thought*, 259.
34. Kreisel, *Maimonides' Political Thought*, 265-266. He acknowledges Dr. Alan Flashman for this "perceptive interpretation."
35. Pines identifies the Aristotelian observation with a passage from *De Caelo* ii.12.291b24 ff. See *GP* I:5:29, n.1.

should not hasten to reach conclusions in "great and sublime" matters without first undergoing extensive training in the sciences (among other things). After he has achieved the requisite knowledge, he should be careful not to make

> categoric affirmations in favor of the first opinion that occurs to him and should not, from the outset, strain and impel his thoughts towards the apprehension of the deity; he rather should feel awe and refrain and hold back until he gradually elevates himself. It is in this sense that it is said, *And Moses hid his face, for he was afraid to look upon God* [Exod. 3:6] ... Moses was commended for this; and God, may He be exalted, let overflow upon him so much of His goodness that it became necessary to say of him: *And the figure of the Lord shall he look upon* [Num. 12:8]. The Sages, may their memory be blessed, have stated that this is a reward for his having at first hidden his face so as not to look upon God.

It is precisely this type of humility to which Maimonides alludes when he says:

> And when he ponders these matters, he will recoil affrighted, and realize that he is a small creature, lowly and obscure, endowed with slight and slender intelligence, standing in the presence of Him who is perfect in knowledge.

In the *Halakhot,* fear of God has been transformed from a commandment to be constantly aware of the inevitability of divine retribution for transgressions into a *counsel* on how to seek metaphysical knowledge. Fear must accompany the love of God, the great longing to know His name, lest one come to erroneous conclusions.

To summarize: "Thou shalt fear the Lord thy God" presents a hermeneutic difficulty. Being a non-specific verse, it cannot qualify as a positive commandment. As a result, in the *Halakhot*, Maimonides designates it as simply a *mitsvah*, a suggested goal, one that can only be attained through immersing oneself in metaphysical contemplation.

* * *

The theme that to love and to fear God simply constitute goals which can only be mandated indirectly returns in the *GP*:

> As for the opinions that the Torah teaches us—namely, the apprehension of His being and His unity, may He be exalted—these opinions teach us *love*, as we have explained several times ... For these two ends, namely, *love* and *fear*, are achieved through two things: love through the opinions taught by the Law, which includes the apprehension of His being as He, may He be exalted, is in truth; while fear is achieved by means of all actions prescribed by the Law, as we have explained. Understand this summary. (*GP* III:52:*630*)

I note that while the goals of loving and fearing God are "achieved through" other actions, in the *GP*, fear is consequent upon obedience to the Law and not upon the feelings of cosmic worthlessness that comes from observing the awesomeness of God and His creation. Moreover, fear no longer acts as a restraint against a premature dive into the secrets of metaphysics, but as a restraint on the basest needs of humans, personal sexual conduct. "Know," says Maimonides, that "when perfect men understand this [that God's presence is felt everywhere], they achieve such humility, such awe and fear of God, such reverence and such shame before Him...that their secret conduct with their wives and in latrines is like their public conduct with other people" *GP* (III:52:*629*).

I also note that, with regard to love, Maimonides returns to a more literal reading of the *Sifre* and reminds us that the idea that "the apprehension of His being as He, may He be exalted, is in truth," exists in Scripture. Maimonides no longer needs to posit that the love of God that comes "when a person contemplates His great and wondrous works and creatures" (the core truths of science and metaphysics) is a truth that exists outside of what Scripture prescribes, as he appears to have done in the *Halakhot*. In the *GP*, "the apprehension of His being as He is in truth" is seen as an opinion taught by divine scriptural law. In this evolved theology, by taking note and studying the Torah's opinions, one can reach the desired goal of loving God.

I must admit, however, that I am not entirely convinced that a change has indeed taken place in the *GP*. Chapter 52 of the *GP* may simply be describing the perfect man, the man who has diligently pursued metaphysical knowledge and moral refinement and thus has reached a new stage in his development. The opinions found in Scripture, apodictic statements on the quiddity and nature of the divine ("the apprehension of His being as He is in truth"), have already been subjected to demonstration and assimilated by the perfect man. Such a perfect man will constantly feel the presence of God and fear transgressing His prohibitions. It may well be that, in the hands of Maimonides, the non-legal, wisdom nature of these passages lend themselves to a variety of interpretations, each to a different audience.

P8. TO IMITATE HIS GOOD AND UPRIGHT WAYS

Maimonides draws scriptural support for this claim from the words "And thou shalt walk in His ways" (Deut. 28:9). Yet this directive, like many similar ones, appears to lack specific content: what exactly can one do to walk in His ways other than obey His commandments? This question was asked of Abraham Maimonides (Maimuni) by a reader who was familiar with the Rules of the *ShM*. This reader called "and thou shalt walk in His ways" "a commandment that included the entire Torah," and referred to the strictures of Rule 4. In his reply, Maimuni insisted that tradition, manifested in the rabbinic warrant cited in the *ShM*, infused the verse with specific content.[36] As we shall see, this assumption is not definitive.

36. Abraham Maimonides, "Teshuvot Rabbenu Abraham ben ha-RaMBaM," 218. Maimuni's second answer is as interesting as it is original. He argued that the phrase that immediately precedes "and walk in His ways," namely, "if thou shalt keep the commandments of the Lord" (Deut. 28:9), is indeed a general, non-specific command, one that encompasses all of the commandments. However, the subsequent phrase, "and walk in His ways," focuses exclusively on the improvement of traits, and thus is quite specific. Maimuni argued that the Torah felt it necessary to spell this out since "it would be possible to think that it [this command] is not obligatory like the [obligatory nature] of the commandments, because commandments are performative [*maasiyot*] and the going in His ways are things that depend on moral virtues, as explained by the tradition 'just as the Holy One, blessed be He, is called Merciful, etc.,' even though the goal of these moral virtues is also actions." Maimuni was addressing an issue that still concerned Jewish theologians: does the Torah command virtues, correct notions, and correct character dispositions, as it commands physical actions? Recall that Maimonides proves that the Torah does command the correct notions of the existence of God, as proved by an explicit rabbinic warrant. See our discussion in chapter 5.

The *ShM* formulates the commandment as stating that we are "to be like God (praised be He) as far as it is in our power." In his argument, Maimonides notes that in addition to "And thou shalt walk in His ways" (Deut. 28:9), the commandment is repeated in two other ways: "to walk in all His ways" (Deut. 10:12 and 11:22) and "After the Lord your God shall ye walk" (Deut. 13:5).

Maimonides cites the following midrash on the verse "to walk in all His ways":

> Just as the Holy One, blessed be He, is called Merciful [*rahum*], so shouldst thou be merciful; just as He is called Gracious [*hanun*], so shouldst thou be gracious; just as He is called Righteous [*tsadiq*], so shouldst thou be righteous; just as He is called Saintly [*hasid*] so shouldst thou be saintly.[37]

He also alludes to a second aggadah (*BT Sotah* 14a), this one on the verse "After the Lord your God shall ye walk," which he summarizes:

> we are to imitate the good deeds and honorable [*MnT*: *hashuvot*, "distinguished"] attributes [*middot*] by which the Lord (exalted be He) is described in a figurative way—He being indeed immeasurably exalted above all such descriptions.

To better understand Maimonides' summation, I quote the entire aggadah in its original context:

> R. Hama son of R. Hanina further said: What does this text mean: *Ye shall walk after the Lord your God?* Is it, then, possible for a human being to walk after the Shekhinah; for has it not been said: *For the Lord thy God is a devouring fire*? But [the meaning is] to walk after the attributes of the Holy One, blessed be He. As He clothes the naked, for it is written: *And the Lord God made for Adam and for his wife coats of skin, and clothed them* [Gen. 3:21], so do thou also clothe the naked. The Holy One, blessed be He, visited the sick, for it is written: *And the Lord appeared unto him by the*

37. *Sifre Deuteronomy* 49 (114), with only minor variants. Some printed editions lack the phrase "just as He is called Righteous, so shouldst thou be righteous." See *Sefer ha-Mitsvot*, ed. Heller, ad loc., n. 18. When quoting this dictum in *Hilkhot De'ot* 1:6, Maimonides omits any reference to "righteous" and "saintly," substituting "holy" (*qadosh*) in their place.

> *oaks of Mamre* [Gen. 18:1], so do thou also visit the sick. The Holy One, blessed be He, comforted mourners, for it is written: *And it came to pass after the death of Abraham, that God blessed Isaac his son* [Gen. 25:11], so do thou also comfort mourners. The Holy one, blessed be He, buried the dead, for it is written: *And He buried him in the valley* [Deut. 34:6], so do thou also bury the dead.[38]

Following a strictly literal reading, the aggadah attributes to God a number of acts of kindness and offers them as examples for man to imitate.

In the *ShM*, Maimonides maintains that to be like God is "to imitate the good deeds and honorable attributes by which the Lord is described." While the phrase "good deeds" clearly refers to the benevolent acts described in the Talmudic aggadah, "honorable attributes" has no specific referent and leaves the full meaning imprecise. I read "honorable attributes" as parallel to "good deeds," both phrases referring to the generally accepted meanings of these terms. The simple understanding of this pair of phrases, "good deeds" and "honorable attributes," is that the former refers to *gemilut h̲asadim,* the kinds of good deeds that were traditionally praised by the Sages, and the latter to attributes generally considered honorable, such as compassion, mercy and righteousness: in sum, both represent different but overlapping aspects of moral excellence.[39] The talmudic aggadah to which Maimonides alluded makes this point well.

---

38. Qayyara's entry Pq32 reads "to go in His ways," and it is immediately followed by "to clothe the naked, to bury the dead, to console the mourner, and to visit the sick." It is not clear if Qayyara intended these special acts of benevolence to represent separate commandments, as Maimonides understood, or if—as is more likely—these attributes explain the general command to "go in His ways," just as the above midrash does. For a useful survey of the issues, see Hildesheimer, *Haqdamat Sefer Halakhot Gedolot*, nn. 329-330.

39. An interesting and illuminating example can be found in *Midrash Zutta (Shir ha-Shirim)*, ed. Buber, sec. 1, no. 15, where God's kind deeds are actually ascribed to His honorable attributes of compassion (*rah̲um*) and mercy (*h̲anun*), showing that in the popular and rabbinic mind, these attributes had been understood in the same sense as (and indeed as the drivers of) good deeds. Some scholars see these "honorable attributes" as referring to the doctrine of the middle way espoused by Maimonides in the *MT*. For example, Würzburger correctly notes that, in the *Halakhot,* Maimonides abandons the idea (proposed in the *ShM*) of imitating God's deeds and "felt constrained to limit the scope of the commandment *Thou shalt walk in His ways* exclusively to the cultivation of virtues." Würzburger understands the ShM's expression "honorable attributes" to be identical with the concept of the mean that lies between the extremes of all character dispositions. Würzburger, "Imitatio Dei in Maimonides' Sefer ha-Mitsvot and the Mishneh Torah." But this is not self-evident.

An important change takes place in the *Halakhot,* a change that was already adumbrated in Maimonides' discussion of Rule 9. There he states that "the Torah commands us to conduct ourselves in certain qualities of character, such as the command to act with kindness, mercy, pity and love, this being contained in the verse *And thou shalt love thy neighbor as thyself.*" In this brief discussion, Maimonides does not categorize acts of kindness under the heading of "and thou shalt walk in His ways." This comment already foreshadows the manner in which Maimonides treats these obligations in the *Halakhot.*[40]

In the *Halakhot*, practicing moral excellence through the benevolent deeds described in the talmudic aggadah is placed in the category of positive commandments ordained by the rabbis (*mitsvat 'aseh shel divrehem*), and the discussion of these rabbinic commandments is moved to *Hilkhot Avel* (14:1).[41] The standard that we are bidden to

40. This again raises questions with regard to the chronological sequence in which Maimonides wrote the *SE, ShM,* and the Rules. See also chapter 5, notes 19 and 52.

41. Three out of the four acts mentioned in the midrash above are discussed there: to visit the sick, to comfort the mourners, and to bury the dead. Maimonides specifies that the fourth benevolent act, to clothe the naked, is part of the positive commandment of charity (*Hilkhot 'Aniyim* 7:3) and is directly covered by the verse "[and thou shalt surely lend him] sufficient for his need [in that which he wanteth]" (Deut. 15:8). He had already suggested in the *ShM* (Rule 1) that to clothe the naked falls under the purview of this verse and attacked Qayyara for listing the obligation to clothe the naked as a separate commandment when it is part of the broader obligation of charity. Strangely, Maimonides was not willing to view Qayyara's claims "to clothe the naked, to bury the dead, to console the mourner, and to visit the sick"—which follow in Qayyara's list immediately after "to go in His ways"—as simply details of this scriptural command, just as the aggadah had suggested. See note 38 above. Maimonides' criticism reveals a certain incongruity in his own work. To explicate the commandment "to go in His ways," P8, Maimonides refers to an aggadah that lists a number of good deeds. One of these good deeds is to clothe the naked. Yet in Rule 1, in addition to castigating Qayyara for listing this deed as a separate entry, Maimonides wonders what might have been Qayyara's source for this claim. He writes: "it is [this point] which has eluded someone [i.e. Qayyara], and for that reason he counted the clothing of the naked [among the commandments] because he found in Isaiah: *When thou seest the naked, thou shalt cover him* (Isa. 58:7)." He appears to shows no awareness of the aggadah to which he himself refers in P8. We might posit that the Rules, or at least Rule 1, may have been written quite a bit earlier; it was only at a later date, when Maimonides was writing the short glosses on each commandment, that he first became aware of this aggadah. An alternative explanation is that he may have known about the aggadah when he criticized Qayyara but temporarily forgot it in the heat of the polemic. A more

imitate is no longer moral excellence, but rather *virtue*, an Aristotelian concept explicated in the *Nicomachean Ethics*.[42]

Virtue (Gr. *arete*), sometimes translated as excellence, is that trait that makes an object or person good at being what they are. So, for example, the virtue of a knife is what makes the knife durable and sharp; the "virtue of eyes," says Aristotle, "makes the eyes and their functioning excellent, because it makes us see well." Aristotle concludes that "the virtue of a human being will likewise be the state that makes a human being good and makes him perform his functions well."[43] When

---

interesting possibility is that Maimonides wrote the Rules after he wrote the glosses on each commandment—by which time he no longer thought that the aggadah represented a valid source for these obligations, since his understanding of *imitatio dei* had taken a dramatic turn away from the idea of imitating God's good deeds. Thus, judging Qayyara generously, Maimonides suggested that Qayyara relied on a prophetic passage rather than a homiletic aggadah. Until we know more about the order of the writing of various sections and compositions of Maimonides' works, we cannot fully understand his train of thought. I want to thank my dear son-in-law, Avi Horowitz, not only for helping me clarify some of these issues but also for making some very insightful and helpful observations throughout the discussion of this commandment.

42. Some enumerators, like the author of the *Sefer ha-Hinukh* (No. 611), seem to have conflated the views of the *ShM* and the *Halakhot*. In the beginning of his discussion, the author of that work paraphrases the *ShM* as he normally does, appearing to emphasize the need to practice moral excellence ("one must lean towards the ways of kindness and compassion"). Later on, however, in his practical discussion, he recommends that one should adopt the middle way and never move to either of the extremes, in line with the *Halakhot*. Hanna Kasher is also of the opinion that both views are similar, although she posits one difference between the definitions proposed in the *ShM* and those in the *MT*: the former, being a more popular work, provides actual examples of good deeds, while the latter, standing on a more sophisticated level, provides abstract principles. Note, however, that the *ShM* only alludes to a talmudic passage: it does not provide actual examples, which would be more fitting if it were trying to reach an unsophisticated audience. Also, the *MT* gives detailed examples of the types of moral dispositions (Kasher, "Does 'Ought' Imply 'Can' in Maimonides?" 27.) As I already stated, I maintain that in the *ShM*, Maimonides discusses general concepts of moral excellence, rather than the doctrine of the mean. Schwarzchild, too, argues that "Maimonides, conspicuously ... makes no reference at all to the doctrine of the mean in defining the commandment of imitation. On the contrary, he places heavy emphasis on the infinite, unattainable, radical character of *imitatio dei*." Here he refers to the closing statement in Maimonides' discussion of P8 in the *ShM*, where the good deeds and honorable attributes are "described in a figurative way—He being indeed immeasurably exalted above all such descriptions." Schwarzchild, "Moral Radicalism and 'Middlingness' in the Ethics of Maimonides," 65-94.

43. Aristotle, *Nicomachean Ethics*, II:6, 42-46.

it comes to human character, Aristotle maintains that excess and deficiency are the characteristics of vice, while balance, maintaining the mean, is the characteristic of virtue. In essence, this is the doctrine of the middle way, a doctrine that took on near-canonical stature, making its way into the minds and writings of all the greatest Islamic medieval thinkers. Maimonides was no exception.

After a thorough discussion of human traits and dispositions at the beginning of *Hilkhot De'ot*, Maimonides states,

> The right way [in moral dispositions] is the mean in each group of dispositions common to humanity; namely that disposition which is equally distant from the two extremes in its class, not being nearer to the one than to the other. Hence, our ancient Sages [*ḥakhamim ha-rishonim*] exhorted us that a person should always evaluate his dispositions and so adjust them that they shall be as the mean between the extremes... whoever observes in his disposition the mean is termed wise.[44]

Following a long introduction, spanning five *halakhot*, Maimonides finally cites the scriptural text that governs this commandment. He writes: "we are bidden to walk in the middle paths which are the right and proper ways, as it is said, *and thou shalt walk in His ways* (Deut. 28:9)." Here he introduces the Aristotelian concept of virtue as an axiom and equates it with God's ways, making no effort to relate the verse specifically to this ethical claim. The notion that this is an established truth that needs no proof gains further strength from what Maimonides writes in the next few lines:

> In explanation of this *mitsvah*, the Sages taught, "even as God is called gracious, so be thou gracious; even as He is called merciful, so be thou merciful; even as He is called Holy, so be thou holy." Similarly [*ve-al derekh zo*], the prophets described the Almighty by all the various attributes [*kinuyim*] "long-suffering and abounding in kindness, righteous and upright, perfect, mighty and powerful," and so forth to teach us that

44. *Hilkhot De'ot* 1:4. Hyamson rendered *ḥakhamim ha-rishonim* as "*our* ancient Sages" (emphasis added). The correct translation is "*the* ancient Sages," which raises the question as to whom Maimonides was referring. One possibility may be Aristotle and the Islamic philosophers who followed him. But see note 47 below.

> these qualities are good and right and that a human being should cultivate them, and to imitate[45] [God], as far as he can. (*Hilkhot De'ot* 1:6)

As we already saw, these divine attributes of graciousness, mercifulness, and holiness likely refer to moral excellence. There is no indication in the rabbinic dictum that the Sages intended to refer to the way of the mean.[46] Nevertheless, Maimonides posits that the Sages bid one "to walk in the middle paths which are the right and proper ways." As Marvin Fox noted, Maimonides treats this theory "as an established truth to which one need only refer but which does not require any evidence to support it."[47]

In sum, in the *Halakhot*, although Maimonides uses the same *Sifre* that he cited in the *ShM*, he effectively voids the terms describing God's attributes of their plain meaning, instead infusing them with

45. *U-le-hidamot*. Hyamson's "thus imitate God" is interpretive.

46. The closest we come to this idea of the mean is the verse and exposition quoted by Maimonides in the introduction to *M Avot*, end of ch. 4: "If a man continually weighs his actions and aims at the mean, he is the highest of human ranks ... The Sages ... referred to this goal, commenting on it, and said: *Everyone who appraises his paths merits and sees the salvation of the Holy One, blessed be He. As it is said: 'And to him who sets his way aright will I show the salvation of God.' Do not read* vesam derekh, *but* vesham derekh. (B Moed Qatan 5a). *Shuma* means 'assessing' and 'appraising,' and this is precisely the meaning that we have explained in this entire chapter." *Ethical Writings of Maimonides*, ed. Weiss and Butterworth, 74.

47. Fox, "The Doctrine of the Mean in Aristotle and Maimonides," 112. He further notes that if one accepts the plausible view that Maimonides is referring to the Sages of Israel in this quotation, "then we have the remarkable situation of Maimonides telling us that the principle that the middle way is good is known as an independent truth, and that because it is known to be true, the Jewish religious authorities accepted it as their rule of conduct and character development." So, too, writes Herbert Davidson in "The Middle Way in Maimonides' Ethics," 64. Raymond L. Weiss, on the other hand, posits that Maimonides here proposes an imitatio dei based on moral excellence since "[t]he qualities of holiness and mercy certainly do not lie in the middle ... Being gracious, like being abundant in loving-kindness, which is also among the ways of God that a Jew must imitate, supplements the essentially self-centered orientation of philosophic ethics." Weiss reasons that since the exegesis does not follow from the verse, Maimonides could not have intended to refer to the middle way. See further *Hilkhot De'ot* 1:7, where Maimonides insists that these attributes are equivalent with the middle path. Weiss is stating the obvious, but his reading runs counter to what Maimonides unequivocally declares in *halakhot* 5-7. Weiss, *Maimonides' Ethics*, 134.

philosophic ethics[48] that appear to have no counterpart in rabbinic writings. Concretely, the idea of imitating God expressed in the *Halakhot* does not require emulating His lofty attributes by cultivating good moral traits, but rather evaluating one's traits and adjusting them so "that they shall be as the mean between the extremes." Maimonides has skillfully and naturally woven Aristotelian ethics into the rabbinic exposition.

By the time he wrote his commentary to the Mishnah, Maimonides had already shown himself to be under the intellectual spell of Aristotelian ethics. Since he lacked a fitting scriptural proof text to support an ethical rule of conduct based on virtue, in his introduction to *M Avot*, popularly called *Shemonah Peraqim* (*SP*), Maimonides offers a rationale for the commandments wholly grounded on philosophic ethics. After stating that "The Law did not lay down its prohibitions or enjoin its commandments except for just this purpose, namely that by its disciplinary effect we may persistently maintain the proper distance from either extreme," he continues at length to demonstrate that wide sections of the laws of the Torah are designed with this goal in mind. In his words: "If you consider most of the commandments in this way, you will find that all of them discipline the powers of the soul."[49] According to the *SP*, the ethical absoluteness of the middle way is implicit in the divine commandments. Nevertheless, no single scriptural proof text commands one to follow the middle way.

In the *Halakhot* (probably a later text than the commentary on the Mishnah, even as the latter was continuously revised), Maimonides connects the task of balancing one's character traits to the command of imitating God. In Fox's words, "while Aristotle construes moral virtue as a case of art imitating nature, Maimonides teaches that the model of human virtue is the standard provided by the ideal of the imitation of God."[50]

48. Term coined by Raymond L. Weiss. See Weiss, "The Adaptation of Philosophic Ethics to a Religious Community."
49. *Ethical Writings of Maimonides*, ed. Weiss and Butterworth, 71-72.
50. Fox, "The Doctrine of the Mean," 115. Menachem Mendel Schneerson, the rebbe from Lubavitch, expounds on this point. He suggests that just as God acts dispassionately, so too must man act dispassionately to imitate God. Citing *GP* I:54:*126*, Schneerson writes that man "should be merciful and gracious, not out of mere compassion and

While the commandments are designed to help a person achieve this ethical goal, as emphasized in the *SP*, they may not be sufficient. In *Hilkhot De'ot*, Maimonides suggests direct exercises:

> How shall a man train himself in these dispositions, so that they become ingrained? Let him practice again and again the actions prompted by those dispositions which are the mean between the extremes, and repeat them continually till they become easy and are no longer irksome to him, and so the corresponding dispositions will become a fixed part of his character. (*Hilkhot De'ot* 1:7)

There is no mention of practicing commandments as exercises in this section. Either Maimonides changed his mind with respect to the character-changing potential of performing the commandments, or more likely, he felt that the duty of *imitatio dei* necessitated a special effort of will apart from keeping the commandments.

I now return to the problem posed to Abraham Maimonides: because the verse "And thou shalt walk in His ways" is a command that includes the entire Torah, classifying it as a commandment violates the strictures of Rule 4. In his reply, Maimuni concedes that this objection may be correct, but insists that tradition provides specific content, as elaborated by the *Sifre*. My analysis indicates, however, that the rabbinic exhortation "Just as the Holy One, blessed be He, is called merciful (*ra<u>h</u>um*), so shouldst thou be merciful" can be read in two ways. Its simple meaning is in prodding the faithful towards moral excellence and thus towards acts of beneficence, as explicated in the *ShM*; a less likely interpretation urges one to balance one's traits towards the mean and thus be virtuous in the philosophical-ethical

---

pity, but in accordance with what is fitting." *Likkutei Sichos*, vol. 34, 153. Absent *imitatio dei*, one might come to adopt an ethic based on moral excellence. Along similar lines, Herbert Davidson suggests that ultimately, Maimonides advocates metaphysically-discovered ethics that lead to dispassionate actions. Maimonides dismisses an ethic based on the perfection of moral qualities, "the perfection consisting in intermediate psychological characteristics." God's ways, he says, are "the acts emanating from Him," not characteristics of His soul. The person that walks in His ways "will not ... be merciful, gracious or vengeful, in the sense that he fosters mercy, graciousness, and anger, in his soul. As far as humanly possible, he will perform merciful or vengeful acts dispassionately, as God does." Davidson, "The Middle Way in Maimonides' Ethic," 66.

sense—an idea that seemed foreign to the rabbinic mind. The rabbinic warrant is inconclusive. If the commandment requires moral excellence, then "and thou shalt walk in His ways" is a redundant proof text, since this requirement could be learned from the verse "thou shalt love thy neighbor as thyself," as detailed in Maimonides' later writings. If, however, the commandment requires balancing one's traits towards the mean, then the verse "and thou shalt walk in His ways" would indeed contain specific content that could justify a *mitsvat 'aseh* designation. Since Maimonides must have been aware that the Sages were unlikely to have intended the doctrine of the mean in their aggadah, he could not elevate the verse to the category of a positive commandment. As a result, he resigned himself in the *Halakhot* to stating that the verse's statement of philosophic ethics represents a counsel of wisdom rather than a scriptural obligation.

The language and structure of the first chapter of *Hilkhot De'ot* confirm this assessment. In the *Halakhot*, Maimonides never designates balancing one's traits towards the mean or imitating God to be a positive commandment, even as he brings a scriptural proof text. In *Hilkhot De'ot* 1:5 he merely states: "we are bidden [*u-metsuvin*, a participle of the root *ts.v.h*] to walk in the middle paths which are the right and proper ways, as it is said, *and thou shalt walk in His ways* (Deut. 28:9)." In 1:6, he writes: "in explanation of this *mitsvah*, the Sages taught," again avoiding the term *mitsvat 'aseh*. The less-forceful character of this command can also be seen in other remarks from the first chapter of *Hilkhot De'ot*. He states, for example, that "to cultivate either extreme in any class of dispositions is not the proper course for any person [*ein ra'ui lo le-adam*] to follow or to teach to oneself" (1:3). If following the middle way were an absolute obligation, one would have expected the more severe expression "it is forbidden" rather than the phrase "not the proper course." Even when Maimonides uses the strong term *h̲ayav* (he is obliged), as in 1:6, he tempers it with the qualifier "as far as he can."

Structural considerations also confirm that we are in the presence of a counsel of wisdom. In 1:4, after explaining the properties of the "right way," Maimonides adds: "hence, *our ancient sages* [emphasis added] exhorted us that a person should always evaluate his dispositions and so adjust them that they shall be at the mean between the extremes." To support his description of the right way, he cites verses from the wisdom literature, Psalms and Proverbs. Significantly, he expounds this law *before* introducing any scriptural proof text.[51]

In sum, *imitatio dei* is characterized as a *mitsvah* in the *Halakhot*, a commendable goal, a suggestion rather than an order. It is never explicitly designated as a positive commandment. It is worth noting that in *Hilkhot De'ot* 1:7, Maimonides traces the philosophic ethics back to Abraham:

> This path is called the way of God and this is what the patriarch Abraham taught his children as it says *For I love him, because he will charge his children and his household after him, that they may keep the way of the Lord* [Gen. 18:19].[52]

Moreover, the way of the mean is the path to earthly happiness: "Whoever walks in this way secures for himself happiness and blessing, as the text continues, *In order that the Lord might bring upon Abraham that which He spoke concerning him.*" Were the way of the mean to be a commandment, one would expect happiness and blessing as a reward in the world to come.[53] Because no timeframe is stipulated for happiness and blessing, one assumes that these benefits are natural outcomes of following a wise counsel in this earthly world.[54]

---

51. Dov Septimus also notes some of these peculiarities and posits that the first few *halakhot* of *Hilkhot De'ot* reflect *normative*, not prescriptive, language. I disagree with his assertion that a *commandment* is what follows this normative introduction. In an attempt to reconcile the literary difficulty, he argues that Maimonides meant to write that the Torah commanded these practices because they are inherently good. As I argue above, I believe that Maimonides never considered "and thou shalt walk in His ways" to be a positive commandment. He certainly did not designate it as such in the *Halakhot*. Septimus, "Mivneh ve-ti'un be-sefer ha-madda," 226-227.
52. This dichotomy between the Abrahamic and Mosaic approaches in Maimonidean writings has been intriguingly explored in Diamond, *Maimonides and the Hermeneutics of Concealment.*_
53. See *Hilkhot Teshuvah* 9:1.
54. Tradition knows of a few types of good deeds that garner divine reward in *both* worlds, but never in only one. See *BT Qiddushin* 40a. As an aside, see Maimonides' interesting comments to *M Peah* 1:1 on the benefits of reciprocity when performing kind deeds.

The way of the mean is a tenet of wisdom rather than a stipulation of the law. Maimonides identifies it with the "way of God," tracing it back to the patriarch Abraham and promising that whoever practices it "secures for himself happiness and blessings."

As I have argued, Maimonides asserts that the so-called commandments to love God, to fear Him, and to imitate His ways are not *mitsvot 'aseh*, orders that one must strive to fulfill, but rather *mitsvot*, suggestions or commendable goals. I would like to suggest that the *mitsvot* just reviewed not only play an important role in Maimonides' jurisprudence, but also, in at least one respect, they move Maimonides' system closer to a modern conception of the law. In analyzing the *ShM*, Hanina Ben-Menahem argues that Maimonides clings to an imperative model of law: Maimonides thought that the faithful were ordered to fulfill all of the 248 positive commandments. Though one might argue with this conclusion—and I have brought some evidence to show that many of the positive commandments in the *ShM* cannot be seen as orders, such as the commandments related to uncleanness (P99-107)—Ben-Menahem does make an interesting observation:

> The thesis advanced by Hart, that the law should be individuated so as to reflect the fact that it directs and guides, not only through commands and prohibitions, but also by outlining the means for achieving desired ends, is *not upheld* by Maimonides [emphasis added].[55]

If my reading of the way in which the *Halakhot* presents these so-called commandments is correct, we find that, at least in the *Halakhot*, the Law is individuated so that it does indeed "[direct and guide], not only through commands and prohibitions, but also by outlining the means for achieving desired ends." In effect, the three commandments reviewed in this chapter suggest ways by which one can come to achieve a highly meaningful mystical-intellectual experience (by loving and fearing God) as well as ways by which one can grow toward the personal excellence that promises to secure "happiness and blessing."

55. Ben-Menahem, "Maimonides' Fourteen Roots," 28-29.

P34. THAT WHEN THE ARK IS CARRIED, IT SHOULD BE CARRIED ON THE SHOULDER

Hilkhot Kele ha-Miqdash 2:12 reads:

> When the ark is being transported [*be-et she-molikhin*] from one place to another, it is not transported [*ein molikhin*] on a beast and not on a wagon. And because David forgot [the law] and carried it on wagons, a bursting-out burst out on Uzza [based on 1 Chr. 13:11.]. It is therefore a *mitsvah* to carry it on one's shoulder, as it says, *because the service of holy things belonged unto them: they bore them upon their shoulders* [Num. 7:9].

The commandment that the ark must be carried on the shoulders of its bearers is not called a *mitsvat 'aseh,* but simply termed a *mitsvah*. As if to dispel any lingering doubts, Maimonides repeats this assessment at the close of the *halakhah*: "It is therefore a *mitsvah* to carry it on one's shoulder." Of further interest is the peculiar structure of the *halakhah*. Rather than opening with the actions that constitute the *mitsvah*, Maimonides begins by cautioning that the ark "is not transported [*ein molikhin*] on a beast and not on a wagon." This peculiar arrangement shifts the emphasis from the positive aspects of the command—to make a deliberate attempt to "exalt" the ark[56]—to a simple warning that the ark may not be treated disrespectfully. These difficulties fall away when we evaluate the pentateuchal proof text in context. In effect, Numbers 7:9 simply states that the sons of Kehat did not receive carts and oxen because their service dealt with the sacred objects, and that "they bore them upon their shoulders." This is a statement of fact: no command is represented by these words. Indeed, there is no indication that there ever was a divine command to this effect. I infer that the manner of porterage was a decision made by the levitical leaders and/or the porters themselves, clearly in deference to the sacredness of the objects. The matter-of-fact statement leaves little doubt that the decision met with the approval of God and Moses. Nevertheless, while this action was taken in recognition of the exalted nature of the sacred objects, it better fits our new definition of *mitsvah* as a desirable or praiseworthy action.

---

56. Cf. *GP* III:45:*580*.

I also note that the David and Uzza story (told in 2 Samuel 6:3-8 and 1 Chronicles 13:7-10) appears to say, at least according to Maimonides, that the immediate cause of God's anger was the manner by which the ark was transported, namely "on wagons." Except perhaps by implication, there is no hint in this story that the ark ought to have been carried on the porters' shoulders. According to Maimonides' reading, the most important lesson learned from this story is that the ark may not be carried on wagons or beasts. This perhaps explains Maimonides' surprising emphasis on the negative aspects of the transport of the ark, the warning that the ark "is not transported [*ein molikhin*] on a beast and not on a wagon."[57]

In conclusion: the designation *mitsvah* is fully consistent with the context of the proof text. In the pentateuchal text, no command appears to have been given to transport the ark on the shoulders of the porters. More likely, this means of transport was a felicitous decision made by those involved in the transport of the ark, in deference to the sacredness of the object. The prohibition to carry the ark on wagons can be deduced by God's displeasure and reaction in the David and Uzza story. When linked exegetically, the passage from Numbers and the implications of the David and Uzza story from Samuel and Chronicles can indeed yield a so-called command that the ark must be carried on the porters' shoulders. But that exercise lies well outside of Maimonides' legal hermeneutics and his *peshateh di qera* approach.

P173. TO APPOINT A KING

In the *ShM*, Maimonides writes that "we are commanded to appoint a king over ourselves that is an Israelite [*mi-yisrael*, lit., from Israel]," implying that the commandment is to appoint an Israelite as king, if

57. Maimonides tells us that "David forgot," causing a divine "bursting-out," but it is not at all clear what it was that David forgot. Perhaps he forgot that the porters of the wilderness had chosen to carry the ark on their shoulders, but, as we pointed out above, this was not a commandment but simply a desirable way of dealing with sacred objects. It is noteworthy that Maimonides leaves out the object of "forgot," supplied by the translator in brackets. Maimonides well knows that what David forgot was not a halakhah or a law but simply a praiseworthy idea.

and when the Israelites choose to appoint a king.[58] Interestingly, this is also the way the commandment is formulated in the Headings to *Hilkhot Melakhim*, prompting Abarbanel to conclude that there is no particular obligation (*mitsvat 'aseh*) to appoint a king.[59] To complicate matters, the *SE* lists the commandment as "to appoint a king" without any qualifiers, leaving little doubt that, at least in the *SE*, Maimonides intended to convey that there is an obligation to appoint a king. Since the *SE* is probably sandwiched chronologically[60] between the *ShM* and the Headings, it is difficult to believe that Maimonides began with the idea that there is no obligation to appoint a king (just an obligation to ensure that he is an Israelite), moved in the *SE* to the notion that there *is* an obligation to appoint a king, and reversed course again when he composed the Headings. It is more likely that the *ShM* was later corrected on the basis of the Headings, perhaps even by Maimonides himself, after he had concluded that there was no absolute obligation, no *mitsvat 'aseh*, to appoint a king. This thesis can be substantiated by a simple fact: the argument in the *ShM* moves unequivocally in the direction of proving that there *is* an obligation to appoint a king.

If this thesis is correct, we can establish that Maimonides originally maintained that there was an absolute obligation to appoint a king. This is seen in the *SE* and in some versions of the *ShM*. By the time Maimonides wrote the Headings, he had reversed course and no longer maintained that position. By adding the phrase "that is an Israelite"

---

58. The term "that is an Israelite" (*mi-yisrael*) is missing in some printed versions. See *Sefer ha-Mitsvot im Hasagot ha-RaMBaN*, ed. Chavel, based on the first printing in Constantinople, 1516; see also *Sefer ha-Mitsvot*, ed. Heller, where an asterisk informs the reader that the word mi-yisrael was missing in one of the ms. that Heller used as a base.

59. See Abarbanel's comments to Deuteronomy 17:14 and I Samuel 8:5. Perla, *Sefer ha-Mitsvot*, vol. 3, 230, s. v. "*ve-raiti*," quotes Abarbanel on Deuteronomy 17:14 and discusses this understanding of Maimonides' position. The correct formula in the heading is "from Israel," as reflected in all the good manuscripts, and not "in Israel," as some printed editions have it, though it is not impossible that Maimonides himself was responsible for the change in formulation. For the variants, see "Yalqut Shinuye Nus<u>h</u>aot," *Mishneh Torah*, ed. S. Frankel,"*Hilkhot Melakhim*," *Perate ha-Mitsvot*. For an understanding of the issues involved, see the discussion that follows in this chapter.

60. A matter which I have alluded to a number of times in this work but, admittedly, have not demonstrated. I hope to do so in a future work.

(*mi-yisrael*) to his formulation, Maimonides effected a radical change in the claim: the only obligation is to ensure that any king chosen would be an Israelite. Indeed, in the *Halakhot*, Maimonides did not treat the appointment of a king as an obligation but rather as a *mitsvah*.

I will now show some evidence for the reversal and the possible reasons behind it. The scriptural source for the commandment of the king is found in Deuteronomy 17:14-15:

> When thou art come unto the land which the Lord thy God giveth thee, and shall possess it, and shalt dwell therein; and shalt say: 'I will set a king over me, like all the nations that are round about me'; thou shalt in any wise set him king over thee, whom the Lord thy God shall choose; one from among thy brethren shalt thou set king over thee; thou mayest not put a foreigner over thee, who is not thy brother.

The interpretation of these verses was the subject of a tannaitic dispute. While there are very significant variants in the sources,[61] the gist of the dispute is clear. In all of the sources, R. Nehorai argues that these verses do not mandate the appointment of a king. Rather, these verses were "spoken only in anticipation of their future murmurings" (*BT Sanhedrin* 20b): they represent a prophecy. The incident to which these verses allude is found in 1 Samuel 8:5, where it is recounted that the Israelites demanded that the prophet Samuel appoint a king "to govern us like all other nations." In response to this demand, God tells Samuel to heed the demands of the people. Sensing Samuel's displeasure and hurt, God says to Samuel: "For it is not you that they have rejected; it is Me that they have rejected as their king." R. Nehorai adds that this section conveyed "a disgrace for Israel" (*Sifre*). In the *Sifre*'s passage, R. Judah views this section as commanding the appointment of a king, in accordance with what he had already stated earlier (Re'eh, piska 67): "Three commandments were given to Israel when they entered the land: [i] to appoint a king, [ii] to cut off the seed of 'Amaleq, and [iii] to build themselves the chosen house." By R. Judah's logic, why would God have shown displeasure? R. Judah answers[62] that it was because

61. *BT Sanhedrin* 20b, *T Sanhedrin* 4:3, and *Sifre Deuteronomy* 156 (208).

62. Reading *T Sanhedrin* 4:3, one cannot be completely certain that R. Judah is the author

they rushed the events.[63] In sum, one mishnaic Sage believes that the passage from Deuteronomy does not mandate the appointment of a king, but instead prophetically anticipates a concession to an unlawful demand that would occur many centuries later. A second Sage believes that the passage does command the Israelites to appoint a king, in accord with the threefold command given to them upon entering the land: to appoint a king, to cut off the seed of ʿAmaleq, and to build the Temple. As an aside, medieval exegetes known for their predilection for reading Scripture according to the plain sense did see these passages as *permitting* the appointment of a king—as a dispensation rather than as an obligation to do so.[64] This sense stems from the fact that verse 15 does not stand by itself but comes in response to a request for a king.

In the *ShM*, Maimonides cites R. Judah's dictum (without attribution) as proof for the claim that there is an obligation to appoint a king. He further cites another unattributed exposition found in the same *Sifre* passage[65] which comments on the verse "Thou shalt in any wise set him king over thee," explaining: "This is a positive commandment (*mitsvat ʿaseh*)." Maimonides continues that the *Sifre* explains this statement as meaning that "he must be held in awe."

If Maimonides' text of the *Sifre* is the same as ours, this last interpretive twist is not entirely persuasive. In the midrash, the comment that appointing a king is a positive commandment is the second of two opinions, introduced by the common formula "another interpretation" (*davar a<u>h</u>er*). The midrash's concern pivots on the unusually strong infinitive-imperative language used by Scripture, *som tasim*, translated here as "thou shalt at any wise set him king over thee."

---

of this comment; the question and answer may well have been posed by the editor of the *baraita*. In the *Sifre*'s version, however, R. Judah explicitly asks and answers the said question.

63. "They rushed the events" seems to be the simple meaning of the phrase *le-fi she-hiqdimu ʿal yadan*. The other rationale for God's displeasure, offered by R. Elazar b. R. Jose, is that the elders made an eminently proper request, asking for a king to serve as a judge and help quash rebellious elements, but the multitudes ruined the request by asking for a king to lead them into war "like all the nations." See RaSHI, *BT Sanhedrin* 20b, s. v. "*amei ha-arets qilqelu*."

64. See the commentaries of Ibn Ezra and Saʿadiah Gaon on Deuteronomy 17:15.

65. *Sifre Deuteronomy* 157 (209).

These two midrashic readings seem to be mutually exclusive, with the *davar aher* offering an alternative interpretation. It may be possible that Maimonides' version of the *Sifre* differed from ours and the two comments were merged (without the *davar a<u>h</u>er* intervening gloss). I do note, however, that both the *baraita* quoted in the Talmud and the Tosefta show that R. Judah interprets the verse "thou shalt at any wise set him king over thee" as meaning "that his fear should lord over you," while both tannaitic sources omit the comment that "this is a positive commandment." It would appear from these sources that R. Judah did not agree with the positive commandment thesis.

In sum, in the *ShM,* Maimonides attempts to prove that appointing a king is a positive commandment, a claim that suffers from a number of hermeneutic weaknesses. Chief among them is that the scriptural command appears to come as a dispensation responding to a request, rather than as an independent commandment. Second, on close analysis, rabbinic interpretation of the critical scriptural passage is ambiguous at best. Crucially, the extant tannaitic sources show no consensus among tannaim that the words "thou shalt at any wise set him king over thee" mandate the appointment of a king, consensus being the sine qua non condition for a positive commandment.

As we move to the *Halakhot*, our initial doubts gain strength. Maimonides opens *Hilkhot Melakhim* as follows:

> Three commandments [*mitsvot*] to be carried out on entering [the land of] Israel were enjoined upon the Israelite nation: to appoint a king as it is said: *Thou shalt in any wise set him king over thee* ... to destroy the seed of 'Amaleq ... and to build the sanctuary.

In *halakhah* 2, Maimonides continues:

> The appointment of a king was to precede the war with 'Amaleq, as it is written: *The Lord sent me to anoint thee to be king over His people ... Now go and smite 'Amaleq* [1 Sam. 15:1, 3]. The destruction of the seed of 'Amaleq was to precede the erection of a sanctuary, as it is written: *And it came to pass, when the king dwelt in his home....* [2 Sam. 7:1-2]. Seeing that the setting up of a king was a commandment [*mitsvah*], why did the Holy One, blessed be He, look with disfavor upon the request [made by the people] of

> Samuel for a king? Because they asked in a querulous spirit. Their request was prompted not by a desire to fulfill the commandment [*ha-mitsvah*] but by a desire to rid themselves of Samuel the prophet, as it is written: *for they have not rejected thee, but they have rejected Me* [1 Sam. 8:7].

Maimonides' introductory remarks alert the sensitized reader to a subtle change from what had been posited in the enumerative works. What stands out is his failure to declare that appointing a king is a *mitsvat 'aseh*. At the same time, it is clear that he describes some sort of desired action, since he uses the term *mitsvah* three times in these two *halakhot*. Similarly puzzling, one wonders why Maimonides cites R. Judah's dictum in the first two *halakhot* of *Hilkhot Melakhim* that the Israelites were given three commandments upon entering the land, instead of simply citing the scriptural proof text from Deuteronomy 17:15.

I believe that the answer lies in R. Judah's remark that the need to appoint a king was only made apparent after the Israelites received a special revelation on their way into the land. The prophetic oracle revealed that the national goals of exterminating 'Amaleq and of building God's abode should be preceded by the appointment of a king. While the oracle's remarks may have been understood as an order or as a suggestion, it is this oracle that I believe forms the basis for the *mitsvah* that he describes, and it is the reason why Maimonides spends time documenting the commandment.[66]

By contrast, the verses at Deuteronomy 17:14-15 only refer to an historical incident that was to take place many centuries later. As R. Nehorai put it, the verses were "spoken only in anticipation of their future murmurings." Collating the various tannaitic sources, one might come to conclude that R. Judah, too, agrees that the verses refer to a future event. While it is true that in the opening *halakhah* of *Hilkhot*

66. Both the commentators *Kesef Mishneh* on 1:1 and *Lehem Mishneh* on 1:2 wonder why Maimonides does not cite the Pentateuchal proof texts offered in the Babylonian Talmud and in the *Sifre*. The latter argues that Maimonides chose the prophetic texts because they were more compelling than the pentateuchal ones and notes that this practice is common in the *Halakhot* whenever the new exegesis does not contain halakhic implications. This is clearly not applicable in this case; extra-pentateuchal proof texts can hardly serve as proof texts for Mosaic law. As I see it, Maimonides' choice fits well with our notion that the command was extra-pentateuchal.

Melakhim, Maimonides resorts to Deuteronomy 17:14-15 in support of the *mitsvah*, we must consider the possibility that this maneuver represents merely an elegant midrashic flourish that *post factum* exploits the latent polyvalence of Torah, since the fusing of the scriptural passage and R. Judah' s tradition is incompatible with Maimonides' *peshateh di-qera* hermeneutics. As a result, Maimonides can cite Deuteronomy 17:15 as the basis for the *mitsvah*, but he does not assign to the command the force of a positive commandment. For Maimonides, the command to appoint a king remains no more than a *mitsvah*, a piece of good advice.

P172. TO HEED THE CALL OF EVERY PROPHET IN EACH GENERATION, PROVIDED THAT HE NEITHER ADDS TO NOR TAKES AWAY FROM THE TORAH

The law is discussed at great length and in great detail in *Hilkhot Yesode ha-Torah* 7:7, 8:2, 9:2 and 9:3. Throughout the discussion of this commandment, Maimonides repeatedly uses the term *mitsvah* rather than the expected *mitsvat 'aseh,* even though the commandment had been identified as a *mitsvat 'aseh* in the *ShM*. To discover why, I turn to *Hilkhot Sanhedrin*, where Maimonides lists all the scriptural violations and their punishments. In 19:3 we read:

> [A] priest who performs service without having washed his hands and feet, though he incurs thereby the penalty of death [by divine intervention], is not flogged, because this is a positive commandment [*mitsvat 'aseh*]. So too, a prophet who suppresses his prophecy, a prophet who acts contrary to his own words, and one who disregards the words of a prophet, are not liable to flogging—though these three offenders incur the penalty of death [by divine intervention]—the prohibition they transgress is derived by implication from a positive command, as it is said *Unto him ye shall hearken* [Deut. 18:15], and a negative command derived by implication from a positive command is treated *as* a positive command [*ke-'aseh*], the violation of which does not entail the penalty of flogging [my emphasis].

Maimonides makes it abundantly clear that while the verse "Unto him ye shall hearken" (Deut. 18:15) is to be treated as a positive commandment, it is actually an inferred prohibition derived from a positive statement, since the verse essentially prohibits one from disobeying a prophet.[67] As I discussed earlier, in the *ShM*, Maimonides uses this hermeneutic device to prove that a given commandment is a *mitsvat ʿaseh*.[68] Once Maimonides' criteria for determining positive commandments changed to require an absolute obligation—as I argue they did in the *Halakhot*—statements that infer a prohibition could no longer be treated as positive commandments. Maimonides confirms this shift away from using this Talmudic principle by ever so subtly changing the talmudic formulation: he adds the preposition *kof* in front of the word *ʿaseh* to read "it is *like* an *ʿaseh*" (though not an *ʿaseh*).[69]

Since the injunction "Unto him ye shall hearken" (Deut. 18:15) is used in the Talmud to convey a prohibition against ignoring the words of a true prophet, the positive statement can only convey a desideratum, not an absolute obligation.[70] In other words, Scripture desires that the Israelites obey their true prophets; it lets us know this by threatening those who *disobey* their messages with divine punishment.[71] As we have seen, a desideratum is best described with the solo term *mitsvah*.

---

67. This is how the *Lehem Mishneh* commentary to *Hilkhot Yesode ha-Torah* 9:2-3 understands the verse, arguing that the command ought to be read as denoting a prohibition, as if to say "do not violate the prophet's words [*de-inyano lav hu, lo taavor al divre ha-navi*]."

68. See chapter 2. The appearance of P172 on the list of the 60 unconditional obligations is quite puzzling, however; even if Maimonides thought it proper to enumerate this commandment in the *ShM* on the basis of the Talmudic principle that says that a prohibition derived by implication from a positive statement is considered a positive commandment, he could not have seen the verse as an absolute obligation. Moreover, if Maimonides follows the prominent rabbinic tradition that prophecy was abolished after the destruction of the Temple, how can P172 be an active commandment in the modern period, appropriate for inclusion on the abbreviated list of obligations? The most likely answer to the first problem is that Maimonides initially read the verse "Unto him ye shall hearken" as a positive commandment; only later, at the time of the composition of the *MT*, did he change his mind and view the verse as an inferred prohibition. See note 67 above. On this topic, see J. Levinger's interesting distinction between prophetic legislation and prophetic advice. Levinger, *Ha-RaMBaM ke-Filosof*, 84-87.

69. But like an *ʿaseh*, he means to say that, just like the non-performance of an *ʿaseh* is not liable to lashes, so too, the transgression of this prohibition does not attract lashes.

70. For the logic of this statement, see above, note 29.

71. As Maimonides makes clear, had this injunction been phrased in the negative form, it would have required the courts to administer lashes to the violator. Perhaps the logic is not as convoluted as it would appear at first. Scripture may have preferred to keep the courts out of having to pass judgment on hard-to-read matters of the heart.

P178. THAT ONE WHO POSSESSES EVIDENCE SHALL TESTIFY IN COURT

This commandment was discussed at some length in chapter 5. Here I discuss Maimonides' formulation of the commandment in the *Halakhot*.

In *Hilkhot 'Edut* 1:1, he writes: "The witness is commanded (*metsuveh*)[72] to provide in Court any testimony he may have...as it says, *he being a witness, whether he hath seen or known, if he do not utter it, then he shall bear his iniquity.*" Note that while Maimonides cites the expected proof text, he fails to declare that providing testimony is a positive commandment.

In the discussion of this commandment in chapter 5, I noted that Scripture provides no explicit command urging one who possesses evidence to come to court. Commentators attempt to find some scriptural basis for this commandment, but these solutions do not follow the grammatical sense of the text. Only an explicit scriptural imperative could convey an absolute obligation and, with it, a *mitsvat 'aseh*. By stating instead that someone who does not appear as witness will "bear his iniquity," Scripture hints, so to speak, about the desirability of appearing in court if and when one is in possession of evidence. This desirability is fully and richly conveyed by the term *mitsvah*.

P201.THAT THE HIRED LABORER EAT [OF THE PRODUCE HE IS REAPING] WHILE HE IS EMPLOYED

In my examination of this commandment in chapter 5, I discussed how the *ShM* defines this commandment as applicable to the worker: he is

72. This term is ambiguous. There are instances where the term *metsuveh* clearly stands for a scriptural obligation. See, for example, *Hilkhot Talmud Torah* 5:1: "Just as a person is commanded [*metsuveh*] regarding the honor of his father and the fear of him, so is he obligated [*hayav*] with regard to the honor and fear of his teacher ..." In this instance we know that *metsuveh* means "scripturally obligated," because in *Hilkhot Mamrim* 6:1 Maimonides declares that to honor and fear one's parents is a *mitsvat 'aseh*. Note the interesting terminological shift in this *halakah*: one is *metsuveh* with regard to one's father, but one is *hayav* with regard to one's teacher. Maimonides was drawing a difference between the obligations—the former is scriptural, the latter merely rabbinic. See our discussion of P209 later in this chapter. At any rate, what is certainly missing is a categorical statement declaring that it is a *mitsvat 'aseh* for one who possesses evidence to testify in court.

permitted to eat the produce while he reaps. We see a different law in *Hilkhot Sekhirut* 12:1:

> Behold, it is a *mitsvah* on the employer that he allow them [the laborers] to eat from [the produce] with which they are working, as it says *When thou comest into thy neighbor's vineyard*, etc. [Deut. 23:25] and it says *When thou comest into the standing corn of thy neighbor*, etc. [Deut. 23:26].

Note the change of focus: in contrast to how he describes this commandment in the *ShM*, the *SE*, and even the Headings, which define it in terms of the rights of the worker, here Maimonides places the emphasis on the landowner. "It is," he writes, "a *mitsvah* on the employer that he allow them [the laborers] to eat from [the produce] with which they are working." Since only absolute obligations can be labeled as positive commandments, it is unsurprising that the *Halakhot* omits any reference to this right being a positive commandment. It is of interest, however, that Maimonides enjoins the landowner to perform a *mitsvah* by allowing the worker to exercise his right. Whence this designation? I believe that the answer lies in Maimonides' unique understanding of Scripture's intention.

We are familiar with the right that Scripture grants workers to eat from the produce that they farm. Problematically, this is a law that does not seem to consider the wide gamut of social realities. Quite conceivably, these rights might be denied under certain circumstances, as in situations where workers exercise very weak economic bargaining power. Thus, as Maimonides may have reasoned, Scripture's true ethical intention is not merely to grant the worker what might be a nominal right, but, more importantly, to enjoin the landowner to exercise economic self-restraint: it attempts to shape the ethical conscience of the landowner. There is no scriptural injunction that obligates the landowner to allow the worker to eat from his produce. Instead, Maimonides reads Scripture as advising the landowner to permit the worker to exercise his rights. Here again we see the principle that law, as Maimonides states, can "direct and guide, not only through commands and prohibitions."

P205 TO REBUKE THE SINNER

In the *ShM*, the commandment is formulated as follows:

> To rebuke one who is sinning or is disposed to sin, to admonish him verbally against sinning[73] and to reprove him ... This injunction is contained in His words, exalted be He, *Thou shalt surely rebuke thy neighbor* [Lev. 19:17].

Immediately thereafter, Maimonides adds:

> Included in this commandment is [the obligation] on anyone who is injured by another to rebuke him, and not to bear him a grudge or entertain any evil thought of him. We are commanded to rebuke [the offender] aloud, so that no [ill-feeling] against him shall be left in our heart.

Though Maimonides does not cite direct rabbinic evidence for either the primary meaning (to rebuke a sinner) or the secondary meaning (to rebuke one who has injured you), it is reasonably clear from his sources that he believes that the Sages understand the term rebuke (*hokhahah*) as referring to rebuking one who sins. This is indicated by his explanation, following a talmudic passage that discusses rebuking a sinner:

> That this commandment is binding upon every person, so that even an inferior is under obligation to rebuke a man of high rank, and even if he is met with curses and insults, he may not desist or cease rebuking him until he is beaten—as explained by those who handed down the tradition: they said "to the point of suffering blows."

Compare this explanation with the following passage found in *BT 'Arakhin* 16b:

> Whence do we know that if a man sees something unseemly in his neighbour, he is obliged to reprove him? Because it is said: *Thou shalt surely rebuke*. If he rebuked him and he did not accept it, whence do we

73. Or, following *MnT*, "to restrain him verbally."

> know that he must rebuke him again? The text states: *surely rebuke* all ways. One might assume [this to be obligatory] even though his face blanched, therefore the text states: *Thou shalt not bear sin because of him*.

Further proof that Maimonides has this Talmudic passage in mind is gathered from his formulation: "As explained by those who handed down the tradition: they said 'to the point of suffering blows.'" Maimonides here alludes to the Talmudic Sage Rav, quoted near the end of the passage, who responds to the question "How far shall reproof be administered?" with "Until he [the reprover] be beaten." Maimonides uses a *midrash halakhah* to further support his idea that one must not desist from rebuking until the message is accepted:

> How do we know that even if one has rebuked the offender four or five times, he must still rebuke him again and again? Because Scripture says *Thou shalt surely rebuke thy neighbor* [Lev. 19:17]—even a thousand times. One might think that in rebuking him you may cause him shame [and should therefore refrain]: Scripture therefore says, *Thou shalt not bear sin because of him*. (*Sifra Qedoshim* 4:8 (89a))

In rabbinic literature, the term *hokhahah* often has the connotation of admonishing to impose discipline or to change wayward behavior, and it is in this sense that it is used in *BT 'Arakhin* 16b. This also appears to be what the *Sifra* intends repeated admonitions to achieve: to change behavior.

Maimonides' second interpretation has a distinctly different flavor, however. In this second type of admonition, the hurt party informs his offender that he has been hurt so that he will not harbor further ill will towards his offender. In this case, the rebuke is of therapeutic benefit to the rebuker. This, I believe, is clearly the intention of his words: "We are commanded to rebuke [the offender] aloud, so that no [ill-feeling] against him shall be left in our heart." In the *Halakhot*, Maimonides is even clearer: "But it is his duty to inform [*mitsvah 'alav le-hodi'o*] the offender and say to him 'Why did you do this to me? Why did you sin against me in this matter?'" Note that one *informs* the offender: one does not rebuke him. That Maimonides believes this to be the plain sense of the verse is evident from his comment at N303. After explaining that the Sages indicated that one must rebuke the sinner repeatedly but stop just before he suffers shame—hence the source for the prohibition against shaming a person—Maimonides says: "The plain sense of the verse, however, is that we are forbidden to retain any thought of his sin or to remember it." Rebuking a sinner does little to erase the memory of the sin. If the sin is an offense done against another person, however, rebuking the offender does help the aggrieved to dismiss the incident.

Two further observations: Maimonides' second interpretation is as psychologically valid and textually sensitive as it is original. He brings no sources for this view, although commentators have put forth one possible rabbinic source.[74] I assume that Maimonides had not seen this source, or he would have cited it to substantiate his case. Second, it is interesting to note that while Maimonides considered the novel and original interpretation secondary, he did think that it was "included in this commandment." This points to an ambiguity in the scriptural text: it apparently expresses two totally unrelated thoughts.

In the *Halakhot*, Maimonides changes direction. He presents both claims side by side, without indicating which of the claims is linked to the primary meaning of the verse and which to the secondary one. Just as importantly, he reverses the order from how he had presented the commandment in *ShM*, implying that the interpretation that is closer to the plain sense is actually the primary commandment. In *Hilkhot De'ot* 6:5, he rules that "[w]hoever entertains in his heart hatred of any Israelite, transgresses a prohibition, as it is said *Thou shalt not hate thy brother in thy heart*." This is followed in *halakhah* 6 by its natural correlative:

> When a man sins against another, the injured party should not hate the offender and keep silent, as it is said concerning the wicked *And Absalom spake to Amnon neither good nor evil, for Absalom hated Amnon* [2 Sam. 13:22]. But it is his duty [*mitsvah*] to inform the offender and say to him "Why did you do this to me? Why did you sin against me in this matter?" And thus it is said *Thou shalt surely rebuke thy neighbor* [Lev. 19:17].

---

74. "R. Elazar b. Matia said: If there is a matter [*davar*] between him and yourself, tell him and do not be a sinner about it [*bo*]. This is the meaning of *Thou shalt not hate thy brother in thy heart*, etc. *and not bear sin because of him*." *Seder Eliyahu Rabah ve-Seder Eliyahu Zuta*, ed. Ish Shalom, ch. 18, 109. See also *Yalqut Shimoni*, ad loc.

Maimonides sees this text as enjoining an injured party to tell his offender that he has been injured, which accords with the plain meaning of the words and with the context of the verse. This interpretation places the utility of the commandment on healing the injured party, lest he come to hate his offender.

It is only in *halakhah* 7 that Maimonides discusses the commandment as he had in the *ShM*:

> If one observes that a person committed a sin or walks in a way that is not good, it is proper [*mitsvah*] to bring the erring man back to the right path and point out to him that he is wronging himself by his evil courses, as it is said *Thou shalt surely rebuke thy neighbor*.

The use of the term *mitsvah* instead of *mitsvat 'aseh* in both *halakhot* calls for an explanation. I contend that these designations are a direct function of how Maimonides read the words "thou shalt surely rebuke thy neighbor." It seems reasonable to conclude that at the time of writing the *Halakhot*, Maimonides had come to see these words as direct and natural complements to the first half of the verse, "thou shalt not hate thy brother in thy heart." By rebuking one's neighbor—by informing the neighbor of what the neighbor had done to him—the offended party would release some of his pain and thus not transgress the prohibition to hate his brother. This constituted for Maimonides the plain reading of the text.[75] As he understood it, "thou shalt surely rebuke they neighbor" is simply a scriptural recommendation, a piece of good advice. Thus, the designation *mitsvah* for this interpretation is fully justified.[76]

By this measure, any other interpretation of "thou shalt surely rebuke they neighbor" takes the words out of context. This is the case

75. In N303, Maimonides offered this interpretation under the method of *peshat*, or *zahir* (in Arabic). At present, I am working on a study to show that *zahir* was a valid and authoritative hermeneutic, one which gained increasing prominence in Maimonides' later writings, contra M. Cohen, who maintains that *zahir al-nass* connotes at times "the apparent sense—which is ultimately incorrect." Cohen, *A Talmudist's Halakhic Hermeneutics*, Appendix A, 69 and n. 292.

76. It is worth noting that Maimonides did not list this commandment among the sixty unconditional obligations (*mitsvot hekhre<u>h</u>iyot*), a sign perhaps that even at an early stage, he did not consider it as an absolute, unconditional obligation.

with the rabbinic midrash, which, by understanding *hokhahah* to mean the reproof of sinful behavior, leaves the sentence logically unattached to the first part of the verse. Since Maimonides views allusively-driven interpretations as no more than rabbinic homilies, he also labels this interpretation as a piece of good advice, a *mitsvah*.

P209. TO HONOR THE WISE

In the *SE*, Maimonides supports this claim by citing the first half of Leviticus 19:32, "Thou shalt rise before the hoary head." In the *ShM*, he cites the entire verse to make an additional point: "to respect scholars and to rise before them in order to do them honor. It is contained in His words *Thou shalt rise up before the hoary head, and honor the face of the old man*." In support of this reading, Maimonides quotes a passage from the *Sifra*[77] that connects the two adjoining verbs in the proof text to produce a meaning of "rising in the manner of manifesting honor." In the *ShM*, Maimonides does not tell us what prompts him to read "wise" into the verse, rather than the literal "old man," though it is clear that the interpretation that he adopts does not follow the plain sense of the text. This alerts us to the possibility that "to respect scholars and to rise before them in order to do them honor" is a non-scriptural commandment. As we shall see below, there are good grounds to believe that this is indeed the case.

A *baraita* cited in *BT Qiddushin* 32b reports a three-way tannaitic controversy on the interpretation of our verse:

> Our Rabbis taught: *Thou shalt rise up before the hoary head*; I might think, even before an aged sinner [*zaqen ashamai*]; therefore it is said, *and honor the face of a zaqen*, and *zaqen* can only refer to a sage, for it is said: *Gather unto me seventy men of the elders of Israel* [Num. 11:16]. R. Yose the Galilean said: *Zaqen* means only he who has acquired wisdom,[78] for it is said: *The Lord possessed me* [sc. wisdom personified] [*qanani*, lit., acquired

77. The midrash cannot be found in our edition of the *Sifra*, but see *ShM*, ed. Heller, note 10.
78. R. Yose the Galilean defines *zaqen* as "one who acquired wisdom" by means of a word play: *ZaQeN=Zeh she-QaNah hokhmah*. The same root *q.n.h.* appears in the adduced proof text from Prov. 8:22, demonstrating that wisdom is acquired.

> me] *as the beginning of his way* [Prov. 8:22]....Issi b. Judah said: *Thou shalt rise up before the hoary head* implies even any hoary head. [Even a gentile and a sinner!]
>
> [*Gemara*:] But is not R. Yose the Galilean identical with the first tanna?—They differ in respect to a young sage: the first tanna holds that a young sage is not [included in the precept], whereas R. Yose the Galilean holds that he is.
>
> Issi b. Judah said: *Thou shalt rise up before the hoary head* implies even any hoary head." R. Yohanan said: The law is as Issi b. Judah. R. Yohanan used to rise before the heathen aged, saying: "How many troubles have passed over these!" Raba would not rise up, yet he showed them respect. Abaye used to give his hand to the aged. Raba sent his messengers.

With the exception of Issi b. Judah, the tannaim in this passage exhibit a strong tendency to stray from the literal and plain sense. Even Issi b. Judah's position is qualified by the later Sages, who refuse to grant the heathen aged a full measure of honor. One might reasonably conclude from the above passage that with their far-fetched interpretations, the tannaim went out of their way to reject the verse's literal sense. Stretching this idea, one could further reason that the authoritative interpreters of Scripture, the rabbinic Sages, had concluded that the verse's literal sense of honoring the old should be taken as a counsel of wisdom rather than as an obligation. In *Hilkhot Talmud Torah* 6:9, Maimonides appears to assume this conclusion when he states that "one rises before an old man" (using the participle), rather than ruling that one *must* stand up before him:

> One rises [*omdin le-fanav*] before an old man, advanced in years, even if he is not a sage. Even a learned man who is young rises up before an old man of advanced age. He is not obliged however to rise to his full height but need only raise himself sufficiently to indicate courtesy. Even a gentile who is aged should be shown courtesy in speech [*mehadrin oto bi-devarim*]; and one should extend a hand to support him, as it is said *Thou shalt rise up before the hoary head, and honor the face of the old man,* without qualification.[79]

---

79. Maimonides here follows the opinions of R. Yohanan, Raba and Abaye, who qualify Issi b. Judah's position. See Karo, *Kesef Mishneh*, ad loc. Qarqovsky, *'Avodat_ha-*

Following this line of thought, I further suggest that the two tannaim that remove the word *zaqen* from its plain meaning are not intending a literal reading of Scripture; rather, they are using the scriptural verse as an *asmakhta*, a support for their ruling concerning honoring the sages. This reading understands honoring the sages to be a non-scriptural or rabbinic precept[80] and justifies Maimonides' use of the term *mitsvah* in describing this commandment: "It is a *mitsvah* to honor every scholar, even if he is not one's teacher, as it is said, *Thou shalt rise up before the hoary head, and honor the face of the old man* [zaqen]. *Zaqen,* he who acquired wisdom."

Maimonides goes out of his way to explain that *zaqen* is not to be understood here in its usual sense of "old," but in the sense of one who acquires wisdom. The purpose of this gloss is not to inform us that he follows R. Yose the Galilean's interpretation (which he appears to do), but to explain why he does not treat the commandment to honor a sage as a *mitsvat 'aseh.* In sum, to render *zaqen* as "one who acquires wisdom" instead of the philologically attested "old man" not only signals a departure from *peshateh di-qera,* it also suggests an exegesis that is characteristic of rabbinic *asmakhta.* By labeling the commandment to honor a scholar a *mitsvah,* Maimonides treats it as a commendable practice.[81]

While for the purpose of our analysis, the use of the solo term *mitsvah* might be a sufficient warrant to claim that the commandment to honor the wise/scholar is not an absolute scriptural obligation, I believe that I have found a subtle confirmation of this view in the peculiar arrangement of chapters 5 and 6 of the *Halakhot.* In his lengthy comments on this commandment in the *ShM,* Maimonides digresses

---

Melekh, citing an earlier authority, wonders why Maimonides does not enumerate the commandment to honor any old man, as per 6:9. See his discussion to the Heading of *Hilkhot Talmud Torah.* Note the use of the participle *'omdin,* an indication that we are dealing with a correct practice or a good counsel rather than an obligation.

80. See chapter 7, n. 10.

81. Maimonides utilizes consensual oral traditions on a few occasions, even as they differed somewhat from the plain sense of the text, and introduces them as *lamdu mi-pi ha-shemu'ah* (see chapter 7). One might wonder if the Talmudic traditions here could serve this purpose. But on the contrary, in this case, the lack of consensus in the oral tradition over the meaning of this verse takes the Talmudic statements out of the category of authoritative traditions.

from the original claim to include a more detailed application of the particular duty to honor one's teacher:

> While this commandment to respect scholars is a duty incumbent on all alike ... it is especially and in a large measure obligatory on a disciple, who owes much greater respect to his teacher than to any other scholar, and has the duty of fearing him as well, since the Sages state clearly that one's duty to one's teacher is greater than one's duty to one's father, whom one is enjoined to honor and to fear.

Maimonides proceeds to prove, in midrashic style, that showing disrespect towards one's teacher is like showing disrespect towards God. He concludes: "All the foregoing is deduced from the scriptural injunction to honor scholars and parents, as is clear from the language of the Talmud, not that this[82] should be an independent commandment."

These comments make clear that the special obligation to honor one's teacher is subsumed under the general obligation to honor a scholar. Yet, in the *Halakhot*, Maimonides places the laws relating to honoring one's teacher in the chapter immediately preceding the one relating to honoring the wise/scholar. Moreover, he completely detaches the commandment to honor one's teacher from that of honoring a scholar, and instead makes it dependent on the commandment to honor and fear one's *father*: "Just as a person is commanded [*metsuveh*] regarding the honor of his father and the fear of him, so is he obligated [*h̲ayav*] with regard to the honor and fear of his teacher" (*Hilkhot Talmud Torah* 5:1).

Why this change? I believe that this literary arrangement reveals Maimonides' new appreciation of the commandment under review. Seeing that no explicit references can be found in Scripture for the duty to honor and fear one's teacher, Maimonides attempts to anchor this important notion in a scriptural commandment. In the *ShM*, Maimonides divides this duty into two: he anchors the duty to fear one's teacher on the commandment to fear one's father, and the duty to honor one's teacher on the commandment to honor scholars in general. Because

82. Chavel adds in brackets "[and the fear of one's teacher]" to indicate that Maimonides was discussing the command to fear the teacher. But this need not be so; Maimonides could be referring to both fear and honor or just referring to honor.

in the *Halakhot,* Maimonides relegates the duty to honor scholars to a simple *mitsvah* instead of a *mitsvat 'aseh,* he could no longer anchor the duty to honor one's teacher in the duty to honor scholars. This would explain the *Halakhot*'s strategic repositioning of the duty to honor and fear one's teacher, making it totally dependent on the commandment to honor one's father, which is an acknowledged *mitsvat 'aseh.*

At the conclusion of chapter 6, I noted that in order to explain the 27 remaining commandments that were not designated as *mitsvot 'aseh* in the *Halakhot,* one must examine Maimonides' approach to the reading of the legal material in Scripture. Based on the implications of the legal/exegetical principles discussed in chapter 7, I proposed two novel ideas to explain the remaining failures to designate. In chapter 8, I argued that Maimonides had, for all practical purposes, reclassified a number of formerly-designated scriptural commandments as *mitsvot mi-divre sofrim*. In this chapter, I have analyzed a number of occurrences in the *Halakhot* in which Maimonides applies the solo term *mitsvah* to commands that had previously been identified in the *ShM* as *mitsvot 'aseh*. I argued that although attached to scriptural texts, these *mitsvot* lack the formal properties of scriptural commandments. Broadly speaking, I found that the commands in question suffer hermeneutically from one of the following deficiencies: they lack specificity; they do not convey the sense of an obligation in their pentateuchal proof texts; they are derived from inferences in the text; or the traditional meaning attributed to them does not conform to the plain sense of the text. In these cases, Maimonides prefers to label the commands as *mitsvot* or as non-absolute obligations, avoiding the language of *mitsvat 'aseh.*

According to this reading, Maimonides' special hermeneutics of *peshateh di qera,* which we extracted from his comments to Rule 2, are seen to have a profound impact on the way he interprets Scriptural law. To state its general conclusions, a necessary (though not necessarily sufficient) condition for a scriptural commandment is that the command be issued in a clear and explicit form. In this chapter, however, I have suggested that forms that do not fulfill this condition nonetheless retain legal standing in Maimonidean theory. Rather than as absolute obligations, they are to be seen in a softer light, as suggestions, recommendations, or pieces of advice. I suggest that in Maimonides' jurisprudence, scriptural legal theory resembles rabbinic legal theory in at least one very important respect: it distinguishes between absolute obligations on the one hand and recommendations on the other, much as rabbinic legal theory clearly and explicitly distinguishes between *ẖovah* and *mitsvah*.

CHAPTER X

SUMMARY AND CONCLUSION

Scholars have ascribed far too much importance to Maimonides' enumeration of the commandments and far too little to the motivations that lay behind his appropriation of R. Simlai's aggadah as the basis for the enumeration and to the significance that Maimonides attached to this aggadah. The proximate reason for creating an enumeration was his need to have a reasoned and methodical outline of all Torah legislation in front of him, a reminder of topics to guide his preparation of the upcoming code of law, a massive and unique undertaking. Thus we find him saying in the introduction to the *ShM*:

> All this [I would do] in order to guard against omitting *any topic* [emphasis added] from discussion, for only by including them in the enumeration of the commandments [heading the various treatises] would I insure against such omission.

This sense is reinforced by some of the Rules, especially Rules 7 and 10-14, which are essentially taxonomic rules rather than definitions of what constitutes a *mitsvah*. I posited that the logically unnecessary identification of this outline with R. Simlai's count of 613 commandments owed its existence to Maimonides' desire to incorporate the two fundamental beliefs of the Jewish faith, God's existence and His oneness, into the legal realm, and thus transform their intellection into obligations, a dramatic departure from the preceding geonic paradigm. I inferred this conclusion from a dispassionate and unapologetic assessment of the *mitsvah* count. Maimonides stretched the meaning of *mitsvat 'aseh* well beyond its common rabbinic usage, relying uncharacteristically on an aggadah of questionable legal worth, a homiletic creation with didactic aims and no pretensions of being precise, and resorted to a contrived and hardly compelling logic to arrive at the numerical target, likely fully aware of the variant results that could be legitimately obtained.

The enumeration, *qua* a reasoned list of commandments, has diverted the attention of the countless students of his works ever since the *ShM* left his hands. But I posit that it was not R. Simlai's dictum that 613 commandments were given to Moses at Sinai that was significant, but rather R. Hamnuna's accompanying exegesis. Maimonides used R. Hamnuna's midrashic exegesis that the verses *I am the Lord thy God* and *Thou shalt have no other God before Me* specifically formed part of the count of 613 commandments to prove that to intellect the existence of God and His oneness constituted a positive, performative obligation. The credibility of R. Hamnuna's exegesis was even more firmly established when Maimonides inferred from its language what he believed was a theological truth: the nature of the commandments to believe in the existence of God and to believe in His oneness was categorically distinct from the nature and motivation underlying the rest of the commandments. He explained this distinction by averring that the former were philosophically demonstrable truths, capable of being apprehended without the medium of revelation, while the latter were only conventions, necessitating the mediation of a lawgiver and prophet.

The two articles of faith occupy the most prominent position in the *MT*, appearing in the opening lines of the *Sefer ha-Madda'*. In a letter to his disciple, Yoseph b. Yehudah, Maimonides wrote that he undertook to compile a code of law in his zeal for the glory of God, "in seeing a nation bereft of a truly comprehensive book (*diwan*) of law, and bereft of clear and correct [theological] notions."[1] Only the inclusion of these two beliefs in the canon of law could have satisfied the requirements of "a truly comprehensive book (*diwan*)" containing "correct theological notions." In sum, the unequivocal and unique statement found in R. Simlai's aggadah, that the beliefs in God's existence and His oneness constituted positive obligations, led

1. *Iggerot ha-Rambam*, ed. Shailat, vol. 1, 301.

Maimonides to appropriate the aggadah, adopt its numerical value of 613, and conflate it with the outline that he was preparing—all despite the constraints that it imposed.

In the second half of the book, I turned my attention to the subsection of positive commandments and drew some conclusions from the way they are described and defined in the *Halakhot*. While my readings hinged on what Maimonides actually wrote, I recognized that, being human, Maimonides was bound to make the occasional mistake. That said, the exceptional (but more than occasional) omission of the formulaic phrase "X is a *mitsvat 'aseh*" at the start of a topical discussion held my special attention because of the implausibility of it being forgotten: the phrase is rich, bold, highly informative, and consistent with Maimonides' sustained interest for making categorical distinctions. Additionally, and just as importantly, my readings focused on *how* Maimonides expressed himself. The rhetoric, the literary presentation of his ideas, and the logic of composition mattered as much to me as the slight inferences one could arrive at by noting the absence or presence of a particular term, elements which have constituted the more traditional way of studying his works.

I began this book's second section by noting that in the *Halakhot*, Maimonides moves away from the contrived artificiality adopted in the *ShM* of using the term *mitsvat 'aseh* to designate all types of legal themes: here he applies the term to a very specific case, that of an absolute and unconditional obligation. Combing scriptural and rabbinic sources, Maimonides searches for clear indications of unconditional commands and imperatives to perform well-defined acts. These he designates boldly and prominently at the commencement of each topical discussion, with a formulaic phrase that states that the directive at hand is a *mitsvat 'aseh*. Where Maimonides withholds the *mitsvat 'aseh* designation, I theorized that he must have done so because the scriptural and/or rabbinic evidence was insufficient to make such a determination. I tested for this evidentiary insufficiency, and when confirmed, I theorized further that under the influence of reigning Islamic legal theory (which was also heavily if not wholly influenced by rabbinic thinking), Maimonides opts for a softer definition. As a result, certain scriptural directives are categorized as recommendations rather than orders, wise pieces of advice rather than commands. Supporting these with scriptural proof texts, he labels them with the solo term *mitsvah*, a label that he also uses to designate rabbinical directives. The scriptural *mitsvot* include such prominent directives as to love and fear God, to imitate Him, to appoint a king, to heed the call of a prophet, to rebuke the sinner, to honor the wise, to testify in court, and a few others.

I conjectured further that Maimonides deliberately withheld the scriptural designation from certain commandments that had been labeled as scriptural in the *ShM* when the plain reading of the scriptural text did not appear to provide sufficient evidence for them, even when rabbinic interpretation suggested otherwise. To this end, he chose an artful but somewhat concealed literary device to designate them as such, the participle of correct practice. This is the case with such prominent practices as the recitation of the Shema, the binding of the tefillin, the writing and placing of the mezuzah and the study of Torah.

In the heavily politicized atmosphere of Cairo, where Rabbanites were both assiduously courted and continuously attacked by sectarian groups (largely Karaites) over the role of the oral law in interpreting Scripture, Maimonides chose to keep his radical opinions hidden yet recoverable. When applied to the legal sections of the Torah, Maimonides' *peshateh di-qera* hermeneutics would likely raise hackles among his own co-religionists and, worse yet, give comfort to the deniers of the oral law. His carefully planted literary cues could lead the reader who is familiar with rabbinic terminology and unburdened by popular and superficial conclusions to discover the Master's true opinion, or at the very least sense his ambivalence.

Maimonides was informed by a hermeneutics of *peshateh di-qera* that was firmly and demonstrably anchored in the Andalusian tradition. His insistence on presumed philological validity, however, left him uneasily placed, uncomfortably close to sectarian investigation and interpretation. Ironically, this led him at times to mount a struggling defense of his own traditional Rabbanite views, well aware that the plain sense of Scripture did not lend convincing support for such a stance.[2]

2. See, for example, *Hilkhot Hovel u-Maziq* 1:1-6, *Hilkhot Temidin u-Musafin* 7:11, and P153 in the *ShM*. On another occasion, I plan to show that Maimonides adopted

Consciously or unconsciously, Maimonides navigated his legal system between the Rabbanites and the Karaites, upholding the former's respect for authoritative tradition and the latter's insistence on relying only on philologically informed readings. Maimonides' extraordinarily novel application of *peshateh di-qera* to the halakhic corpus threatened the very foundations of a Rabbanism, one that was intimately intertwined with the Talmud and its authority. Nahmanides understood this all too well when he criticized Rule 2:

> [F]or this book of the master, its content is *delightful, full of love* [based on Song 5:16] except for this principle, which uproots great mountains of the Talmud and throws down fortified walls of the Gemara. For the students of the Gemara, this notion is evil and bitter. Let it be forgotten and not said.[3]

Of course, Maimonides would not have conceded this point: he would have maintained that his paradigm flowed quite naturally from the pages of the Talmud. Did not the Talmud's quest for *peshateh di-qera* support the distinction between divine and man-made law? Did not the rabbis of the Talmud acknowledge that explicitly stipulated scriptural laws enjoyed an epistemic advantage over and a distinction from man-made laws? To Maimonides the answer to these two questions was a resounding yes.

Thanks to his remarkable codification, Maimonides left an indelible mark on Jewish law. Unfortunately, an important part of his jurisprudence, the exquisitely fine distinctions he made between divine and human law and between command and advice, was never fully appreciated, perhaps because of its radical import—or perhaps because Maimonides, for his own good reasons, hid many of these contributions behind formulaic omissions, terminological nuances, and subtle literary devices. It is this rich and layered nuancing that, in some modest way, I have tried to recover.

---

purely polemical positions in some of these instances.

3. *Hasagot* to Rule 2.

EXCURSUS

An estimate of the number of entries that Maimonides omitted from Qayyara's list of positive commandments and possible reasons for these omissions

This exursus is a speculative exercise. In the methodological section (Rules) of his *Sefer ha-Mitsvot*, Maimonides provides a number of examples of the erroneous enumerations proposed by Qayyara and his followers. These examples only yield a partial list of disqualifications. One might think that a careful comparison of Qayyara's and Maimonides' lists would give a full account of the omissions. Unfortunately, as I have explained in this work, Qayyara's entries are terse and often vaguely worded, and the entries require careful interpretation. As in most subjective exercises, the range of meanings is quite wide: Qayyara's interpreters, often driven by both intuition and imagination, differed a great deal in their readings. Their differing analyses, in turn, have a meaningful impact on our conclusions. Matters are further complicated by the existence of a number of recensions of this list, each containing important variants. Since we have no way to identify which version Maimonides saw and critiqued, our conclusions must remain tentative, at best. Finally, all the lists suffer from the crucial inconvenience of lacking punctuation; where one commandment ends and a new one begins is itself a matter of interpretation. Most of these problems have been highlighted by Naftali Tsvi Hildesheimer.[1]

In the list below, I have identified entries in Qayyara's list of Positive Commandments (Pq) that the Rules appear to disqualify. Where relevant, I have noted Maimonides' reason for the disqualification. For simplicity's sake, I have adopted Hildesheimer's version of the list[2]

1. Hildeshimer, *Haqdamat*, 18-24.
2. Hildesheimer, *Haqdamat,* based on ms. Oxford Genizah, c18. In Hildesheimer's opinion, this version is similar in many respects to the B version and to ms. Ambrosiano (Milan) # Sup. C116.

and his parsing of the commandments. Hildesheimer's notes on the individual commandments provide a brief but informative survey of commentators' interpretations and are helpful in choosing the meaning that comes closest to the plain sense of the entry.

This exercise can be said to be highly conjectural, though I believe that regardless of the particular text, interpretation, and application of Rules that one might use, the conclusion would not vary greatly. Maimonides reduced Qayyara's count of positive commandments by approximately 60, and the total count (not dealt with here) by as many as 100.

Pq #	**Description**	**Eliminated by Rule**
20[3]	"the hides of the most consecrated offerings"	12
21[4]	"that which is raised from thanksgiving offering"	12
22[4]	"the breast and thigh (of the peace offering)	12
27	"one-hundred blessings each day"	1
33[5]	"to clothe the naked"	1
34[5]	"to bury the dead"	1
35[5]	"to console the mourner"	1
36[5]	"to visit the sick"	1
37[6]	"the love of peace"	1
38[7]	"righteousness"	1
39[8]	"faith"	1
49	"joy of Sabbath"	1

3. Pq 20. In V (Venice edition), but missing in B (Berlin edition). Maimonides makes it part of the commandment outlining the procedure of the burnt offering (P 63).

4. Pq 21-22. Maimonides makes it part of the commandment outlining the procedure of the burnt offering (P 66).

5. Pq 33-36. These entries follow Pq 32 "to walk in His ways." Maimonides understood that each of these entries represented a separate commandment (Cf. Rule 1). Arguably, these four entries could represent details of Pq 32, in accordance with the talmudic tradition, and not separate commandments. See chapter 9, note 38.

6. Pq 37. My explanation is conjectural and is based on understanding this entry as enjoining peace with other members of society. See the *baraita* cited in BT Shabbat 127a. It appears to me that Maimonides excluded this entry because, like other rabbinic commandments, it lacked an explicit scriptural proof text. It is not clear, however, what Qayyara meant here; moreover, we find a number of significant variants in the various recensions. See Hildesheimer, *Haqdamat*, n. 333.

7. Pq 38. Rabbinic commandment? See previous note. Alternatively, Rule 4, for being nonspecific. See also Hildesheimer, *Haqdamat*, n. 334.

8. Pq 39. "Faith," as in dealing with honesty (*nasata be-emunah*), a rabbinic precept. See chapter 5. V has here "truth." Hildesheimer, *Haqdamat*, equates this entry with religious faith and finds its correlate in Maimonides' P1 and P2.

Pq #	Description	Eliminated by Rule
50[9]	"its pleasure"	1
80[10]	"to keep it [Passover] seven days"	Redundant
83-90[11]	"kiddush eight days"	1
103-121	"18 days and one night to recite the full *Hallel*"	1
134-138[12]	"the five [restitutions of] one fifth"	7
139	"the Sabbath candle"	1
140	"the *Hanukah* candle"	1
141[13]	"to give the carcass of an animal (*nevelah*) to a *ger toshav*"	7
143[14]	"to uphold [the righteousness of] judgement"	1
145[15]	"to be whole"	4
147[16]	"to pursue justice"	7
148[17]	"to do (or repay) kindness"	2
155	"to fear the Sages"	2

9. Pq 50. To delight in Sabbath is a *mitsvah mi-divre sofrim* (*MT Hilkhot Shabbat* 30:1).
10. Pq 80. This entry has puzzled commentators, who offer a variety of interpretations. According to Eliezer ben Shmuel me-Mitz, *Sefer Yereim*, it is a general commandment that covers all the injunctions of the Passover, in accordance with "Thou shalt therefore keep this ordinance in its season from year to year" (Exod. 13:10). As such, it can be considered redundant. For other possibilities, see Hildesheimer, *Haqdamat*, n. 361.
11. Pq 83-90. Refers here to the recitation of the kiddush that introduces the Sabbath and the seven festival days (A. S. Traub). According to Maimonides, only the Sabbath kiddush is scriptural. Maimonides would therefore be eliminating here seven entries out of eight. For other interpretations, see Hildesheimer, *Haqdamat*, n. 364.
12. Pq 134-138. Five commandments, following A. S. Traub, see Hildesheimer, *Haqdamat*, 84n376. Maimonides enumerates three of these under P 118 (see Hurewitz, *Yad ha-Levi*, ad loc.); the other two should not be enumerated since they would constitute details of "holy things," as mentioned in Rule 7.
13. Pq 141. Detail of P 195, the obligation to give charity (so Nahmanides' additions to the positive commandments, #16). Ibn Ezra (Abraham ibn Ezra, *Yesod Mora*, Second Gate, 105) and Simeon Duran (Duran, *Zohar ha-Raqia*, positive commandments, *siman* 77) consider the verse *reshut* and not a *ẖovah*. This rationale, however, cannot be adduced in favor of Maimonides' omission in view of the broad typology of commandments claimed in the *SE/ShM* enumerations.
14. Pq 143. A number of commentators have understood it as the rabbinic precept urging one to accept divine judgement (*tsidduq ha-din*). If taken instead in a juridical context, Pq 143 would be subsumed under P 177. See Hildesheimer, *Haqdamat*, n. 382.
15. Pq 145. Not specific. This probably refers to various forms of witchcraft (so *Megillat Esther*, on Nahmanides' additions to the positive commandments, #8).
16. Pq 147. Meaning uncertain. Possibly subsumed under P 177.
17. Pq 148. At any rate, Maimonides notes (Rule 2) that this obligation is subsumed under the scriptural commandment to love one's neighbor as oneself (P 206). See Hildesheimer, *Haqdamat*, n. 329.

Pq #	Description	Eliminated by Rule
164[18]	"you shall sanctify yourself and you shall be holy"	4
165[19]	"be lowly in spirit"	1
181[20]	"pourings (*yetsiqot*)"	12
182	"minglings (*belilot*)"	12
183	"crumblings (*petitot*)"	12
185	"liftings (*tenufot*)"	12
186	"the bringing near (*hagashot*)"	12
187	"fist-fulls (*qemitsot*)"	12
188	"the offerings of incense (*haqtarot*)"	12
189[21]	"slaughterings"	12
190[22]	"nipping off (*meliqot*)"	12
191[23]	"receiving [the blood]"	12
192[24]	"sprinkling [the blood]"	12
200[25]	"reading the *megillah*"	1

The above deletions total 64.

18. Pq 164. Based on Leviticus 11:44. In his discussion of Rule 4, Maimonides criticizes those who counted a similar injunction based on a slightly different verse (Lev. 19:2).
19. Pq 165. M Avot 4:4. This is possibly subsumed under P8, the commandment to imitate God.
20. Pq 181-188. This lists various steps in the preparation of the meal offerings. Maimonides refers to these in his discussion of Rule 12 and points out the error in enumerating them as separate commandments rather than as parts of bringing a meal offering. I have omitted "saltings (*meli<u>h</u>ot*)" from this list because Maimonides also enumerates "salting," though in connection with all offerings (P 62).
21. Pq 189. Maimonides would make this procedure a part of bringing the various offerings (P 63-66).
22. Pq 190. Maimonides would make this procedure a part of bringing various bird offerings included in P 63 and P 64.
23. Pq 191. See note on Pq 189, above.
24. Pq 192. See note on Pq 189, above.
25. Pq 200. A rabbinic precept (Rule 1).

POSTSCRIPT

Readers of chapter 7 of this book will be aware that Maimonides uses two technical terms in the *Sefer ha-Mitsvot* when referring to the plain meaning (*peshat*) of Scripture: the Aramaic *peshateh di-qera* as well as its equivalent, *gufeh di qera*, and the Arabic *zahir al-nass*. At the time of writing the dissertation, and through the subsequent period of revising it for publication, I maintained the intention to return to this matter, since I felt that a precise definition and the relation between these terms had eluded me (see footnote 30, chapter 7). Just as this book goes to print, I have had the opportunity to read the recently published (and anxiously anticipated; see chapter 7, footnote 26) monograph *Opening the Gates of Interpretation: Maimonides' Biblical Hermeneutics in Light of His Geonic-Andalusian Heritage and Muslim Milieu* (Leiden: Brill, 2011), by Mordechai Cohen, in which he tries to shed light on this question. Cohen has the great merit of having noticed and investigated the precise contours of these two terms by which Maimonides describes the plain sense of the text. In fact, to the best of my knowledge, he may be the first Maimonidean scholar ever to have done so. Space and time considerations allow me neither to detail his arguments nor to offer my rebuttal and my own views in more than a summarizing fashion; these will have to await a future article. Still, the main conclusions are worth presenting as they bear on what is discussed in the second half of this book. I beg the reader to review the analysis conducted in chapter 7 before reading this postscript, as I plan to allude or briefly refer to, but not to repeat, some of the evidence drawn from the *Sefer ha-Mitsvot*.

Cohen begins by distinguishing between the meaning of a term, i.e., its strict definition, and its use, that is, "the specific connotations it conveys in a particular context." He concludes that *peshateh di-qera*, meaning an "unfolding of the text," simply represents the plain and straightforward sense of the verse, much as Sarah Kamin describes its Hebrew equivalent, *peshuto shel miqra*. Concerning the *use* of the term, Cohen argues that Maimonides reserves it for halakhically authoritative readings, even when these readings depart from the philological contextual sense of the verse. *Peshateh di-qera,* then, is a marker for *peshat* as sanctioned by the oral Sinaitic tradition. *Zahir al-nass*, on the other hand, denoting that which becomes visible, i.e., the external sense, has generally been understood as the literal sense by Maimonides' Andalusian predecessors. But Maimonides *uses* it, *pace* Cohen, in a number of ways, sometimes to express the manifestly correct sense or the obvious sense of the text, and sometimes, by contrast, to denote the apparent sense of the text. The latter somewhat negative judgment of *zahir al-nass*—"apparent," with the connotation of insufficient or essentially incorrect—is primarily driven by the fact that Maimonides in the Guide faults *zahir al-nass* for the mistaken conceptions of God that unsophisticated readers acquire on reading anthropomorphic passages in the Bible (*Open the Gates*, 105). To be sure, Cohen maintains that "the term *zahir* in the *Sefer ha-Mitsvot* generally connotes the contextual-philological interpretation," a statement with which one can whole-heartedly concur, but then adds, in line with his thesis, that *zahir* may represent the apparent sense, "which would be correct if not for an opposing authoritative rabbinic interpretation" (*Opening the Gates*, 118). That is, *zahir* is a marker for a rejected view.

Peshateh di-qera and *zahir al-nass* are close enough equivalents that both Ibn Tibbon and Kafih, the two main translators of the *Sefer ha-Mitsvot,* rendered these terms simply as *peshat*. Cohen acknowledges this very close connection when he says that "Maimonides regarded *zahir al-nass* as a key component in determining the correct meaning of *peshateh di-qera*, and he did not ignore the close relation between the two concepts, notwithstanding the distinction he made between them in the Book of Commandments. In fact, in his Hebrew writings ... he at times does use the term *peshat* in the sense of Arabic *zahir*, which further indicates the link between the two concepts in his view" (*Opening the Gates*, 436 n.12). The "distinction he made between them" is more imagined than real, as we find only one case, N165, in which Maimonides contrasts, and then only indirectly, these two hermeneutics. In his summary of the nine instances in which *peshateh di-qera* appears in the *Sefer ha-Mitsvot*, Cohen admits that in as many as seven instances, *peshateh di-qera* adheres to *zahir al-nass*, while in two other instances it does not (*Opening the Gates*, 331-334). What Cohen sees as divergence from *zahir al-nass* is based on a subjective appreciation of what the contextual meaning of the verse should convey, hardly a solid basis for such a determination. A methodological caution is in order with respect to other writings since it is entirely possible that Maimonides used these terms differently throughout his literary career and therefore they may not shed useful light on their usage in the *Sefer ha-Mitsvot*—despite Cohen's valiant efforts. For example, in the Guide Maimonides may have taken *zahir al-nass* to refer simply to the literal sense of words, as opposed to their figurative or philosophical sense, in the same way Saadia and some of his other predecessors did, and much as modern scholarship has understood it.

I remain unconvinced of Cohen's precisions, as I have adumbrated in footnote 30 of chapter 7, particularly with respect to Maimonides' *use,* though not the *meaning,* of the terms. Nevertheless, Cohen's thorough analysis and my own recent research on *zahir al-nass* as used in the Guide have led me to make a slight and important correction in the definition of these two terms. In my revised opinion, *peshateh di-qera* stands for the straightforward sense of a verse, one that results from being able to explain all the grammatical components of the sentence as they are commonly used and applying to the verse the minimum amount of force. In the *Sefer ha-Mitsvot,* Maimonides uses *peshateh di-qera* specifically to reject the fanciful, homiletic alternative interpretations that the Talmudic rabbis offer for certain verses, i.e., *derashot,* which, in his view, do not represent Scripture's true intention. Therefore, these interpretations cannot be said to attain the status of scriptural law. Significantly, the context in which the verses are presented plays no role in this exegesis.

These criteria are mostly or wholly consistent with the nine appearances of *peshateh di-qera* in the *Sefer ha-Mitsvot*. The atomistic reading of Exodus 18:20 (see Rule 2) and Deuteronomy 23:24 (P94) proposed by some *midrashim* and cited by Maimonides as invalid interpretations of scriptural laws because they chop the various parts of the verse into unintelligible utterances, are good examples of *derashot* that violate *peshateh di-qera* (see my chapter 7, pages 249-250). Along similar objections, the rabbinic *derashah* to Deuteronomy 14:1 (cited by Maimonides at N45) that forbids the dividing of people and causing strife works by uprooting the words *lo titgodedu* from the rest of the verse and must therefore be rejected as an interpretation that does not follow *gufeh di-qera* (the equivalent to *peshateh di-qera).* Again, by the same token, the prohibition against eating filthy or repulsive things derived by the rabbis homiletically from the words "ye shall not make yourselves detestable" (Leviticus 11:43) works only by reading this sentence in isolation from the rest of the verse. As Maimonides avers, *peshateh di-qera*, a look at the entire verse, reveals that the prohibition concerns itself only with creeping things (*sherets*). In Rule 3, Maimonides places *peshateh di-qera* in apposition to a textual intimation (*remez*) and reveals a similar criterion. The short passage reads as follows: "Now although (the rabbis) do say: 'An intimation against stealing a holy vessel (is found in the verse) "And they shall not go in to see as they dismantle (or ruin) (*kevalla*') the holy..."'—it is sufficient that they labeled it [i.e., this *derashah*] an intimation (*remez*); the *peshateh di-qera* does not carry this sense." The short clause containing the difficult *kevalla*' is homiletically read as a warning against stealing or hiding holy vessels (see Rashi, bSanhedrin 81b). However, the entire verse, governed by the predicate "go in to see" as well as the sense provided by the immediately prior verse to which this verse is connected via the conjunctive *vav*, makes it clear that the straightforward sense is about the prohibition against Levites seeing the holy vessels as the sanctuary is being dismantled and moved to another location.

The historical explanation that Maimonides gives, in the name of *peshateh di-qera*, to harmonize the plain sense of Exodus 20:24 with normative *halakhah* rather than to adopt the forced midrash of Rabbi Yishmael (at P20), is proof evident of the high regard Maimonides has for *peshateh di-qera* (P20). In effect, the *midrash* succeeds in reconciling the text with *halakhah* only by assuming an unlikely and unexpected ellipsis in a perfectly readable text and by supplying the elided term. This type of violence to the text is inimical to *peshateh di-qera* hermeneutics. And yet it is worth noting that the *derashah* carries the day, and it is so codified in *MT*, *Hilkhot Bet ha-Be<u>h</u>irah* 1:13. Here, then, *peshateh di-qera* is not necessarily the authoritative interpretation that Cohen makes it out to be.

One might be tempted to question Maimonides' use of *peshateh di-qera* in connection with Leviticus 19:14 at N299 in light of the fact that he adopts a figurative rather than a simpler and more literal sense for the verse. We should note, however, that *peshateh di-qera* does not necessitate literal readings; a figurative interpretation can also do, as long as the interpretation "fits" the entire verse, and in this case, as the cited Sifra makes clear, it unquestionably does. Maimonides' preference for the figurative over the literal sense on this occasion may be a function of such things as the belief that the physical sense has already been covered by a different proof-text (see the immediately preceding N298), the unexpected appearance of the word "give" (*titen*) where one might have expected "put" (*tasim*) if a physical obstacle was being planted, or simply aesthetic considerations. The point is that the choice between literal and figurative, all else being equal, is a matter of subjective preference rather than the application of the hermeneutics of an "unfolding of the text." Moreover, Maimonides uses *peshateh di-qera* on this occasion not to reject the literal sense but, as always, to reject the multiple rabbinic interpretations—some of which he cites—that are appended to this verse.

In connection with Exodus 20:20, Cohen argues that Maimonides adopts the *peshateh di-qera* (as substantiated by *Mekhilta*) that reads the verse as a prohibition to make graven images even for non-worship purposes, in opposition, so he argues, to the philological-contextual construal (*zahir al-nass*), which sees the verse as a prohibition to make graven images, i.e. idols, for the purposes of worship. In his words, "In this case, the rabbinic commentary [referring to *Mekhilta*'s interpretation] is an authoritative 'transmitted interpretation' that overrides *zahir al-nass* ... that would have been correct otherwise." Besides committing the error of subjective preference discussed earlier, Cohen fails perhaps to appreciate *Mekhilta*'s close reading of the verse and all its parts, in this case the play on the preposition-plus-plural-pronoun *lakhem*, for yourselves, which follows the verb "to make" and yields "to make for yourselves," i.e. for your pleasure and benefit. As usual, the *peshateh di qera* comes to disavow the reader from other far-fetched *derashot*, as Cohen correctly points out, "Maimonides here invokes the rule of *peshat* to choose the rabbinic interpretation that is more reasonable ... as opposed to other laws attached to the text by way of *derash*" (*Opening the Gates*, 318).

The use of *gufeh di-qera* (equivalent to *peshateh di-qera*) at N165 requires a short introduction because the discarded view is not as obvious as those we have examined earlier. The commandment that forbids priests to leave the Sanctuary while ministering is based on two verses. The first verse addresses the common priest with the words, "You shall not go out from the door of the tent of meeting" (Leviticus 10:7), while the second refers to the High Priest and says, "He shall not go outside the sanctuary and he shall not profane the sanctuary of his God" (Leviticus 21:12). In Rule 5 of the *Sefer ha-Mitsvot*, Maimonides deals with motive clauses framed in the form of negative injunctions, and states that these clauses are not to be enumerated as independent commandments. One of the examples he provides is Leviticus 21:12. He points out that the sentence "and he shall not profane the sanctuary" must be understood as a motive clause explaining why the High Priest is prohibited from going out: the High Priest must not go out of the sanctuary lest he profane the sanctuary. This, he argues, is the correct way of reading the verse; the negative injunction must not be read out of context to support a second and independent prohibition, to wit, that the High Priest must not profane the Sanctuary, as other enumerators of the commandments seem to have done. It follows that the prohibition to go out of the sanctuary is effective only when the opportunity to profane the sanctuary presents itself, that is, while the High Priest is ministering. Maimonides, with the help of Sifra, extends this rationale to all priests, thus the prohibition for priests to go out of the sanctuary while ministering. At any rate, through the correct, or straightforward, way of reading the "second" prohibition, Maimonides manages to add an important qualification to the prohibition against priests leaving the sanctuary. Hence Maimonides is justified in saying that *gufeh di-qera* supports his reading of the verse.

In sum, *peshateh di-qera* in the *Sefer ha-Mitsvot* stands for a method of interpreting Scripture that features the straightforward, plain sense reading of texts, one that requires the least amount of grammatical and syntactical manipulation and that takes special care in reading the verse as a whole; words or groups of words may not be taken out of context. The interpretative unit in which *peshateh di-qera* operates, however, is the individual verse and not the larger passage in which the verse is embedded. *Peshateh di-qera* makes its appearance in the *Sefer ha-Mitsvot* wherever fanciful and forced interpretations or *derashot* are mentioned, referred to or alluded to, and it is used as a categorical foil to these *derashot*.

Zahir al-nass is a creative hermeneutic with an illustrious Andalusian pedigree, as Cohen demonstrates, that follows philologically sound principles and takes into account both context and the logic of an entire passage. *Zahir al-nass* reflects the intention of the author and therefore, contra Cohen, is deemed to reflect the correct sense of Scripture. This is so in the Guide, as I have recently argued in "Maimonides on Anthropomorphism: Should Scripture be Read Philosophically?" (*As a Perennial Spring: A Festschrift Honoring Rabbi Dr. Norman Lamm*, ed. Bentsi Cohen, David B. Greenberg [NY: 2013]), and this is true also in the *Sefer ha-Mitsvot*. Cohen tries to show that *zahir al-nass* in the *Sefer ha-Mitsvot* is trumped by tradition in N46, proving therefore that it yields an incorrect, non-authoritative meaning (*Opening the Gates*, 118-120). However, puzzlingly, Maimonides appears to contradict here his own Rule 8, which states that the determination of whether a negative particle stands for a prohibition or a negation can be made only by the logic of the passage and not by tradition. In Maimonides' words, "there is no clear-cut rule for distinguishing a negative statement from an admonition, except by the purport of the statement." Cohen appears to overlook this point and therefore regards *zahir al-nass* here as "incorrect." (Tantalizingly, Maimonides may in fact be protesting the rabbinic tradition!)

This is not to deny that *zahir al-nass* may in fact be trumped by a received tradition, as Maimonides suggests in Rule 9 with respect to otiose scriptural passages, where these redundancies are expected to be taken as stylistic variations or for the purpose of emphasis. As Cohen notes, "... where the rabbis attribute a new meaning to the seemingly redundant verse, their interpretive tradition, in his opinion, is 'most correct' and overrides the *zahir*, which would otherwise have been more reasonable" (*Opening the Gates*, 121). As we saw earlier, this is also true for *peshateh di-qera*.

In this book, I have shown that Maimonides minimizes the number of traditional interpretations that are not compatible with plain meaning and makes strong efforts to make the traditional interpretation conform to the plain sense of the text. My argument is not that *zahir* must at times take a backseat to tradition, but rather that Maimonides will not cite a *zahir* interpretation in the *Sefer ha-Mitsvot* in the sense of "apparent meaning" for the purpose of rejecting it.

As we saw earlier, Maimonides applies (at N165) *peshateh di-qera* to Leviticus 10:7 in support of a general scriptural claim that priests are forbidden to go out of the Sanctuary while ministering. In that same comment to N165, Maimonides applies a *zahir al-nass* interpretation to the parallel passage (Leviticus 21:12), which refers, as we saw earlier, to the High Priest and determines that the High Priest is forbidden to accompany the bier of a near relative (*M Sanhedrin* 2:1 attributes this opinion to R. Judah). The exegesis is based on the fact that the verse appears in a section discussing the manner in which the High Priest should behave when one of his relatives dies. The context is therefore critical to this interpretation. The subsequent Talmudic discussion attributes R. Judah's view not to a contextual reading of the verse but to rabbinic concerns that the grieving High Priest may come to defile himself by touching the corpse during the funeral procession. At the same time, Maimonides does not enumerate this prohibition in his count of the 613 scriptural commandments. On this evidence, Cohen deduces that *zahir al-nass* does not represent the authoritative interpretation of the verse and therefore *zahir al-nass* can only be said here to be the *apparent* sense of Scripture (but see *Opening the Gates*, 127 and footnote 132, where Cohen seems to waver), in glaring contrast with *peshateh di-qera*, which, as we saw, yields a scriptural law. This conclusion is unwarranted in my view. Maimonides' comments in the *Sefer ha-Mitsvot* seem to indicate quite clearly that he holds the *zahir al-nass* interpretation to be genuine and scriptural in nature, rather than the product of a rabbinic precautionary decree, but that it would not affect the enumeration of commandments because of a principle enunciated in Rule 9, namely, that two verses that repeat the same law, as in this case, must not be counted separately. Moreover, in his comment to that same *mishnah*, Maimonides states that the *halakhah* follows R. Judah's view, suggesting that at least at an earlier stage he adhered to the *zahir al-nass* (Maimonides' opinion with respect to the scriptural status of R. Judah's law may have changed in the later *MT*; but see Kafih, *Sefer ha-Mitsvot*, N165 n. 17, and see *Hilkhot Biat ha-Miqdash* 2:6, which seems to presuppose this exegesis).

At N181, Maimonides clearly endorses *zahir al-nass* and adopts it as the primary meaning of Exodus 22:30. Cohen's explanation for the reason Maimonides calls this construal *zahir al-nass* rather than *peshateh di-qera* as he should, in view of the fact that the latter term denotes authoritative meaning, is highly convoluted and must be rejected.

Cohen wavers with respect to Leviticus 19:17 (at N303), where Maimonides registers, "somewhat surprisingly" in Cohen's words, "his understanding of *zahir al-nass*." On the one hand, Cohen renders *zahir al-nass* in this gloss as "the apparent sense of the text," meaning the incorrect or superficial sense, but on the other he suggests that "Maimonides does not seem to relinquish the contextual (meaning), and states that it appears to have influenced his halakhic thinking, as implied by his formulation of P205" (123-124). I have already shown in my book (see pages 318-320) that Maimonides in the *MT* treats the *zahir al-nass* reading as fully authoritative.

In conclusion, *zahir al-nass* in the *Sefer ha-Mitsvot* is a philological-contextual reading of the scriptural text that Maimonides attempts to incorporate into the body of scriptural law even absent an oral tradition to this effect. *Peshateh di-qera* and *zahir al-nass* are two distinct *peshat* tools that operate tangentially to each other in Maimonides' legal scriptural hermeneutics and that accomplish different objectives. In broad strokes, Maimonides uses the former as a bulwark against fanciful interpretations, and he uses the latter as a way to plumb the true intentions of the law. None of these serve as markers of authoritativeness or lack thereof as Cohen has strenuously but unsuccessfully, in my opinion, argued.

BIBLIOGRAPHY

1. *Sacred Literature*

Babylonian Talmud. 20 vols. Vilna, Poland: Romm, 1898.

Bereshit Rabbah. Edited by J. Theodor and Ch. Albeck. Jerusalem: Wahrmann, 1965.

The JPS Torah Commentary. Philadelphia: Jewish Publication Society, 1989.

Masekhet Derekh Erets Zuta u-Pereq ha-Shalom. Edited by D. Sperber. Jerusalem, 1994,

Mekhilta de-Rabbi Ishmael. Edited by H. S. Horowitz and Y. A. Rabin. Jerusalem, 1998.

Mekhilta de-Rabbi Shimon Bar Yohai. Edited by Y. N. Epstein and A. S. Melamed. Jerusalem: Yeshivat Sha'are Rachamim ve-Bet Hillel, 1988.

Mekhilta im Perush Middot Sofrim. Edited by I. H. Weiss. Vienna: 1865.

Midrash Rabbah. Standard editions.

Midrash Tanhuma. Edited by S. Buber. Vilna: 1883. Reprint, Jerusalem: 1964.

Midrash Tannaim al Sefer Devarim. Edited by D. Z. Hoffmann. Vol. 1. Berlin: 1908.

Midrash Zuta al Shir ha-Shirim, Ruth, Eichah, ve-Qohelet. Yalqut Shimoni al Echah. Edited by S. Buber. Berlin: 1894.

Mishnat R. Eliezer. Edited by H. Enelow. New York: 1934.

Otzar ha-Geonim. Edited by B. M. Lewin. Haifa, Jerusalem: 1928-1943.

Palestinian Talmud. Reprint, New York: Shulsinger, 1948.

Pentateuch and Haftorahs. Edited by J. H. Hertz. Brooklyn: Soncino Press, 2001.

Pesikta de Rav Kahana. Edited by Bernard Mandelbaum. New York: Jewish Theological Seminary, 1987.

Pesiqta de-Rav Kahana. Edited by S. Buber. Lyck: 1868. Reprint, Jerusalem: Meqitze Nirdamim, 1983.

Seder Eliyahu Rabah ve-Seder Eliyahu Zuta. Edited by Meir Ish Shalom. Jerusalem: Sifre Wahrmann, 1969.

Shir ha-Shirim Rabbah. Standard editions.

Sifra. Edited by L. Finkelstein. 5 vols. Jerusalem and New York: Jewish Theological Seminary, 1989-1991.

Sifra. Edited by I. H. Weiss. Vienna: 1862.

Sifra de-ve Rav (Based on the Rome MS). Edited by Abraham Shoshanah. Jerusalem: Makhon Ofeq, 1991.

Sifra de-ve Rav (Im Perush Derekh ha-Qodesh le-ha-Gaon Vidal ha-Tsorfati). Jerusalem: Doveve Sifte Yeshenim, 1985.

Sifre 'al Bamidbar ve-Sifre Zuta. Edited by H. S. Horowitz. Leipzig: Shalem Books (Facsimile Reproduction, Leipzig 1917), 1992.

Sifre de-ve Rav (Im Tosefot Meir 'Ayin). Edited by Meir Ish Shalom. Vienna: 1864.

Sifre on Deuteronomy. Edited by L. Finkelstein. New York: Bet ha-Midrash le-Rabbanim be-America, 1993.

Tanakh: JPS Hebrew-English Tanakh—The Traditional Hebrew Text and the New JPS Translation. Philadelphia: Jewish Publication Society, 2003.

Targum Neofiti. Edited by Alejandro Diez Macho. Madrid: 1974.

Torat Chaim Chumash. Jerusalem: Mosad he-Rav Kook, 1993.

Yalqut Shimoni. 2 vols. Saloniki: 1521-1527. Reprint, Jerusalem: 1968-1973.

2. Works authored by Moses Maimonides

2.1 *Sefer ha-Mitsvot*

The Book of Commandments. Translated by C. D. Chavel. London: The Soncino Press, 1984.

Sefer ha-Mitsvot. Edited by S. Frankel. Jerusalem, 1995.

Sefer ha-Mitsvot. Translated by Moshe ibn Tibbon. Edited by Hayim Heller. Jerusalem: Mosad ha-Rav Kook, 1981.

Sefer ha-Mitsvot. Edited and translated by Joseph Kafih. Jerusalem: Mosad ha-Rav Kook, 1971.

Sefer ha-Mitsvot im Hasagot ha-RaMBaN. Edited by C. D. Chavel. Jerusalem: Mosad ha-Rav Kook, 1981.

2.2 Mishneh Torah, Code of Maimonides

The Code of Maimonides: Book 1, The Book of Knowledge. Edited and translated by Moses Hyamson. Boys Town Jerusalem Publishers, 1965.

The Code of Maimonides: Book 2, The Book Of Love. Translated by Menachem Kellner. Yale Judaica Series. New Haven: Yale University Press, 2004.

The Code of Maimonides: Book 3, The Book Of Seasons. Translated by Solomon Gandz and Hyman Klein. Yale Judaica Series. New Haven: Yale University Press, 1961.

The Code of Maimonides: Book 3, Treatise 8, The Sanctification of the New Moon. Translated by Solomon Gandz, Julian Obermann and Otto Neugebauer. New Haven: Yale University Press, 1956.

The Code of Maimonides: Book 4, The Book Of Women. Translated by Isaac Klein. New Haven: Yale University Press, 1972.

The Code of Maimonides: Book 5, The Book Of Holiness. Translated by Leon Nemoy, Louis I. Rabinowitz, and Philip Grossman. New Haven: Yale University Press, 1965.

The Code of Maimonides: Book 6, The Book Of Asseverations. Translated by B. D. Klein. New Haven: Yale University Press, 1962.

The Code of Maimonides: Book 7, The Book Of Agriculture. Translated by Isaac Klein. New Haven: Yale University Press, 1979.

The Code of Maimonides: Book 8, The Book Of Temple Service. Translated by Mendell Lewittes. New Haven: Yale University Press, 1957.

The Code of Maimonides: Book 9, The Book Of Offerings. Translated by Herbert Dan. New Haven: Yale University Press, 1950.

The Code of Maimonides: Book 10, The Book Of Cleanness. Translated by Herbert Dan. New Haven: Yale University Press, 1954.

The Code of Maimonides: Book 11, The Book Of Torts. Translated by Hyman Klein. New Haven: Yale University Press, 1954.

The Code of Maimonides: Book 12, The Book Of Acquisitions. Translated by Isaac Klein. New Haven: Yale University Press, 1951.

The Code of Maimonides: Book 13, The Book Of Civil Laws. Translated by Jacob J. Rabinowitz. New Haven: Yale University Press, 1949.

The Code of Maimonides: Book 14, The Book Of Judges. Translated by Abraham M. Hershman. New Haven: Yale University Press, 1949.

A Collection of Important Commentaries on the Code of Maimonides [Mefarshe Yad ha-Hazaqah]. 20 vols. Jerusalem: Otzreinu, 2006.

Madd'a, Ahavah: Ha-Sefer ha-Mugah. Introduction by S. Z. Havlin. Facsimile edition of MS. Huntington 80. Jerusalem: 1997.

Mahadurat Menuqedet im Perush le-Am. 10 vols. Jerusalem: Mosad ha-Rav Kook, 1987.

Mishneh Torah. Edited by S. Frankel. 15 vols. Bnei Brak: Hotsaat Shabse Frankel, 1975-2006.

Mishneh Torah. Edited by Joseph Kafih. 23 vols. Jerusalem: 1984-1996.

Mishneh Torah Hu ha-Yad ha-Hazaqah le-Rabbenu Moshe b. Maimon: Haqdamah u-Minyan ha-Mitsvot im Perush Yad Peshuta. Edited by Nachum L. Rabinovitch. Jerusalem: Hotsaat Maaliyot, 1997.

Mishneh Torah Hu ha-Yad ha-Hazaqah le-Rabbenu Moshe b. Maimon: Sefer Ahavah im Perush Yad Peshuttah. Edited by Nachum L. Rabinovitch. Jerusalem: Hotsaat Maaliyot, 1984.

Mishneh Torah: The Book of Adoration. Edited by Moses Hyamson. Jerusalem: Feldheim, n.d.

RaMBaM Meduyaq. Edited by Y. Shailat. 4 vols. Ma'aleh Addumim: Hotsaat Shailat, 2004.

"Sefer ha-Liquttim." In *Mishneh Torah*. Edited by S. Frankel, 1975-2006.

"Sefer ha-Mafteah." In *Mishneh Torah*. Edited by S. Frankel, 1975-2006.

"Yalqut Shinuye Nushaot." In *Mishneh Torah.* Edited by S. Frankel, 1975-2006.

2.3 Guide of the Perplexed

The Guide of the Perplexed. Translated by Shlomo Pines. Chicago: Chicago University Press, 1963.

Guide of the Perplexed of Maimonides. Translated by M. Friedlander. 3 vols. London, 1881-1885. Reprint, New York: Hebrew Publishing Company, n. d.

Les Guide des Egarés. Translated by S. Munk. Paris: 1856. Reprint, Paris: 1960.

Moreh ha-Nevukhim. Edited and translated by Joseph Kafih. Jerusalem: Mosad ha-Rav Kook, 1984.

Moreh Nevukhim. Translated by R. Judah b. R. Shlomo Al-Harizi. Warsaw: 1904.

Moreh Nevukhim. Edited by Michael Schwarz. 2 vols. Tel Aviv: Tel Aviv University Press, 2002.

Moreh Nevukhim (with the Commentaries of Efodi, Shem Tov, Crescas and Abarbanel). Translated by Shmuel ibn Tibbon. Warsaw: 1872. Facsimile reprint, Jerusalem: 1960.

2.4 Letters, Epistles

Epistles of Maimonides: Crisis and Leadership. Translated by A. S. Halkin. Edited by David Hartman. Philadelphia: Jewish Publication Society, 1993.

Iggerot ha-RaMBaM. Translated and Edited by Y. Shailat. 2 vols. Maaleh Addumim: Ma'aliyot Press, 1987-1988.

Iggerot ha-RaMBaM. Translated by D. Baneth. Jerusalem: 1985.

2.5 Treatise on Logic

"Maimonides' Treatise on Logic [English Translation]." Edited and translated by Israel Efros. *PAAJR* 8 (1938): 34-65.

2.6 Responsa

Responsa of Moses b. Maimon. Edited and translated by Jehoshua Blau. 4 vols. Jerusalem: Meqitze Nirdamim, 1960.

Sheelot u-Teshuvot ha-RaMBaM "Peer ha-Dor." Edited by David Yosef. Jerusalem: Makhon Yerushalayim, 1980.

Teshuvot. Edited by A. Freimann and S. Goiten. Jerusalem: 1937.

2.7 *Commentary on the Mishnah*

Ethical Writings of Maimonides. Edited by Raymond L. Weiss and Charles E. Butterworth. New York: Dover Publishing, 1975.

Haqdamot ha-RaMBaM la-Mishnah. Edited and translated by Y. Shailat. Jerusalem: Hotsaat Maaliyot, 1992.

Perush ha-Mishnah. Edited and translated by Joseph Kafih. 3 vols. Jerusalem: Mosad ha-Rav Kook, 1984.

3. *General Bibliography*

Aaron ben Elijah of Nicomedia. *Sefer Gan Eden.* Eupatoria, 1864. Reprint, Ramla: 1972.

———. *Sefer Keter Torah.* Eupatoria: 1867. Reprint, Ramla: 1972.

Aaron ha-Levi of Barcelona. *Sefer ha-Hinnukh.* Edited by C. D. Chavel. Jerusalem: 1952.

Abarbanel, Yitshaq ben Yehudah. *Commentary on the Torah [Perush al ha-Torah].* Jerusalem: 1994.

———. *Rosh Amanah.* Edited by Menachem Kellner. Ramat Gan: Bar Ilan University Press, 1993.

Abramson, Shraga. "Arbaah Peraqim be-Inyan ha-RaMBaM." *Sinai* 60 (1972): 24-33.

———. "Inyanot be-Sefer Mitsvot Gadol." *Sinai* 80 (1976-77): 203-213.

———. "Le-Mavo ha-Talmud le-Rav Shmuel ben Hofni." *Tarbiz* 26 (1957): 421-424.

Ahai Gaon. *Sheiltot.* Edited by S. K. Mirsky. 3 vols. Jerusalem: 1947-1952, 1959.

Al-Bargeloni, Yitshaq ben Reuven. *Azharot.* Livorno: 1841.

———. *Sefer Mitsvot he-Arukh.* Jerusalem: Mifal Taryag Mitsvot, 1999, 222-282

Albeck, H. *Mavo la-Talmudim.* Tel Aviv: Devir, 1969.

Alegre, Abraham. "Lev Sameah." *Sefer ha-Mitsvot.* Edited by S. Frankel. Jerusalem: 1995.

Alexander, Philip S. "The Rabbinic Hermeneutical Rules and the Problem of the Definition of Midrash." In *Proceedings of the Irish Biblical Association*, vol. 8, 97-125. Edited by A. D. Mayes. Dublin: 1984.

Al-Farabi. *Al-Farabi on the Perfect State*. Revised edition. Translated by Richard Walzer. Oxford: Oxford University Press, 1985.

———. *Al-Farabi's Commentary and Short Treatise on Aristotle's De Interpretatione*. Translated by F. W. Zimmermann. Oxford: Oxford University Press, 1981.

———. *Aphorisms of the Statesman*. Translated by D. M. Dunlop. Cambridge: Cambridge University Press, 1961.

———. "Enumeration of the Sciences." Translated by Fauzi M. Najjar. In *Medieval Political Philosophy: A Sourcebook*. Edited by Ralph Lerner, Muhsin Mahdi, and with the collaboration of Ernest L. Fortin, 22-30. Ithaca, NY: Cornell Paperbacks, 1984.

———. *La 'Classificazione delle Science' di Alfarabi nella Tradizione Hebraica (Edizione Critica e Traduzione Annotata della Versione Hebraica di Qalonymos ben Meir)*. Edited by Mauro Zonta. Vol. 29. Torino: Universitá degli Studi di Venecia, 1992.

Alfasi, Isaac. *Hilkhot ha-RIF*. In standard editions of Babylonian Talmud.

———. *Sefer ha-Halakhot*. Edited by N. Zaks. 2 vols. Jerusalem: Mossad ha-Rav Kook, 1969.

Altmann, A. "Maimonides' 'Four Perfections'." In *Essays in Jewish Intellectual History*, 65-76. Lebanon: University Press of New England, 1981.

———. "Review of G. Vajda's L'amour de Dieu dans la théologie juive du Moyen Age." *Sefarad* 10 (1950): 25-71.

———. "Saadya's Conception of the Law." *Bulletin of the John Rylands Library* 28 (1944): 320-239.

———. "Saadya's Theory of Revelations: Its Origins and Background." In *Studies in Religious Philosophy and Mysticism*, 140-160. London: Routledge, 1969.

Ankori, Tsvi. *Karaites in Byzantium, The Formative Years: 970-1100*. New York: Columbia University Press, 1959. Reprint, New York: AMS Press, 1968.

Appel, G. *A Philosophy of Mizvot*. New York: Ktav Publishing House, 1975.

Aristotle. *Nicomachean Ethics*. Translated and edited by Terence Irwin. Indianapolis: Hackett Publishing Company, 1985.

Aristotle. *Posterior Analytics, Topica*. Translated by Hugh Tredennick and E.S. Forster. Loeb Classical Library. Cambridge, MA: Harvard University Press, 1960.

Assaf, S. "He'arah al Yahaso shel ha-RaBaD el ha-RaMBaM." In *Rabbenu Moshe ben Maimon*, edited by Y. L. Fishman, 276-287. Jerusalem: 1935.

———. "Mi-Shiyare Safrutam shel ha-Geonim." *Tarbiz* 15 (1954): 31-33.

———. "Qeta'im mi-Sefer Yad ha-Hazaqah...be-Etsem Ketav Yado shel ha-RaMBaM." *Qeriyat_Sefer* 18 (1941): 150-155.

———. "Sifre Rav Hai u-Teshuvotav ke-Maqor le-ha-RaMBaM." *Sinai* 2 (1938): 522-526.

———. *Tequfat ha-Geonim ve-Safrutah*. Edited by M. Margoliyot. Jerusalem: Mossad ha-Rav Kook, 1955.

Atlas, Samuel H., ed. *Qeta'im mi-Sefer Yad ha-Hazaqah le-ha-RaMBaM*. London: Ha-Itim, 1940.

Averroes. *Averroes' Commentary on Plato's Republic.* Edited and translated by E. I. J. Rosenthal. Cambridge: Cambridge University Press, 1969.

Ayyash, Yehudah. "Lehem Yehudah." In *A Collection of Important Commentaries on the Code of Maimonides [Mefarshe Yad ha-Hazaqah]*. Original publication, Livorno: 1745-1758. New edition incorporating "Ve-Zot le-Yehudah," Jerusalem: 1986. Reprint, Jerusalem: Otzreinu Toronto, 2006-2007.

Babad, Joseph. *Minhat Hinnukh*. 3 vols. Jerusalem: Makhon Yerushalayim, 1988.

Bacharach, Yair. *Sheelot u-Teshuvot Havvot Yair*. Lemberg: 1896. Reprint, Jerusalem: 1987.

Bacher, W. *Ha-RaMBaM ke-Farshan ha-Miqra*. Translated by A. Z. Rabinovitz. Tel Aviv: 1932.

———. "Zum Sprachlichen Charakter des Mischne Thora." In *Moses ben Maimon: Sein Leben, Seine Werke und Sein Einfluss,* vol. 1, edited by W. Bacher, M. Brann, and D. Simonsen, 296-305. Leipzig: 1908. Reprint, New York: Georg Olms Verlag Hildesheim, 1971.

Bacher, Yitshaq. *Divre Emet*. Halberstat: 1861.

Baḫya ibn Paquda. *The Book of Direction to the Duties of the Heart*. Translated by Menachem Mansoor. London: Routledge, 1973.

———. *Hovot ha-Levavot*. Translated by Judah ibn Tibbon. Edited by A. Zifroni. Jerusalem: 1928.

———. *Hovot ha-Levavot*. Translated and edited by Joseph Kafih. Jerusalem: 1973.

Baneth, D. "Hathalat Sefer ha-Mitsvot le-RaSaG." In *Qovetz Rav Saadia Gaon*, edited by J. L. Fishman, 365-382. Jerusalem: 1943.

Baron, S. W., ed. *Essays on Maimonides: An Octocentennial Volume*. New York: Columbia University Press, 1941.

Baron, S. W. "The Historical Outlook of Maimonides." *PAAJR* 6 (1935): 5-113.

Bashyatsi, Eliyahu. *Sefer ha-Mitsvot Aderet Eliyahu*. Ramla: 1966.

Bekhor-Shor, Joseph. *Perushe R. Yosef Bekhor Shor*. Edited by Y. Navo. Jerusalem: 1994.

Ben Barzilai, Judah. *Perush Sefer Yetsirah*. Berlin: S. J. Halberstamm, 1885.

Benedict, B. Z. "Ha-RaMBaM be-Pesiqah, be-Parshanut, be-Hagut u-be-Hanhagah - Derekh Ahat Lo." In *Asufat Maamarim*, 118-130. Jerusalem: Mosad ha-Rav Kook, 1994.

———. *Ha-RaMBaM le-lo Setiyah min ha-Talmud*. Jerusalem: Mosad ha-Rav Kook, 1985.

Ben-Menahem, Hanina. "Maimonides' Fourteen Roots: Logical Structural and Conceptual Analysis." *Jewish Law Annual* 13 (2000): 3-30.

Ben Manoah, Hizkiyahu. "Hizkuni (Commentary on the Pentateuch)." In *Torat Chaim Chumash*. 1993.

Benor, Ehud. *Worship of the Heart*. Albany: State University of New York Press, 1995.

Ben Porat, Eliezer. "Emunot ve-De'ot le-Mitsvot le-Da'at ha-RaMBaM ve-R. Hasdai Crescas." *Sinai* 120 (1997): 216-229.

Ben Shlomo, Hoter. *Commentary to the Thirteen Principles of Maimonides*. Edited by D. Blumenthal. Leiden: Brill, 1974.

Benveniste, H. *Dina de-Hayy*, 2 vols. Original printing, Constantinople: 1742-1747. Reprinted with citations of the SMaG. Edited by Moses Batzri. 4 vols. Jerusalem: Makhon Ketav, 1997.

Ben Yafet, Levi. *Sefer ha-Mitsvot*. Edited by Y. Algamil. Ashdod: Makhon Tiferet Yosef, 2004.

Ben Yatsliah, Hefets. *A Volume of the Book of Precepts*. Edited by B. Halper. 2 vols. Philadelphia: Dropsie College for Hebrew and Cognate Learning, 1915.

Berman, Lawrence V. "The Ethical View of Maimonides within the Context of Islamicate Civilization." In *Perspectives on Maimonides*, edited by Joel Kraemer, 13-32. Oxford: Oxford University Press, 1991.

———. "Ibn Bajjah and Maimonides: A Chapter in the History of Political Philosophy [Hebrew]." Ph.D. dissertation: Hebrew University of Jerusalem, 1959.

———. "The Ideal State of the Philosophers and Prophetic Laws." In *A Straight Path: Studies in Medieval Philosophy and Culture: Essays in Honor of Arthur Hyman*, edited by Ruth Link-Salinger, 10-22. Washington D.C.: The Catholic University of America Press, 1988.

———. "Maimonides on the Fall of Man." *AJS Review* 5 (1980): 1-16.

———. "Maimonides, the Disciple of Alfarabi." *Israel Oriental Studies* 4 (1974): 154-178.

———. "The Political Interpretation of the Maxim: The Purpose of Philosophy is the Imitation of God." *Studia Islamica* 15 (1961): 53-61.

———. "A Reexamination of Maimonides' Statement on Political Science." *Journal of the American Oriental Society* 89 (1969): 106-112.

———. "The Structure of the Commandments of the Torah in the Thought of Maimonides." In *Studies in Jewish Religious and Intellectual History*, edited by S. Stein and R. Loewe, 51-66. Tuscaloosa: University of Alabama Press, 1979.

Birnbaum, Philip, ed. *Karaite Studies*. New York: Hermon Press, 1971.

Bland, Kalman. "Moses and the Law According to Maimonides." *Mystics, Philosophers and Politicians*, edited by J. Reinharz and D. Swetschinski, 49-66. Durham: Duke University Press, 1982.

Blidstein, Gerald (Yaaqov). "Ha-Gishah le-Qaraim be-Mishnat ha-RaMBaM." *Tehumin-Torah* 8 (1987): 501-510.

———. "Maimonides on Oral Law." *Jewish Law Annual* 1 (1978): 108-122.

———. "Mesorat ve-Samkhut Mosdit le-Ra'ayon Torah she-be-al-Peh be-Mishnat ha-RaMBaM." *Da'at* 16 (1986): 11-27.

———. "Where Do We Stand in the Study of Maimonidean Halakhah?" In *Studies in Maimonides,* edited by I. Twersky, 1-30. Cambridge, MA: Harvard University Press, 1990.

Bloch, Moise. "Les 613 Lois." *REJ* 1 (1880): 197-211.

Bloomberg, Jon Irving. "Arabic Legal Terms in Maimonides." Ph.D. dissertation: Yale University, 1980.

Blumenfeld, S. M. "Towards a Study of Maimonides the Educator." *HUCA* 23 (1950-51): 555-591.

Boccaccini, Gabriele. *Roots of Rabbinic Judaism: An Intellectual History, from Ezekiel to Daniel.* Grand Rapids, MI: William B. Eerdmans Publishing Company, 2002.

Boyarin, Daniel. "On the Status of the Tannaitic Midrashim." *Journal of the American Oriental Society* 112.3 (1992): 455-466.

Braner, Baruch. "Yahaso shel ha-RaLBaG le-Darko shel ha-RaMBaM be-Minyan ha-Mitsvot." In'*Iyyunim u-Biurim be-Divre ha-RaMBaM*, vol. 12, 224-242. Ma'aleh Addumim: 1998.

Braude, William G. "Maimonides' Attitude to Midrash." In *Studies in Jewish Bibliography, History and Literature*, edited by C. Berlin, 75-82. New York: Ktav Publishing House, 1971.

Brody, H. "Miqtamim al ha-RaMBaM." *Moznayim* 3 (1935): 402-413.

Brody, Robert. *Zohar le-Sifrut ha-Geonim.* Jerusalem: Ha-Kibbutz ha-Meuchad, 1998.

Bromberg, A. J. "Hashpaat Rabbenu Hananel al ha-RaMBaM." *Sinai* 33 (1953): 43-55.

———. *Meqorot le-Pisqe ha-RaMBaM.* Jerusalem: Mosad ha-Rav Kook, 1947.

———. "Meqorot ve-He'arot le-Perush ha-Mishnayot le-ha-RaMBaM." *Sinai* 29 (1950): 146-172.

———. "Rabbenu Hananel ve-ha-RaMBaM." *Sinai* 22 (1948): 4-13.

Chajes, Tsvi Hirsh. *Kol Sifre Maharats Chajes.* Jerusalem: Divre Hakhamim, 1958.

Chinitz, J. "Ten Terms in the Torah for Teachings, Commandments and Laws." *Jewish Bible Quarterly* 3, no. 2 (2005): 113-119.

Cohen, B. "Classification of Law in the Mishneh Torah." *JQR* 25 (1934-1935): 519-540.

Cohen, Mordechai Z. "The Best of Poetry: Literary Approaches to the Bible in the Spanish Peshat Tradition." *Torah u-Madd'a Journal* 6 (1995-6): 15-57.

———. "A Talmudist's Halakhic Hermeneutics: Maimonides on 'Scripture Does Not Leave the Hand of Its Peshat.'" Unpublished paper, 13 December 2008.

———. *Three Approaches to Biblical Metaphor: From Abraham ibn Ezra and Maimonides to David Kimhi*. Leiden: Brill, 2003.

Cohen, Naomi G. "TaRYaG and the Noachide Commandments." *Journal of Jewish Studies* 43 (1992): 46-57.

Cohen, Shaul. *Netiv Mitsvotekha*. Livorno: 1841.

Cook, Michael. "Anan and Islam: The Origins of Karaite Scripturalism." *Studies in Arabic and Islam* 9 (1987): 161-82.

Crescas, Don Hasdai. *Or Adonai*. Original publication, Vienna: 1859. Reprint, Tel Aviv: 1963.

Danzig, Neil. "The First Discovered Leaves of Sefer Hefets." *JQR* 82 (1991): 51-136.

Daube, David. "Haustafeln." In *New Testament Judaism: Collected Works of David Daube*, edited by Calum Carmichael, 295-306. Studies in Comparative Legal History, vol. 2. Berkeley, CA: University of California for the Robbins Religious & Civil Law Collection, 2001. Originally published in *The New Testament and Rabbinic Judaism*. London, 1956.

Davidson, Herbert. "The First Two Commandments in Maimonides' List of the 613 Believed to Have Been Given to Moses at Sinai." In *Creation and Re-Creation in Jewish Thought: Festschrift in Honor of Joseph Dan on the Occasion of His Seventieth Birthday*, edited by Rachel Elior and Peter Shafer, 113-145. Tübingen: Mohr Siebeck, 2005.

———. "Maimonides on Divine Attributes as Equivocal Terms." In *Minchah Le-Michael (Michael Schwartz Festschrift)*, 37*-51*. Tel Aviv: 2009.

———. "Maimonides' Secret Position on Creation." In *Studies in Medieval Jewish History and Literature*, edited by I. Twersky, 16-40. Cambridge, MA: Harvard University Press, 1979.

———. "Maimonides' Shemonah Peraqim and Alfarabi's Fusul al-Madani." *PAAJR* 31 (1963): 33-50.

———. "The Middle Way in Maimonides' Ethic." *PAAJR* 54 (1987): 31-72.

———. *Moses Maimonides: The Man and His Work.* Oxford: Oxford University Press, 2005.

de Leon, Isaac ben Eliezer. "Megillat Esther." In *Sefer ha-Mitsvot*, edited by S. Frankel. 1995.

DeVreis, Binyamin. "Ha-Categoriyot ha-Hilkhatiyot." *Bar-Ilan Annual, Dedicated to the Memory of Professor Shmuel Bialobilotsky* (1964).

Diamond, James. *Maimonides and the Hermeneutics of Concealment: Deciphering Scripture and Midrash in the Guide of the Perplexed.* Albany: State University of New York Press, 2002.

di Boton, Abraham. *Le<u>h</u>em Mishneh.* Printed in standard editions of Mishneh Torah.

Dienstag, J. I. "A Bibliography of Editions of the *Sefer ha-Mitsvot.*" *Areshet* 5 (1972): 34-80.

———. "Ha-Rav S. Assaf ke-Hoqer ha-RaMBaM." *Sinai* 56 (1962): 100-116.

Diesendruck, Z. "Maimonides' Theory of Teleology and the Divine Attributes [Hebrew]." *Tarbiz* 1-2 (1930-31): 106-136 (vol. 1), 27-32 (vol. 2).

———. "On the Date of the Composition of the Moreh Nebukim." *HUCA* 12-13 (1937-1938): 461-497.

di Tolosa, Vidal. *Maggid Mishneh.* Printed in standard editions of *Mishneh Torah.*

Duran, Profiat. *Ma'aseh Efod.* Vienna: 1865. Reprint, Jerusalem: 1969.

Duran, Simeon ben Tsema<u>h</u>. *Zohar ha-Raqia (im perush Ziv ha-Zohar).* Edited by D. Abraham. Jerusalem: 1987.

Efros, Israel. *Philosophical Terms in the Moreh Nebukim.* Columbia University Oriental Studies, vol. 22. New York: Columbia University Press, 1966.

Ehrlich, Baruch. "Laws of Sabbath in Yehudah Hadassi's Eshkol ha-Kofer." Ph.D. dissertation: Yeshiva University, 1975.

Eichenstein, M. M. "Be-Inyan Mahloqet be-Halakhah le-Moshe mi-Sinai." In *Moriah*, vol. 24, copy 10-12, 286-288. Jerusalem: Makhon Yerushalayim, 2002.

Eliezer ben Shmuel me-Mitz. *Sefer Yereim*. Vilna: 1904.

Elijah ha-Zaqen. "Azharot R. Elijah ha-Zaqen." In *Sefer Mitsvot he-Arukh*, 180-220. Jerusalem: Mifal Taryag Mitsvot, 1999.

Elon, Menachem. *Jewish Law: History, Sources, Principles*. Translated by Bernard Auerbach and Melvyn J. Sykes. 4 vols. Philadelphia: Jewish Publication Society, 1994.

Entsiklopedyah Talmudit. Jerusalem: 1947-2007.

Epstein, I. "The Distinctiveness of Maimonides' Halakhah." In *Leo Jung Jubilee Volume: Essays in his Honor on the Occasion of his Seventieth Birthday*, edited by M. Kasher, N. Lamm, and L. Rosenfeld, 65-75. New York: Shulsinger, 1962.

Epstein, Jehiel Michel. *Arukh ha-Shulhan he-Atid*. Jerusalem: Mosad ha-Rav Kook, 1969-1975.

Epstein, Baruch ha-Levy. *Torah Temimah*. New York: Hotsaat Otzer ha-Sefarim, 1962.

Epstein, Y. N. "Mekhilta ve-Sifre be-Sifre ha-RaMBaM." *Tarbiz* 6 (1935): 99-138.

Fackenheim, Emil L. "The Possibility of the Universe in Al-Farabi, Ibn Sina and Maimonides." *PAAJR* 16 (1946-47): 39-70.

Fakhry, Majid. *Al-Farabi: Founder of Islamic Neoplatonism: His Life, Works and Influence*. Oxford: Oneworld Publications, 2002.

Faur, José, *'Iyyunim be-Mishneh Torah le-ha-RaMBaM: Sefer ha-Madd'a*. Jerusalem: Mosad ha-Rav Kook, 1978.

———. "La doctrina de la ley natural en el pensamiento judío del medioevo." *Sefarad* 27 (1967): 239-268.

———. "Law and Hermeneutics in Rabbinic Jurisprudence: A Maimonidean Perspective." *Cardozo Law Review* 14.6 (1993): 1657-1679.

———. "Maimonides' Starting Precept" (Hebrew), available at http://faur.derushapublishing.com/maimonides-starting-precept.shtml.

———. "Meqor Hiyyuvan shel ha-Mitsvot le-Da'at ha-RaMBaM." *Tarbiz* 38 (1969): 43-53.

———. "The Origin of the Classification of Rational and Divine Commandments in Medieval Jewish Philosophy." *Augustinianum* 9 (1969): 299-304.

Federbush, Shimon. *Ha-RaMBaM: Torato ve-Ishiyyuto*. New York: Mahloqet ha-Tarbut shel ha-Congres ha-Yehudi ha-Olami, 1956.

Feintuch, A. "Ha-Munah de-Oraita ve-ha-Middot she-ha-Torah Nidreshet ba-Hen." *Sinai* 119 (1997): 150-160.

———. *Sefer ha-Mitsvot im Perush Pequde Yesharim*. Jerusalem: Hotsaat Maaliyot, 2000.

Feldblum, Meyer S. "Criteria for Designating Laws: Derivations from Biblical Exegesis, and Legislative Enactments." In *Maimonides as Codifier of Jewish Law*, edited by N. Rakover, 45-49. Jerusalem: The Library of Jewish Law, 1987.

———. "Pisqav shel ha-RaMBaM le-Or Gishato le-Homer ha-Setami she-be-Bavli." *PAAJR* 46 (1979-80): 111-120.

Finkel, J. "Maimonides' Treatise on Resurrection." *PAAJR* 9 (1939): 57-105.

Finkelstein, L. "Ha-De'ah ki 13 ha-Middot hen Halakhah le-Moshe mi-Sinai." In *Sefer ha-Zikaron le-Rabbi Shaul Liebermann*, edited by S. Friedman, 79-84. New York: JTS, 1993.

———. "Maimonides and the Tannaitic Midrashim." *JQR* 25 (1935): 469-517.

Fogelman, Mordechai. "Haqdamat ha-RaMBaM le-Perusho la-Mishnah, Seder Zera'im." *Sinai* 44 (1960): 339-346.

Fox, Harry. "Maimonides on Aging and the Aged in Light of the Esoterist/Harmonist Debate." In *The Thought of Moses Maimonides: Philosophical and Legal Studies*, edited by I. Robinson, L. Kaplan, and J. Bauer, 319-383. Lewiston, NY: Edwin Mellen Press, 1990.

———. "Neusner's The Bavli and its Sources: a Review Essay." *Jewish Quarterly Review* 130, 3-4 (1990): 349-361.

Fox, Marvin. "The Doctrine of the Mean in Aristotle and Maimonides: A Comparative Study." In *Interpreting Maimonides: Studies in Methodology, Metaphysics and Moral Philosophy*, 93-123. Chicago: University of Chicago Press, 1990.

Frank, Daniel. *Search Scripture Well: Karaite Exegetes and the Origins of the Jewish Bible Commentary in the Islamic East*. Leiden: Brill, 2004.

———. "The Study of Medieval Karaism, 1989-1999." In *Hebrew Scholarship and the Medieval World*, edited by N. de Lange, 3-22. Cambridge: Cambridge University Press, 2001.

Frank, Daniel H. "The End of the Guide: Maimonides on the Best Life for Man." *Judaism* 34 (1985): 485-495.

———. "Humility as a Virtue: A Maimonidean Critique of Aristotle's Ethics." In *Moses Maimonides and His Time*, edited by Eric Ormsby, 89-99. Washington: Catholic University of America Press, 1989.

———. "Review of Raymond Weiss' 'Maimonides' Ethics: The Encounter of Philosophic and Religious Morality'." *Journal of Religion* 74, no. 1 (1994): 116-117.

Frankel, Carlos. "Ma'avar le-Talmid Ne'eman: Biqoroto shel Shmuel Ibn Tibbon al ha-RaMBaM." *Da'at* 57, no. 9 (2006): 61-82.

Frankel, David. *Qorban ha-'Edah and Shiare Qorban*. In standard editions of the Jerusalem Talmud.

Friedberg, Albert. "Cross-Cultural Influences and the Possible Role of Competition in the Selection of Some Commandments." In *Vixens Disturbing Vineyards: The Embarassment and Embracement of Scriptures: A Festschrift Honoring Harry Fox*. Edited by Tzemah Yoreh, Aubrey Glazer, Justin Jaron Lewis, and Miryam Segal, 410-414. Boston: Academic Studies Press, 2010.

Galston, Miriam. "Philosopher-King vs. Prophet." *Israel Oriental Studies* 8 (1978): 204-218.

———. *Politics and Excellence: The Political Philosophy of Alfarabi*. Princeton: Princeton University Press, 1990.

———. "The Purpose of Law According to Maimonides." *JQR* 69 (1978-9): 27-51.

Gandz, D. "Date of the Composition of Maimonides' Code." *PAAJR* 17 (1948): 1-7. Reprinted in *Studies in Hebrew Astronomy and Mathematics*, edited by D. Gandz and S. Sternberg, 113-120. New York: Ktav Publishing House, 1970.

Gersonides, Levi. *RaLBaG's Commentary to the Pentateuch*. Edited by Baruch Braner and Carmiel Cohen. Ma'aleh Adumim: Hotsa`at Maaliyot, 2002.

Gertner, M. "Terms of Scriptural Interpretation: A Study of Hebrew Semantics." *Bulletin of the School of Oriental and African Studies, University of London* 25, no. 1/3 (1962): 1-27.

Gil, Moshe. "Qadmoniyyot ha-Qaraim." *Teudah* 15 (1999): 71-107.

Ginzberg, Louis. *Geonica.* 2 vols. New York: Jewish Theological Seminary, 1909.

———. *Ginze Schechter.* 2 vols. New York: Jewish Theological Seminary, 1928.

Glick, Aharon. "'Iyyunim be-Darko shel ha-RaMBaM be-Sefer ha-Yad." In *Nitte Naamanim Makhon Mishnat Rabbi Aharon,* 478-481. Lakewood, NJ: 2000.

Goitein, S. "Hayye ha-RaMBaM le-Or Gilluyim Hadashim." *Peraqim* 4 (1966): 29-42.

———. *A Mediterranean Society: The Jewish Communities of the Arab World as Portrayed in the Documents of the Cairo Geniza.* 3 vols. Berkeley: University of California Press, 1967-1978.

Goldfield, Lea Naomi. *Moses Maimonides' Treatise on Resurrection: An Inquiry into its Authenticity.* New York: Ktav Publishing House, 1986.

Goldman, Eliezer. "On the Purpose of the World in the Guide of the Perplexed [Hebrew]." In *Studies in Honor of Yeshayahu Leibowitz,* edited by A. Kasher and Y. Levinger, 164-191. Tel Aviv: Papyrus, 1982.

———. "Political and Legal Philosophy in the Guide for the Perplexed." In *Maimonides as Codifier of Jewish Law,* edited by N. Rakover, 155-164. Jerusalem: The Library of Jewish Law, 1987.

Goldman, S. "The Halakhic Foundations of Maimonides' Thirteen Principles." In *Essays Presented to Chief Rabbi Israel Brody On the Occasion of His Seventieth Birthday,* edited by H. J. Zimmels et al, 111-118. Jews' College, London: The Soncino Press, 1967.

Gotthelf, Allan, and James G. Lennox, eds. *Philosophical Issues in Aristotle's Biology.* Cambridge: Cambridge University Press, 1987.

Guttmann, Y. M. *Behinat ha-Mitsvot u-Behinat Qiyyum ha-Mitsvot.* Breslau: 1931. Facsimile edition, 1978.

———. "The Decisions of Maimonides in his Commentary on the Mishnah." *Hebrew Union College Annual* 2 (1925): 228-268.

Hadassi, Judah ben Elijah. *Eshkol ha-Kofer.* Goslaw: Mordechai, 1835. Reprint, Jerusalem: Maqor, 1968.

Haggai ben Shammai. "Haluqqat ha-Mitsvot u-Musag ha-Hokhmah be-Mishnat RaSaG." *Tarbiz* 41 (1972): 170-182.

———. "Jewish Thought in Iraq in the 10th Century." In *Studies in Muslim-Jewish Relations: Judeo-Arabic Studies*, edited by N. Golb, 15-32. Amsterdam: Harwood Academic, 1997.

———. "The Karaite Controversy: Scripture and Tradition in Early Karaism." In *Religionsgespräche im Mittelalter*, edited by Bernard Lewis and Friedrich Niewöhner, 11-27. Wolfenbütteler Mittelalter-Studien Bd. 4. Wiesbaden: Otto Harrassowitz, 1992.

Hagiz, Moses ben Jacob. *Sefer Eleh ha-Mitsvot.* Amsterdam: 1713.

Hai-Raqah, Masud. *Ma'aseh Roqeah*. Venice: Meir Da Zarah, Nella Stamparia Vendramina, 1742 (vol. 1); Livorno: 1862-1863 (vols 2-3). Facsimile reproduction (4 vols), Jerusalem: 1976.

ha-Kohen, Shaul. *Netiv Mitsvotekha (on the Azharot of Yitshaq al-Bargeloni and ibn Gabirol).* Livorno: 1841.

Halbertal, Moshe. "Maimonides' Book of Commandments: The Architecture of the Halakhah and its Theory of Interpretation [Hebrew]." *Tarbiz* 59, nos. 3-4 (1990): 457-480.

———. "What is Mishneh Torah? On Codification and Ambivalence." In *Maimonides After 800 Years*, edited by Jay Harris, 81-111. Cambridge, MA: Harvard University Press, 2007.

Halivni, David Weiss. *Peshat and Derash: Plain and Applied Meaning in Rabbinic Exegesis.* New York and Oxford: Oxford University Press, 1991.

Halkin, A. S. "Sanegoryah al Sefer Mishneh Torah." *Tarbiz* 25 (1956): 413-428.

Hallaq, Wael B. *A History of Islamic Legal Theories: An Introduction to Sunni Usul al-Fiqh.* Cambridge: Cambridge University Press, 1997.

Harkavy, Abraham E. "Heleq me-Sefer ha-Mitsvot le-Rav Shmuel ben Hofni Gaon." *Ha-Qedem* 3 (1909-1910): 107-110.

———. *Sefer ha-Mitsvot le-Anan ha-Nasi.* St. Petersburg: 1903.

———. *Zikhron ha-Gaon Shmuel ben Hofni u-Sefarav*. Jerusalem: Kedem, 1969.

Harris, Jay M. *How Do We Know This? Midrash and the Fragmentation of Modern Judaism.* Albany: State University of New York Press, 1995.

Hartman, David. *Maimonides: Torah and Philosophic Quest*. Philadelphia: Jewish Publication Society, 1976.

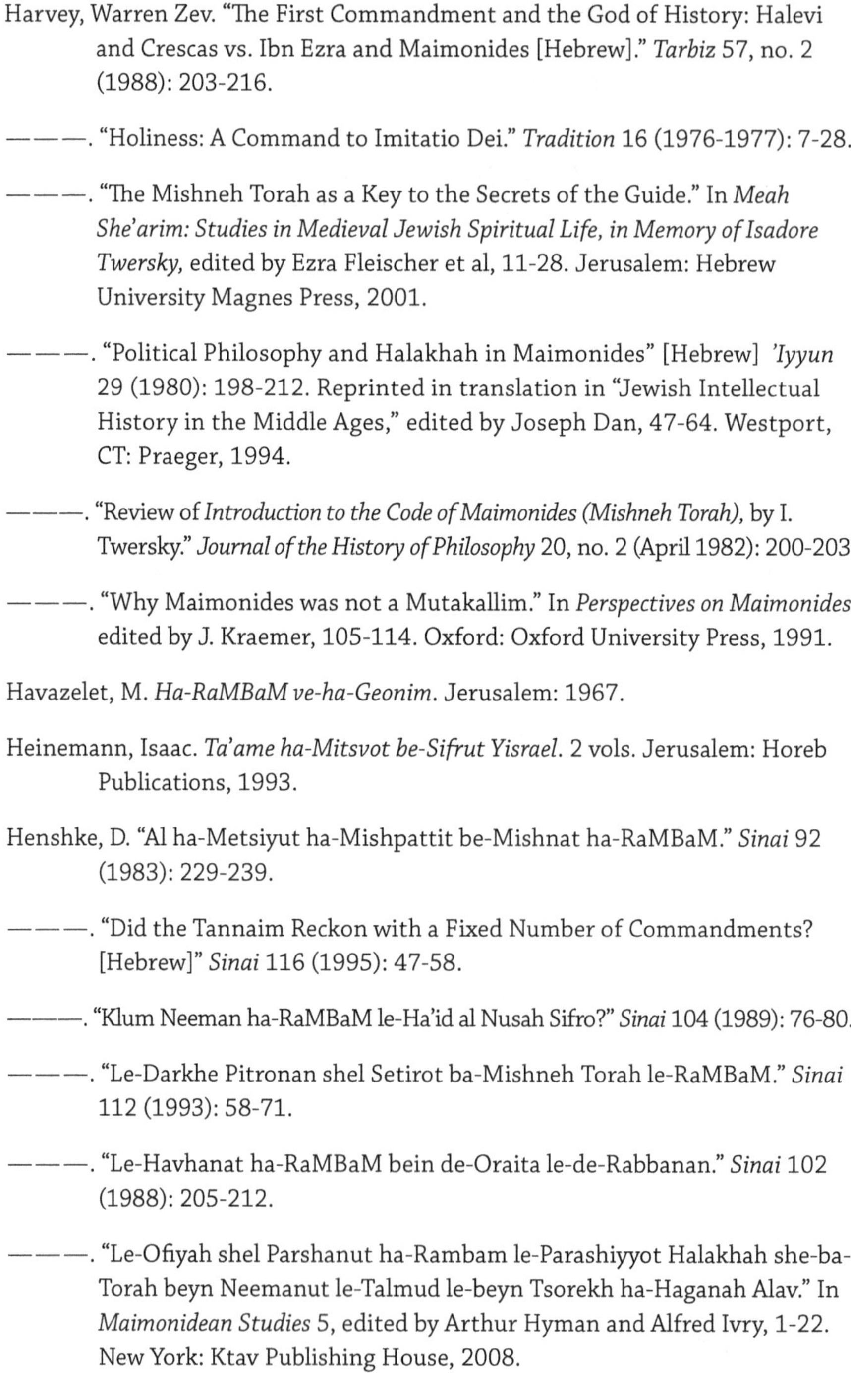

Harvey, Warren Zev. "The First Commandment and the God of History: Halevi and Crescas vs. Ibn Ezra and Maimonides [Hebrew]." *Tarbiz* 57, no. 2 (1988): 203-216.

———. "Holiness: A Command to Imitatio Dei." *Tradition* 16 (1976-1977): 7-28.

———. "The Mishneh Torah as a Key to the Secrets of the Guide." In *Meah She'arim: Studies in Medieval Jewish Spiritual Life, in Memory of Isadore Twersky,* edited by Ezra Fleischer et al, 11-28. Jerusalem: Hebrew University Magnes Press, 2001.

———. "Political Philosophy and Halakhah in Maimonides" [Hebrew] *'Iyyun* 29 (1980): 198-212. Reprinted in translation in "Jewish Intellectual History in the Middle Ages," edited by Joseph Dan, 47-64. Westport, CT: Praeger, 1994.

———. "Review of *Introduction to the Code of Maimonides (Mishneh Torah),* by I. Twersky." *Journal of the History of Philosophy* 20, no. 2 (April 1982): 200-203.

———. "Why Maimonides was not a Mutakallim." In *Perspectives on Maimonides*, edited by J. Kraemer, 105-114. Oxford: Oxford University Press, 1991.

Havazelet, M. *Ha-RaMBaM ve-ha-Geonim*. Jerusalem: 1967.

Heinemann, Isaac. *Ta'ame ha-Mitsvot be-Sifrut Yisrael*. 2 vols. Jerusalem: Horeb Publications, 1993.

Henshke, D. "Al ha-Metsiyut ha-Mishpattit be-Mishnat ha-RaMBaM." *Sinai* 92 (1983): 229-239.

———. "Did the Tannaim Reckon with a Fixed Number of Commandments? [Hebrew]" *Sinai* 116 (1995): 47-58.

———. "Klum Neeman ha-RaMBaM le-Ha'id al Nusah Sifro?" *Sinai* 104 (1989): 76-80.

———. "Le-Darkhe Pitronan shel Setirot ba-Mishneh Torah le-RaMBaM." *Sinai* 112 (1993): 58-71.

———. "Le-Havhanat ha-RaMBaM bein de-Oraita le-de-Rabbanan." *Sinai* 102 (1988): 205-212.

———. "Le-Ofiyah shel Parshanut ha-Rambam le-Parashiyyot Halakhah she-ba-Torah beyn Neemanut le-Talmud le-beyn Tsorekh ha-Haganah Alav." In *Maimonidean Studies* 5, edited by Arthur Hyman and Alfred Ivry, 1-22. New York: Ktav Publishing House, 2008.

———. "Le-Toldot Parshanutan shel Parashiyyot Ma'aser: Bein Megillat ha-Miqdash le-Hazal." *Tarbiz* 72 (2003).

———. "Le-Yesode Tefisat ha-Halakhah shel ha-RaMBaM." *Shenaton ha-Mishpat ha-Ivry* 20 (1997): 103-149.

———. "Maimonides as His Own Commentator [Hebrew]." *Sefunot* 23 (2003).

———. "On the Question of Unity in Maimonides' Thought [Hebrew]." *Da'at* 37 (1995): 37-52.

———. "Seride Sefer ha-Mitsvot le-RaMBaM be-Mishneh Torah." In *Proceedings of the Tenth World Congress on Jewish Learning,* section 3, vol. 1, 180-186. Jerusalem: 1990.

———. "Ve-Simah et Ishto: Le-Toldot Shitat ha-RaMBaM." In *Qovetz ha-RaMBaM (Sinai),* edited by Yosef E. Mobshobitz, vol. 135-136, 22-30. Jerusalem: Mosad ha-Rav Kook, 2005.

Herzog, I. "Seder ha-Sefarim." In *Qovetz ha-RaMBaM*, edited by J. L. Maimon, 257-264. Jerusalem: Mosad ha-Rav Kook, 1935.

Heschel, Abraham J. "Did Maimonides Believe He Had Attained the Rank of Prophet?" In *Prophetic Inspiration after the Prophets: Maimonides and Other Medieval Authorities*, edited by M. Faierstein, 69-126. Hoboken NJ: Ktav Publishing House, 1996.

———. *Maimonides: Eine Biographie.* Berlin: E. Reiss, 1935.

Hildesheimer, Naftali Tsvi. *Haqdamat Sefer Halakhot Gedolot*. Jerusalem: 1986.

Hilvitz, A. *Li-Leshonot ha-RaMBaM.* Jerusalem: Mosad ha-Rav Kook, 1950.

———. "Seder ha-Mitsvot be-Minyan shel ha-RaMBaM." *Sinai* 19 (1946): 258-267.

Hirschenfeld, Hartwig. "Early Karaite Critics of the Mishnah." *JQR* 8 (1918): 157-257.

Horowitz, Y. "Le-Mishneh Torah u-le-Perush ha-Mishnayot shel ha-RaMBaM." *Sinai* 15.

Hurewitz, I. S. *Sefer ha-Mitsvot im Perush Yad ha-Levi.* Jerusalem: 1926.

Hyamson, Moses. Review of Guttman's *Behinat ha-Mitsvot*. *JQR*: 205-211.

Hyman, A. "Rabbi Simlai's Sayings and Beliefs Concerning God." In *Perspectives on Jewish Thought and Mysticism*, edited by A. L. Ivry, Elliot Wolfson, and Allan Arkush, 49-62. Amsterdam: 1998.

Hyman, Arthur. "Maimonides' Thirteen Principles." In *Jewish Medieval and Renaissance Studies*, edited by Alexander Altmann, 119-145. Cambridge, MA: Harvard University Press, 1967.

———. "A Note on Maimonides' Classification of the Law." *PAAJR*, Jubilee Volume 46-47 (1979-1980): 323-343.

Ibn Daud, Abraham. *Sefer ha-Qabbalah: A Critical Edition With a Translation and Notes*. Edited by Gerson D. Cohen. Philadelphia: Jewish Publication Society, 1967.

Ibn Ezra, Abraham. *Perush al ha-Torah*. Edited by Asher Weiser. 3 vols. Jerusalem: Mosad ha-Rav Kook, 1976.

———. *Yesod Mora ve-Sod Torah*. Edited by Joseph Cohen and Uriel Simon. Ramat Gan: Bar Ilan University Press, 2002.

Ibn Gabirol, Solomon. "Azharot." In *Zohar ha-Raqia*, edited and annotated by D. Abraham. Jerusalem: 1987.

Ibn Habiba, Yosef. "*Niemuqe Yosef*." Printed in standard editions of the Babylonian Talmud containing the commentary of Isaac Alfasi.

Ibn Kaspi, Joseph. "Maskiyot Kesef." In *Sheloshah Qadmone Mefarshe ha-Moreh*. Vienna: 1853. Reprint, Jerusalem: 1961.

Ibn Tibbon, Samuel. *Maamar Yiqqavu ha-Mayim*. Pressburg: M. Bisliches, 1837.

Ivry, Alfred. "Ismaili Theology and Maimonides' Philosophy." In *The Jews of Medieval Islam: Community, Society and Identity*, edited by Daniel H. Frank, 271-299. Leiden: E. J. Brill, 1995.

———. "Neoplatonic Currents in Maimonides' Thought." In *Perspectives on Maimonides*, edited by J. Kraemer, 115-140. Oxford: Oxford University Press, 1991.

Jospe, Raphael. "Rejecting Moral Virtue as the Ultimate Human End." In *Studies in Islamic and Judaic Traditions*, edited by W. Brinner and S. Ricks, 185-204. Atlanta: Scholars Press, 1986.

Kadushin, Max. *The Rabbinic Mind*. New York: Block Publishing Company, 1972.

Kafih, Joseph. *Ha-Miqra ba-RaMBaM*. Jerusalem: Mosad ha-Rav Kook, 1972.

———. *Ketavim*. 3 vols. Jerusalem: HaVa'ad ha-Klali li-Qehilat ha-Temanim bi-Yerushalayim, 1989-2002.

———. "Sheelot Hakhme Lunel u-Teshuvot ha-RaMBaM, Klum Meqoriyot Hen?" In *Sefer Zikaron le-ha-Rav Yitshaq Nissim 2*, 243-245. Jerusalem: 1985. Reprinted in Kafih, *Ketavim*.

Kahana, I. "Ha-Polmos mi-Saviv le-Qeviat ha-Halakhah ke-ha-RaMBaM." *Sinai* 26 (1955): 391-411. Reprinted in *Mehqarim be-Sifrut ha-Teshuvot*. Jerusalem: 1973.

Kahana, Kalman. "Al Harazotav shel ha-RaMBaM." *Ha-Ma'ayan* 17 (1977): 5-27.

———. *Heqer ve-'Iyyun: Qovetz Maamarim*. Tel Aviv, 1960.

Kahana, Menahem. "The Biblical Text as Reflected in Ms Vatican 32 of the Sifre [Hebrew]." In *Mehqere Talmud*, edited by Y. Sussman and D. Rosenthal, vol. 1, 1-10. Jerusalem: Magnes Press, 1990.

———. *The Geniza Fragments of the Halakhic Midrashim* [Hebrew]. *Part I: Mekhilta de-Rabbi Ishmael, Mekhilta de-Rabbi Shimon ben Yohai, Sifre Numbers, Sifre Zuta Numbers, Sifre Deuteronomy, Mekhilta Deuteronomy.* Vol. 1. Jerusalem: Hebrew University Magnes Press, 2005.

Kalinberg, Y. Y. *Seder ha-Mitsvot*. Warsaw: N. D. Zisberg, 1861.

Kamin, Sarah. *RaSHi's Exegetical Categorization in Respect to the Distinction Between Peshat and Derash [Hebrew]*. Jerusalem: Hebrew University Magnes Press, 1986.

Kaplan, Lawrence. "'I Sleep, But My Heart Waketh': Maimonides' Conception of Human Perfection." In *The Thought of Moses Maimonides: Philosophical and Legal Studies*, edited by I. Robinson, L. Kaplan, and J. Bauer, 130-166. Lewiston, NY: Edwin Mellen Press, 1990.

———. "An Introduction to Maimonides' Eight Chapters." *Edah Journal* 2, no. 2 (2002): 1-18.

———. Review of Josef Stern's "Problems and Parables of the Law: Maimonides and Nahmanides on Reasons for the Commandments (Ta'ame ha-Mitsvot)." *AJS Review* 26, no. 2 (2002): 361-364.

———. "The Unity of Maimonides' Thought: The Laws of Mourning as a Case Study." In *Judaism and Modernity: The Religious Philosophy of David Hartman*, edited by Jonathan W. Malino, 393-412. Hampshire, UK, and Burlington, VT: Ashgate, 2004.

Karl, Z. "Ha-RaMBaM ke-Farshan ha-Torah." *Tarbiz* 6, nos. 99-138 (1935).

Karo, Joseph. "Kesef Mishneh." Printed in standard editions of *Mishneh Torah*.

Kasher, Hannah. "Does 'Ought' Imply 'Can' in Maimonides? [Hebrew]" *Iyyun* 36 (1987-1988): 13-34.

Kasher, Hannah. "Talmud Torah as a Means of Apprehending God in Maimonides [Hebrew]." *Jerusalem Studies in Jewish Thought* 5 (1986): 71-82.

Kasher, Menachem M. *Ha-RaMBaM ve-ha-Mekhilta de-RaSHBY*. Jerusalem: Hotsaat Bet Torah Shelemah, 1980.

———. *Torah Shelemah*. 44 vols. Jerusalem: 1992-1995.

Kazis, Hananiah. "Qinat Sofrim." In *Sefer ha-Mitsvot*, edited by S. Frankel. Jerusalem: 1995.

Kellner, Menachem. *Dogma in Medieval Jewish Thought*. Oxford: Oxford University Press, 1986.

———. "The Literary Character of the Mishneh Torah." In *Meah She'arim: Studies in Medieval Jewish Spiritual Life, in Memory of Isadore Twersky*, edited by Ezra Fleischer et al, 29-45. Jerusalem: Hebrew University Magnes Press, 2001.

———. *Maimonides' Confrontation With Mysticism*. London: Littman Library of Jewish Civilization, 2006.

———. *Maimonides on Human Perfection*. Brown Judaic Studies 202. Atlanta, GA: Scholars Press, 1990.

Kimhi, David. Commentary on the Bible. Printed in standard editions of *Mikraot Gedolot*.

Kirschner, Robert. "Maimonides' Fiction of Resurrection." *Hebrew Union College Annual* 52 (1982): 163-193.

Kohen, Meir Simhah. *Or Sameah*. Warsaw: A. Boymeryettar, 1910.

Kraemer, Joel. "Alfarabi's Opinions of the Virtuous City and Maimonides' Foundations of the Law." In *Studia Orientalia Memoriae D. H. Baneth Dedicata*, edited by Joshua Blau, 107-153. Jerusalem: Hebrew University Magnes Press, 1979.

———. "Hashpaat ha-Mishpat ha-Musalmi al ha-RaMBaM." *Teudah* 10 (1996): 225-244.

———. "Maimonides' Intellectual Milieu in Cairo." In *Maimonide: philosophe*

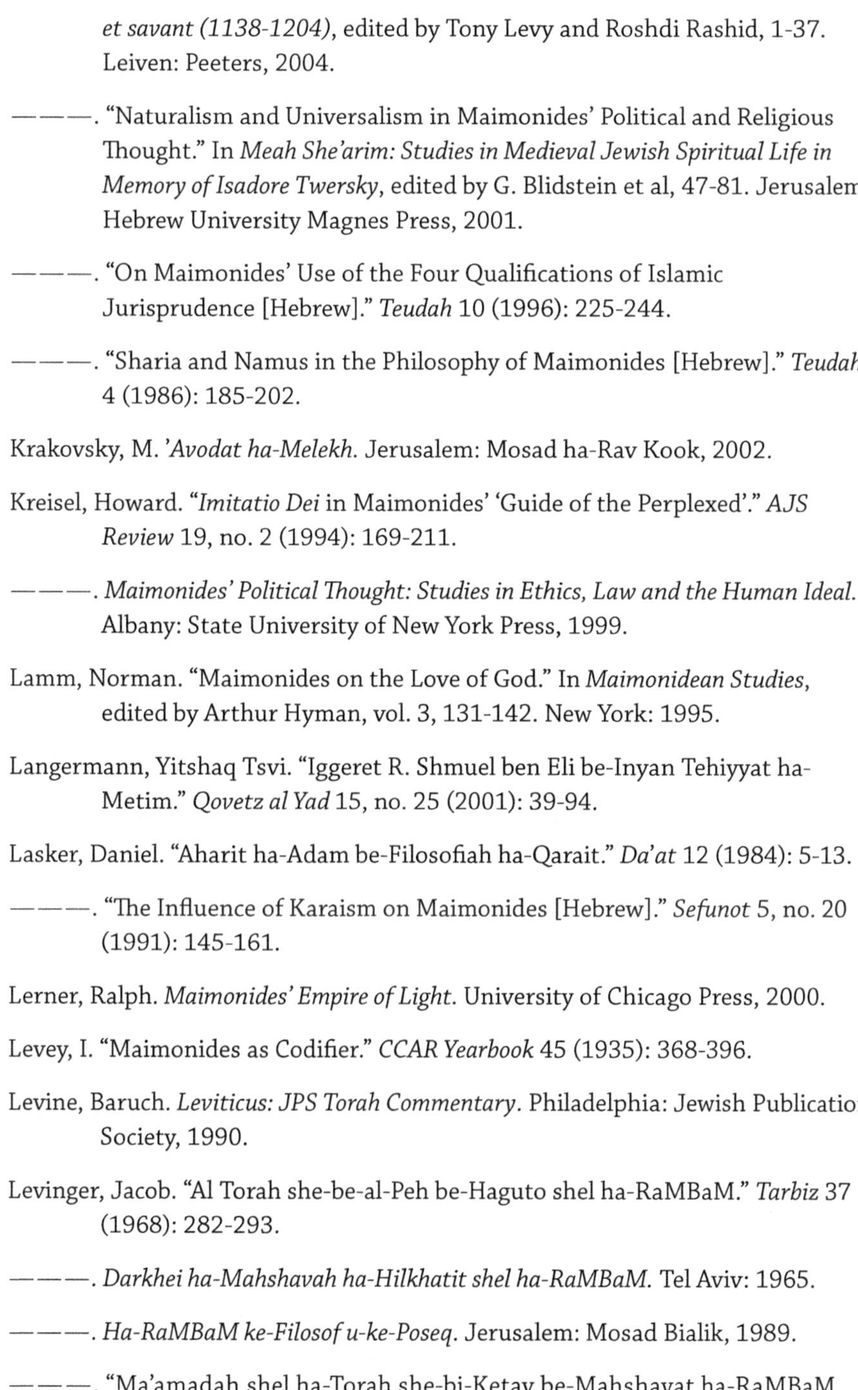

et savant (1138-1204), edited by Tony Levy and Roshdi Rashid, 1-37. Leiven: Peeters, 2004.

———. "Naturalism and Universalism in Maimonides' Political and Religious Thought." In *Meah She'arim: Studies in Medieval Jewish Spiritual Life in Memory of Isadore Twersky*, edited by G. Blidstein et al, 47-81. Jerusalem: Hebrew University Magnes Press, 2001.

———. "On Maimonides' Use of the Four Qualifications of Islamic Jurisprudence [Hebrew]." *Teudah* 10 (1996): 225-244.

———. "Sharia and Namus in the Philosophy of Maimonides [Hebrew]." *Teudah* 4 (1986): 185-202.

Krakovsky, M. *'Avodat ha-Melekh*. Jerusalem: Mosad ha-Rav Kook, 2002.

Kreisel, Howard. "*Imitatio Dei* in Maimonides' 'Guide of the Perplexed'." *AJS Review* 19, no. 2 (1994): 169-211.

———. *Maimonides' Political Thought: Studies in Ethics, Law and the Human Ideal.* Albany: State University of New York Press, 1999.

Lamm, Norman. "Maimonides on the Love of God." In *Maimonidean Studies*, edited by Arthur Hyman, vol. 3, 131-142. New York: 1995.

Langermann, Yitshaq Tsvi. "Iggeret R. Shmuel ben Eli be-Inyan Tehiyyat ha-Metim." *Qovetz al Yad* 15, no. 25 (2001): 39-94.

Lasker, Daniel. "Aharit ha-Adam be-Filosofiah ha-Qarait." *Da'at* 12 (1984): 5-13.

———. "The Influence of Karaism on Maimonides [Hebrew]." *Sefunot* 5, no. 20 (1991): 145-161.

Lerner, Ralph. *Maimonides' Empire of Light*. University of Chicago Press, 2000.

Levey, I. "Maimonides as Codifier." *CCAR Yearbook* 45 (1935): 368-396.

Levine, Baruch. *Leviticus: JPS Torah Commentary*. Philadelphia: Jewish Publication Society, 1990.

Levinger, Jacob. "Al Torah she-be-al-Peh be-Haguto shel ha-RaMBaM." *Tarbiz* 37 (1968): 282-293.

———. *Darkhei ha-Mahshavah ha-Hilkhatit shel ha-RaMBaM*. Tel Aviv: 1965.

———. *Ha-RaMBaM ke-Filosof u-ke-Poseq*. Jerusalem: Mosad Bialik, 1989.

———. "Ma'amadah shel ha-Torah she-bi-Ketav be-Mahshavat ha-RaMBaM ke-Tsiyyun Derekh Didakti bi-sh-Vilenu." In *Ha-Miqra ve-Anahnu*, edited by Uriel Simon, 120-132. Tel Aviv: Hotsaat Devir, 1979. Reprinted (with slight modification) in Levinger, *Ha-RaMBaM ke-Filosof u-ke-Poseq*, 56-66.

Lewin, B. M. "Midreshe Halakhah u-Pisqe ha-RaMBaM le-fi Seder ha-Torah." *Rabbenu Moshe ben Maimon,* edited by Y. L. Fishman, 101-145. Tel Aviv: Ha-Merkaz ha-Olami shel ha-Mizrahi, 1935.

Libson, Gideon. "A Guarantee to Present the Debtor: Shmuel ben Hofni's Treatise on Surety, the Responsa of the Geonim, Maimonides and Analogous Muslim Legal Literature." *Shenaton ha-Mishpat ha-Ivry* 13 (1987): 121-184.

———. *Jewish Law and Islamic Law: A comparative Study of Custom During the Geonic Period*. Cambridge, MA: Harvard University Press, 2003.

———. "Maimonides and Muslim Law [Hebrew]." In *Mehqere Talmud*, edited by Y. Sussman and D. Rosenthal, vol. 1, 305-322. Jerusalem: 1967.

———. "Parallels Between Maimonides and Islamic Law." In *The Thought of Moses Maimonides: Philosophical and Legal Studies*, edited by I. Robinson, L. Kaplan and J. Bauer, 209-248. Lewiston, NY: Edwin Mellen Press, 1990.

———. "Surety for Liability in Geonic Literature, Maimonides and Muslim Law [Hebrew]." In *Mehqere Talmud*, edited by Y. Sussman and D. Rosenthal, vol. 1, 305-322. Jerusalem, 1990.

Lieberman, S. *Hellenism in Jewish Palestine: Studies in the Literary Transmission, Beliefs and Manners of Palestine in the I Century B.C.E.-IV Century C.E.* New York: Jewish Theological Seminary, 1962.

———. *Hilkhot ha-Yerushalmi le-Rabbenu Moshe ben Maimon*. New York: Jewish Theological Seminary, 1947.

Loewe, Raphael. "The 'Plain' Meaning of Scripture in Early Jewish Exegesis." In *Papers of the Institute of Jewish Studies, London*, edited by J.G. Weiss, 140-186. Jerusalem: Hebrew University Magnes Press, 1964.

Macy, Jeffrey. "The Rule of Law and the Rule of Wisdom in Plato, al-Farabi and Maimonides." In *Studies in Islamic and Judaic Traditions*, edited by W. Brinner and S. Ricks, 205-232. Atlanta: Scholars Press, 1986.

———. "The Theological-Political Teaching of Shemonah Peraqim: A Reappraisal of the Text and of its Arabic Sources." In *Proceedings of the Eighth World Congress of Jewish Studies (Division C)*, 31-40. Jerusalem: Hebrew University Magnes Press, 1982.

Maimonides, Abraham. *Birkat Abraham*. Edited by B. Goldberg. Lyck: 1859.

———. *Ma'aseh Nissim*. Edited and translated by B. Goldberg. Paris: 1867.

———. "Teshuvot Rabbenu Abraham ben ha-RaMBaM le-Sheelot Rabbi Daniel ha-Bavli be-Inyane Sefer ha-Mitsvot." In *Sefer ha-Mitsvot*. Translated by D. Z. Hilman and edited by S. Frankel. Jerusalem: 1995.

———. *Torah Commentary: Genesis and Exodus [Hebrew]*. Original Arabic text edited and translated into Hebrew by Efraim Weisenberg and S. Sasson. London: 1959; Jerusalem: Qeren Hotsaat Sifre Rabbenu Bavel, 1984.

Malachi ben Yaaqov ha-Kohen. *Yad Malachi, Kelalei ha-Gemara u-Kelalei ha-Posqim u-Kelalei ha-Dinim*. N.p., n.d.

Malbim, Meir Leibush. *Ha-Torah ve-he-Mitsvah*. Jerusalem, 1969.

Malter, H. *Saadya Gaon*. Philadelphia, 1942.

Mann, J. *The Jews in Egypt*. 2 vols. New York: 1970.

———. *Texts and Studies in Jewish History and Literature*. 2 vols. New York: Ktav Publishing House, 1972.

Margoliyot, M. *Sefer Hilkhot ha-Nagid*. Jerusalem: 1962.

Marmorstein, A. "The Place of Maimonides' *Mishneh Torah* in the History and Development of the Halakhah." In *Moses Maimonides*, edited by I. Epstein, 159-179. London: Soncino, 1935.

Marx, A. "The Correspondence between the Rabbis of Southern France and Maimonides about Astrology." *HUCA* 3 (1926): 311-358.

———. "Texts by and about Maimonides." *JQR* 25 (1935): 371-428.

Meacham (le Beit Yoreh), Tirzah. "Introduction." In *Introducing Tosefta: Textual, Intratextual and Intertextual Studies*, edited by Harry Fox and Tirzah Meacham, 1-37. Hoboken, NJ: Ktav Publishing House, 1999.

Milgrom, Jacob. *Leviticus: The Anchor Bible*. New York: Doubleday, 1991.

Miller, Philip E. "Karaite Perspectives in Yom Teru'ah." In *Ki Baruch Hu: Ancient*

Near Eastern, Biblical, and Judaic Studies in Honor of Baruch A. Levine, edited by Robert Chazan, William W. Hallo, and Lawrence H. Schiffman, 537-41. Winona Lake: Eisenbrauns, 1999.

Mizrahi, Eliyahu. Super-commentary on RaSHI, in *Otsar Pirushim al ha-Torah–Mizrahi*. New York: Defus ve-Hotsaat Avraham Yitzhak Friedman, 1965.

Moran, W. L. "The Ancient Near Eastern Background of the Love of God in Deuteronomy." *CBQ* 25 (1963): 77-87.

Moses ben Joshua of Narbonne. *Commentary on the Guide of the Perplexed*. Edited by J. Goldenthal. Printed in *Sheloshah Qadmone Mefarshe ha-Moreh*. Vienna: 1853. Reprint, Jerusalem: 1961.

Mosse, Martin. *The Three Gospels: New Testament History Introduced by the Synoptic Problem*. Paternoster Biblical Monographs. Colorado Springs: Milton Keynes, 2007.

Nagar, Eliyahu. "Fear of God in Maimonides' Teaching [Hebrew]." *Da'at* 39 (1997): 89-99.

Nahmanides, Moses. "Hasagot ha-RaMBaN." In *Sefer ha-Mitsvot,* edited by S. Frankel. Jerusalem: Bnei Brak, 1995.

———. *Perush al ha-Torah*. Edited by C. D. Chavel. Jerusalem: Mosad ha-Rav Kook, 1966-1967.

———. *Sefer ha-Mitsvot le-ha-RaMBaM im Hasagot ha-RaMBaN*. Edited by C. D. Chavel. Jerusalem: Mosad ha-Rav Kook, 1994.

Nehorai, Michael. "Maimonides' System of the Commandments [Hebrew]." *Da'at* 10 (1983): 29-42.

———. "Torat ha-Mitsvot shel ha-RaMBaM." *Da'at* 13 (1984): 29-42.

Nemoy, L. "Al-Qirqisani's Account of the Jewish Sects." *HUCA* 7 (1930): 317-398.

———. "Karaites." In *The Encyclopedia of Religion*, edited by Mircea Eliade. New York: Macmillan, 1987.

———. "Maimonides' Epistle to Yemen." Review of *Moses Maimonides' Epistle to Yemen: The Arabic Original and the Three Hebrew Versions*, edited by A. Halkin. *JQR* 44 (1953-1954): 170-175.

Nemoy, L., ed. and trans. *Karaite Anthology*. New Haven: Yale University Press, 1952.

Neubauer, A. "Miscellanea Liturgica, II: Azharot on the 613 Precepts." *JQR* 6 (1894): 698-709.

Neubauer, J. *Ha-RaMBaM al Divre Sofrim*. Jerusalem: 1957.

Novak, David. *Natural Law in Judaism*. Cambridge: Cambridge University Press, 1998.

———. *The Theology of Nachmanides Systematically Presented*. Atlanta: 1992.

Nuriel, Abraham. "Musag ha-Emunah etsel ha-RaMBaM." *Da'at* 2-3 (1979): 43-47.

Olszowy-Schlanger, Judith. *Karaite Marriage Documents from the Cairo Geniza: Legal Tradition and Community Life in Medieval Egypt and Palestine*. Leiden: E. J. Brill, 1998.

Parens, Joshua. "Maimonidean Ethics Revisited: Development and Asceticism in Maimonides?" *The Journal of Jewish Thought and Philosophy* 12, no. 3 (2006): 33-61.

Peritz, Moritz. "Das Buch der Gesetze, Nach Seiner Anlage un Seinem Inhalt Untersucht." In *Moses ben Maimon: Sein Leben, Seine Werke und Sein Einfluss*, edited by W. Bacher, M. Brann, and D. Simonsen, vol. 1, 439-474. Leipzig: 1908. Reprint, New York: Georg Olms Verlag Hildesheim, 1971.

Perla, Yeruham Fischel. *Sefer ha-Mitsvot le-RaSaG*. 3 vols. Jerusalem: Hotsaat Qeset, 1973.

Pines, Shlomo. "The Limitations of Human Knowledge According to Al-Farabi, Ibn Bajja and Maimonides." In *Studies in Medieval Jewish History and Literature*, edited by I. Twersky, 82-109. Cambridge, MA: Harvard University Press, 1979.

———. "The Philosophic Sources of the Guide of the Perplexed." *The Guide of the Perplexed*, translated by Shlomo Pines, lvii-cxxxiv. Chicago: University of Chicago Press, 1963.

———. "The Philosophical Purport of Maimonides' Halakhic Works and the Purport of the Guide of the Perplexed." In *Maimonides and Philosophy: Papers Presented at the Sixth Jerusalem Philosophical Encounter, May, 1985*, edited by S. Pines and Y. Yovel, 1-14. Dordrecht: M. Nijhoff, 1986.

Pinsker, Simhah. *Liqqute Qadmoniyyot*. Vienna: 1860. Reprint, Jerusalem: 1968.

Polak, Gabriel J. *Huqe ha-Eloqim*. Amsterdam, 1831.

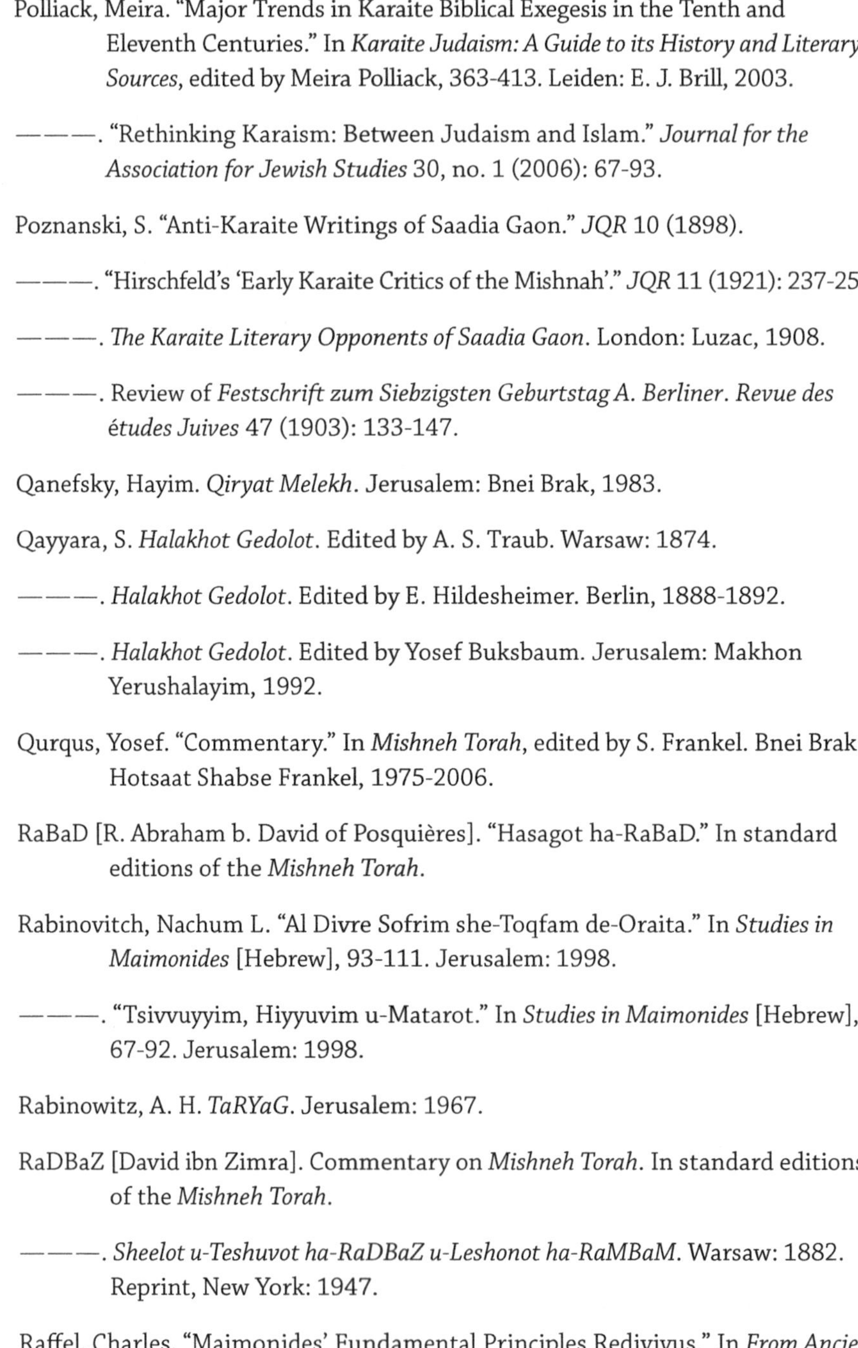

Polliack, Meira. "Major Trends in Karaite Biblical Exegesis in the Tenth and Eleventh Centuries." In *Karaite Judaism: A Guide to its History and Literary Sources*, edited by Meira Polliack, 363-413. Leiden: E. J. Brill, 2003.

———. "Rethinking Karaism: Between Judaism and Islam." *Journal for the Association for Jewish Studies* 30, no. 1 (2006): 67-93.

Poznanski, S. "Anti-Karaite Writings of Saadia Gaon." *JQR* 10 (1898).

———. "Hirschfeld's 'Early Karaite Critics of the Mishnah'." *JQR* 11 (1921): 237-257.

———. *The Karaite Literary Opponents of Saadia Gaon*. London: Luzac, 1908.

———. Review of *Festschrift zum Siebzigsten Geburtstag A. Berliner*. *Revue des études Juives* 47 (1903): 133-147.

Qanefsky, Hayim. *Qiryat Melekh*. Jerusalem: Bnei Brak, 1983.

Qayyara, S. *Halakhot Gedolot*. Edited by A. S. Traub. Warsaw: 1874.

———. *Halakhot Gedolot*. Edited by E. Hildesheimer. Berlin, 1888-1892.

———. *Halakhot Gedolot*. Edited by Yosef Buksbaum. Jerusalem: Makhon Yerushalayim, 1992.

Qurqus, Yosef. "Commentary." In *Mishneh Torah*, edited by S. Frankel. Bnei Brak: Hotsaat Shabse Frankel, 1975-2006.

RaBaD [R. Abraham b. David of Posquières]. "Hasagot ha-RaBaD." In standard editions of the *Mishneh Torah*.

Rabinovitch, Nachum L. "Al Divre Sofrim she-Toqfam de-Oraita." In *Studies in Maimonides* [Hebrew], 93-111. Jerusalem: 1998.

———. "Tsivvuyyim, Hiyyuvim u-Matarot." In *Studies in Maimonides* [Hebrew], 67-92. Jerusalem: 1998.

Rabinowitz, A. H. *TaRYaG*. Jerusalem: 1967.

RaDBaZ [David ibn Zimra]. Commentary on *Mishneh Torah*. In standard editions of the *Mishneh Torah*.

———. *Sheelot u-Teshuvot ha-RaDBaZ u-Leshonot ha-RaMBaM*. Warsaw: 1882. Reprint, New York: 1947.

Raffel, Charles. "Maimonides' Fundamental Principles Redivivus." In *From Ancient Israel to Modern Judaism: Intellect in Quest of Understanding: Essays in*

Honor of Marvin Fox, edited by J. Neusner, E. Frerichs, and N. Sarna, vol. 3, 77-88. Atlanta: Scholars Press, 1989.

Ratteh, Meshulam. "Shitat ha-RaMBaM be-Bedrashot HaZaL ve-Asmakhtot u-Peshuto shel Miqra." In *Qol Mevasser: Sheelot u-Teshuvot*, vol. 2, 34-35. Jerusalem: Mosad ha-Rav Kook, 1962.

RaShBaM [R. Samuel b, Meir]. "Perush ha-Torah." In standard editions of *Miqraot Gedolot*.

RaSHi [R. Solomon b. Isaac]. "RaSHi: Commentary on the Pentateuch." *Torat Chaim Chumash*. 1993.

———. Commentary on the Babylonian Talmud. In standard editions of the Babylonian Talmud.

———. Commentary on the Torah. In standard editions of *Miqraot Gedolot*.

Rawidowicz, Simon. "On Maimonides' Sefer ha-Madd'a." In *Studies in Jewish Thought*, edited by Nahum N. Glatzer, 317-323. Philadelphia: Jewish Publication Society, 1974.

———. "Sefer ha-Mitsvot ve-Sefer ha-Madd'a le-RaMBaM." *Metsudah*, Sivan 1945, 181-213.

Raz, Joseph. "Legal Principles and the Limits of Law." *Yale Law Journal* 81 (1972): 823-834.

Reines, H. Z. "Ha-Muvan shel ve-Ahavta le-Reakha Kamokha." In *Sefer Yovel le-Shimon Federbush*, edited by J. Maimon, 304-315. Jerusalem: 1961.

RiBaSH [Yitzhaq b. Sheshet]. *Sheelot u-Teshuvot*. Riva di Trento: 1559.

Romney-Wegner, Judith. "Islamic and Talmudic Jurisprudence: The Four Roots of Islamic Law and their Talmudic Counterparts." *American Journal of Legal History* 26, no. 1 (1982): 24-71.

Rosanes, Y. "Derekh Mitsvotekha." In *Sefer ha-Mitsvot*, edited by S. Frankel, 416-436. Jerusalem: 1995.

Rosenberg, Shalom. "Ethics." In *Contemporary Jewish Religious Thought: Original Essays on Critical Concepts, Movements, and Beliefs*, edited by Arthur A. Cohen and Paul Mendes-Flohr, 195-202. New York: C. Scribner's Sons, 1983.

———. "The Interpretation of the Torah in the Guide [Hebrew]." *Jewish Studies in Jewish Thought* 1, no. 1 (1981): 85-157.

Rosenthal, Erwin I. J. "Maimonides' Conception of State and Society." In *Moses Maimonides*, edited by I. Epstein. London: The Soncino Press, 1935. Reprinted in Rosenthal, E. I. J., ed., *Studia Semitica*, vol. 1 (Jewish Themes), Cambridge: Cambridge University Press, 1971, 275-288.

Rubenstein, Jeffrey L. *The History of Sukkot in the Second Temple and Rabbinic Periods*. Brown Judaic Studies 302. Atlanta: Scholars Press, 1995.

Sa'adiah Gaon. *The Book of Beliefs and Opinions*, edited by Samuel Rosenblatt. Yale Judaica Series. New Haven: Yale University Press, 1976.

———. *The Book of Beliefs and Opinions (Arabic Text and Hebrew Translation)*. Translated by Joseph Kafih. Jerusalem: Sura, 1970.

———. *Siddur*. Edited by I. Davidson, S. Assaf, and B. I. Joel. Jerusalem: Meqitze Nirdamim, 1985.

Sàenz-Badillos, A. "The Biblical Foundation of Jewish Law According to Maimonides." In *Maimonides as Codifier of Jewish Law: Proceedings of the Second International Seminar on the Sources of Contemporary Law*, edited by Nahum Rakover, The Library of Jewish Law, 61-73. Jerusalem: Jewish Legal Heritage Society, 1987.

Safrai, S. "Halakhah le-Moshe mi-Sinai - Historiah o Teologiah?" In *Mehqere Talmud*, edited by Y. Sussman and D. Rosenthal. Jerusalem: Hebrew University Magnes Press, 1990.

Salman ben Yeruham. *Milhamot ha-Shem*, edited by Y. El-Gamil. Ramla: Institute Tireret Yosef, 2000.

Schacht, Joseph. *An Introduction to Islamic Law.* Oxford: Oxford University Press, 1982.

———. *The Origins of Muslim Jurisprudence.* Oxford: Oxford University Press, 1950.

Schechter, S. "The Dogmas of Judaism." In *Studies in Judaism*, 147-181. Philadelphia: Jewish Publication Society, 1915.

———. *Saadyana: Geniza Fragments of Writings of R. Saadya Gaon and Others.* Cambridge: Deighton and Bell, 1903.

Schneerson, Menachem Mendel. *Likkutei Sichos*, vol. 34. Kehot Publication Society, 1995.

———. "Mitsvat Yedi'at ha-Shem." In *Hiddushim u-Biurim be-Shas u-be-Divre ha-RaMBaM*. New York: Yeshivat Tomkhe Temimim ha-Merkazit, 1985.

Schwarz, A. *Der Mischneh Thorah: Ein System der Mosaisch-Talmuchischen Gesetzeslehre. Zur Erinnerung an den Siebenhundertjährigen Todestag Maimuni's*. Karlsruhe: G. Braun, 1905.

Schwarzchild, S. "Do Noachites Have to Believe in Revelation?" *JQR* 52-3 (1962): 297-308, 30-65.

———. "Moral Radicalism and 'Middlingness' in the Ethics of Maimonides." In *Studies in Medieval Culture*, edited by John R. Sommerfeldt and Thomas H. Seiler, vol. 11, 65-94. Kalamazoo, MI: The Medieval Institute, Western Michigan University, 1978.

Schweid, E. *'Iyyunim bi-Shemonah Peraqim*. Jerusalem: 1969.

Sefer Mitsvot he-Arukh. 3 vols. Jerusalem: 1999.

Segal-Horowitz, Aryeh-Leib. "Marganita Taba." In *Sefer ha-Mitsvot*, edited by S. Frankel, 1995.

Septimus, Bernard. "What Did Maimonides Mean by *Madd'a*?" In *Meah She'arim: Studies in Medieval Jewish Spiritual Life, in Memory of Isadore Twersky*, edited by E. Fleischer and J. Blidstein, 83-110. Jerusalem: Hebrew University Magnes Press, 2001.

Septimus, Dov. "Mivneh ve-ti'un be-sefer ha-madda." In *Ha-Rambam: Shamranut, Meqoriyut, Mahepkhanut*, edited by A. Ravitzky, 223-246. Jerusalem: Mercaz Zalman Shazar le-Toldot Israel, 2009.

Shailat, Y. "Perush ha-Mishnah le-RaMBaM ve-Hadarato be-Dorenu." In *Beit ha-Va'*

ad le-'Arikhat Kitve Rabbotenu, edited by Yoel Qatan and E. Soloveitchik, 65-74. Jerusalem, 2003.

Shapira, Tsvi Elimelekh. *Sifre me-HaRTSa mi-Dinov*, vol. 2 (*Devarim Nehmadim*). Jerusalem: 1987.

Shapiro, Marc B. *The Limits of Orthodox Theology: Maimonides' Thirteen Principles Reappraised*. Portland, OR: The Littman Library of Jewish Civilization, 2004.

———. *Principles of Interpretation in Maimonidean Halakhah*. Scranton, PA: University of Scranton Press, 2008.

———. *Studies in Maimonides and His Interpreters*. Scranton, PA: University of Scranton Press, 2008.

Shatz, D. "Maimonides' Moral Theory." In *The Cambridge Companion to Maimonides*, edited by Kenneth Seeskin, 167-192. Cambridge: Cambridge University Press, 2005.

Shem Tov ibn Gaon. "Migdal 'Oz." Printed in standard editions of the *Mishneh Torah.*

Shemesh, Aaron. "Le-Toldot Mashmaam shel ha-Musagim Mitsvot Aseh u-Mitsvot lo Ta'aseh." *Tarbiz* 72, nos. 1-2 (2003): 133-150.

Sherira Gaon. *Iggeret Rav Sherira Gaon.* Edited by B. M. Lewin. Haifa: 1921.

Shiloh, S. "Yahaso shel R. Yosef ibn Megas le-Geonim." *Sinai* 66 (1970): 263-268.

Shlomo b. Eliezer ha-Levi. *'Avodat ha-Levi.* Venice: 1546.

Shohetman, Eliav. "'Halakhah mi-Pi ha-Qabbalah' ve-'Halakhah le-Moshe mi-Sinai': 'Iyyun bi-Leshonot ha-RaMBaM." *Shenaton ha-Mishpat ha-Ivry* 22 (1961-1963).

Silver, Daniel J. *Maimonidean Criticism and the Maimonidean Controversy 1180-1240.* Leiden: E. J. Brill, 1965.

Sklare, E. David. *Samuel ben Hofni Gaon and His Cultural World.* Leiden: E. J. Brill, 1996.

———. "Yusuf al-Basir: Theological Aspects of his Halakhic Works." In *The Jews of Medieval Islam: Community, Society and Identity,* edited by Daniel Frank, 249-270. Leiden: E. J. Brill, 1995.

Sofer, Moses. *Sheelot u-Teshuvot Hatam Sofer.* Pressburg, 1841-1862.

Soloveitchik, Hayim. "Maimonides' Iggeret ha-Shemad: Law and Rhetoric." In *Rabbi Joseph H. Lookstein Memorial Volume,* edited by Leo Landman, 281-319. New York: 1980.

Sonne, I. "A Scrutiny of the Charges of Forgery against Maimonides' 'Letter on Resurrection'." *PAAJR* 21 (1952): 101-117.

Sperber, D. *Masechet Derekh Erets Zuta.* 2nd ed. Jerusalem: 1982.

Spiegel, S. "Le-Parshat ha-Polmos shel Pirqoi ben Baboi." In *Harry Austryn Wolfson Jubilee Volume: On the Occasion of his Seventy-Fifth Birthday*, edited by S. Lieberman et al, vol. 3, 243-274. Jerusalem: American Academy for Jewish Research, 1965.

Stern, Josef. "The Idea of Hoq in Maimonides' Explanation of the Law." In *Maimonides and Philosophy: Papers Presented at the Sixth Jerusalem*

Philosophical Encounter, May, 1985, edited by S. Pines and Y. Yovel, 92-130. Dordrecht: Martinus Nijhoff, 1986.

———. "Maimonides on ʾAmaleq, Self-Corrective Mechanisms and the War against Idolatry." In *Judaism and Modernity: The Religious Philosophy of David Hartman*, edited by Jonathan W. Malino, 359-392. Burlington: Ashgate Publishing Company, 2004.

———. *Problems and Parables of Law: Maimonides and Nahmanides on Reasons for the Commandments*. Albany: State University of New York Press, 1998.

Stern, S. *Calendar and Community*. Oxford: Oxford University Press, 2001.

Strack, H. L., and G. Stemberger. *Introduction to the Talmud and Midrash*. Translated by Markus Bockmuehl. 2nd ed. Minneapolis: Fortress Press, 1992.

Strauss, Leo. "How to Begin to Study the Guide of the Perplexed." In Maimonides, *The Guide of the Perplexed,* translated by Shlomo Pines, xi-lvi. Chicago: University of Chicago Press, 1963.

———. "Maimonides' Statement on Political Science." *PAAJR* 22 (1953): 115-130.

———. "Notes on Maimonides' Book of Knowledge." In *Studies in Mysticism and Religion: Presented to Gershom G. Scholem on His Seventieth Birthday by Pupils, Colleagues and Friends*, edited by E. Urbach, 269-283. Jerusalem: Hebrew University Magnes Press, 1967.

———. *Persecution and the Art of Writing*. Glencoe, IL: Free Press, 1952.

———. *Philosophy and Law*. Translated and with an introduction by Eve Adler. SUNY Series in the Jewish Writings of Strauss. Albany: State University of New York Press, 1995.

———. "Quelques remarques sur la science politique de Maïmonide et de Farabi." *Revue des Etudes Juives* 100 (1936): 1-37.

Stroumsa, Sarah. *The Beginning of the Maimonidean Controversy in the East: Yosef ibn Shimon's Silencing Epistle Concerning the Resurrection of the Dead*. Jerusalem: Ben Tsvi Institute, 1999.

Talmage, Frank. "Apples of Gold: The Inner Meaning of Sacred Texts in Medieval Judaism." In *Jewish Spirituality: From the Bible through the Middle Ages*, edited by Arthur Green. London: Crossroads, 1986.

Ta-Shema, I. "Review of J. Levinger: Darkhe ha-Mahshavah ha-Halakhtit shel ha-RaMBaM." *Qiryat Sefer* 41 (1966): 138-144.

Tchernowitz, C. *Toldot ha-Halakhah*. 4 vols. New York: Hamul, 1935-1950.

———. *Toldot ha-Posqim*. 3 vols. New York: Va'ad ha-Yovel, 1946-1947.

Touati, Charles. "Croyances vraies et croyances necessaires (Platon, Averroes, philosophie juive et Spinoza)." In *Hommage A Georges Vajda*, edited by Gerard Nahon and Charles Touati, 169-182. Louvain: Editions Peeters, 1980.

Toulmin, Stephen E. *The Uses of Argument*. Cambridge: Cambridge University Press, 2003.

Towner, W. Sibley. "Hermeneutical Systems of Hillel and the Tannaim: A Fresh Look." *HUCA* 53 (1982): 101-135.

Twersky, I. "The Beginnings of Mishneh Torah Criticism." In *Biblical and Other Studies*, edited by A. Altmann, Studies and Texts, 161-183. Cambridge, MA: Harvard University Press, 1963.

———. "Did Ibn Ezra Influence Maimonides? [Hebrew]." In *Rabbi Abraham ibn Ezra, Studies in the Writings of a Twelfth-Century Jewish Polymath*, edited by Isadore Twersky and Jay M. Harris, 21-48. Harvard Judaic Texts and Studies. Cambridge, MA: Harvard University Press, 1993.

———. *Introduction to the Code of Maimonides (Mishneh Torah)*. New Haven: Yale University Press, 1980.

———. *RaBaD of Posquières: A Twelfth-Century Talmudist*. Cambridge, MA: Harvard University Press, 1962.

———. "Some Non-Halakhic Aspects of the Mishneh Torah." In *Jewish Medieval and Renaissance Studies*, edited by A. Altmann. Studies and Texts, 95-119. Cambridge: Harvard University Press, 1967.

Urbach, Ephaim E. "Ha-Derashah ke-Yesod ha-Halakhah u-Ba'ayat ha-Sofrim." *Tarbiz* 27 (1957): 166-182.

———. *The Sages – Their Concepts and Beliefs*. Translated by Israel Abrahams. Cambridge, MA: Harvard University Press, 1997.

Vajda, Georges. *L'amour de Dieu dans la théologie juive de moyen* âge. Études de philosophie médiévale 46. Paris: Librairie Philosophique J. Vrin, 1957.

Waxman, M. "Maimonides as Dogmatist." *CCAR Yearbook* 45 (1935): 397-418.

Weis, P. R. "Abraham ibn Ezra ve-ha-Qaraim." *Melilah* 1 (1944): 35-53.

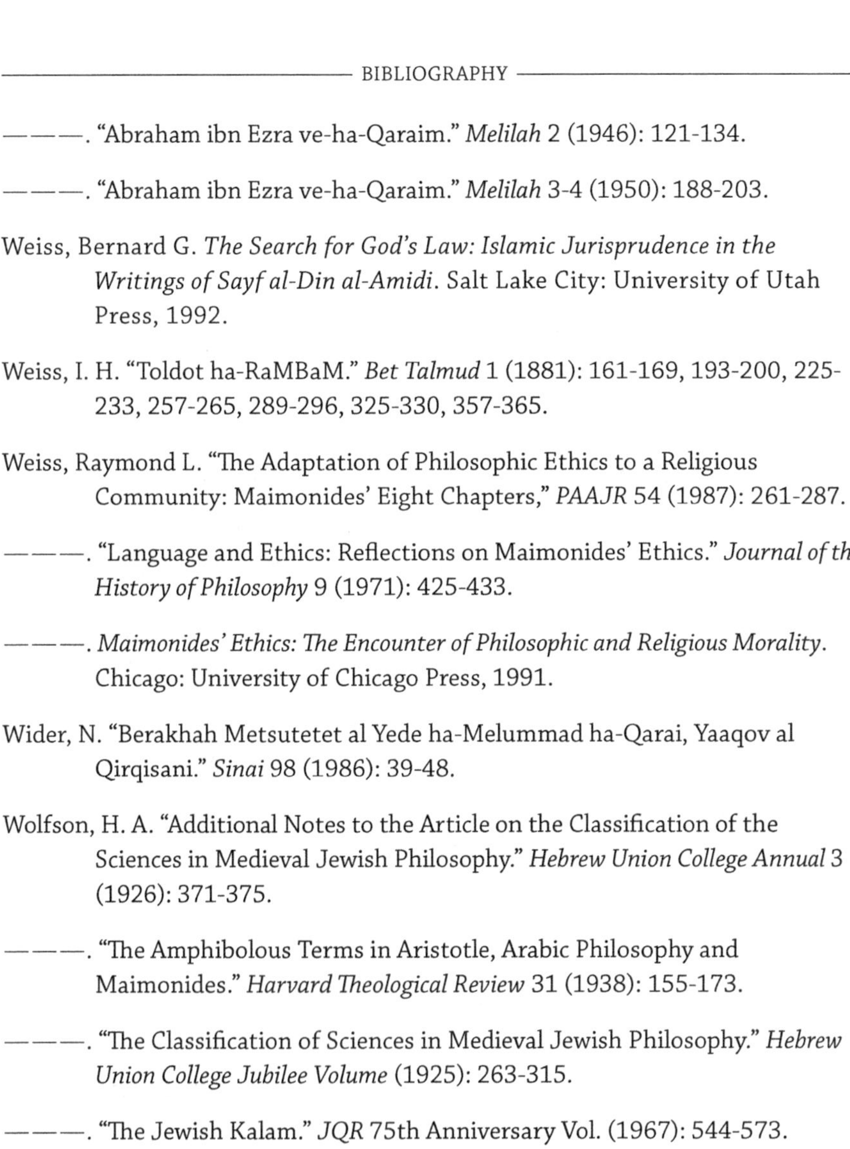

———. "Abraham ibn Ezra ve-ha-Qaraim." *Melilah* 2 (1946): 121-134.

———. "Abraham ibn Ezra ve-ha-Qaraim." *Melilah* 3-4 (1950): 188-203.

Weiss, Bernard G. *The Search for God's Law: Islamic Jurisprudence in the Writings of Sayf al-Din al-Amidi*. Salt Lake City: University of Utah Press, 1992.

Weiss, I. H. "Toldot ha-RaMBaM." *Bet Talmud* 1 (1881): 161-169, 193-200, 225-233, 257-265, 289-296, 325-330, 357-365.

Weiss, Raymond L. "The Adaptation of Philosophic Ethics to a Religious Community: Maimonides' Eight Chapters," *PAAJR* 54 (1987): 261-287.

———. "Language and Ethics: Reflections on Maimonides' Ethics." *Journal of the History of Philosophy* 9 (1971): 425-433.

———. *Maimonides' Ethics: The Encounter of Philosophic and Religious Morality*. Chicago: University of Chicago Press, 1991.

Wider, N. "Berakhah Metsutetet al Yede ha-Melummad ha-Qarai, Yaaqov al Qirqisani." *Sinai* 98 (1986): 39-48.

Wolfson, H. A. "Additional Notes to the Article on the Classification of the Sciences in Medieval Jewish Philosophy." *Hebrew Union College Annual* 3 (1926): 371-375.

———. "The Amphibolous Terms in Aristotle, Arabic Philosophy and Maimonides." *Harvard Theological Review* 31 (1938): 155-173.

———. "The Classification of Sciences in Medieval Jewish Philosophy." *Hebrew Union College Jubilee Volume* (1925): 263-315.

———. "The Jewish Kalam." *JQR* 75th Anniversary Vol. (1967): 544-573.

———. "Note on Maimonides' Classification of the Sciences." *JQR* n.s. 26 (1936): 369-377.

———. *Repercussions of the Kalam in Jewish Philosophy*. Cambridge, MA: Harvard University Press, 1979.

Würzburger, Walter. "Imitatio Dei in Maimonides' Sefer ha-Mitsvot and the Mishneh Torah." In *Tradition and Transition: Essays Presented to Chief Rabbi Sir Immanuel Jakobovits*, edited by Jonathan Sacks, 321-324. London: Jews College, 1986.

Yehoshua, H. "Be-Biur Shitat ha-RaMBaM be-Shoresh ha-Rishon ve-ha-Sheni be-Sefer ha-Mitsvot." *Moriah* 5, nos. 11-12 (1975): 43-48.

Yehoshua ha-Nagid. *Teshuvot*. Edited and translated by Yehudah Ratzaby. Jerusalem: Makhon Mishnat ha-RaMBaM, 1989.

Zeidman, J. "Signon Mishneh Torah." *Sinai* 3 (1938): 112-121.

Ziadeh, Faraht J. "Adab al-Qadi and the Protection of Rights at Court." In *Studies in Islamic and Judaic Traditions: Papers Presented at the Institute of Islamic-Judaic Studies*, edited by William M. Brinner and Stephen D. Ricks. Brown Judaic Studies, 143-150. Atlanta: Scholars Press, 1986.

Zonta, Mauro. "Maimonides as Zoologist? - Some Remarks on Aristotle's Zoology Ascribed to Maimonides." In *Moses Maimonides (1138-1204): His Religious, Scientific and Philosophical Wirkungsgeschichte in Different Cultural Contexts*, edited by G. K. Hasselhoff and O. Fraisse, Ex Oriente Lux: Rezeptionen und Exegesen als Traditionskritik, 83-94.Würzburg: Ergon-Verlag, 2004.

Zucker, Moshe. *Al Targum RaSaG la-Torah*. New York: Feldheim, 1959.

———. "He'arot le-Haqdamat RaSaG le-Tehillim." *Leshonenu* 33, no. 2/3 (1969): 223-230.

———. "Mi-Perusho shel RaSaG la-Torah." *SURA* 2,[Jerusalem and New York] (1955-56): 313-355.

———. "Mi-Sefer ha-Mitsvot shel Hefets b. Yatsliah." *PAAJR* 29 (1960-1961): 1-68.

———. *Perush Rav Saadia Gaon le-Bereshit*. New York: Jewish Theological Seminary, 1985.

———. "Qeta'im le-Rav Saadia." *PAAJR* 43 (1976): 29-36.

———. "Qeta'im mi-Ketav Tahazil al-Sharia al-Semayh le-RaSaG." *Tarbiz* 41 (1971-72): 373-410.

CITATIONS INDEX

5. Babylonian Talmud and Extra-canonical Tractates

Negative Commandments
(Sefer ha-Mitsvot and Minyan ha Qatsar)

MISHNEH TORAH

I. Sefer ha-Madda‘

Hilkhot Yesode ha-Torah

II. Sefer Ahavah

III. Sefer Zemanim

IV. Sefer Nashim

INDEX OF NAMES

I

J

K

CPSIA information can be obtained
at www.ICGtesting.com
Printed in the USA
BVHW040839230720
584407BV00006B/129